PEOPLE OF THE SPIRIT

Exploring Luke's View of the Church

GRAHAM H. TWELFTREE

Baker Academic

a division of Baker Publishing Group
Grand Rapids, Michigan

First published in Great Britain in 2009

Society for Promoting Christian Knowledge
36 Causton Street
London SW1P 4ST

Published in the United States by Baker Academic
a division of Baker Publishing Group
P.O. Box 6287, Grand Rapids, MI 49516-6287
www.bakeracademic.com

British Library Cataloguing-in-Publication Data
A catalogue record for this book is available from the British Library

Library of Congress Cataloging-in-Publication Data is on file at the Library of Congress,
Washington, DC

SPCK ISBN 978–0–281–05536–4

Baker Academic ISBN 978–0–8010–3880–8

1 3 5 7 9 10 8 6 4 2

Typeset by Graphicraft Ltd, Hong Kong
Printed in Great Britain by Ashford Colour Press

Produced on paper from sustainable forests

Contents

About the author

Graham H. Twelftree is Distinguished Professor of New Testament, School of Divinity, Regent University, Virginia Beach. He is the author of a number of books, including *Christ Triumphant: Exorcism Then and Now* (1985), *Jesus the Exorcist: A Contribution to the Study of the Historical Jesus* (1993), *Jesus the Miracle Worker: A Historical and Theological Study* (1999) and *In the Name of Jesus: Exorcism among Early Christians* (2007). He is a member of the editorial board of the *Journal for the Study of the Historical Jesus*.

Preface

What follows arises out of a desire to hear afresh Luke's message in relation to the Church in the twenty-first century. So I have two aims in this book: first, looking back across a two-thousand-year cultural chasm to a unique pair of books in a very different world, I want to see what was important to Luke in relation to the Church. Also, I want to see what implications Luke's views might have for the way we think about and go about living in the Church. If Luke was involved in one of our conversations about the Church – its origins, its nature, its leadership, its purpose, its problems and their solutions – what, if anything, would he have to contribute?

So small and straightforward was this book to be that it was expected to write itself – and quickly. Alas, this did not happen. Along the way issues I had not anticipated arose from what Luke seemed to be saying – his views of mission and worship, for example. Writing slowed to a crawl and sometimes stopped as I set it aside and processed what I was learning. Therefore, this book has turned out to have a long history, and it still reflects no more than a work in progress.

Some parts, especially those dealing with the mission of the Church, first saw the light of day in the form of the 1991 Magarey Lectures, which I was honoured to deliver at the annual conference for the Churches of Christ pastors in South Australia. There are also ideas that received their first expression in my 'Church Agenda: The Lucan Perspectives' in R. Dean Drayton and Graham H. Twelftree, eds, *Evangelism and Preaching in Secular Australia* (Melbourne: JBCE, 1989).

An early draft of this book took shape when I had access to the Löhe Memorial Library, Australian Lutheran College, Adelaide. South Australia is fortunate to have such a library with its skilled and friendly staff. More recently, I have been part of the Regent University School of Divinity in Virginia Beach. Not only am I grateful to my deans and colleagues, but also special thanks are due to the librarians – preeminently Bob Sivigny, the Divinity Librarian, and Patty Hughson and her Interlibrary Loans team – for their ready and gracious support. Further, I gratefully acknowledge the support I have received for this project from a Regent University sabbatical and a faculty research grant. Thank you.

To others who have helped along the way I offer my sincere thanks. Reactions to an early version of these pages from Kevin Giles, Philip Muston, Gregory Pearce, Stephen Travis and David Wenham helped develop my initial thinking. Then, Rodger Bassham, Robert Berg, Robert Menzies, Steve Moyise, David Pao, Skip Horton-Parker, Clark Pinnock, Mark Roberts, John Roth, Charles Talbert, Richard Thompson, Joseph Tyson, Brenton Wait, Catherine Wait and Steve Walton interacted with more recent parts or versions.

Moreover, two anonymous readers of the press offered helpful comments. In thanking these people I do not – I cannot! – imply that they agree with all that is found in these pages.

The practical help of assistants over the years – Enoch Charles, Jacqueline Duckett, Christopher Emerick, Ian Hackmann, Rodney Platt Jr, Kathy Schultz, Jeremy Smith, Andrew Whitaker, Natasha Zhurauliova and especially, most recently, Alicia Eichmann – has considerably lightened the load of research and writing. These individuals have also spurred me on with their interest and enthusiasm. Ruth McCurry and latterly Rebecca Mulhearn have been faultless editors and with the copy-editor Peter Andrews, the proof-reader Gillian Wallis and the SPCK editorial and production teams, as well as Jim Kinney's team at Baker Academic, are also to be thanked for their part in bringing this book to life. Much appreciated help of a different kind has come from Panera Bread® bakery-cafes; they have provided a congenial environment in which to 'hide' for many hours of productive reading. Very generously, my wife continues to offer what she calls assisted living in aid of my work. A few words in a preface are clearly inadequate thanks for her sacrifices.

I owe a special and longstanding debt of gratitude to Mel Gilmour and Ivan Wallis for their loyal friendship, support and desire to explore with me in practical ways what the biblical writers have to contribute to our understanding of the Church. I am only sorry that Ivan did not live to see in print some of the fruit of our discussions.

Although this book seeks to contribute to scholarly conversations about Luke and the Church, in order to increase its accessibility I have refrained from the luxury of footnotes other than for primary evidence. The list of selected items for further reading will stand as part of the evidence of my frequent and significant debt to others, as well as a guide to pursue topics further.

Graham H. Twelftree
Regent University

Abbreviations

BCE	Before the common era
BDAG	F. W. Danker, *Greek-English Lexicon of the New Testament and Other Early Christian Literature*, 3rd edn (Chicago and London: Chicago University Press, 2000)
CE	Common era
CIJ	Jean Baptiste Frey, ed., *Corpus inscriptionum Iudaicarum* (Rome: Pontificio Istituto di Archeologia Cristiana, 1936–52)
LSJ	Henry George Liddell, Robert Scott, Henry Stuart Jones, Roderick McKenzie and Eric Arthur Barber, *A Greek–English Lexicon* (Oxford: Clarendon Press, 1968)
LXX	Septuagint, the most influential Greek translations of the Old Testament
MM	James Hope Moulton and George Milligan, *The Vocabulary of the Greek New Testament* (London: Hodder and Stoughton, 1972)
NRSV	New Revised Standard Version Bible
NT	New Testament
OT	Old Testament
P	Papyrus
RSV	Revised Standard Version Bible

Old Testament

Gen.	Genesis
Exod.	Exodus
Lev.	Leviticus
Num.	Numbers
Deut.	Deuteronomy
Jos.	Joshua
Judg.	Judges
1 Sam.	1 Samuel
2 Sam.	2 Samuel
1 Kgs	1 Kings
1 Chr.	1 Chronicles
2 Chr.	2 Chronicles
Neh.	Nehemiah
Ps./Pss.	Psalms
Prov.	Proverbs
Eccl.	Ecclesiastes
Song	Song of Songs
Isa.	Isaiah

Jer.	Jeremiah
Ezek.	Ezekiel
Dan.	Daniel
Hos.	Hosea
Jon.	Jonah
Mic.	Micah
Hab.	Habakkuk
Zeph.	Zephaniah
Hag.	Haggai
Zech.	Zechariah
Mal.	Malachi

New Testament

Matt.	Matthew
Rom.	Romans
1 Cor.	1 Corinthians
2 Cor.	2 Corinthians
Gal.	Galatians
Eph.	Ephesians
Phil.	Philippians
Col.	Colossians
Philem.	Philemon
1 Thess.	1 Thessalonians
2 Thess.	2 Thessalonians
1 Tim.	1 Timothy
2 Tim.	2 Timothy
Heb.	Hebrews
Jas.	James
1 Pet.	1 Peter
2 Pet.	2 Peter
Rev.	Revelation
Q	*Quelle* (a supposed source for Matthew and Luke)

Apocrypha and Septuagint

Ecclus.	Ecclesiasticus
1 Esd.	1 Esdras
2 Esd.	2 Esdras
1 Macc.	1 Maccabees
2 Macc.	2 Maccabees
3 Macc.	3 Maccabees
4 Macc.	4 Maccabees
Wis.	Wisdom

Old Testament Pseudepigrapha

As. Mos.	*Assumption (or Testament) of Moses*
2 Bar.	*2 Baruch*
1 En.	*1 Enoch*
2 En.	*2 Enoch*
Jub.	*Jubilees*
Pss. Sol.	*Psalms of Solomon*
Sib. Or.	*Sibylline Oracles*

Church Fathers

1 Clem.	*1 Clement*
Did.	*Didache*
Barn.	*Barnabas*
Ign. *Eph.*	Ignatius, *To the Ephesians*
Ign. *Magn.*	Ignatius, *To the Magnesians*
Ign. *Phld.*	Ignatius, *To the Philadelphians*
Ign. *Smyrn.*	Ignatius, *To the Smyrnaeans*
Ign. *Trall.*	Ignatius, *To the Trallians*
Pol. *Phil.*	Polycarp, *To the Philippians*

Dead Sea Scrolls and related texts

CD	Cairo Genizah copy of the *Damascus Document*
CD-A	Cairo Genizah copy of the *Damascus Document*, Manuscript A
1QH^a	Thanksgiving Hymns
1QM	*War Scroll*
1QS	*Rule of the Community*
1Q28a	*Rule of the Congregation* (Appendix a to 1QS)
1Q28b	*Rule of the Blessings* (Appendix b to 1QS)
1QpHab	*Pesher to Habakkuk*
4Q171	*Psalms Pesher*
4Q173	*Psalms Pesher*
4Q174	*Florilegium*
4Q177	*Catena A*
4Q184	*Wiles of the Wicked Woman*
4Q265	Miscellaneous Rules
4Q400–407	*Songs of the Sabbath Sacrifice*
4Q427	*Hymns*
4Q503	*Daily Prayers*
4Q504	*Words of the Luminaries*
4Q511	*Songs of the Sage*
4Q521	*Messianic Apocalypse*
11Q13	*Melchizedek*
11Q17	*Songs of the Sabbath Sacrifice*
11Q19	*Temple Scroll*

Philo

Abraham	*On the Life of Abraham*
Eternity	*On the Eternity of the World*
Cherubim	*On the Cherubim*
Confusion	*On the Confusion of Tongues*
Contempl. Life	*On the Contemplative Life*
Decalogue	*On the Decalogue*
Worse	*That the Worse Attacks the Better*
Drunkenness	*On Drunkenness*
Flaccus	*Against Flaccus*
Flight	*On Flight and Finding*
The Heir	*Who Is the Heir?*
Hypoth.	*Hypothetica*
Embassy	*On the Embassy to Gaius*
Moses	*On the Life of Moses*
Names	*On the Change of Names*
Posterity	*On the Posterity of Cain*
Rewards	*On Rewards and Punishment*
Good Person	*That Every Good Person Is Free*
Sacrifices	*On the Sacrifices of Cain and Abel*
Spec. Laws	*On the Special Laws*
LAB	Pseudo-Philo, *Liber antiquitatum biblicarum*

Josephus

Ag. Ap.	*Against Apion*
Ant.	*Jewish Antiquities*
J.W.	*Jewish War*
Life	*The Life*

Mishnah, Talmud and related literature

m.	*Mishnah*
t.	*Tosefta*
y.	*Jerusalem Talmud*
b.	*Babylonian Talmud*
B. Bat.	*Baba Batra*
B. Meṣi'a	*Baba Meṣi'a*
Ber.	*Berakhot*
Meg.	*Megillah*
Ned.	*Nedarim*
Shabb.	*Shabbat*
Sanh.	*Sanhedrin*
Tg. Ps.-J.	*Targum Pseudo-Jonathan*

Greek and Latin works

Author	*Abbreviation*	*Full title*
Augustine	*Conf.*	*Confessions*
Cicero	*Div.*	*On Divination*
Dio Cassius	*Hist.*	*Roman History*
Dio Chrysostom	*1 Serv. lib.*	*De servitute et libertate i (Or. 14)*
Diodorus Siculus	*Hist.*	*Historicus*
Diogenes Laertius	*Lives*	*Lives of Eminent Philosophers*
Eusebius	*Hist. eccl.*	*Ecclesiastical History*
Herodotus	*Hist.*	*Histories*
Homer	*Il.*	*Iliad*
Irenaeus	*Haer.*	*Against Heresies*
John Chrysostom	*Adv. Jud.*	*Adversus Judaeos (Discourse against Judaizing Christians)*
Justin	*1 Apol.*	*First Apology*
Justin	*2 Apol.*	*Second Apology*
Justin	*Dial.*	*Dialogue with Trypho*
Lucian	*History*	*How to Write History*
Origen	*Cels.*	*Against Celsus*
Origen	*Comm. Rom.*	*Commentarii in Romanos*
Origen	*Hom. Lev.*	*Homiliae in Leviticum*
Plutarch	*Alex.*	*Alexander*
Plutarch	*Is. Or.*	*Isis and Osiris*
Plutarch	*Nic.*	*Nicias*
Plutarch	*Num.*	*Numa*
Plutarch	*Obs.*	*The Obsolescence of Oracles*
Quintilian	*Inst.*	*Institutio oratoria*
Seneca	*Letters*	*Moral Letters*
Tacitus	*Ann.*	*Annales*
Tertullian	*Apol.*	*Apology*
Tertullian	*Bap.*	*On Baptism*
Tertullian	*Marc.*	*Against Marcion*

1

The issues

The way we understand our lives has changed. In the last generation or so a cultural shift – at least in the West – has taken place that could be as profound as, for example, that which took place in the Enlightenment of the eighteenth century. In most areas of intellectual inquiry, confidence has been lost in proceeding on the basis of foundational appeals to dogmas, texts or intuition. There is also now a deep suspicion among ordinary people about absolutes for personal living or for society as a whole. At best, in this pluralistic age perhaps we could hope only to stitch together a tapestry of ideas by which to live.

Whether or not this changed cultural climate is to be called the 'after-life of religion' or 'late modernism' or 'self conscious modernism' or, as it generally is, 'postmodernism', or cannot be given a name, may not be important. What is important for this study is that scholarly as well as popular discussions of the way people understand the Church, both in terms of its essential ideas (orthodoxy) and the way it should function (orthopraxy), are taking place in response to the cultural climate change. This study seeks to contribute to that discussion. For those Christians for whom ecclesiology is a low priority, this book seeks to be a stimulation to discussion.

Besides the cultural shift that has had an impact on the way the Church is understood, there has been a geographical shift in the centre of the Church. Although there may be a 'global church', in the West, despite occasional flickers of light, the Church appears to be dying out, especially its mainline or traditional expressions. Yet, across the world Christianity is often reported to be the fastest growing religion and the largest church congregations in the world are all in South Korea, South America and Africa; notable is Yoido Full Gospel Church in Seoul with its 830,000 members. Christians in the West, it could be suggested, are being forced to face the question of why their church is becoming irrelevant, little more than a relic of a previous culture. In contrast, Christians in South Korea and the global south will soon, if not already, face the question of how a church should relate to a culture that it has come to dominate.

There are those who suggest that the Western Church has sold out to its surrounding culture. It is not that this is seen as a recent change. Critics point out that, since the time of Constantine (died 337 CE), the first Christian emperor, the Western Church has taken on the role of chaplain or even custodian of the culture, too uncritically supporting the political, military, social and intellectual status quo. However, as Western culture has, at least formally, become

1

less and less interested in spiritual issues – privatizing them and leaving them to the individual – and has drifted to more pluralistic attitudes to religion, the Church has found itself increasingly marginalized and uncertain of its role in society.

In turn, one of the recurring ideas expressed by those involved in the Emergent or Emerging Church movement is a disillusionment with church initiatives from the late twentieth century that are interpreted as part of an acquiescence to a feel-good, self-centred culture that focused on individual felt needs The result, they are quick to point out, has often been the growth of culturally benign mega churches. These, they say, have inadvertently adopted tragic aspects of modernism, sacrificing the notion of community. Indeed, in both the Emerging Church movement and in more theoretical discussions on ecclesiology, the idea of community is increasingly seen as one of the major marks of the Church, even able to capture the essence of its nature and function.

§1.1 Back to the Bible?

One response to the angst of our age could be for the Church to ignore it. It is not that postmodernism is to be seen as little more than a media event staged by some French intellectuals. Rather, even while acknowledging the magnitude of the cultural transformations, it could be maintained that Christian theology should carry on its deliberations as if nothing has happened. This approach might arise out of the justifiable conviction that culture is not to determine theology, or it could come from a confidence in the autonomy of theology. However, while theological discussions are responsible for articulating the voice and activity of God for the Church, a lack of dialogical engagement with our culture assumes that God does not speak to us through it or that he is not interested in it. Importantly, carrying on theological speculation without due regard for our culture and changes in it also potentially diminishes our ability to understand and communicate with those involved in it.

Alternatively, in times of stress during a cultural crisis the plea could be heeded that the Church return to its roots. In his tempestuous times, for his paraphrase of Acts, Erasmus of Rotterdam, the Renaissance humanist, wrote a dedicatory letter (31 January 1524) to Pope Clement VII. Erasmus lamented not only the contrast between the very turbulent and corrupt state of the Church known to them and the wonderful picture of the Church in Acts, but also hoped, under Clement, the Church would be reborn, presumably to reflect Luke's picture more nearly. Today, it could be assumed that our troubled churches are simply to be debugged of contemporary cultural viruses and rebooted with the software of the New Testament Church. However, if in a primitivist way this is understood as an attempt to rewind history, to do so would be to ignore – and lose! – all that we learn about the Church from such people as Justin Martyr, Basil of Caesarea, Augustine of Hippo,

Thomas Aquinas, Martin Luther, John Calvin, John Wesley and, more recently, Yves Congar, Hans Küng, Jürgen Moltmann or Miroslav Volf, for example. While the early Church may appear vibrant and innocent to tired or disillusioned Western eyes, to turn a blind eye to the intervening two millennia of reflection on the nature and function of the Church is to run the invariable risk of repeating all the intervening errors.

At first sight a return to the New Testament should, surely, be applauded. For, in these turbulent times, a call to hear again from foundational literature of the Church would appear to be beneficial. However, at least as some approach the exercise, the search is fraught with problems and potential disappointment. First, the potential disappointment. As we will discover, from the reflections in Luke and Acts, there never was a time when the Church was free of problems; even the very earliest days of the Church were far from utopian. There is no lost ecclesiastical utopia to recover. Indeed, if we are going to look anywhere in the New Testament for help in understanding the Church, such inquiry would need to be done knowing that we will find neither the simplicity Erasmus sought nor the model of utopia we may seek. What we will find in Luke–Acts – and throughout the New Testament – is a church familiar to us in the problems and issues it confronted. Nevertheless, importantly, we will also find these problems are being lived through and dealt with by a writer who is informed by very early traditions about Jesus and his followers and who, in his writings, sought to give practical expression to what he understood to be Jesus' intentions.

Second to be confronted are the problems of turning to the New Testament for help. To return to the computer metaphor, there is more than one piece of software or, more accurately, there are entirely different disk or church operating systems advertized in the New Testament. Biblical scholarship has shown us that each of the ten or a dozen New Testament writers portrays a different view of the Church, some very different from and incompatible with others. For example, it does not seem that Paul thought of the Church as having a universal dimension – the sum of all the individual congregations.[1] It was those who followed him, writing in his name, who developed the idea of the universal Church and it having a cosmic reality to which local Christians belonged.[2] From Matthew we hear that the Church consists not in an intellectual body or an organization but in a brotherhood or egalitarian group of people[3] led initially by Jesus the Master[4] and then by Peter (Matt. 16:18). In turn, for Matthew, the Church is only the Church when it functions as a community (e.g. 18:15–20). Although the Fourth Gospel has some interest in church order (John 17:20–21), it appears to have little

---

[1] However, see the problem texts, esp. 1 Cor. 10:32; 12:28; Gal. 1:13.
[2] See Eph. 1:22; 3:10, 21; 5:23–24, 27, 29, 32; cf. Col. 1:18; 1:24. Both Eph. and Col. are often considered to have been written by followers of Paul.
[3] Matt. 9:37; 10:1, 24–25, 42; 11:1.
[4] See Matt. 23:1–12; and 5:22–24, 47; 7:3–5; 12:49–50; 18:15, 20, 21, 35; 25:40.

concern for organization; the Church seems understood as a collection, or a number of collections,[5] of individuals bound together primarily by their separate union to Christ.[6]

Therefore, mindful not only that there is no lost ecclesiological paradise to be found, but also of the variety of ecclesial voices in the New Testament, this book seeks to draw attention to the voice of Luke for those who wish to hear again what one writer in the New Testament has to say about the Church in a time of tectonic change. This is not to deny that it is possible or wise to ignore all that we have learnt from the Calvins and the Küngs of history. Rather, given the frequently declared ongoing significance of Jesus as the root and focus of the Church, it behoves his followers, no matter how far removed in time, to reflect on their life together in the light of the writings of those closest to him and early traditions about him. Also, the deep interest of the global south and east church in the Bible intensifies the need to make clear what it has to say about the Church.

§1.2 Why Luke?

Coming to Luke it could be said that he elaborates no doctrine of the Church, for he only once uses the word 'church' (*ekklēsia*) to mean more than the local congregation (see §1.6), and then it refers not to the universal Church but to the church in Judea, Galilee and Samaria (Acts 9:31; see §5.5 below). Yet, if the Church is taken to be the post-Easter corporate life and activity of the groups of followers of Jesus, in the very act of writing Acts, Luke shows himself profoundly interested in the Church.

What Luke has to say about the Church is well worth our attention, for the writings of Luke are without parallel in the history of Christian literature. More than half of the Gospel of Luke is not found elsewhere.[7] Without Luke's Gospel the Church would suffer an irreplaceable loss. Also, Luke offers the greatest amount of material in the New Testament for us to examine in relation to our subject. He has written over one-quarter of the New Testament[8] and no early Christian has written so plainly and extensively about the corporate life and function of Christians. Further, although Luke is by no means the earliest New Testament writer and, on

---

[5] See John 10:16. Cf. 1 John 1:9–11; 2:19; 2 John 9–10; Rev. 2—3.

[6] Cf. John 10:11–16; 13—17. Also see 1 John 2:7–8; 3:23; 2 John 5–6.

[7] E.g. the birth stories of John the Baptist and Jesus (Luke 1—2), the large catch of fish (5:1–11), the parable of the good Samaritan and Jesus' visit to Mary and Martha (10:25–41), the parables of the lost sheep, the lost coin and the lost son (15:3–32), and the stories of Zacchaeus (19:1–10), the widow's gift (21:1–4) and the walk to Emmaus (24:13–35) are all unique to Luke.

[8] The Johannine writings come to about 27,835 words, or 20 per cent of the NT; Paul's work (even including the Pastoral Epistles) comes to about 32,300 words, that is 24 per cent of the NT. Luke, however, wrote more than any other NT writer – about 37,780 words, or 28 per cent of the text.

his own admission, was not an eyewitness of any of the early years of the Church (Luke 1:1–4), he does set out to tell his readers about the first Christian community. Although he might be more impressionistic than we would wish and has obscured the events and intentions of the characters involved in his narrative, as I will argue, his portrayal of that community as a model to his readers means that we would do well to take a careful account of what he, one of our canonical writers, has to say as we articulate and practise our ecclesiologies.

Moreover, we focus on Luke because, beyond a superficial reading concentrating on the early chapters of Acts, his contribution to our understanding of the early churches has gone largely untapped, even by the Pentecostals who so venerate him. Paul's signed and, at times, intensely personal letters have long dominated popular impression of what the life and theology of the early church was like in the New Testament period. These letters have also provided the yardstick for much of post-Reformation Protestant orthodoxy and practice. Perhaps Luke's neglect in the shadow of Paul is because his work is later than Paul's, or because it is less personal, or (apparently!) less theological and less prescriptive. Equally likely, Luke is neglected because his too-obviously ecstatic, experiential and miracle-ridden, mission-focused, ecclesiology is not to the taste of these more enlightened times.

If not always neglected, Luke's work has been used to support a variety of views. He has been used to 'prove' that the threefold ministry of deacon, priest and bishop is irrevocably God-given. He has been called upon to support the charismatic and Pentecostal churches in their style and models of leadership. Some use Luke-Acts to affirm that all Christians must speak in tongues. For some mainline churches, Luke is used to affirm the view that elders and deacons are inherently part of God's plan for ministry. Luke-Acts has also been used to support the view that baptism in water confers the gift of the Spirit. Therefore, Luke is of special interest to us because, of all the New Testament views of the Church, it is that portrayed in the writings of Luke which provides us with the greatest and most striking challenges.

§1.3 Luke?

For Luke's work to be understood as clearly as possible we need to know as much as we can about those involved in its writing and initial reading, as well as the circumstances that gave rise to this literature. For example, if we know who wrote these two documents – the Gospel of Luke and Acts – we may be able to establish some of the writer's interests and approaches to his themes. Thus, knowing if Luke was a Jew or a Gentile may help us determine his understanding of the relationship between the Church and the Jews. Also, if we can discern why this literature was written, our understanding of Luke's message to his first hearers or readers is likely to be more obvious to us.

§1.3.1 Who?

Although, from time to time, the view is challenged, it remains generally agreed that the third Gospel and Acts came from the same pen and are to be read together as a whole.[9] For more than his name, which was likely to have been associated very early with the two works,[10] we are wholly dependent upon what he wrote. The opening words of the Gospel show that he was at least a second-generation Christian (Luke 1:1–4). In the light of his knowledge of the church at Antioch[11] we could probably agree with church tradition that he was a Syrian, a native of Antioch.[12] However, since Antioch plays no part in Luke's narrative after Acts 15 (though we see the fleeting reference in 18:22 about Paul going from Jerusalem to Antioch), he may no longer have been associated with the church there when he was writing.

Even though it remains a popular view that the author of Luke and Acts was a medical doctor (cf. Col. 4:14), the style of Luke bears no more evidence of medical training and interest than does the language of other writers whom we know were not physicians. The so-called 'we'-passages[13] assume that Luke was a companion of Paul, at least for parts of his second and third journeys, and the final trip to Rome. But we cannot be sure these sections are autobiographical, they could be either the creation of the author or taken up by him from another source. In any case, they become part of the author's idealization of Paul, holding him up as the one taking the mission of the Church to Rome and the ends of the earth.

Whether or not Luke was a Jew or a Gentile is difficult to determine. On the one hand, there is evidence he was not familiar with some aspects of Jewish life and, therefore, could be a Gentile.[14] On the other hand, his desire to cast his characters as faithful Jews (§5.1 below) shows a deep veneration of Judaism. The solution to Luke's cultural identity is probably, then, to see him as a so-called God-fearer: a Gentile who, though not a proselyte, was in general acceptance of Judaism.[15] It is not surprising, then, that Luke shows a great deal of interest in the gospel and the Gentiles. From what he

---

[9] See, e.g. Luke 1:1–4 and Acts 1:1–2. Also cf. Luke 24:1–53 and Acts 1:3; perhaps Luke 22:12 and Acts 1:13, though different Greek words (respectively *anagaion* and *huperōon*) are used for the room.

[10] Cf. e.g. P[75]; Irenaeus, *Haer.* 3.11.8.

[11] Acts 6:5; 11:19–20, 27 (Codex Bezae); 13:1–4; 14:26–28; 15:1–3, 13–40; 18:22–23.

[12] Eusebius, *Hist. eccl.* 3.4.6; Jerome, *On Illustrious Men* 7; *Preface to Matthew.*

[13] Acts 16:10–17; 20:5—21:18; 27:1—28:16. Though, in this case, probably not representing what Luke wrote, the so-called Western text (e.g. Codex Bezae, Old Latin) also uses the third person plural at 11:28.

[14] E.g. if the most likely reading of Luke 2:22 is accepted ('their' rather than, e.g. 'her' purification), Luke shows he is not familiar with Jewish customs (cf. Lev. 12:4, 6); and in Luke 3:2 it seems as if Luke thinks that there were two high priests in office. Also, in Acts 18:18 Luke says Paul had his hair cut as he was under a vow; but in Num. 6:5 the hair is to be cut only to mark the end of the Nazarite vow.

[15] For *phoboumenos* [*ton theon*] ('God-fearer') see Acts 10:2, 22, 35; 13:16, 26 and, thereafter its equivalent, *sebomenos* [*ton theon*] ('devout') at 13:43, 50; 16:14; 17:4, 17; 18:7.

writes, socially, Luke is at home in cities and villages, and moves easily among travellers, the wealthy, as well as administrators and the cultured.

§1.3.2 When and where?

As with most ancient documents, dating Luke's work is difficult; suggestions range from the mid–60s to the early second century (see below). I am happy to follow the majority view that Luke wrote after both the fall of Jerusalem in 70 CE (cf. Luke 19:41–44; 21:20–24) and the writing of Mark around the same time, his major source for his Gospel. Perhaps Luke wrote before the Pauline letters gained sufficient status to warrant quoting them (by the end of the first century CE).[16] For, though he does not explicitly cite them, he may well have known them.[17] In other words, Luke wrote somewhere between about 70 and 80 CE. Since Luke shows a remarkable interest in and knowledge of the Church at Syrian Antioch on the Orontes river – at least in its early stages (see above, n. 11) – it remains the best contender for the place of origin of Luke-Acts.[18]

§1.3.3 What?

As the genre of a text is a major part of what informs readers about the author's intention, we need to give attention to the question of the genre of Luke's work. In attempting to understand what he wrote we have to keep in mind that we are probably dealing with a work in two parts, a Gospel and Acts; what we propose for one must also work for the whole. For, as we will see, in the preface of his second part, Luke signals his intention to continue the same genre and subject, the deeds and teaching of Jesus (cf. Chapter 3 below).

Particularly obvious in the prologues (Luke 1:1–4; Acts 1:1–2), Luke gives the impression of intending to narrate some form of history, even if, by our standards, he does it differently or badly. However, regardless of the historical accuracy – or otherwise – of the details of the work, it has to be kept in mind that biographical material dominates both the Gospel and Acts. Yet, Luke's preface at the beginning of his Gospel does not suggest that biography is his primary concern. Instead, his concern is with undertaking 'an orderly account' or narrative (Luke 1:1).

In determining what Luke thought he was writing we can note that although, theoretically, the diverse genre of history[19] was understood to be distinct from

---

[16] Cf. Ign. *Eph.* 12.2; 2 Pet. 3:15–18. Referring to Paul's letters in the plural (2 Pet. 3:16) is not support in itself of a collection of them, for *epistolas* ('letters', Pol. *Phil.* 3.2) could refer to a single letter. In Luke's period, 1 Macc. 5:14; 10:3, 7; 11:29; 12:5, e.g. refer to a single document.

[17] See 1 Cor. 8–10; and Acts 15:29; see 1 Cor. 10:27; and Luke 10:8; see 2 Cor. 11:32–33; and Acts 9:23–25; see Gal. 1:13–14, 16, 23; and Acts 9:20–21; 22:3; see Gal. 2; and Acts 10:45; 11:2–3; 12:25; 15; 16:1–3; 21:18–28.

[18] Cf. the anti-Marcionite Prologue to the Gospel, perhaps from the third quarter of the second century, begins: 'Luke is a Syrian of Antioch' (*estin ho Loukas Antiocheus Suros*).

[19] See Quintilian, *Inst.* II.4.2–3; Plutarch, *Alex.* 1.3.

biography,[20] in practice the distinction could be blurred or interrelated.[21] Moreover, Plutarch, the Greek philosopher and biographer writing in the same period as Luke, is helpful to us. For, in saying that he was writing a biography not a history of Alexander, he was setting aside exhaustive narrative, not the need for the careful selection of material and detail.[22] Thus, although Luke states he is writing an orderly narrative and gives the impression of narrating real events in the context of world history, he does so primarily through using a series of biographical narratives, first of Jesus, then, in his second volume, through a series of interconnected brief biographical narratives of Jesus' early followers.

Given there was, at the time, an interest not only in the deeds of the persons depicted but also in how the deeds reflected on the character of the person,[23] the hero or heroes of the ancient biography also became models for the lives of his readers.[24] That is, in his biographical interests, Luke is most likely portraying at least his lead characters as models for his readers to follow. This leads us to the question of Luke's purpose.

§1.3.4 Why?

Our answer to this question is of pivotal importance: if Luke intended his work to be prescriptive in some way this will have implications for how we should hear what he would say if he was involved in one of our conversations about the Church. There are several possible motives to Luke's writing.

Defending Paul at his trial[25] cannot be Luke's primary purpose, for he was probably writing too late, though, in part, he is probably attempting to rehabilitate the reputation of the apostle and the mission he embodies (cf. Acts 25:1—26:32). Neither can Luke be defending the Christians before the Roman government for it is unlikely a Roman official would have been able to detect such an apology. Luke is also unlikely to be solving the problem of the delay of the return of Jesus: he includes material that does not serve such a cause[26] and, along with the rest of the Church, he saw in Jesus that judgement, salvation and the overthrow of Satan had become a present reality.[27] Also, even though Christian literature was read by others,[28] it cannot reasonably be suggested that Luke thought he was writing an evangelistic document; his representative reader, Theophilus ('lover of God', Luke 1:3;

---

[20] E.g. Plutarch, *Alex.* 1.1–3; *Galba* 2.3.
[21] E.g. Polybius, *Histories* 10.21.8; Cicero, *Letter to His Friends* 5.12.6.
[22] Plutarch, *Alex.* 1.1–3; *Galba* 2—3; see also *Nic.* 1—2.
[23] Ion of Chios, *Epidemiai*; Plutarch, *Alex.* 1.3; *Nic.* 1.5.
[24] E.g. Seneca, *Letters* 98.12; 104.22, 27–33; Epictetus, *Enchiridion* 5, 33, 46.
[25] Cf. Acts 25:1–12; 28:16, 30–31.
[26] See Luke 12:38–48; 12:54—13:9; 18:8; 21:32.
[27] Luke 10:17–20; 11:14–22; cf. Acts 2:1–42.
[28] See, e.g. Plutarch, *Aristides* 16.3.5; Justin, *Dial.* 10; 18; Athenagoras, *Embassy* 9.3; Tertullian, *Apol.* 31; Origen, *Cels.* 1.34, 40, 58, 68; 3.24, 27, 34, 36; 5.52; 6.16; 7.18.

Acts 1:1) is unlikely to be an outsider, and the large concluding section of his work deals with Paul's trials and travels (21—28).

It could be, in drawing attention to the Jewishness of Jesus, his birth and the importance of the fulfilment of prophecy, that Luke was writing in re-action to Marcion of Sinope. Marcion was the very influential heretic in the early second century, who rejected the Old Testament and 'the bodily substance of Christ'.[29] However, direct connections between Luke and Marcion are difficult to establish.

A view that does considerable justice to the narrative and emphases of his work is that Luke's principal aim was to show his readers that the message they had heard concerning Jesus – probably in the Pauline tradition – is reli-able. Jesus and the salvation associated with him are the subject of Acts as well as the Gospel (cf. Acts 1:1; 28:31). Through his two-volume narrative-biographical approach, Luke binds together what happened before and after Easter and links them to the time of his readers. Readers of Luke can thus be assured that God's salvation – spoken of in the Old Testament and dem-onstrated in the life, ministry, death and resurrection of Jesus, as well as witnessed to in their predecessors after Easter – has not passed them by. For example, the significance for Luke of the number of apostles being twelve (see Luke 22:28–30 and §2.5.2 below) signals that God's salvation in Jesus, experienced by the readers, is a faithful fulfilment of the ancient hopes of Israel. That is, in the risen life of Jesus and the activity of the Holy Spirit among his readers the hoped-for blessings of God have flowed straight into their life together; their Christian experience is analogous to and continuous with that of the first followers.

This perspective is confirmed by Luke's prologue (Luke 1:1–4). Prologues in the ancient world could pertain to all the parts of a multi-volume work,[30] and in Acts 1:1 Luke ties the volumes together, so we can take it that Luke's purpose expressed in the first few verses of his Gospel is most likely to express his purpose for the whole of his work. In other words, Luke was writing to reassure his readers that what they had been taught about Jesus, as well as the Christian life, is no aberration of a message from God but the true goal towards which God's dealings with Israel were moving. Therefore, Luke emphasizes that what had taken (and was taking) place in and within the group of followers of Jesus fulfilled Old Testament hopes.

Another way that Luke bridges the gap between his readers, on the one hand, and his story of salvation in Jesus and the coming of the Spirit, on the other hand, is his use of the first person plural, 'we'. Even if this came to him from his sources, his experience or his own literary creativity (see above, n. 13), used in the latter part of his story, this form of speech not only involves Luke with the story of Paul, but also brings his readers into contact with the

---

[29] Tertullian, *Marc.* 3.8; cf. 1.19; 5.1–21.
[30] E.g. see Josephus, *Ag. Ap.* 1.1–18; *J.W.* 1.17–18.

narrative. This effectively connects the readers not only to Paul, but also, in turn, to his predecessors and the origins of the faith.

Turning to the open-ended closing of Acts we see Luke further involving his readers. An unresolved narrative was a literary device well known at the time, a means of keeping the narrative open for the readers' involvement (see §3.3 below). Thus, the summary of Paul's unhindered yet imprisoned missionary activities in Rome (Acts 28:30–31), echoing the ideal Christian individuals and communities engaged in mission earlier in Acts[31] and even that of Jesus (28:31), provides readers with the mandate to see their own potentially unstoppable mission as the resolution of the incomplete mission of Paul to Gentiles (28:28). Moreover, given that biographies were to be taken as model lives for readers to follow, it is likely that Luke's descriptions of his heroes are intended to become prescriptions for his readers. This is a significant conclusion in the light of our hope that Luke might contribute to our conversations on the Church.

There is another important implication for us that arises from this discussion of Luke's purpose. We have to acknowledge that Luke does not see his purpose as writing an ecclesiology or even, directly, about the Church. Yet, as we have already noted, Luke at least implies a deep interest in ecclesiology by the very writing of his second volume. Therefore, even though his ecclesiology will have to be inferred, our seeking his views on the subject are entirely reasonable, if not intended by Luke.

§1.4 The readers?

According to the opening statements of Luke and Acts the writer is addressing a certain Theophilus (Luke 1:3; Acts 1:1). Literary conventions meant that the relation between author and dedicatee was generally formal and did not govern the contents or restrict readership.[32] So, from the opening words of Luke-Acts, it cannot be assumed that Luke was writing to a particular individual or community. That he intended his work to have a wide-ranging audience is enhanced by the probability that Luke was a travelling missionary[33] whose heroes are itinerant evangelists or, as in the case of the story of Stephen, encouraging missionaries to travel (cf. 8:1).

Luke's readers are likely to be Christians. For, if his Gospel and Acts had come into the hands of pagans, it is doubtful if they would have understood them very well, unless they were already well informed about the Christian life and its origins. Before their conversion, the Jewish Christians,

---

[31] Acts 28:30; cf. e.g. 2:42–47; 5:12–16; 8:4–40.
[32] See Onasander, *The General*; Lucian, *How to Write History* 52–55; and, the most striking parallel to Luke's dedication, Josephus, *Ag. Ap.* 1.1; 2.1.
[33] Note the impression conveyed by the 'we'-passages: Acts 16:10–17; 20:5—21:17; 27—28.

as well as most of the Gentile Christians Luke has in mind, probably had been associated with the synagogue.[34] However, by the time Luke was writing, the Church seems to have been under stress because at least some of the Christians had probably been excluded from the synagogue.[35]

§1.5 Which Church?

In Luke and Acts we are reading about both the early historical churches as well as Luke's ideal Church. It is to be stressed that the focus of this study is not on the recovery of the historical early Christian communities, nor even in discovering very much about the Church to which Luke may have belonged. Instead, the purpose of this book is to describe the main features of what Luke thinks the Church should be like; we are trying to set out the characteristics of what seem – implicitly or explicitly – to be his ideal Church. Nevertheless, at times, we will want to know how far what Luke says about the early Church (or churches) differs from possible historical reality, for that will give us clues as to what he wants to say or emphasize concerning the Church.

§1.6 'Church'

Before we can go much further we need to consider some issues concerning Luke's vocabulary in relation to the Church. We have derived the word 'church' from the Greek adjective *kuriakos* ('the Lord's') and use it to describe a local group of Christians, the world-wide community of followers of Jesus, the 'communion of saints' past and present, as well as to translate *ekklēsia*. For Luke, the word *ekklēsia* ('church') was of no special interest. Instead, he uses a variety of terms for the group of followers of Jesus.[36] The word 'disciples' is the most common (27 times), though it is not used in Acts until 6:1.[37]

---

[34] Acts 13:13–52; 14:1; 17:1–4; 18:8, 14–26; 22:19.

[35] See Acts 14:1–7; 17:1–9; 18:1–17.

[36] Apart from 'disciple' (see below, n. 37) and 'church' (see below, n. 38), the statistics are as follows: brethren (*adelphoi*; Acts 1:15, 16; 2:37; 6:3; 9:30; 10:23; 11:1, 12, 29; 12:17; 14:2; 15:1, 3, 7, 13, 22, 23, 32, 33, 36, 40; 16:2, 40; 17:6, 10, 14; 18:18, 27; 21:7, 17; 28:14, 15), 'friends' (*philoi*, 27:3), 'witnesses' (*martures*, 1:8, 22; 2:32; 3:15; 5:32; 10:39, 41; 13:31; 22:15, 20; 26:16), 'saints' (*hagioi*, 9:13, 32, 41; 26:10), 'believer(s)' or 'those believing' (*pisteuō*, 2:44; 4:32; 5:14; 11:21; 15:5; 16:34; 18:27; 19:18; 21:20, 25; 22:19), 'saved' (*sōzomenoi*, 2:47), 'Christians' (11:26; 26:28), 'Nazarenes' (*Nazōraioi*, 24:5), 'group', 'community' or 'congregation' (*plēthos*, 4:32; 6:2, 5; 15:12, 30), 'sect' (*hairesis*, 24:5, 14; 28:22), 'flock' (*poimnion*, 20:28) and 'Way' (*hodos*, 9:2; cf. 18:25, 26; 19:9, 23; 22:4; 24:14, 22). Also to be considered are 'faith' (*pistis*, 6:7; 13:8; 14:22; 16:5), 'word of God' (*logos*, 12:24; 19:20) and those who call on the name of the Lord (9:14, 21).

[37] Acts 6:1, 2, 7; 9:1, 10, 19, 25, 26 (twice), 38; 11:26, 29; 13:52; 14:20, 22, 28; 15:10; 16:1; 18:23, 27; 19:(1?), 9, 30; 20:1, 30; 21:4, 16 (twice).

Though not used in his Gospel, Luke has the word 'church' 23 times in Acts, first in Acts 5:11.[38] As we will eventually see, it cannot be that Luke thought the Church came into existence at this point; there is nothing in the context of Acts 5:11 to suggest Luke thought there was a change in the constitution of the followers of Jesus around that moment. In any case, throughout Acts, Luke does not draw special attention to *ekklēsia* in his portrayal of the Church. (Though, as we will see, at Acts 8:1 Luke probably uses the word in a significant way.) What this lack of focus on the word 'church' means is that we need to look beyond particular vocabulary if we are to see more clearly what Luke is saying about the corporate life and function of the post-Easter group of followers of Jesus – what we call the Church.

Now that we understand both why Luke is so important as a contributor to our conversations about ecclesiology, as well as some things about him that will help us tune into his voice – who he was, when and where he wrote, and what he was writing and why – we can set out the issues on which we would like to hear what Luke has to say.

§1.7 The issues

I have no intention of claiming that this modest book is a comprehensive study of Luke's view of the Church. It is, instead, an attempt to identify and elucidate only what I take to be the major issues in relation to his ecclesiology. Some of these issues have been generated by scholarship; some questions arise from the sheer force of Luke's writing; other questions come from our experience of being part of the Church in the twenty-first century and being interested in what one of the Church's formative writers has to say. This means that, in the pages that follow, we are bound to tackle a number of issues.

From ongoing work among theologians, as well as New Testament scholars, come questions of the origin and basic nature of the Church, which we will address in Chapter 2. From Luke's perspective, we will need to ask when the Church was conceived, in the ministry of Jesus or in the Pentecost story or at some other time. Our answer to this question has important implications for understanding Luke's view of the nature of the Church. In turn, this enquiry will lead us to explore the most fundamental aspect of Luke's view of the Church: in Jesus the life, character and mission of the Church is prefigured – Jesus is the Church modelled (Chapter 3).

This gives rise to the question, addressed in Chapter 4, is the Church now the source of salvation? That is, what does Luke see as the relationship between the Church and salvation? For example, since Easter, does the Church offer salvation or is salvation attainable apart from the Church?

---

[38] Acts 5:11; 7:38; 8:1, 3; 9:31; 11:22, 26; 21:1, 5; 13:1; 14:23, 27; 15:3, 4, 22, 41; 16:5; 18:22; 19:32, 39, 40; 20:17, 28, excluding 2:47 where copyists have added *en tē ekklēsia* ('in the Church').

In Chapter 5 we will explore how Luke describes the relationship between the Church and Israel and the Jews. Is the Church now Israel or is it a new or renewed Israel? Having attempted to settle that question we will have to ask how, then, is the Church to be described; is the Church to be seen as a sect of Judaism, or a household, or a brotherhood, or should it be described in other ways?

The importance of the Holy Spirit in the writings of Luke has been long and widely recognized. Indeed, the presence and power of the Spirit is almost everywhere palpable, most noticeably in Acts. Our exploration of various aspects of Luke's view of the Spirit in relation to the Church will take us into a cadre of controversies, especially regarding the nature of Pentecost (Chapter 6), and the debates about the relationship between baptism in water, and the reception of the Spirit and speaking in tongues (Chapter 7).

Chapter 8 begins conscious that some readers of Luke-Acts today find a contrast between a relatively problem-free church that Luke describes and their observation or experience of the Church with a myriad of problems. However, as has already been suggested, a more careful reading of Luke shows that he is writing in relation to a church with many and deep problems. From Luke's perspective, life in the Church probably involved, at least, rivalry between Hebrews and Hellenists, inequalities between rich and poor, the pain of suffering and persecution, as well as the issue of the role of women in the Church.

From our experience we are also interested in what Luke says about worship, including the Lord's Supper (Chapter 9). What he says about the place of Scripture in knowing God is also of interest to us in the light of our struggle with the place of Scripture in theological speculation (Chapter 10). Further, reading Luke-Acts against the backdrop of modern Pentecostalism and the charismatic movement, presently the fastest growing wing of the Church, raises the question of the place of religious experience in the life of the Church (Chapter 11).

In relation to Luke's views on leadership or ministry and the attendant structures of the Church, scholarly work on the New Testament has drawn attention to the question of whether or not his writings betray evidence of an early catholicism. That is, could it be that Luke was promoting an authoritative ecclesiastical system with Jerusalem as the headquarters? At the same time, instead of an episcopal order – with the so-called three-fold ministry of deacon, priest and bishop – Luke could be taken to favour an egalitarian or congregational model of the Church. Or, perhaps Luke understands the Church as charismatic, involving not positions in a hierarchy, but God giving his Spirit to whom he wills for service that is modelled on Jesus. Alternatively, perhaps Luke can be mined for a whole series of views. To nuance this even further, perhaps, as we shall discuss in Chapter 12, we are dealing not only with a range of views but also a progression through time in the way Luke portrays the Church being governed.

In the opening of Chapter 13 I shall argue that the most significant problem Luke saw facing the Church was its failure in mission. In going on to discuss what he has to say about mission we will have to take into account how he understands the relationship between eschatology and ecclesiology. For example, does the Church have a role in affecting the end of time? In other words, does Luke urge the early completion of the mission of the Church in order to bring about the day of the Lord 'ahead of schedule'?

Until recent times, one of the great divides among Christians, and a driving question in the contemporary Church, has been the place of social action and justice in the mission of the Church. In our time, for many churches, the issue is settled: social action and working for social justice in the world is integral to the mission of the Church. Yet, for some, the question remains, is the Church to be involved in social action or is it to be involved only in converting people? At the risk of preempting a part of what is to follow, we shall see that Luke has an understanding of mission that is likely to be deeply disturbing for most readers. Whereas, generally, we preach the good news to each other in our churches and attempt to apply justice to a pagan world, Luke's view is that the followers of Jesus should present the good news in a pagan world and apply social action and justice to the Christian community. Hopefully, this issue will receive careful and sensitive handling before our study culminates with suggestions (Chapter 14) on what Luke might contribute to our conversations on the Church.

§1.8 Our goal

Given that our approach to Luke and Acts is not always narratological, but often thematic and synthetic, we will not always be able to draw attention to all the nuances involved in Luke's descriptions as they relate to his plot and the various scenes. However, within the space available, our approach does enable us to identify Luke's major interests and may bring him more nearly into our contemporary conversations.

Also, given that our purpose is to pay attention only to what one writer, Luke, has to say about the Church, at the end of this study we will not have produced a first-century, let alone a twenty-first-century, ecclesiology. Rather, we can anticipate identifying aspects of Luke's ecclesiology, what he would contribute to one of our conversations on the Church. That is, I am not intending that the results of our enquiry concerning Luke's ideas about the Church are to be supplied as something like an ecclesiastical straight-jacket into which the contemporary Church is to be forced. Instead, our goal is to provide some of the raw material for modern theologians and church leaders in taking the next step in shaping the way we should understand and be the Church. I have already argued that Luke's voice in the New Testament is so important that any conversation about the Church that wishes to take account of the canon must give heed to his contribution. We begin by enquiring about what Luke has to say about the origins and purpose of the Church.

2

Origins and purpose

Here we will put to Luke questions concerning the origins of the Church. When does he think the Church came into existence? Was it born in the event or events of Pentecost so that he would, perhaps, see the Church as a product of the Spirit? Or, perhaps, Luke would place the origin of the Church earlier – in the life of Jesus – in which case Luke's ecclesiology is likely to be more Christo- than pneumo-centric. As Luke's views on the origins of the Church become clearer, so also do some of his views on the purpose of the Church.

§2.1 Between Easter and Pentecost

We could expect the beginning of Acts to shed light on what Luke might contribute to a discussion on the origins of the Church. In turn, with the second chapter of Acts marking such a clear new beginning in the narrative (Acts 2:1; see §6.1), giving attention to his portrayal of the group of followers of Jesus up to this point could be expected to uncover clues on Luke's view of the origins, as well as other fundamental aspects of the Church.

In the first section of the book (Acts 1:1–26) the characters involved are described as consisting of the apostles (1:2, 12–13) and a company of people including 'the women' and Mary the mother of Jesus, as well as his brothers, to total about 120 persons (1:14–15). One hundred and twenty persons was one of the numbers of people required before Jews could have a Sanhedrin (*m. Sanh.* 1.6). And those at Qumran – the site of a monastic-like Jewish community on the edge of the Dead Sea – arranged for a leader to be over every ten people.[1] It is reasonable, therefore, to think that Luke's readers would have inferred that this group was being portrayed as an established one with its twelve leaders.[2] There may be hints that Luke intends this inference. He says in 1:15 that 'there was a crowd numbering together (*epi to auto*) about one hundred and twenty' (my translation). As Luke uses the phrase *epi to auto* in 6 of its 10 occurrences in the New Testament[3] and 5 of these relate to the early community being together or gathered in Jerusalem, it is likely that he is being quite intentional about his use of the term. This likelihood is increased when we take into account that in the opening chapters of Acts he also describes the early Christians as being *homothumadon* ('together'),

---

[1] 1QS 6.3–4; 1Q28a 2.22; CD 13.1–2.
[2] See Exod. 18:21; Luke 22:29; 1QS 8.1.
[3] In the NT *epi to auto* ('together') appears in Matt. 22:34; Luke 17:35 (probably from Luke's hand; see Matt. 24:41); Acts 1:15; 2:1, 44, 47; 4:26; 1 Cor. 7:5; 11:20; 14:23.

another distinctively Lukan word.[4] What is conspicuous about this dual description of the followers of Jesus is that in the Greek translations of the Old Testament the phrase *epi to auto*, as well as *homothumadon*, are often used for the Hebrew term *yaḥad* ('together').[5] Then, notably, near Luke's time, the term *hayaḥad* ('the gathering' or 'the community') was frequently used by the people at Qumran to refer to their community.[6] And, not long after Luke's time, *epi to auto* was used by Christians of their gatherings.[7] In short, through the number 120, and the terms he used for 'together' or a 'gathering', Luke probably intends his readers to understand that the community of followers of Jesus that existed in the period between Easter and Pentecost was one that had already been formed, even though it still had not received the resources for mission.[8]

Moreover, the readers probably could not avoid concluding that this community had not been formed recently but had it roots firmly established in the ministry of Jesus: the apostles had been introduced in Luke 6:13–16; Mary the mother of Jesus is well known from early in the Gospel,[9] and Luke has already mentioned the brothers of Jesus (Luke 8:19, 20). 'The women' in Acts 1:14, most naturally, means 'the wives'. But, as 'the brothers' are mentioned separately here, and Luke's story does not generally involve the wives of his characters,[10] the women are more likely intended to be those who appear in the Gospel narrative as supporters of Jesus.[11] Besides, in Peter's speech to the 120, it is directly implied that some of these had been involved with Jesus for some or all of his ministry (Acts 1:21–22), and the list of the apostles (1:1) returning from Olivet to Jerusalem (1:12–13) is – apart from Judas – the same as that in Luke 6:13–16.

The readers also probably could not avoid concluding that this community described in the opening scenes of Acts is continuous not only with that found in the Gospel narrative but also with the community Luke describes after Pentecost. Although Mary is not mentioned after Pentecost, James, one

---

[4] See esp. Acts 1:14; 2:1 (some texts), 46; 4:24; 5:12. Elsewhere in the NT: Acts 7:57; 8:6; 12:20; 15:25; 18:12; 19:29; Rom. 15:6.

[5] In the OT *yaḥad* ('together') occurs 49 times (Gen. 49:6; Deut. 33:5; 1 Sam. 11:11; 17:10; 2 Sam. 10:15; 14:16; 21:9; 1 Chr. 12:18; Ezra 4:3; Job 3:18; 6:2; 10:8; 16:10; 17:16; 19:12; 21:26; 24:4; 31:38; 34:15, 29; 38:7; 40:13; Pss. 2:2; 31:14; 33:15; 40:15; 41:8; 49:3, 11; 62:10; 74:6, 8; 86:11; 88:18; 98:8; 133:1; 141:10; Isa. 14:20; 22:3; 27:4; 42:14; 43:26; 44:11; 45:8; 50:8; Jer. 48:7; Hos. 11:7, 8; Mic. 2:12) and is translated *epi to auto* ('together') 13 times (2 Sam. 10:15; 21:9; Ezra 4:3; Pss. 2:2; 41[40]:8; 49:2[48:3], 10[48:11]; 61[62]:10; 74[73]:6, 8; 98[97]:8; 133[132]:1; Mic. 2:12) and *homothumadon* ('together') 10 times (Job 3:18; 6:2; 16:10; 17:16; 19:12; 21:26; 24:4; 31:38; 34:15; 40:13).

[6] E.g. 1Q28a 1.26; 2.17; 1Q28b 4.26; 4Q184 1 1.2; and especially in the *Rule of the Community*, e.g. 1QS 1.1, 16; 5.1, 3, 7, 16; 6.10.

[7] See *Barn.* 4.10; (cf. 12.7); *1 Clem.* 34.7; Ign. *Eph.* 5.3; 13.1; *Magn.* 7.1; *Phld.* 6.2; 10.1.

[8] Cf. Acts 1:5, 8. See also §8.2 below.

[9] Luke 1:27, 30, 34, 38, 39, 46, 56; 2:5, 16, 19, 34.

[10] For exceptions see Acts 5:1 (Ananias and Sapphira); 18:2, 18, 26 (Priscilla and Aquila) and, possibly, Luke 24:10 (*maria hē Iakōbou*, 'Mary of James'); though, as the Mary is probably intended to be the same as that of Mark 15:40, 47; and 16:1, 'mother of James' would be intended.

[11] Luke 8:2–3; 23:49, 55; cf. 23:27; 24:10.

of Jesus' brothers, remains significant[12] and the story of the death of James, the son of Zebedee, will be told in Acts 12:2.[13] Peter, especially, plays a leading role in the ensuing narrative, and is particularly important in providing narrative continuity. He is introduced before the formation of the twelve apostles (Luke 5:8) and plays a significant role through much of Luke's two volumes (from Luke 5:8 to Acts 15:7). Emerging progressively, acting first with the group,[14] then with John,[15] then alone,[16] Peter also moves Luke's narrative focus in Acts from one involving corporate and relatively minor figures to one dominated by two major characters (Peter and Paul) who, successively, take the story to a wider audience and towards the world of the readers.

This apparent intention to convey a continuity between the community described in Acts 1 and that after Pentecost is also seen in his description of the followers of Jesus as 'devoted' (*proskartereō*). The characteristic of devotion, especially to prayer, is not unique to this pre-Pentecost group; it is also said to be true of the followers of Jesus after the coming of the Spirit.[17]

In other words, through the early scenes in Acts, Luke gives the strong impression of a continuity between the followers of Jesus in his Gospel narrative as well as with those in his post-Pentecostal narrative. This impression is very much strengthened when we take into account what he says about the apostles. For, in relation to the continuity between the followers of Jesus in his Gospel and in Acts (before and after Pentecost), what interests Luke are the apostles.

§2.2 The apostles

In the introductory chapter of Acts, as a group, the apostles provide the connection between the risen Jesus (at the Ascension, Acts 1:2–11) and the community in Jerusalem (1:14–15). Then, among these people, the apostles remain the centre of attention: they are said to have received instruction from the risen Jesus through the Holy Spirit (1:2), they are the only characters to speak,[18] and they alone converse with Jesus (1:6–8). They alone witness the Ascension (1:9–11), all their names are set out (1:13), as a group they head the list of followers of Jesus gathered in the room upstairs in Jerusalem (1:14), and – not least because it is the only story Luke uses to fill the period between the Ascension and Pentecost – there is an importance placed on the election of Matthias to reconstitute their number (1:15–26). Even after Pentecost the new converts are said to devote themselves to the apostles' teaching

---

[12] Acts 12:17; 15:1–20; 21:18.

[13] In the Gospel see Luke 5:10; 6:14; 8:51; 9:28, 54.

[14] Acts 1:13, 15; 2:14, 37, 38; and the group could be implied (see 5:2) in 5:3, 8, 9, 29.

[15] Acts 3:1, 3, 4, 6, 11, 12; 4:8, 13, 19; 8:14, 20. Note Luke 8:51/Mark 5:37; and Luke 9:28/Mark 9:2 where Luke changes lists to bring Peter and John together.

[16] Acts 5:15; 9:32, 34, 38, 39, 40; 10:5, 9, 13, 14, 17, 18, 19, 21, 25, 26, 32, 34, 44, 45, 46; 11:2, 4, 7, 13; 12:3, 5, 6, 7, 11, 14, 16, 18; 15:7.

[17] Acts 1:14; 2:42, 46; 6:4.

[18] Acts 1:6, 16–22 and, perhaps, 24–25.

(2:42) and the apostles appear to function as central or leading figures for the group.[19]

While the apostles are of central importance to Luke in the narrative of the Church early in Acts, and it is conspicuous that 'apostles' is the first term Luke uses of the post-Easter group of followers of Jesus (Acts 1:2), it is equally conspicuous that the term 'disciple' is not used until 6:1, even though it turns out to be the most common term for the followers of Jesus in Acts (see ch. 1, n. 37). This interesting hiatus in the narrative has the effect of both detaching the idea of discipleship in Acts from being with and following the earthly Jesus, as well as enhancing and establishing the apostles as the core of the Church in early Acts.

Already, therefore, from the opening scenes of Acts, it is clear that Luke sees the Church as having its origins before Easter. Then, given the significance of the apostles in early Acts and Luke dominating the use of the term in the New Testament,[20] an understanding of Luke's portrayal of this group is likely to yield a more precise understanding of what he wants to convey to his readers about the origins of the Church.

§2.3 Apostles and the nature of the Church

Before the word 'apostle' (*apostolos*) was adopted by Christians it was associated primarily with naval expeditions[21] and also with colonists and their settlement,[22] as well as with a commander of an expedition (Hesychius).[23] Herodotus twice used the word to mean messenger, as in one place did the Septuagint, the Greek translation of the Old Testament.[24]

Yet, with the rich sending tradition in the Old Testament,[25] and the early Christians' frequent dependence on the Septuagint for the raw material of their theology, their Scriptures are more likely to provide the roots of *apostolos*. This is increasingly likely in the light of Paul seeing his call and being sent in terms that echo Old Testament prophetic traditions.[26] Thus, in taking up

---

[19] Acts 5:2, 12, 18, 29, 40; 6:2 (the twelve), 6.

[20] In the NT, *apostolos* ('apostle') is found once in Matt. (10:2), Mark (3:14?; 6:30) and John (13:16), and 34 times in Luke-Acts: 6 times in Luke (6:13; 9:10; 11:49; 17:5; 22:14; 24:10) and 28 times in Acts (1:2, 26; 2:37, 42, 43; 4:33, 35, 36, 37; 5:2, 12, 18, 29, 40; 6:6; 8:1, 14, 18; 9:27; 11:1; 14:4, 14; 15:2, 4, 6, 22, 23; 16:4). The term appears 34 times in the Pauline and later Pauline corpus: Rom. 1:1; 11:13; 16:7; 1 Cor. 1:1; 4:9; 9:1, 2, 5; 12:28, 29; 15:7, 9 (twice); 2 Cor. 1:1; 8:23; 11:5, 13; 12:11, 12; Gal. 1:1, 17, 19; Eph. 1:1; 2:20; 3:5; 4:11; Phil. 2:25; Col. 1:1; 1 Thess. 2:7; 1 Tim. 1:1; 2:7; 2 Tim. 1:1, 11; Titus 1:1. In the remainder of the NT *apostolos* appears in Heb. 3:1; 1 Pet. 1:1; 2 Pet. 1:1; 3:2; Jude 1:17; Rev. 2:2; 18:20; 21:14.

[21] E.g. Plato, *Letters* 7.346a; Pseudo-Herodotus, *Life of Homer* 19; Lysias, *Speeches* 19.21; Demosthenes, *Oration* 18.3, 5, 80, 107.

[22] Dionysius of Halicarnassus, *Antiquitates romanae* 9.59.

[23] BDAG, 122.

[24] Herodotus, *Hist.* 1.21; 5.38; 1 Kgs 14:6.

[25] Well illustrated in Isa. 61:1. See also Isa. 6:8; 42:19; 48:16; 49:1–6; Jer. 1:7; 7:25; 14:14–15; 23:21, 32, 38; 26:5, 12; 27:15; 28:9, 15; 29:9, 19; 35:15; 43:1, 2; 44:4; 49:14; Ezek. 2:1–4; 3:4–6; Dan. 10:11.

[26] See Rom. 1:1–2; 10:15–16 (cf. Isa. 52:7; 53:1); Rom. 10:20 (cf. Isa. 65:1); Rom. 15:21 (cf. Isa. 52:15); 2 Cor. 6:2 (cf. Isa. 49:8); Gal. 1:15–17 (cf. Isa. 41:9; 42:6; 49:6; Jer. 1:5).

the term, Luke and his readers would have understood themselves to be using a word with religious connotations that had, in particular, a prophetic dimension. Also, part of the semantic field of the term would have been the importance and urgency of any mission associated with the word, the authority yet insignificance of the one being sent, as well as the priority of the call of the sender (God!) to go to a particular people.[27]

In bringing the word to significance in Christian vocabulary, Paul and then Luke each use the idea of 'apostle' in different ways, though holding in common the idea that being sent involved a commission with a special message or task.[28] In particular, Paul used the word to describe his calling,[29] which he strongly defended on the basis of having 'seen Jesus our Lord' (1 Cor. 9:1), and which he considered was sealed or authenticated by his ministry (1 Cor. 9:2; 2 Cor. 12:12). Thus, Paul can also use the term to describe his relationship to people: 'If I am not an apostle to others, at least I am to you' (1 Cor. 9:1), and in Romans 11:13 he describes himself as 'an apostle to the Gentiles' (cf. Phil. 2:25). In 1 Corinthians 12:28 an apostle is the first *charisma* or gift and appointment by God in the Church, by which he probably does not mean delegate sent to a church (as in 2 Cor. 8:23; Phil. 2:25) for the apostle here is appointed 'in the Church'. Nor, obviously, are they the super apostles of 2 Corinthians 10–13. Rather, as elsewhere in Paul, the apostle is a church founder.[30] Not surprisingly, then, Paul also uses the term of his significant predecessors or church leaders, though they are a wider group than the twelve.[31]

For Luke, as he makes plain in his Gospel, the twelve are the apostles chosen from among the wider group of disciples: 'And when day came, he called his disciples and chose twelve of them, whom he also named apostles' (6:13; cf. Matt. 10:1). In the addition of the last phrase, 'whom he also named apostles', Luke is likely to be the first to equate the twelve with the apostles.[32] This idea is important to him, even though, as we will see, he later includes others as apostles (see §2.5.3). As a named group, the apostles go on to play a larger part in his narrative than in any other Gospel. Luke achieves this not only through taking up the one certain reference to the apostles in his sources,[33] but also through twice introducing the term 'apostles'.[34]

---

[27] See Exod. 3:10; Judg. 6:8; Isa. 6:8; Jer. 1:7; Ezek. 2:3; Hag. 1:12; Zech. 2:11.

[28] Cf. e.g. (LXX), Gen. 32:4; Num. 20:14; Jos. 7:22; Judg. 6:35; 7:24; 9:31; 2 Chr. 36:15; Mal. 3:1.

[29] Rom. 1:1; 11:13; 1 Cor. 1:1; 4:9; 9:1–2, 5; 15:9; 2 Cor. 1:1; Gal. 1:1, 17; Col. 1:1; 1 Thess. 2:7.

[30] Rom. 1:5; 11:13; 15:20; 1 Cor. 3:5–6, 10; 9:2; 15:9–11; Gal. 1:15–16.

[31] See Rom. 16:7; 1 Cor. 1:1; 4:9; 9:1, 5; 12:28, 29; 15:7–9; 2 Cor. 8:23; Gal. 1:17, 19; Phil. 2:25.

[32] Those texts of Mark 3:14 which carry the phrase 'whom he also names apostles' have probably been assimilated to Luke 6:13. Before Luke, Mark probably did not understand his use of *apostolos* ('apostle', Mark 6:30) as a formal equivalent for 'the twelve' but as a nominalization of the sending (*apostellein*, 'to apostle' or 'to send') just reported of Jesus in 6:7: In 1 Cor. 15:5–7 Paul may be equating the twelve with the apostles. More likely, he sees the apostles as a wider group than the twelve; see 1 Cor. 15:7–9; also see ch. 2, n. 31.

[33] Mark 6:30/Luke 9:10, which refers to those returning to Jesus after he had sent them out on mission. On Mark 3:14/Luke 6:13 see ch. 2, n. 35.

[34] See Luke 17:5/Matt. 17:19 ('disciples'); and Luke 22:14/Mark 14:17 ('twelve').

On three other occasions Luke introduces the term 'apostle'; two of these strengthen his identification of the disciples or the twelve with the apostles.[35] This identification of the apostles with the disciples, and especially the twelve, is further heightened by Luke writing out a number of the references to the disciples in his sources[36] and referring to the disciples as the 'twelve', either through maintaining the word[37] or introducing it.[38]

A third introduction of the term 'apostle' makes more obvious Luke's agenda in equating the terms 'disciples', 'twelve' and 'apostles'. Whereas Luke's source has Jesus say, 'I send [*apostellō*, present tense] you prophets and sages'[39] Luke has 'I will send [*apostelō*, future tense] them prophets and apostles' (Luke 11:49). That is, in both the tense change and the appearance of the term 'apostle', Luke is able to strengthen the bridge between the ministry of Jesus in his Gospel narrative and the activity of the followers of Jesus after Easter in his Acts narrative.[40]

In addition, through the identification of the apostles with the twelve, this interpretive bridge is able to take traffic in the opposite direction. That is, congruent with details in Acts,[41] Luke establishes the apostles of the early Church in Jerusalem as the twelve that tradition knows Jesus chose in his ministry.[42] Thus, Luke defines 'apostleship' (*apostolē*, Acts 1:25) as being part of the group accompanying Jesus from the baptism of John until the Ascension and being witnesses, particularly of the resurrection (1:22; cf. Luke 24:48). In view of the significance of the twelve or the apostles, it is not surprising that Luke rehabilitates them from their poor showing in Mark. In two places Luke writes out the disciples so they are not seen to be rebuked by Jesus (Mark 8:33/Luke 9:23) or to argue with each other (Mark 9:14/Luke 9:37); he softens their ignorance (Mark 9:28/Luke 17:6) and their incomprehension is excused (Mark 8:32/Luke 9:45); Jesus' indignation at them (Mark 10:13/Luke 18:15) and criticism of them is removed (Mark 10:23/Luke 18:24), as is mention of them all forsaking Jesus (Mark 14:50/Luke 22:53). Luke also increases their involvement in Jesus' ministry.[43]

---

[35] Luke 6:13. Assuming Luke was here relying on Mark, the phrase 'whom he also named apostles' (Mark 3:14) is insufficiently secure to know whether or not it would have been known to Luke. See also Luke 24:10, on which Mark 16:10, part of the second-century longer ending of Mark, is likely to be partly dependent.

[36] Mark 2:24/Luke 6:2; Mark 3:7/Luke 6:17; Mark 6:1/Luke 4:16; Mark 7:2, 5/Luke 11:37; Mark 8:33/Luke 9:22; Mark 8:34/Luke 9:23; Mark 9:14/Luke 9:37; Mark 10:10/Luke 16:18; Mark 10:23/Luke 18:24; Mark 10:46/Luke 18:35; Mark 13:1/Luke 21:5; Matt. 8:21/Luke 9:59.

[37] See Mark 3:14/Luke 6:13; 9:1; Mark 6:7/Luke 9:1; Mark 10:32/Luke 18:31; Mark 14:10/Luke 22:3.

[38] Matt. 9:35/Luke 8:1; Mark 6:35/Luke 9:12. At Luke 24:9 Luke inserts 'the eleven'. Cf. Matt. 28:8; Mark 16:8.

[39] Probably his Q source; see Matt. 23:34.

[40] See also the changes Luke makes to his sources to help readers identify with the followers of the pre-Easter Jesus: Matt. 10:37–38/Luke 14:26–27; Mark 8:34/Luke 9:23; Mark 10:10/Luke 16:18; Mark 11:1/Luke 19:29; Mark 16:7/Luke 24:7.

[41] Acts 1:2; see §2.5.1 and 2.5.2 below.

[42] Cf. Mark 3:14, 16; 4:10; 6:7; 9:35; 10:32; 11:11; 14:10, 17, 20, 43: Cf. Luke (Q) 22:28, 30.

[43] See Mark 6:6/Luke 8:1; Mark 6:39, 41/Luke 9:14, 16; Mark 11:9/Luke 19:37.

These perspectives on the apostles – particularly their being sent on mission, their equation with the twelve whom Jesus chose and their being part of the bridge between the ministries of Jesus before and after Easter – prepare the reader of Acts for what Luke has to say there about the apostles and their part in the origins of the Church. What Luke has to say through the apostles about the purpose and life of the Church we will come to presently.

§2.4 Apostles and the origin of the Church

Early in this chapter we saw that Luke is probably giving signals that, even before Pentecost, the community of followers was already formed (§2.1). Looking more closely we see that, in Luke's first description of the post-Easter group of Jesus' followers as the apostles whom 'he had chosen' (*exelexato*, Acts 1:2), he uses the aorist indicative tense of the verb 'to choose'. This points to the choosing having taken place at some point in the past. Indeed, the appointment of the apostles implied here is most obviously reported in Luke 6:13: 'he called his disciples, and chose (*eklexamenos*) from them twelve, whom he named apostles'.

The election of Matthias is further confirmation of Luke's view that the origin of the Church was in Jesus choosing the twelve. The election (Acts 1:23–26) takes place before the coming of the Spirit (2:4), who plays no part in this story. The Spirit does not lead Peter to choose between candidates, nor does the Spirit call on Matthias to be set apart (cf. 13:2). Instead, the company of followers of Jesus put forward two men who had been with them for the whole of Jesus' ministry. Then they pray to the 'Lord' (*kurios*, 1:24, most probably Jesus)[44] to make the choice. The choice is determined through prayer and the casting of lots (1:23–26), which would have been understood as revealing God's choice. With the widespread use of casting lots,[45] and the addition of the specific phrase 'and the lot fell on Matthias' (1:26), it is likely that Luke's readers would have taken the casting of lots to have been used rather than it being a figure of speech for a decision.

The importance of Jesus for the origin and ongoing focus of the Church is seen in other ways in Acts. For example, we find, even immediately after

---

[44] Cf. Acts 1:24. In Acts, 'Lord' (*kurios*) is most obviously used of Jesus in 1:6, 21 (Lord Jesus); 2:36; 4:33 (Lord Jesus); 7:59 (Lord Jesus), 60; 8:16 (Lord Jesus); 9:1, 5, 10 (twice), 17 (Lord Jesus), 27, 28(?), 35, 42; 11:16, 17 (Lord Jesus), 20 (Lord Jesus), 21 (twice), 24; 15:11 (Lord Jesus), 26 (Lord Jesus); 16:31 (Lord Jesus); 19:13 (Lord Jesus), 17 (Lord Jesus); 20:1 (Lord Jesus), 24 (Lord Jesus), 35 (Lord Jesus); 21:13 (Lord Jesus); 22:8, 10 (twice), 19; 26:15 (twice); 28:31 (Lord Jesus).

[45] On casting lots as a way of gaining God's guidance (even by those not of the people of God, Jon. 1:7; though see Hos. 4:12) see Prov. 16:33. Cf. 1 Sam. 10:19–22; 14:36–42; Prov. 16:1, 9; Isa. 34:17; Ecclus. 33:3; Homer, *Il.* 171.592–93; Plato, *Laws* 690c; 741b; 757e; 759c; *LAB* 49.1–5; Lucian, *Sects* 40, and note the combination of casting of lots and prayer: Homer, *Il.* 170.140–41, 314–17; 1 Sam. 14:41; *LAB* 25.5.

See also Homer, *Il.* 3.310–28; Cicero, *Div.* 2.41; 1QS 2.23; 5.3; 6.13–23; 1Q28a 1.16; Josephus, *Ant.* 5.43, 81; 6.61; 7.367; 9.211; *J.W.* 3.390; 4.153, 155; 5.511; 7.396; Tacitus, *Germany* 10.

Pentecost, that it is the Lord (possibly Jesus, see ch. 2, n. 44) who adds to their number those being saved (Acts 2:47), even though the Spirit is involved (e.g. 10:44). Also, it is not the name of the Spirit but the name of Jesus that gives them identity (9:21) as well as forgiveness (10:43), and in whose name they speak and teach,[46] baptize,[47] suffer (5:41; 9:16), heal (4:10), exorcise (19:18), perform miracles (4:30; 19:17) and die (21:13).

§2.5 Apostles and the purpose of the Church

The particular bridge of interpretation Luke has built between his Gospel and Acts – in the construction of the first sentence of Acts (see Chapter 3), and his use of the term apostles and their appointment by Jesus before Easter – implies that the purpose of the Church after Easter is to continue what Jesus did and taught. This is made more explicit and comprehensible in both the Gospel portraits of the apostles, as well as in the roles and descriptions he gives of them in Acts.

§2.5.1 The apostles (the Church) in the Gospel

One of the most significant points about the apostles is that there were twelve of them. Luke and his readers shared the view that the number was an analogue for the twelve tribes of Israel: the entire people of God.[48] In taking up the number twelve Luke is not claiming that in the apostles the origin of the Church was to be traced to the Old Testament. But, along with his tradition, he is affirming that the followers of Jesus are claiming all the promises God made to his people. In that twelve was also the number in which the hopes of all Israel resonated, Luke agreed that the future of the entire people of God was to be found in the Church (Luke 22:30; Acts 26:7). The past promises and future hopes of the people of God find their realization in the Church. That Luke calls these twelve apostles is doubly significant.

In the gospel story of the call of the twelve nothing is said regarding their mission other than the adumbration involved in the term 'apostle' (Luke 6:13–16). Luke does not say that the twelve were chosen 'to be with him' (cf. Mark 3:14). Nor does he say that the twelve were chosen 'to preach and to have authority to cast out demons' (3:14–15, my translation). Instead, following the story of the call of the twelve there is a succession of stories of Jesus involved in ministry during which, at one point, it is said, 'the twelve were with him' (Luke 8:1). In this demonstration of what he meant by being with Jesus, Luke has not allowed the idea to be divorced from being on mission; they are, for him, the same thing. Thus, even though the twelve are sent on mission, readers will understand they are not being separated from Jesus (cf. Chapter 3).

---

[46] Acts 4:18; 5:28, 40; 8:12; 9:15, 27, 28.
[47] Acts 8:16; 10:48; 19:5.
[48] Acts 7:8; cf. Gen. 49; Exod. 24:4; 28:21; 39:14; Jos. 3:12; 4:8; 1 Kgs 18:31; Ezek. 47:13.

Luke says, 'He called the twelve and gave them power (*dunamis*) and authority over all the demons and to cure the sick, and sent (*apostellō*) them to preach the kingdom of God and to heal' (Luke 9:1–2, my translation). A number of aspects of this statement deserve attention in order to elucidate what it implies about Luke's understanding of the purpose of the Church.

To begin with, from Acts 1 readers know that the twelve, or the apostles, are the core of the Church, so that the descriptions of them would be read as a proleptic portrayal of the Church. Second, the mission to which the twelve are being commissioned is the same as that ascribed to Jesus: casting out demons, healing the sick and preaching the kingdom of God.[49] In other words, the ministry of Jesus is mirrored and understood to be continued in the ministry of the apostles (see Chapter 3). Third, in view of the Septuagintal roots of the word, the use of *apostellō* could hardly fail to alert readers to the apostles functioning in Jesus' place (see §2.3 above). Indeed, in the story of the feeding of five thousand (which closely follows this one), the twelve are said to act for Jesus in arranging the crowd and in distributing the bread and fish (Luke 9:14–16). Fourth, Luke's addition of the word 'power' (*dunamis*) to his source (Mark 6:7) draws attention to two things. On the one hand, power has enabled Jesus to preach, to cast out demons and to heal.[50] On the other hand, power is also what the risen Jesus promises the apostles for their mission (Luke 24:49; Acts 1:8). Or, seeing this point from the narrative perspective of Acts, the power involved in the coming of the Holy Spirit to the apostles at Pentecost for their mission is a reflection of both what Jesus had for his mission and what he had given his followers in the Gospel for theirs. This reinforces the point that the post-Easter ministry of the apostles is a reflection and continuation of Jesus' ministry, though now not just to the Jews but also to the Gentiles.

§2.5.2 The Church (the apostles) in Acts

Not only in the Gospel but also in the early chapters of Acts, Luke has the ministry of Jesus mirrored and maintained through the twelve apostles speaking 'the word of God'[51] and performing miracles.[52] Luke also spells out that the ministry of Jesus continues through the apostles' teaching in the name of Jesus (Acts 5:28). And, in response to being asked, 'By what power or by what name did you do this?' (4:7), Peter says the man is in good health 'by the name of Jesus' (4:10).

In these stories not only is the ministry of the apostles as a group of twelve centred in Jerusalem (Acts 8:1, 14), the eschatological city,[53] but also particular attention is drawn to their role in the eschatological coming of the Spirit.

---

[49] See, e.g. Luke 4:43; 8:1; 9:11; 11:20.
[50] See Luke 4:14, 36; 5:17; 6:19; 8:46; cf. 10:13; 19:37; Acts 10:38.
[51] On Jesus speaking the word of God see Luke 5:1; cf. 8:21; on the apostles speaking the word of God see 4:31; 6:2; cf. 8:14; 11:1. See also ch. 13, n. 51.
[52] Acts 2:43; 3:1–10; 5:12–16.
[53] Cf. e.g. Isa. 52:7–8; 60—62; Ezek. 5:5; 38:12; Zech. 9:9; Mal. 3:1–4; esp. Luke 2:25, 38.

Immediately before the coming of the Spirit Luke says Matthias 'was added to the eleven apostles', restoring their full number (1:26). Narratively, Luke has prepared (or repaired) the twelve, the embryonic people of God to receive Pentecost. Then, immediately after the coming of the Spirit, Peter is said to stand 'with the eleven' to give an eschatological interpretation of the Spirit's arrival (2:14, 17).

The importance of the twelve in the preparation for and involvement in the coming of the Spirit has already been signalled and explained in the Gospel. In the main scene of the Last Supper Luke has Jesus say to the apostles: 'I confer on you, just as my Father has conferred on me, a kingdom,[54] so that you may eat and drink at my (*mou*) table in my (*mou*) kingdom, and you will sit on thrones judging (*krinō*) the twelve tribes of Israel' (Luke 22:29–30). The imagery of the banquet is clearly eschatological[55] so that Luke intends Jesus to be referring to his future kingdom that the apostles will share with him (note the double *mou*) and judge the twelve tribes. In view of the regal rather than judicial context here, and Luke generally using *krinō* to mean 'decide' in such contexts,[56] he likely had in mind the apostles leading the twelve tribes, that is, renewed Israel.

When Luke thinks this will take place is shown by a small change he makes in his tradition. If, as is likely, Luke is depending on Q for his material here (cf. Matt. 19:28), he has left out reference to the leading taking place in the future new age or 'new creation' (*tē palingenesia*).[57] This term was used of a world beyond the present material one, and of an individual's entry into it[58] and, more simply, of life after death (e.g. Philo, *Posterity* 124; *Cherubim* 114). By leaving out reference to *tē palingenesia* Luke has brought the apostles' leading forward from the future to the present time of the people of God. That this is what Luke has in mind can be seen in noting that the next time Jesus is discussing the kingdom with the twelve is in Acts 1:3. They respond by asking whether he is now going 'to restore the kingdom of Israel' (Acts 1:6). Importantly, in a 'No, but' answer Jesus promises the coming of the Holy Spirit (1:8). That is, the present coming of the Spirit on the followers of Jesus is the restoration of the kingdom of Israel.[59] In the coming of the Spirit the followers of Jesus are shown to be the true Israel.

---

[54] For Jesus' kingdom and regal status see Luke 1:32–33; 19:11–27, 28–40; 23:42.

[55] See Isa. 25:6–7; 64:3; 65:13–14; Ezek. 32:4; 39:17–20; *1 En.* 62.14; 25.5; *2 Bar.* 29.4–8; *4 Ezra* 6.49–51; *2 En.* 42.5; Luke 12:37; 13:29.

[56] For Luke, *krinō* ('judge') could mean to 'pass judgement', as in Acts 7:7 (cf. Gen. 15:14); 13:27; 17:31; 23:3; or to be tried in court, as in 23:6; 24:21; 25:9, 10, 20; 26:6; or 'decide', as in Acts 15:39; 13:46 (negatively); 16:15; 20:16; 25:25; 26:8; 27:1; or (in the plural) 'decisions', as in Acts 16:4; 21:25.

[57] *Palingenesia* ('rebirth' or 'new age') does not appear in the LXX, though Job 14:14 has the phrase *palin genōmai* ('exist again'). In the NT *palingenesia* occurs in Matt. 19:28; and Titus 3:5.

[58] See, e.g. Marcus Aurelius, *Meditations* 9.1; Plutarch, *The E at Delphi* 389a; *Is. Or.* 364; *On the Eating of Flesh* 996c; 998c; *Obs.* 438d; Lucian, *The Fly* 7; and, notably, Terentius Varro, cited by Augustine, *The City of God* 22.28.

[59] On the relationship between the Church and Israel see Chapter 5 below.

After providing the eschatological interpretation of the coming of the Spirit (esp. Acts 2:14–21), as a numbered group, the twelve only appear again to oversee the election of the seven (6:1–3) and to assert their role to be devoted to prayer and serving the word (6:4). The group of twelve has witnessed to the resurrection and Ascension – the enthronement of Jesus as Messiah of Israel. They have prepared for, received and interpreted the coming of the Spirit – the inauguration of the new Israel. They have also initially mirrored and maintained the ministry of Jesus in the power of that Spirit. The numbered group of twelve has accomplished its primary roles. It is in noting this that we have the reason why James is not replaced; the twelve, though not the apostles, had fulfilled their role (cf. 12:2).

§2.5.3 Extending the apostolate

Having used the twelve to witness to the enthronement of Jesus and to establish and interpret the coming of the kingdom in the Spirit, as well as having depended on the apostolate to establish the function of the Church as receiving the eschatological promises of God and mirroring and maintaining the ministry of Jesus, Luke has to bridge the gap between the first and later generations of followers of Jesus. One of the ways Luke achieves this is by extending his definition of an apostle.

One of the puzzles of Luke's definition of an apostle is that, as we have seen, he closely identifies the apostles with the twelve appointed by Jesus, including Matthias, and reserves the title for them. Yet, later in Acts, he calls Barnabas and Paul apostles[60] and, as we will see, portrays them in that role. The puzzle of this apparent contradiction is not even partially solved by suggesting that one of Luke's sources is responsible for the term 'apostle'.[61] For, most easily in his Gospel, Luke can be shown to be in full control of his material and able to be held responsible for the views expressed in his text.[62]

A closer look at how Luke defined the apostles shows that early in Acts he has paved the way for the possibility of others being apostles and carrying on their ministry. That is, the criteria set out for the replacement of Judas emphasize the person being with the group of followers rather than just Jesus. Peter says: 'one of the men who have accompanied *us* during all the time that the Lord Jesus went in and out *among us*, beginning from the baptism of John until the day when he was taken up *from us* – one of these must become a witness *with us* to his resurrection (Acts 1:21–22). Thus, it is not that the twelfth apostle simply had to have been with Jesus before Easter. Rather, the person had to belong to the wider group of his followers, among whom Jesus

---

[60] Acts 14:4, 14. In 15:13, Luke is probably including James among the apostles. Cf. 1 Cor. 15:7; Gal. 1:19; §12.1.2 below.

[61] A separate source is perhaps evident in the unexpected order in which Barnabas and Paul are mentioned. For Barnabas and Saul see Acts 11:30; 12:25; 13:2, 7; for Paul and Barnabas see 13:43, 46, 50; 14:1; 15:22, 35; and for Barnabas and Paul see 14:14; 15:12, 25; cf. 14:12.

[62] Luke's otherwise consistent use of 'apostle' means that its absence in some texts of Acts 14:14 is to be explained as copyists attempting to conform Acts to their views.

moved. In this way Luke has loosened or broadened the readers' understanding of an apostle.

Also, in relation to defining the apostles, Luke shares with his predecessors the understanding that witnessing the resurrection was seeing the risen Jesus rather than seeing the event of the resurrection.[63] Notably, it is in the penultimate scene in the Gospel that Luke introduces the idea of being a witness (Luke 24:44–49).[64] In Jerusalem (24:33), immediately before the Ascension story (24:50–53), Jesus summarizes both what he has said to them in his ministry (24:44), as well as what has just happened to the Christ in the Easter events (24:46). He goes on to say, 'you [the eleven and those with them, 24:33] are witnesses to these things' (24:48). 'These things' refers, then, both to the entire ministry of Jesus but particularly to the Easter events. This is all but confirmed in noting that the only time the apostles speak after Easter in the Gospel is to say, 'The Lord has risen indeed, and he has appeared to Simon!' (24:34). And, in Acts, witnessing by the apostles is generally related to or restricted to the resurrection.[65] However, it is not that Luke is saying the apostles are to bear testimony to seeing Jesus rise from the dead. Rather, it is reports of appearances of the risen Jesus that are the basis of witnessing to the resurrection.

Defining witnesses as those to whom Jesus appears enables others to witness the resurrection, pass this test, and be called apostles. In turn, this provides Luke with a further basis for extending the notion of an apostle beyond the twelve. In particular, this is seen in Luke's development of his portrait of Paul in which he is eventually accorded full status as an apostle.

Luke's development of the role of Paul in Acts is reflected in the three separate stories of Paul's conversion. In the first story a light from heaven is seen by Paul alone, who falls to the ground, as Ezekiel did on seeing the glory of the Lord in his call (Ezek. 1:28). Although Luke probably intends his readers to understand that Paul has encountered the glory of God, Jesus is heard but not seen (Acts 9:3–7).

Nevertheless, on Paul having trouble joining the disciples, Barnabas successfully introduces him to the apostles on two grounds: 'he had seen the Lord' and 'had spoken boldly in the name of Jesus' (Acts 9:27, see 19–22). These are the same two characteristics mentioned of the apostles and define them at the end of Luke: to have seen the risen Jesus and to witness in the sense of speaking about something known (Luke 24:48).[66]

---

[63] For *martus* ('witness') in relation to the apostles see Luke 24:48; Acts 1:8, 22; 2:32; 3:15; 5:32; 10:39, 41.

[64] The only other occurrence of *martus* ('witness') in Luke's Gospel refers to the scribes (Luke 11:48).

[65] See Acts 1:22; 2:32; 3:15; 10:41; 13:31. *Martus* is used in a general sense in Acts 1:8 (though following so close to Luke 24:48 it would retain an echo of its reference to the resurrection); 5:32 (which echoes 24:47–48); and 10:39 (which is overshadowed by another use of *martus* in 10:41 that refers to the resurrection); also see 6:13 (false witness); 7:48 (witnesses of Stephen's speech); and 22:20 (epithet for Stephen).

[66] On 'witness' as testifying see Matt. 18:16; 26:65; Mark 14:63; Acts 7:58; 2 Cor. 13:1; 1 Tim. 5:19; Heb. 10:28.

The result of the introduction of Paul to the apostles is particularly important in Luke's portrait of Paul. He sketches a picture of Paul as almost one of the apostles, saying he 'went in and out among them in Jerusalem'. Moreover, he goes on to say that Paul was 'speaking boldly in the name of the Lord' (Acts 9:28). This is reminiscent of the prayer of the group to which Peter and John went after being released by the authorities: 'Lord, look at their threats, and grant to your servants to speak your word with all boldness' (4:29). Boldness is a description used a number of times of the apostles.[67] Thus, although Luke does not yet promote Paul into the apostolate, he certainly pictures Paul as having their imprimatur, as associating very closely with them and as performing the same ministry. Readers are well prepared for Paul (and Barnabas) to be called apostles (Acts 14:4, 14).

When Paul and Barnabas are called apostles it is conspicuous that it occurs in the story of Paul's first mission to the Gentiles, when he is reported as doing the work of an apostle (Acts 13:4—14:28). It is also notable that, following this mission, his ministry is authenticated by the apostles in Jerusalem (15:1–35).

At the same time that Paul is increasingly described as, and doing the work of, an apostle, the twelve (apostles) fade from Luke's narrative. After the sanctioning of Paul's ministry, Peter and the other eleven apostles are not mentioned. Once Peter was charged with 'strengthening' the Church (Luke 22:31–32), now Paul is fulfilling that role.[68] Paul even takes the place of Peter as the central character in the last part of Acts. It is these observations that help make sense of Luke calling both the twelve and Paul and Barnabas apostles.

Luke continues to bring Paul closer to his portrait of the apostles in the second conversion story (Acts 22:1–21). This time Paul is said 'to see[69] the Righteous One' as well as hear his voice. Paul goes on to say this was so he would 'be his witness (*martus*)' of what he had 'seen and heard' (22:14–15). Again, along with using the term 'witness', this echoes Luke's description of the apostles in what Jesus says to them in the penultimate scene in his Gospel (Luke 24:44–49).

In the third story of Paul's conversion, the parallel between the description of Paul and the portrait of the apostles is drawn even more closely. The risen Lord says to Paul, 'I have appeared to you for the purpose, to appoint you to serve and testify (*martus*) to the things in which you have seen me and to those in which I will appear to you' (Acts 26:16; cf. 9:17). Just as Jesus appeared to Peter (Luke 24:34; cf. Acts 13:31), he has also appeared to Paul. Readers would now reasonably conclude that Paul (and Barnabas) have continued the ministry of the twelve, or expressed the purpose of the Church,

---

[67] Acts 2:29; 4:13, 31.

[68] Acts 14:22 (with Barnabas); 15:41; 16:5; 18:23. That Judas and Silas are also seen taking up this task (15:32) further broadens the 'apostolic' base of the Church for Luke.

[69] The use of *eidon*, the aorist of *horaō* ('see'), in Luke-Acts can involve seeing with the eyes (e.g. Luke 2:15; 7:22; Acts 3:3; 8:18) as well as seeing in visions (e.g. Luke 1:12; Acts 9:12; 10:3, 17; 11:5; 16:10).

in mirroring and maintaining the ministry of Jesus and have accorded them full status as apostles.[70]

§2.6 Conclusions

In considering Luke's view of the origin and purpose of the Church, two points can be made. First, an unavoidable conclusion to be drawn from this chapter is that from Luke's perspective the Church has its origin in the ministry of Jesus and is recreated by the risen Jesus to be the renewed people of God.[71] In the simple unaided call of the apostles and the collection of them around Jesus, the Church had its origins or birth. The Church is, then, based on the apostles, not in that they initiate or inaugurate it but in that they are the Church, and that it continues to grow from them.

In coming to this conclusion we have found no evidence that Luke would consider a sacramental act – baptism or the Eucharist, for example – to be involved in the origin of the Church. Moreover, the Church was not conceived at Pentecost. For Luke, the Church is not the product of the Spirit; the Spirit has not created the Church. The nascent Church was in existence before the coming of the Spirit.

We can see that Luke would not call Pentecost the birth of the Church. For him the origins of the Church is in the call and community of followers of Jesus during his ministry. Perhaps Luke would say that what was born in hope in the ministry of the earthly Jesus was given the 'breath' (*pneuma*) of life and power in the promised coming of the 'Spirit' (*pneuma*). This means that, for Luke, the Church does not occupy a period in history separate from that of Jesus. Rather, the Church was called into existence by him and is a continuation or ongoing expression of his ministry. Indeed, as Acts 1:1 intimates, by saying that the Gospel concerned what 'Jesus began to do and teach', the ministry of the Church is not seen as distinct from but continues the ministry of Jesus and is even to be identified with the continuing ministry of the risen Lord. As important as the Spirit is for Luke's understanding of the corporate life of the believers after Easter (see Chapters 6 and 7 below), the Church in it origins and fundamental purpose is firmly Christo-centric.

Of course, in the light of the significance and interpretation Luke gives to the Pentecost story, he does not understand the Church in the same way after Pentecost – he even calls it a beginning (Acts 11:15). In Pentecost the Church is not born but established as the heir of the eschatological kingdom, the hope of Israel. Given that Luke believed the Church was conceived

---

[70] The parallels between Peter and Paul are particularly noticeable in Acts 2—5 and 16:16–40. E.g. Peter (5:19; cf. 12:7–11) is described as miraculously escaping from prison, so also is Paul (16:25–34), and Paul (16:16–18; cf. 13:4–12; 14:8–18; 19:11–12; 20:7–12) performs the same kinds of miracles as Peter (3:1–10; 5:15; cf. 9:32–43).

[71] Acts 1:24; cf. 9:4–6, 15–16.

and began its life in the election of the apostles before Easter we are obliged to return to Luke's story of Jesus in order to increase our understanding of his views about the Church and its origins (see Chapter 3 below).

Second, in his characterization of both those who associated with Jesus before Easter and those eventually included among them, Luke gives expression to a number of his views about the purpose of the Church. In the very name 'apostle', with its roots in the Old Testament prophetic call stories, there is the notion of a summons to be sent to represent God. Perhaps with this in mind, it is notable that Luke leaves out the idea of the apostles being with Jesus, one of Mark's defining characteristics of the followers of Jesus or the Church. For Luke, being with Jesus is not separated from being on mission – they are the same thing.

At one level, as seen in the mission of the apostles, Luke's purpose for the Church is to mirror and maintain the ministry of Jesus: to cast out demons, heal the sick and preach the kingdom of God. Yet, on closer examination, the function of the Church is not a mere emulation of the speech and activity of Jesus. For, when we take into account the apostles preparing for, receiving and explaining the coming of the Spirit we see that their apparent activities are expressions of a more profound purpose of the Church. That is, the Church receives, embodies and expresses the same kingdom, Spirit or powerful presence of God that Jesus embodied and expressed in his activities. At least to this extent, the Church is sacramental in being a visible form of the now invisible activity of God in Jesus (cf. Augustine, *Letter* 105.12). The purpose of the Church, then, arises out of being obedient to what is both expressed and possible in the power of the Spirit – embodying the ministry of Jesus. We will return to this theme when we examine Luke's portrait of Jesus, in the next chapter, and also when we look at the major problems facing the Church as Luke describes it (see Chapter 8).

In eventually promoting Barnabas and particularly Paul to the rank of apostle, Luke is able to show his readers that the purpose of the Church portrayed in his Gospel and the early parts of Acts is to be the same as for the Church in the life of the readers. There is no closing of one age (the apostolic) and the initiating of another (post-apostolic) period. The kingdom, inextricably bound to the notion of mission, is conferred on the apostles, and experienced by them and expressed by them. The kingdom is also the subject of Paul's attention as Acts closes. But this closing is the opening for the readers to continue experiencing and expressing the kingdom in their lives. Already we are beginning to see some of the fundamental aspects of Luke's view of the Church; these will be even more obvious as we turn to the way he portrays the single most important character who appears in both volumes of his work.

3

Jesus: the Church modelled

At the opening of Acts, Luke offers his readers an important entrée into his view of the Church. The NRSV translates the first words of Acts: 'In the first book, Theophilus, I wrote about all that Jesus did and taught from the beginning'. However, a more literal translation is to be preferred indicating that, in his Gospel, Luke was writing about 'all that Jesus began to do and teach' (RSV). This would imply that Acts was about what Jesus continued to do and teach. Such a reading allows 'began' (the aorist *ērxato* from *archō*, 'begin') its natural meaning. Thus, in these opening words, Luke is probably signalling to his readers not only that his second volume continues the ministry of Jesus but also that in the first volume the ministry of the Church began and can be seen in what Jesus was doing and teaching.

Our confidence in this observation that Jesus, even if generally unseen and unnamed, continues to play the lead role in Acts is reinforced in a number of ways that we shall explore later (§11.1). However, perhaps most significantly, there is the long-recognized tapestry of parallels Luke weaves between his portraits of Jesus and the post-Easter group of his followers, parallels that maintain Jesus in active ministry beyond the Gospel and through Luke's second volume.

We turn attention to these parallels in this chapter for they yield important results in relation to our study of Luke's view of the nature and function of the Church. This will lead us to include a discussion of the two-part structure of his work. In turn, as we follow the progress of Luke's thinking in chapters below about Jesus in relation to the nature and function of the Church, we are obliged not only to look back from Acts to the Gospel but also forward to the relationship between the Church and the end of time.

§3.1 Jesus paralleled

The most heavily concentrated set of parallels between Jesus and the post-Easter group of his followers revolves around the inauguration of the ministry of Jesus in Luke and the beginning of the Church in Acts. In preparation for the coming age in which Jesus will feature, the people ask John, 'What shall we do?'[1] and in preparation for the coming of the Spirit on the first converts the people ask Peter, 'What shall we do?' (Acts 2:37). When he is

---

[1] Luke 3:10, 12, 14.

baptized, Jesus is portrayed as praying (Luke 3:21) and, prior to their being baptized in the Spirit, his followers are also described as praying people (Acts 1:14, cf. 24). Visionary experiences are associated with the coming of the Spirit on both Jesus and his followers (Luke 3:22; Acts 2:1–13). Then, Luke has the ministry of Jesus begin with a sermon explaining the fulfilment of prophecy in events associated with him (Luke 4:16–21) and Peter, representing the twelve (Acts 2:14), preaches a sermon in which prophecy is said to be fulfilled in events that had just taken place in the coming of the Spirit (2:14–40). Each of these sermons mentions the Holy Spirit coming to the speaker and the associated offer of 'release' (*aphesis*, Luke 4:18; Acts 2:38). In both the ministry of Jesus (Luke 4:31—5:26) and his followers (Acts 3:1–10) miracles are then depicted. Then, for both Jesus and his followers in Acts, opposition from religious authorities follows (Luke 5:29—6:11; Acts 4:1—8:3). From this it is reasonable to maintain the conclusion that Luke is developing the theme foreshadowed in the first line of his second work, that what was begun in the activity and teaching of Jesus is to be continued in the life of his followers after Easter. On closer examination a number of themes emerges as important to Luke in these parallels between Jesus and his post-Easter followers.

§3.1.1 The Holy Spirit

The first set of parallels that becomes obvious in Luke's work is the Holy Spirit anointing and filling both Jesus and his followers. When the angel Gabriel came to Mary, he said that the Holy Spirit would come upon her (Luke 1:35). When Jesus was baptized in the Jordan by John, the heavens opened and the Holy Spirit descended upon him (3:22). Full of the Holy Spirit, Jesus returned from the Jordan and was led by the Spirit for forty days in the wilderness (4:1). Then, when Jesus began his ministry he is said to 'return in the power of the Spirit into Galilee' (4:14). And, in the synagogue, the passage Jesus reads out from Isaiah begins: 'The Spirit of the Lord is upon me, for he has anointed me. He has sent me to preach' (4:18; cf. Isa. 61:1). It is notable that all of these references to Jesus being filled or empowered by the Spirit are related to Jesus' conception and the inauguration of his ministry. This emphasis is paralleled in the early days of the Church in Acts.

On the day of Pentecost all the followers of Jesus are filled with the Holy Spirit.[2] Being filled with the Spirit, Peter stands up and speaks to the crowd (Acts 2:14). Also, said to be filled with the Spirit, Peter makes his defence before the Sanhedrin (4:8). At the beginning of the Church among the Gentiles Luke says that 'the Holy Spirit fell on all who heard the word' (10:44). Then, throughout Acts those said to be filled with the Spirit are the seven (6:3), Stephen (6:5; 7:55), Barnabas (11:24) and the disciples (13:52). From this series of parallels it is obvious that just as Jesus' ministry was inaugurated and

---

[2] Acts 2:4; see also 2:17, 18, 33, 38.

empowered by the Spirit so the followers of Jesus were and, by implication, should continue to be empowered by the same Spirit.

§3.1.2 Teaching and preaching the good news[3]

We have already noted that, in summarizing his Gospel, Luke said that it contained 'all that Jesus began to do and teach' (Acts 1:1). Indeed, Luke depicts Jesus teaching in the synagogues, in the temple, from a boat, in the street and in the villages.[4] Then, in Acts, Luke says Peter and John teach, and the apostles teach in the temple and in Jerusalem.[5] Barnabas and Paul teach for a whole year in Antioch (11:26; 15:35) and for eighteen months Paul teaches the word of God in Corinth (18:11). Luke reports Paul saying that he had taught the Ephesians in public and in their homes (20:20). Acts ends with Paul in Rome 'teaching about the Lord Jesus Christ quite openly and unhindered' (28:31).

Similarly, Luke describes both Jesus and his immediate disciples, as well as his post-Easter followers, as preaching the good news. Jesus preaches about the good news of the kingdom of God,[6] so also do the disciples.[7] After Easter the apostles, Peter and John, and those scattered from Jerusalem and Philip, are depicted as preaching the good news.[8] In the cities he enters, Paul is also often said to be preaching the good news.[9]

In more detail, we see that Jesus said that he had not come to call the righteous, but sinners to repentance (Luke 5:32), and the parables of the lost sheep, the lost coin and the lost son tell of the joy over a sinner who repents.[10] Then, Jesus sent out the seventy-two[11] to preach, that is, it is assumed, to call for repentance (cf. 10:13). In Acts, Peter tells the crowd to repent to receive forgiveness of their sins[12] and Paul says that God commands everyone to repent (Acts 17:30; 26:20). Also, there is a correspondence between the message of the risen Jesus (Luke 24:44–47) and that of Paul (Acts 26:22–23). This series of parallels shows that just as Jesus proclaimed good news, so the followers of Jesus had a message of good news. So important is this theme that we shall explore it further when we discuss the mission of the Church.

---

[3] That Luke does not wish readers to draw any particular distinction between the two words, 'to preach' (*euangelizesthai*) and 'to teach' (*didaskein*) seems apparent from Luke 20:1 and Acts 15:35.

[4] Luke 4:15, 31–32; 5:3, 17; 6:6; 11:1; 13:10, 22; 19:47; 20:1, 21; 21:37.

[5] Acts 4:2; 5:21, 25, 28, 42.

[6] Luke 4:43; 8:1, 10; 9:11, 62.

[7] Luke 9:2, 60; 10:9, 11.

[8] Acts 5:42; 8:4, 12, 25, 35, 40; 11:20.

[9] Acts 13:32; 14:7, 15, 21; 15:35; 16:10; 17:18.

[10] Luke 15:7, 10, 22–24, 32.

[11] The numbers, 'seventy-two' and 'seventy' are both well attested in the manuscripts. As the number is probably a reference to the number of nations of the world (cf. Luke 10:3), and Luke follows the LXX, which has the number 'seventy-two' in Gen. 10 for the nations of the world (the Hebrew has 'seventy'), 'seventy-two' is probably the number Luke wrote, which was changed by later copyists familiar with the Hebrew.

[12] Acts 2:38; 3:19; 8:22.

§3.1.3 Healing and exorcizing

It must not be missed that, summarizing Jesus' ministry, Luke says that Jesus 'went about doing good and healing all that were oppressed by the devil' (Acts 10:38). Indeed, after announcing his ministry through reading and explaining a passage from Isaiah, the first thing Jesus does is cast out a demon (Luke 4:31–37). There follows story after story of Jesus healing the sick and exorcizing demons. When Jesus sent his followers out he not only called them together to commission them to proclaim the kingdom of God but also 'gave them power and authority over all demons and to cure diseases' (9:1). Further, the seventy-two are also told to heal the sick (10:9) and they return from their mission with joy that even the demons were subject to them in Jesus' name (10:17).

Turning to Acts, we see both Jesus' ministry and that of his followers portrayed in the Gospel paralleled in the characters of Luke's second volume. For example, Peter and John heal a lame man at the temple gate (Acts 3:1–10).

> [People] even carried out the sick into the streets, and laid them on beds and pallets, that as Peter came by at least his shadow might fall on some of them. The people also gathered from the towns around Jerusalem, bringing the sick and those afflicted with unclean spirits, and they were all healed. (5:15–16)

In Philip's ministry, unclean spirits come out of many, and many who were lame were healed (8:7). In Joppa, Peter raises a dead girl (9:36–43). At Lystra, Paul healed a man who had been crippled from birth (14:8–18), and at Philippi he cast a spirit of divination out of a girl (16:16–18). Luke says that, at Ephesus, 'God did extraordinary miracles by the hands of Paul, so that handkerchiefs or aprons were carried away from his body to the sick, and diseases left them and the evil spirits came out of them' (19:11–12). Again, just as Jesus' ministry included healing and exorcizing, the disciples in the Gospel and then his followers in Acts are portrayed as continuing the same activity.

§3.1.4 Parallels in prayer

Luke portrays prayer as being very important to Jesus. Before choosing the twelve from among the disciples Jesus spent a whole night in prayer (Luke 6:12). At or before other important times Jesus prays. He prays at his baptism (3:21), he prays alone before speaking to the disciples about his death (9:18), he was praying as he was transfigured (9:28–29), and he prayed about his willingness to die and before he was arrested (22:39–46). In Luke 11:1 Jesus was praying in a certain place, and when he stopped one of his disciples asked if he would teach them to pray.

In Acts, the first thing the eleven, along with the women and Jesus' mother and brothers do after the Ascension is, with one accord, devote themselves to prayer (Acts 1:14). The followers of Jesus also pray before or in relation to important events. After being arrested for the first time and then being released the followers of Jesus pray (4:23–31). When the seven are chosen the apostles pray and lay their hands upon them (6:6). Then, throughout Acts, Peter[13] and Paul[14] are depicted as praying, often before key events.

§3.1.5 Parallel qualities

Luke parallels his description of Jesus and the disciples before and after Easter not only in their activities but also in the qualities or description of their lives. For example, Jesus is described as being filled with 'wisdom' (*sophia*, Luke 2:40) and increasing in wisdom (2:52), just as are the seven (Acts 6:3, 10). 'Power' (*dunamis*) is another quality paralleled in the lives of both Jesus and his followers. The angel says that Jesus' conception will involve 'the power' of the Most High overshadowing Mary (Luke 1:35). Jesus' ministry begins 'in the power' of the Holy Spirit (4:14) and power characterizes his authority over the unclean spirits (4:36). This power of the Lord determined his ability to heal.[15] When Luke sums up Jesus' ministry in Acts 10:38 he mentions the 'power' which characterized his ministry. Then, 'power' was given to the twelve in relation to healing and exorcism (9:1). In Acts the apostles are promised to receive 'power' when the Holy Spirit has come upon them (Acts 1:8). And, with great power, the apostles are said to give their testimony to the resurrection (4:33).

Stephen is said not only to be full of power but also of grace (Acts 6:8). 'Grace' (*charis*, sometimes better translated 'favour') also characterizes Luke's portrait of Jesus. The grace or favour of God was upon the boy Jesus (Luke 2:40) who also found favour with other people (2:52). On hearing Jesus' interpretation of Scripture, the audience wondered at his 'gracious' words (4:22). Then, in Acts, the group of believers is said to find 'favour' with everyone (Acts 2:47). Also, great 'grace' was said to be upon all the believers (4:33). That a great number of people at Antioch believed is said to be the 'grace' of God (11:23), and remaining a believer is called 'continuing in the grace of God' (13:43). Further, the work of Paul and Barnabas arose out of the Antiochene Christians committing them to the 'grace' or favour of God (Acts 14:26; see also 15:40).

'Fear' (*phobos*) is said to be one of the responses to Jesus' ministry. When the crowd, including Pharisees and teachers of the law, saw the paralysed man get up and go home glorifying God they were filled with fear (Luke 5:26). The same thing is reported when Jesus raised the widow's dead son (7:16), as well as when he cast out many demons from Legion (8:37). Similarly, fear is said to come upon people in Jerusalem as they observed the miracles of the apostles and the life together of the believers (Acts 2:43; see also 5:5, 11).

Another characteristic shared by Jesus and his followers, to which Luke draws attention in his portraits, is 'joy' (*chara*). Even the coming of Jesus was heralded by the angel as joyful news (Luke 2:10) and the parable of the sower

---

13 Acts 8:15; 9:40; 10:9; 11:5.
14 Acts 9:11; 14:23; 16:13, 16, 25; 20:36; 21:5; 22:17; 28:8.
15 Acts 5:17; 6:19; 8:46.

highlights the joy of receiving the word of God (8:13). The appearance of the risen Jesus is greeted with joy (24:41) and the disciples return from the Mount of Olives to Jerusalem with great joy (24:52). Likewise, the seventy-two returned from their mission with joy (10:17). So also the ministry of the disciples in Acts produces joy in the audience. Philip's ministry for example, produces much joy in Samaria (Acts 8:8). This theme turns out to be so important that we will devote more attention to it when we look at the kind of church Luke encourages his readers to be, not least in the face of their difficulties.

§3.1.6 Jesus, Stephen and Paul

In Luke's portrait of Stephen and Paul the parallels between Jesus and his followers are particularly heightened and obvious. Luke says that people spoke well of both Jesus and Stephen (Luke 4:22; Acts 6:3), that they were filled with the Holy Spirit,[16] that the grace or favour of God was on each,[17] that power characterized both,[18] and that each performed wonders and signs (Acts 2:22; 6:8). Also, in the story of the transfiguration, Jesus' face was changed (Luke 9:29) and at his trial Stephen's face was like that of an angel (Acts 6:15). Both Jesus and Stephen spoke of the prophets which the ancestors of the audiences had persecuted and killed (Luke 11:47–50; Acts 7:51–52).[19]

Paul's life is even more extensively paralleled to that of Jesus in Luke's writing. In the Gospel of Luke Jesus is depicted as journeying toward Jerusalem as is Paul in Acts.[20] In Jerusalem both Jesus and Paul are well received (Luke 19:37; Acts 21:17–20) and visit the temple (Luke 19: 45–48; Acts 21:26). Both Jesus and Paul interact with Sadducees who do not believe in the resurrection and are supported by scribes (Luke 20:27–39; Acts 23:6–9). Luke similarly describes meals hosted by Jesus and Paul (Luke 22:19; Acts 27:35) and each are seized by a gang or crowd (Luke 22:54; Acts 21:30) and are struck (Luke 22:63–64; Acts 23:2). Moreover, each character is depicted as standing trial four times: before a gathering of Jews, the Sanhedrin, a Roman governor and a member of Herod's family;[21] of each the crowd shouts, 'Away with him';[22] three times, each is said to be innocent;[23] of each a centurion

---

[16] Luke 4:1; Acts 6:3, 5; 7:55.

[17] Luke 2:40, 52; Acts 6:8.

[18] Luke 4:14, 36; 6:19; Acts 6:8.

[19] If we could be confident in the status of Luke 23:34 ('Then Jesus said, "Father, forgive them; for they do not know what they are doing"'), which is absent from a variety of early witnesses, it would form a parallel with Stephen asking the Lord not to hold this sin against those stoning him (Acts 7:59–60).

[20] Cf. Luke 9:51, 53 and Acts 19:21; Luke 13:22 and Acts 20:22; Luke 13:33 and Acts 21:4; Luke 17:11 and Acts 21:11–12; Luke 18:31 and Acts 21:13; Luke 19:11 and Acts 21:15; Luke 19:28 and Acts 21:17.

[21] See Luke 23:13–25 and Acts 21:27–22:29; Luke 22:66–71 and Acts 23:1–10; Luke 23:1–5 and Acts 24:1–21; Luke 23:6–12; Acts 25:23–26:32.

[22] Luke 23:18: *aire touton* ('Away with this man'); Acts 21:36: *aire auton* ('Away with him').

[23] See Luke 23:4, 14, 22; and Acts 23:29; 25:25; 26:31–32.

passes a favourable remark (Luke 23:47; Acts 27:3, 43); and, despite remark-able setbacks, the ministry of each is similarly depicted as ending well (Luke 24:36–53; Acts 28:23–31).

§3.1.7 Conclusions

In the light of these extensive and detailed parallels between Jesus and his followers, the question remains, what was Luke attempting to convey to his readers? It could be argued, for example, that the story of Paul is a retelling of the Jesus story so that Paul's journey to Rome is a retelling of the death and resurrection of Jesus. However, this does not take sufficient account of the parallels we have noted between the early stages of the ministry of Jesus and that of the early Church. Rather, keeping in mind the opening words of the second volume, in these parallels Luke is more likely encouraging his readers to draw the important conclusion that all the followers of Jesus, in-dividually (notably Paul) as well as collectively, do not simply mirror and maintain his ministry but are visible forms of the activity of God in Jesus. Further, in so far as Luke is using the figures in his narrative as models for his readers (§1.3 above), they are to draw the contingent conclusion that they, the readers, are also to be visible forms of the activity of God in Jesus.

This means, as we saw in the last chapter, that a sharp distinction between the time of Jesus and the time of the Church is more in the minds of modern readers than in Luke's (see §2.6 above). For, if anything, Luke blurs potential distinctions between the so-called epochs of Jesus and the Church. Thus, in the time of the Church the disciples continue to consult Jesus (Acts 1:24) and heal in the name of Jesus (3:6; 4:10), as they are said to do before Easter (Luke 10:17). Even in visions, his followers still see and meet him (Acts 7:56; 9:5). And, as we have noted more than once, in the opening words of Luke's second volume the point is signalled that he is about to relate what Jesus continued to do and teach (1:1). The continued activity of Jesus is also sig-nalled in various aspects of the structure of Acts, to which we now turn.

§3.2 The Church: Jesus modelled

We have just seen that one of the important implications of Luke produc-ing his narrative in two parts is that he is able to reinforce in the second vol-ume what was already in the traditions of his first: the Church is to be a visible form of the activity – as well as the character – of God in Jesus. Also, aspects of Luke's structuring of his work further contribute to showing that not only is Jesus the Church modelled but also the Church models Jesus. In turn, we will examine Luke's use of the Ascension, the structure of Acts, as well as the ending of his two-part narrative.

§3.2.1 The Ascension story repeated

An aspect of the overall structure of Luke-Acts which could tell something of Luke's views about the Church is his characteristic retelling of some stories. Paul's conversion is told three times[24] and the story of the conversion of Cornelius in Acts 10:1–47 is repeated in 11:2–18: Clearly, these stories are important to Luke. The importance of the Ascension story is obvious not only in its repetition (Luke 24:50–53;[25] Acts 1:9–11) but also in that Luke is the only New Testament writer to propose that the Ascension was an event that was visible in time and space.[26] The Ascension is further emphasized because of its appearance at the end of the first volume and at the beginning of the next. However, it is unnecessary for us to engage in an extended discussion of Luke's Ascension stories; we need only to note those aspects reflecting most directly on his understanding of the Church.

At the end of the Gospel, the Ascension story becomes the climax and an interpretive lens for the life, death and resurrection of Jesus (Luke 24:50–53). Indeed, the Ascension enables the revelation of the true destiny of Jesus. The glory anticipated (2:32–34; 4:5–6), but only prefigured (9:28–36) and glimpsed previously (19:28–40; 20:1–8), is now shown to have been realized in the resurrection (cf. 24:1 and 13). For only now do the followers of Jesus worship him, worship that is said to be with great joy and continual (24:52–53).

The raised hands for blessing,[27] bowing or kneeling by witnesses, and the subsequent worship of Jesus reflect Ben Sira's description of the high priest Simon II, the last of the famous men he praises (Ecclus. 50:1–24, esp. 21). In most probably echoing this description of Simon, Luke creates the final image of Jesus as the climactic figure among Israel's greatest figures: priests[28] and especially prophets, many of whom Ben Sira says were miracle workers.[29] Notably, when Elijah, who is among these prophets and miracle workers, is 'enveloped in the whirlwind', Elisha, his follower, is filled with his spirit (48:12–14). From this readers would conclude that, just as Elisha inherited the spirit as well as the prophetic and miracle-working ministry of Elijah, the same can be expected of Jesus' followers.

The second Ascension story being at the head of Acts also positions the idea of Ascension as the lens through which to view the nature and destiny

---

[24] Acts 9:1–30; 22:1–29; 26:1–29.

[25] Although a few manuscripts (e.g. Codex Bezae from the fourth to sixth centuries) omit from Luke 24:51 the phrase 'and he was carried up into heaven' (*kai anephereto eis ton ouranon*), the remainder of the manuscript tradition, including P[75] (*c.* 200 CE), is most probably to be followed, not least, because, in Acts 1:2, Luke refers to the end of his Gospel as where Jesus was 'taken up' (*analambanō*).

[26] For the perspective of other NT writers see, e.g. John 3:13; 6:62; 7:33; 8:14, 21; 13:1–3, 33; 14:2, 4, 13, 28; 16:5, 7, 10, 17, 28; 20:17; Rom. 10:6–8; Eph. 4:7–10; Phil. 2:8–11; 1 Thess. 1:10; 4:16; 1 Tim. 3:16; Heb. 4:14; 6:19–20; 9:24; 1 Pet. 3:22; Rev. 1:12–18; 3:21; 6:1–7; 7:17.

[27] The Levitical or Aaronic gesture is only found in Lev. 9:22; Ecclus. 50:20; and Luke 24:50. In that, as well as here at the end of the Gospel (Luke 24:30, 50, 51, 53), there is also a concentration of the use of *eulogeō* ('bless') at the beginning of the Gospel (1:42, 64; 2:28, 34) where the temple forms a back drop to the narrative and a priest, mute, was unable to bless the people (1:22; cf. *m. Tamid* 7.2), Jesus' blessing after his own sacrifice, appears to function as a figure completing the Tamid left open by Zechariah.

[28] Ecclus. 45:6–22, 23–25; 50:1–24.

[29] See Ecclus. 45:3; 45:19; 46:4, 15–18; 47:3; 48:4–6, 12–14, 23; and, perhaps, 49:10.

of the followers of Jesus. Thus, the focus of attention in the Acts story is not on Jesus (cf. Luke 24:50–52) but on his followers;[30] the Ascension is brought from the day of the resurrection (24:51) into proximity to Pentecost (Acts 1:3–9) so that the glory of Jesus is now also to be associated with, and seen in, the new life of the Church.

The use of the term 'to take up'[31] maintains the stories of Enoch and Elijah as interpretive figures for this story. For, otherwise, in Ascension stories, which were familiar to readers in the ancient world,[32] this word is only found associated with stories of Enoch and Elijah in the Septuagint.[33] And, as anticipated, the followers of Jesus receive the same Spirit.[34]

At the end of the Gospel the disciples had been told that they are to be witnesses, and that Jesus is sending the promise of the Father; or, to be clothed with power from on high (Luke 24:49). Then, in more detail in the beginning of Acts, they are told that the witnessing for Jesus is to be done until he comes again (Acts 1:9, 11), and the promise is not only specified as being the Spirit but also that the empowerment is to be for this mission (1:8). In this way, Luke is able to assure his readers that the Holy Spirit, who has clothed them with power for mission, has been sent to them from heaven by the same Jesus who was empowered by the same Spirit for his mission.

Thus, the Ascension can probably be taken as one of the keys to understanding the whole of Luke's work, an important interpretive bridge between the two parts of his narrative and also between what he has to say about Jesus as well as the Church. The Church is not simply the end of the story of Jesus, the Church is the continuation of his ministry in which his glory is also now seen (cf. Acts 1:1), as it was and is in the resurrection. That the Church continues the ministry of Jesus is a point also seen from the structure of Acts.

§3.2.2 The structure of Acts

It is not obvious how Luke has structured his work, particularly Acts. He could be structuring Acts around what appear as breaks or points of transition.[35] However, we also have to keep in mind that Luke uses a number of summary statements (see below), and that Acts 1:8 appears to function as an organizing statement for the narrative.

That it is difficult to discern how Luke has structured his work, particularly Acts, probably has a great deal to do with our habit of looking for discrete tidy sections rather than understanding how ancient writers formed their work. In setting out *How to Write History*, Lucian of Samosata, the second

---

[30] Acts 1:6, 9, 10.

[31] *Analambanō*; Acts 1:2, 11, 22.

[32] See, e.g. Plutarch, *Num.* 2.3; Antoninus Liberalis, *Metamorphōseōn synagōge* 25; annotation to Apollonius of Rhodes, *Argonautica* 4.57; Dio Cassius, *Hist.* 56.42; cf. Wisd. 4:10. The relation of *Barn.* 15.9 to the writings of Luke is not clear.

[33] 1 Macc. 2:58; Ecclus. 48:9; 49:14.

[34] Luke 3:16, 21; 4:1; Acts 1:5; 2:4.

[35] See Acts 2:1; 6:1; 9:32; 11:19; 13:1; 15:36; and 19:21.

century (CE) author and wit, writes of the expectation of a writer to inter-weave and overlap subject matter (*History* 55). Given, therefore, that Luke is likely to be using a number of overlapping structures, in order to understand what he says about the Church we can direct our attention to those signals of structure which are clearest and have most to do with the Church.

The promise and command of Acts 1:8, to which we have just referred ('you shall be my witnesses in Jerusalem and in all Judea and Samaria and to the end of the earth'), is reasonably understood as a broad outline of the Acts story as it describes the expansion of the Church. Jerusalem is the setting of the story up to Acts 8:4. From there until 11:18 Judea and Samaria can be taken as the arena of activity, and the remainder of the book shows the wit-nessing proceeding to the ends of the world. Taking into account what we have just seen about the invitation implied in the ending of Acts, this verse reinforces the point that the readers are to continue the expanding mission described in Acts.

The broad narrative sweep of the growth of the Church anticipated in the promise and command of Acts 1:8 then appears to be fulfilled through a more detailed structuring of Acts (cf. Luke 24:47). Luke has punctuated his second volume with six summary statements of the progress of the spread of the good news: Acts 6:7; 9:31; 12:24; 16:5; 19:20; and 28:30–31. Taking these statements as important in how Luke expected his work to be read, the first part of the book focuses on the establishment of the followers of Jesus in Jerusalem and the preaching of Peter to Jews – Hebrews and Hellenists (cf. Acts 6:1). Then comes the statement: 'And the word of God increased; and the number of the disciples multiplied greatly in Jerusalem, and a great many of the priests were obedient (*hupakouō*) to the faith' (6:7). From this section Luke is drawing attention not only to the increase in the numbers in the Church but also, in the mention of 'a great many priests' being obed-ient to the faith, to the direct continuity between the people of God and the Church. Even Luke's rare use of 'obey' (*hupakouō*),[36] which is sometimes used in the Greek Old Testament to translate 'hear' (*shm‘*),[37] a word that involves the idea of obeying,[38] may be intended to hint that 'the faith' was not a diver-sion from that of the people in the Old Testament.

The second section of Acts relates the growth of the Church in Palestine (Acts 6:8—9:31), despite the martyrdom of Stephen and conflict with the Jewish authorities. Luke says: 'Then the Churches throughout the whole of Judea and Galilee and Samaria all had peace and were walking in the fear of the Lord and . . . were multiplied' (9:31). The third section (9:32—12:24),

---

[36] Luke 8:25; 17:6; Acts 6:7; 12:13. Otherwise in the NT see: Matt. 8:27; Mark 1:27; 4:41; Rom. 6:12, 16, 17; 10:16; Eph. 6:1, 5; Phil. 2:12; Col. 3:20, 22; 2 Thess. 1:8; 3:14; Heb. 5:9; 11:8; 1 Pet. 3:6.

[37] See Gen. 26:5; 27:13; 39:10; Deut. 17:12; 21:18, 20; Jer. 16:12.

[38] Cf. Deut. 21:18–21; 1 Kgs 12:24/2 Chr. 11:4. See also, e.g. Deut. 4:1; 11:13, 27–28; 28:13; Jer. 7:23; 26:13; 38:20.

on the good news being received by the Gentiles through Peter, ends with the words: 'But the word of God grew and multiplied' (12:24). Thus, the spread of the Church is not only geographic but also moves out from the Jews to include others, here Gentile God-fearers, and eventually all Gentiles (28:28).

This is the second of three times in these summaries Luke refers to the word of God increasing or growing.[39] We could take this puzzling expression to mean that the message (cf. Acts 8:14; 11:1) or preaching[40] of God's word was spreading. Or, it could also be a way of referring to the faith or Christianity (cf. 8:14; 11:1). But these suggestions probably miss something important in the range of meanings Luke gives to 'the word of God'. In his parable of the sower, Luke also has the idea of the word being spread and growing (Luke 8:4–15). In that story, the apparent tangible activity of and independence of the word from God reflect ideas found in the Old Testament. There, particularly in the later material, the word of God is not simply the content of utterances directly from God (cf. Jer. 46:13). It is also the presence or hand of God (Ezek. 1:3) realized in the speech (3:27) as well as the activity of a prophet (cf. Hos. 1:2). Sometimes the word of God is the activity of God[41] or its explanation (Ezek. 6:3), or even God himself (e.g. Zeph. 2:5; Zech. 9:1). The word of God can be understood as the expression or manifestation of God, including his activity. Similarly, Philo of Alexandria, the Jewish philosopher and biblical interpreter, writing just before Luke, equates God's word with his activity (Philo, *Sacrifices* 65). With these things in mind, Luke saying that the word of God grew or multiplied can be seen as a way of including the idea that what was taking place in the growth of the Church and the increasing numbers involved the realization of the activity or presence of God.

The fourth section in Acts marks a change in mission strategy (Acts 12:25—16:5). Peter, the central figure, is replaced by Paul who will dominate the remainder of Acts and, as we will see, provide Luke with an ending that takes the implications of the narrative into the world of the readers. Also, up until Acts 12:24 missions – including Philip's (8:4–5) – took place as a result of persecutions. From Acts 13:1–3 there begins the first planned and organized full-time mission work with the deliberate setting apart of Barnabas and Saul to go to Asia. In this section Luke also deals with the problem and solution of how Gentiles could be included in the group of followers of Jesus. Luke then says: 'So the churches were strengthened in the faith, and they increased in numbers daily' (16:5).

In the fifth section those preaching the gospel are called to Europe (Acts 16:6—19:20). Again Luke says, depending on how the text is to be translated: 'So, by the might of the Lord, the word increased and was strong' or 'So the word of the Lord grew mightily and prevailed' (19:20). This is the third time

---

[39] Acts 6:7; 12:24; and 'word of the Lord' in 19:20.
[40] Cf. Acts 13:5, 7, 46; 18:11.
[41] E.g. Ezek. 5:13, 15, 17.

in the summaries Luke has used the word 'to grow'.[42] We will need to keep this in mind when we discuss Luke's view of the mission of the Church (see Chapter 13 below).

In the final and longest section of Acts, Luke tells the story of Paul's missionary work leading to Rome, carried forward in the face of suffering and persecution (Acts 19:21—28:31). As we have noted, Luke concludes with Paul preaching and teaching about the Lord Jesus Christ quite openly and unhindered for two years (28:30–31). There is no reference to growth or increase in numbers here; yet the open ending of Acts takes the narrative into the broader world of the mission of the readers (see below).

These six summary statements, reporting the progress of Luke's story, have the effect of emphasizing the missional nature of the Church, as if it was inherently meant to grow. It is not that these indications of a structure are to be seen in conflict with what Luke set out in Acts 1:8. Rather, the purpose of the Church adumbrated in the broad structure suggested by Acts 1:8 is elucidated through these six statements.

There have been a variety of suggestions as to how Luke may have structured Acts, so we ought to be cautious about claiming too much for what we have observed. Nevertheless, we are probably justified in assuming Luke was using both the broad as well as the more detailed structure of his second volume to communicate with his readers – the first to show the broad sweep of the scope of the spread of the narrative (Acts 1:8) and the more detailed six summaries to provide a measured reminder of the progress of his story towards the life of his readers. In other words, what we have called the promise and command of Acts 1:8 is shown to be realized in more detail through the six summary statements: as the followers of Jesus witness – achievable in the face of profound difficulties, persecutions and seemingly insurmountable defeats – the word of God or saving, powerful presence of God grows and the number and racial groups of followers are multiplied.

According to the summaries, we can see that the measure of success of this mission was particularly in the growth in numbers of followers of Jesus. Also important to Luke was obedience, strength of faith, walking in the fear of the Lord and the continuation of preaching and teaching despite opposition. From Acts 19:20 it is clear Luke believes all this is possible 'by the power of the Lord' which, we have seen, is a synonym for the Holy Spirit (§3.1.5). Again, we will need to take this into account when dealing in more detail with the mission of the Church according to Luke (see Chapter 13 below).

§3.2.3 The invitation of the end of Acts
Perhaps the most pressing question about the structure of Luke-Acts is the way it finishes. The final scene in Acts is of Paul in Rome receiving local leaders of the Jews at his lodgings (Acts 28:17–30): 'From morning until evening

---

[42] Acts 6:7; 12:24; 19:20.

he explained the matter to them, testifying to the kingdom of God and trying to convince them about Jesus' (28:23). However, the members in his audience disagreed among themselves and left (28:26). In response to this, the last thing Paul says in Acts is: 'Let it be known to you [Jewish leaders] then that this salvation of God has been sent to the Gentiles; they will listen' (28:28). Despite this rejection, Luke goes on to comment positively: 'And he lived there two whole years at his own expense, and welcomed all who came to him, preaching the kingdom of God and teaching about the Lord Jesus Christ quite openly and unhindered' (28:30–31, my translation). At this point Luke's work ends.

This abrupt and, at first, surprising ending has given rise to a number of theories that fit into two broad categories. One set of theories suggests Luke intended to write a third part – or we have lost a volume – telling of Paul's release, later journeys, second arrest (see 2 Tim. 4:16–17) and martyrdom. However, we have no evidence that Paul was released from the house arrest of Acts 28:16. It is true that, in the first verse of Acts, Luke refers to his 'first' (*prōtos*) rather than 'former' (*proteros*) book which, strictly speaking, could imply a 'third' (*tritos*) volume. However, the word *prōtos* can mean 'former' and, in Acts 12:10, Luke uses it without intending a third. Further, the view that Acts was to be followed by a third volume does not take into account the well-balanced plan of the existing two-part work in which themes are held over from the first to be dealt with and, importantly, resolved in the second.[43] Moreover, as we will see, a third volume would ruin the ending of Acts.

Other theories attempting to explain the ending of Acts revolve around the idea that Luke's story finishes because he did not know what was going to happen next. This means that Luke-Acts was written about 62 CE, two years after Paul arrived in Rome (Acts 28:30). However, Luke and his readers seem to know of the death of Paul,[44] as well as the fall of Jerusalem in 70 CE (cf. Luke 21:20–24). In any case, for Luke to say that Paul remained under house arrest for two years (Acts 28:30) implies both a later perspective and a knowledge that there was a change in circumstances at that point.

The failure to spell out this probably shared knowledge of Paul's martyrdom is a puzzle that is important to solve. For, understanding the way Luke has ended his two-part work is likely to hold important clues to his message.

It is clear that, although the great missionary Paul was killed by the Romans, this has not stopped the spread of the gospel to the heart of the Roman empire and, therefore, potentially, to the Gentiles to the ends of the earth. Despite

---

[43] E.g. see Mark 7:1–23 which receives only scant attention in Luke 11:37–41, but the theme is treated more fully in Acts 10. Also, Mark 15:58 is omitted by Luke but see Acts 6—7.

[44] Acts 20:24–25 (includes echoes of John's fate in Luke 13:25); Acts 20:36–38 (the response of grief at Paul's parting); 21:11 and 13–14 (echoes of Jesus' fate); and 28:30 (assumes an unspecified fate after two years). Moreover, readers may have seen echoes of the last days of Socrates in the closing scene of Acts. Cf. Plato, *Crito*; *Phaedo*. Also, *1 Clem.* 5.5–7, written in the mid-90s, mentioning Paul's death suggests that, apart from Acts, Luke's readers could have otherwise known of Paul's fate.

suffering, persecutions and terrible setbacks, including martyrdoms, nothing has and, by implication, nothing can halt the open, unhindered proclamation of the good news about Jesus. In the light of this, the last four words of Acts – 'with all boldness unhindered' (*meta pasēs parrēsias akōlutōs*), which tell of the way Paul was able to preach and teach for two years in Rome – are expected to realize their significance in the lives of the readers. This would be a great encouragement to a church perhaps experiencing failure in its mission, a point we will develop later (see §13.2 below).

This view needs to be nuanced, however, when we take into account a wider perspective on Luke's structure. When we notice both the parallel endings of the Gospel and Acts (each involving the departure from the narrative of a living hero), as well as the life and ministry of the hero of the first volume (Jesus) continuing in the life of his followers in the second, it is reasonable to suppose that Luke was inferring that his readers were to take up the bold unhindered ministry of the main hero of the second volume (Paul) in their own lives. Indeed, in Luke's world, the open ending of a book was taken as an invitation for the readers to continue the story in their own narrative.[45] Therefore, through his abrupt yet poignant ending to Acts, Luke has issued an invitation for the ministry of Jesus in his first volume, reflected in his followers in the second volume, to be modelled by readers in their own lives. In other words, through the two-part open-ended structure of his work, Luke signals that the Church is to be a reflection of the lives of the earliest Christians and, therefore, a continuation of the ministry of Jesus, 'with all boldness unhindered', to the ends of the earth.

§3.3 Conclusions

We have been able to see that key aspects of the way Luke has structured his work – the parallels between Jesus and his followers, and the subtle structuring of Acts, including the open end of the entire work – contribute to his view that Jesus is the Church modelled and the Church is modelled on Jesus.

From the extensive and detailed parallels between Jesus and his followers before and after Easter, readers can be expected to conclude that Jesus is the principal actor of Acts as well as of the Gospel so that the Church exists not simply to mirror and maintain Jesus' ministry but to be a visible form of the activity of God in Jesus (note Acts 1:1). The Church is, then, those in obedience continuing the life and ministry of Jesus. In this Luke is blurring and drawing together the epochs of each of his volumes.

In the structuring of Luke-Acts the Ascension stories provide two lenses through which to see the true glory of Jesus: his destiny as enthroned Messiah

---

[45] See the endings of Herodotus, *Hist.* 9; Lucretius, *On the Nature of Things*; and the advice of Quintilian, *Inst.* II.13.12–13. Cf. Silius, *Punicia* 1.8–14.

and his life in the Church. Thus, the Church is not simply the second part of the story of Jesus but its continuation. While being cautious about any claims concerning Luke's structure of Acts, it seems reasonable to conclude that Luke used the promise and command of Acts 1:8 to show the broad sweep or universal scope of the spread of the narrative; the six summaries provide a measured reminder of the ever-growing realization of the word or saving, powerful presence of God in the face of profound difficulties.

Perhaps the most engaging aspect of Luke's narrative structure is its poignant ending. We have seen that what appears as an abrupt and uncertain end was most likely intended to be read as a call to continue the ministry of Jesus in the ministry of the readers. It is an invitation for the ministry of Jesus in the first volume, reflected in his followers in the second volume, to be taken up by readers in their own lives. Again, just as Jesus is the Church modelled, the Church is to be Jesus modelled. This suggests the Church now dispenses salvation, an issue to which we now turn.

4

Salvation and the Church

If, as we have just seen, the Church embodies and continues the mission of Jesus, the question arises as to whether or not Luke thinks that the post-Easter Church now dispenses salvation. Or, if the Church does not dispense salvation, is salvation possible apart from the Church, and what is the precise relationship between the Church and salvation? Put another way, is salvation being incorporated into the Church or, perhaps, is incorporation part of salvation? It is necessary to begin our enquiry by setting out how Luke understood salvation.

§4.1 Salvation

It is not to be doubted that salvation is a very important theme to Luke. His salvific vocabulary is considerable;[1] and it is a prominent theme in the introduction to his Gospel – seen mostly through citations of the Old Testament,[2] as well as in the conclusions of his two volumes (Luke 24:47; Acts 28:28). However, although the theme of salvation may arguably be the centre of his theology, its explication is not the purpose of his writing. His purpose, we have argued, is to show his readers that the message of salvation concerning Jesus is to be trusted and continued in the life of the readers (see §1.3 above). In any case, our immediate task is to distil from Luke's two volumes a description of salvation that he would acknowledge.

§4.1.1 The scope of salvation

If we take into account what is said about salvation in the Septuagint, Luke's Scriptures, his ideas on salvation are seen more clearly. In the Old Testament

---

[1] E.g. in his Gospel, Luke uses *apolutrōsis* ('redemption', 21:28), *diasōzein* ('to rescue', 7:3), *lutrousthai* ('to redeem', 24:21), *lutrōsis* ('ransom', 1:68; 2:38), *sōtēr* ('saviour', 1:47; 2:11), *sōtēria* ('deliverance', 1:69, 71, 77; 19:9), *sōtērion* ('bringing salvation', 2:30; 3:6) and *sōzein* ('to save,' 7:50; 8:12, 36, 50; [9:56 in some manuscripts]; 13:23; 17:19; 19:10; 23:37, 39), in places where there is no parallel in his sources.

In Acts, Luke uses *diasōzein* (23:24; 27:43, 44; 28:1, 4), *sōtēr* (5:31; 13:23); *sōteria* (4:12; 7:25; 13:26, 47; 16:17; 27:34), *sōterion* (28:28) and *sōzein* (2:21, 40, 47; 4:9, 12; 11:14; 14:9; 15:1, 11; 16:30; 27:20, 31).

Luke rarely drops salvific language: at Luke 8:42 (cf. Mark 5:23) a whole sentence is recast to keep the attention on Jesus and to conform to what happens later in the story; Luke 21:19 clarifies Mark 13:13; and in Luke 21:24 the interest is in a military siege rather than Mark's vague reference to salvation and the days of tribulation (Mark 13:19).

[2] Luke 1:47, 69, 71, 77; 2:30; 3:6. See also 2:11.

45

the great act of salvation was the deliverance of the whole people of God from Egypt.[3] Yet, God is not only saviour of his people as a whole,[4] but also, occasionally, of groups of them.[5] There are also instances in the Old Testament of salvation being for a remnant of God's people (e.g. Gen. 7:1–7; Isa. 10:20–23); in other places salvation is related more broadly to all the oppressed of the earth (e.g. [LXX] Ps. 75:10), or even expected for all people.[6] Nevertheless, particularly in the Psalms,[7] God is declared to be the saviour of individuals,[8] who – sometimes representing the people of God (cf. e.g. [LXX] Ps. 117:21) – call out for salvation[9] or are said to have experienced salvation.[10] Thus, while the rescue of his people in the Exodus was God's prime and exemplary salvific deed, throughout the biblical story salvation was also sought, expected and received by groups as well as individuals.

When we turn to Luke we also note there is the expectation not only that the whole people of God will be saved[11] but also, at times, including in Acts, that any or all people can anticipate salvation[12] – including Gentiles[13] and those who fear God (Acts 13:26). With this theme of universal inclusion echoing that of the Old Testament and it being found across Luke's work,[14] including being emphasized early in both of his books,[15] it is reasonable to take the universal offer of salvation as undergirding Luke's theology of salvation. How this salvation is received and worked out or applied is illustrated through his stories of individuals and groups.[16]

§4.1.2 The nature of salvation

If, so far, Luke seems largely content with the perspective on the scope of salvation offered by his Scriptures, when we consider his view of the nature of salvation, he makes a radical departure from them. For example, the Septuagint almost always uses *sōzein* ('to save') to refer to military victory or winning wars (e.g. [LXX] Ps. 32:16), or escaping danger (e.g. Gen. 19:20) so that salvation could be characterized as God expressing his powerful and tangible care of

---

[3] See, e.g. Exod. 14:1—15:21; Judg. 4–5; 6:8–9, 13; 1 Sam. 12:6, 8; 2 Sam. 8:1–14; 1 Kgs 8:51; 2 Chr. 7:22; Neh. 9:9–11; Pss. 77:14–20; 78:12–55; 80:8; 114:1–8; Jer. 7:21–24; 11:1–8; 34:13; Dan. 9:15; Hos. 11:1.

[4] E.g. (LXX) Pss. 67:21; 68:36; 97:1.

[5] E.g. (LXX) Pss. 71:4; 107:13, 19.

[6] See, e.g. Isa. 2:1–4; 49:6, 22–23; 60:1–14; Amos 9:7.

[7] Though see Hannah rejoicing in her salvation in 1 Sam. 2:1.

[8] E.g. (LXX) Pss. 42; 86; 50:14; 108:31.

[9] E.g. (LXX) Pss. 3:8; 6:5; 17:4; 30:3, 17; 58:3; 68:2, 15; 69:2; 70:2, 3; 85:2, 16; 108:26.

[10] E.g. (LXX) Pss. 29:4; 30:8; 33:7; 114:6.

[11] See Luke 1:69, 71, 77; Acts 5:31; 13:23, 26; cf. 2:40, 47; 7:25.

[12] Luke 2:10–11, 30; 3:6; 9:24; 18:26; Acts 2:21; 4:12; 15:1, 11. Cf. 1:8.

[13] Acts 11:14; 13:47; 28:28.

[14] Luke 2:30–32 (cf. Isa. 42:6; 46:13; 49:6, 9); 3:6 (cf. Ps. 67:1–7); Acts 2:21 (cf. Joel 2:32); 13:47 (cf. Isa. 45:22; 49:6).

[15] Luke 2:29–32; Acts 2:21; cf. 3:11–12.

[16] Noting only those stories that include the vocabulary of salvation: Luke 1:47; 6:9; 7:50; 8:36, 48, 50; 17:19; 18:42; 19:9–10; Acts 4:9; 14:9; 16:30–31.

his people in the face of danger or their enemies. Even references to future salvation generally maintain this theme.[17]

Over against this Old Testament notion of salvation dominated by the military and political, what is striking is that only twice does Luke echo this theme (Luke 1:69–71; Acts 7:25). Instead, the spiritual and personal aspects loom large in his view of salvation. Luke characterizes salvation most often as forgiveness,[18] as well as the gift of repentance,[19] and also as various forms of healing,[20] including exorcism (Luke 8:36), raising the dead (8:50) and, perhaps, spiritual healing (Acts 28:28). Salvation can also be equated with eternal life (13:46–47) and can mean being blessed,[21] the coming of peace (Luke 2:14; cf. 2:11) and receiving revelation and glory (2:30).

As we will see in a moment, when we turn to some stories of salvation, being saved can mean not being lost (esp. Luke 15:3–32) and not belonging to 'this corrupt generation' (Acts 2:40). Salvation can also mean escaping from the horrors of the last days (2:17, 21). In two places in Acts salvation is equated with receiving the gift of the Holy Spirit (2:38–40; 11:14–15). Added to all this, in the light of the ministry of Jesus, Luke is convinced that salvation is a present experience.[22] Thus, it is reasonable to agree that, for Luke, salvation does not have a political or military dimension but is the present (generally individual) experience of wholeness or the Spirit or the kingdom – the powerful presence of God. Indeed, in his Gospel salvation can be characterized as either eating in (Luke 13:23, 29) or entering the kingdom of God.[23] We must note that to this Luke adds the theme of joy and gratitude both in the experience of salvation,[24] including seeing others saved (e.g. Acts 11:23; 13:48), and in joyously awaiting the return of the ascended Jesus (Luke 24:52–53).

§4.2 Salvation and the Church

From this discussion, the relationship between individual salvation and the Church is not immediately clear. It is in looking beyond the particular vocabulary of salvation (see ch. 4, n. 1) to other passages in Luke-Acts that brings Luke's view into focus.

Of the considerable material we have to take into account, we begin with Luke's well-known trilogy of parables of the lost to help understand Luke's perspective on the relationship between the Church and salvation.

---

[17] E.g. Isa. 12:2; 33:22; Zech. 9:16.
[18] Luke 1:77; 3:6; (cf. 3:3); 7:50; (cf. 7:48); Acts 2:40; (cf. 2:38); 5:31; 13:38–39; (cf. 13:23).
[19] Acts 5:31; 11:18; cf. 11:14.
[20] Luke 6:9; 7:3; 8:48; 17:19; 18:42; Acts 4:9; (cf. 3:8); 14:9.
[21] Luke 1:47; cf. 1:42, 48.
[22] Luke 4:21; 11:20; 14:17; 17:20–21; 19:9.
[23] Luke 18:24–26. See also, e.g. 8:1; 9:2; 10:9, 11; 11:20; 14:15–24; 16:16; 17:20, 21, 18:17, 24, 25, where salvation and the kingdom are synonyms or most obviously and closely related.
[24] E.g. Acts 3:8; 5:41; 8:8, 39; 15:3.

1 In the story of the lost sheep (Luke 15:3–15), the mark of not being saved is being separated from the flock. However, rescue or salvation is not equated with rejoining the group but with the act of being found by the shepherd (15:5). Nevertheless, the reasonable assumption is that the straying animal will rejoin the others for whom the shepherd is responsible.

2 In the parable of the lost coin, as the number ten was thought to be the number of perfection,[25] it is in being separated from a complete set that the lost state of the coin is defined. However, it is noticeable that the rejoicing is not over the coin taking its place among others, but simply in its being found (Luke 15:8–10). Yet again, the reasonable assumption is that the misplaced coin will be returned to the collection.

3 Similarly, the younger son is deemed to be lost because he is away from home. Also, he is deemed to be found not when he rejoins the family but when he and his father meet and embrace (Luke 15:22–24). Nevertheless, in this case, the story follows through what can only be assumed in the other two stories: re-entry into the family (15:24b). That is, the lost is returned to the former place. A similar scenario is to be imagined in the story of the ten lepers. On being cleansed they can be assumed to re-enter society.[26]

4 We can also note that, in a final summary line of the story, Zacchaeus is described as lost (Luke 19:10). Not only through the socially isolating profession of Zacchaeus being a tax collector[27] but also in a clear allusion to Ezekiel 34:16,[28] Luke continues to show that he considers separation from God's people to indicate the need for salvation. Again, not least from this allusion to Ezekiel, the reader could assume that, having been saved, Zacchaeus is able to join the people of God.

5 Turning to Acts, in considering the relationship between salvation and the Church, Acts 2:47 is significant. Luke says that the Lord added to the existing followers of Jesus 'those who were being saved'. In line with what we have seen in the Gospel, here joining the Church – or the followers of Jesus – is not depicted as a part of salvation. Rather, joining the group is a natural, perhaps assumed, consequence of salvation.

Confirmation of this apparent distinction between salvation and joining the Church comes from the conversion stories in Acts.

1 Although the eunuch in Acts 8 is not described as joining a group of followers of Jesus, he is baptized (Acts 8:36–39). As baptism is a rite offered by other followers of Jesus as a symbol of belonging to the group (cf. §7.3 below), this is at least consistent with the perspective that joining the Church is acceptance by or a response to salvation rather than a cause or part of what had already happened to the man (cf. 8:36).

---

25 See, e.g. Philo, *Moses* 1.96; *Spec. Laws* 2.201; 4.105.
26 Luke 17:19. Cf. Lev. 13:45–46; 14:2–20.
27 See Diogenes of Sinope, *Letter* 36.2; Dio Chrysostom, *1 Serv. lib.* 14; Matt. 5:46; 9:10; 11:19; 18:17; 21:31; Mark 2:15; Luke 7:34; 15:2; 18:11; *m. Teharot* 7.6; *m. Ned.* 3.4; *b. Sanh.* 25b.
28 Ezekiel (LXX) 34:16: 'I will seek what was lost and turn back what is going astray'.

2 Similarly, in the story of the conversion of Cornelius and his family, the reception of the Holy Spirit (Acts 10:44) or their salvation[29] takes place before baptism, which is offered in response to their conversion (10:47–48).

3 In the story of Lydia's conversion the relationship between conversion and baptism is not as clear. However, most naturally, Luke is to be read as intending that her conversion – or heart being opened[30] – was distinct from and prior to baptism (Acts 16:15).

4 Finally, this distinction between the receiving of salvation and the subsequent joining the Church is played out in the story of Paul. In Acts 9:26–30, Luke describes Paul, not long after his conversion, as attempting to join the disciples in Jerusalem as if this was the natural response to becoming a disciple.

In these stories Luke's view of the relationship between the Church and an individual's present experience of salvation becomes clear. It is not that salvation is dependent on being part of the Church, nor even that entry into the Church is part of salvation. Rather, salvation comes about distinct from and prior to joining the Church. Yet, taking up one's place among the other people of God is a natural and assumed consequence of being saved – being found or made whole. In short, for Luke, while salvation is not joining or re-entering the community of God's people – the Church – it is a natural (perhaps expected or unavoidable) consequence or expression, even ongoing benefit, of it.

§4.3 The Church dispenses salvation?

With such an emphasis on the topic, the question of whether or not the followers of Jesus (i.e. the Church) dispense salvation was clearly an important problem for Luke and his readers. On the one hand, looking over the way Luke has used the vocabulary of salvation,[31] in his Gospel he depicts salvation being brought by God[32] and his word (Luke 8:12), but primarily by Jesus[33] or his power (8:48), word[34] or command (8:36). Indeed, three of the four of Luke's uses of 'saviour' (*sōtēr*) refer to Jesus.[35] Notably, Jesus assumes the title from his birth (2:11; cf. 2:30) and the role of saviour, not after Easter but from the inauguration of his ministry (cf. 4:18–19). In Acts, salvation is also brought by God[36] but more often by (the Lord) Jesus,[37] as well as by the

---

[29] Acts 11:18. For the relationship between salvation and 'repentance' (*metanoia*, Acts 11:18), see Acts 2:38; 3:19; 5:31; 20:21; 26:20.

[30] Acts 16:14: For the 'heart' as part of a metaphor for conversion see Luke 1:17; 8:12, 15; Acts 7:39; 8:21; 28:27.

[31] *Diasōzō, sōtēr, sōtēria, sōtērion* and *sōzein*.

[32] Luke 1:47, 69, 71; 18:26.

[33] Luke 2:11 ('the Messiah, the Lord'), 30; 7:3; 17:19; 19:9–10.

[34] Luke 6:9; 7:50; 8:50; 18:42.

[35] Luke 1:47 refers to God. Luke 2:11; Acts 5:31; and 13:23 refer to Jesus.

[36] Acts 11:4; (cf. 11:17); 27:20, 31, 34, 43; (cf. 27:23); 28:20.

[37] Acts 15:1, 11; 16:30–31; cf. 2:21.

exalted[38] or risen Jesus[39] or his grace (Acts 15:11). In addition, the name of Jesus is also seen as bringing salvation.[40] In all this there is no hint that the Church, or joining a group of people, brings salvation. Indeed, when it is obvious, in Luke's Gospel it is typically faith that is the means of reception.[41] Faith also dominates Acts as the means of receiving salvation,[42] with repentance also being mentioned in Acts 2:38. This verse also appears to contain an exception to the pattern: baptism or being accepted by the group of believers is integral to receiving salvation. However, with the explanation that baptism was to take place 'in the name of Jesus', Luke was thinking of baptism as an expression of trust in Jesus rather than joining the group.

Yet, so readily did he understand the followers of Jesus to use the name of Jesus, and so closely did he see their identity with him that, when they were involved in the coming of salvation, Luke could say that 'signs and wonders were done among the people through the apostles' (Acts 5:12) and that the crowds could see 'the signs that he [Philip] did' (8:6). The problem of potential misunderstanding is addressed most directly in a couple of stories. First is the story of Philip in Samaria to which we have just alluded. Simon, the so-called magician, is portrayed as assuming that Philip and the apostles from Jerusalem simply dispensed the Holy Spirit at will (8:9). He is roundly corrected, with Peter making clear that the Holy Spirit is God's gift (8:20).

Second, if there was any doubt that Luke did not think that the Church – the people – could bring or dispense salvation, the story of Paul in Lystra makes it clear. Luke says that there was a man who had never walked listening to Paul. When Paul saw that he had faith to be healed, Luke says Paul looked intently at him and said, 'Stand upright on your feet' (Acts 14:10). It appears as if it is Paul who is offering healing or salvation (cf. *sōzō*, 14:9) for, uncharacteristically, there is no mention of the source of Paul's power or authority for this command (3:6). Thus, Luke reports that, in response to the man springing up and walking, the crowds wanted to offer sacrifices to Paul and Barnabas, shouting, 'The gods have come down to us in human form!' (14:11). The extended section that Luke dedicates to clarifying that Paul was not acting on his own, but was a mortal and bringing good news that people should turn to the living God (14:14–18), is an unavoidable indication that Luke did not think that the Church or those belonging to it offered salvation. Indeed, when Luke portrays the Church in its first public encounter with the Jewish authorities regarding by 'what power or by what name' they

---

[38] Acts 2:40; (cf. 2:33); 5:31.

[39] Acts 13:23, 26; cf. 13:32–39.

[40] Acts 4:9; (cf. 3:15); 4:12.

[41] See Luke 1:47; 7:50; 8:12, 48, 50; 17:19; 18:42. In 3:6 John's baptism, in 9:24 self-denial, in 13:23 striving and in 19:9, 10 renunciation are linked with salvation.

[42] Acts 4:9; (cf. 3:16); 11:14; (cf. 11:17); 13:23, 26; (cf. 13:39); 14:9; 16:30–31 and, perhaps, 27:20, 31, 34, 43 (cf. 27:31). Calling on the name of the Lord (2:21) is also to be seen as expressing faith. The 'listening' of 28:28 is also to be placed under the category of faith for hearing was considered to include understanding and acceptance. See, e.g. Deut. 6:4–9; 11:13–21; Num. 15:37–41; Isa. 1:2, 10; Jer. 2:4; Amos 7:16; cf. Acts 13:48.

were bringing salvation (cf. *sōzō*, 4:9), the climax of Peter's defence is his statement that, 'There is salvation in no one else, for there is no other name under heaven given among mortals by which we must be saved' (4:12). That name, from the context, is Jesus.

§4.4 Conclusion

In our setting out aspects of Luke's view of the Church, so far we have established that the Church has its origins not, as is often thought, in Pentecost but in Jesus' call to the twelve. Further, we have seen that the purpose of the Church is to represent God not by emulating Jesus but by being an ongoing embodiment of his ministry. This became particularly clear as we saw that Luke portrays Jesus as modelling the Church. However, this raised the question for this chapter as to whether or not the Church dispenses salvation. Involved in this discussion has been a consideration of the nature of salvation.

As Luke describes it, the universal scope of salvation has been taken up from his Scriptures. However, he makes a radical departure from the military and material understanding of salvation that dominates what he read in the Old Testament. Instead of salvation being primarily political, salvation is seen in spiritual and personal terms. Forgiveness, the gift of repentance, the gift of the Spirit, various kinds of healing, 'being found', escaping from the last days, eternal life, blessedness, peace, revelation and glory are ideas that better capture aspects of his understanding of salvation. *For Luke, salvation is the realization of the powerful presence of God in present as well as future experience.* This is generally described in terms of the individual. It bears repeating that this point is not only important in understanding the nature of the Church, but will also be particularly critical in understanding the mission of Jesus and the Church (Chapter 13).

In our consideration of the corporate dimension of salvation it has become clear that, although Luke thinks the Church embodies and continues the ministry of Jesus, he does not think that the Church dispenses salvation. The story of Paul in Lystra makes this most plain. Luke is at pains to depict, despite appearance, Paul and Barnabas not as bringing or dispensing salvation but as mortals bringing this news. Yet, further, while salvation is prior to and distinct from becoming part of the Church, Luke portrays belonging to the people of God as an assumed, natural response to, and expression of, being saved. Thus, though salvation is prior to the Church, it is inconceivable without the Church. While one may have been saved individually, on being saved, one was expected to live corporately.

5

The Church as the people of God

We have already seen that Luke identified the origins of the Church with Jesus choosing twelve of his followers to designate them as apostles. We have also seen that Luke envisaged the Church as a continuation of the ministry of Jesus, though the source of salvation shown and told by the Church is still Jesus.

Yet, for Luke, the Church as an identifiable organization was still both new – recently estranged and emerging from Judaism – as well as a relatively unknown minority among many other religions, sects and schools. To increase our understanding of some of the fundamental aspects of Luke's view of the Church we turn to investigate how he describes the Church in relation to the cultural and religious milieu of his time. We will discuss Luke seeing the Church in synagogue terms, and as a sect. We will note what it means for him to use the term 'the Way' for the followers of Jesus and how he uses of the term 'church' (*ekklēsia*) and how his understanding of the local group of followers of Jesus is informed by the idea of the household. But we begin with the broader issue of the relationship of the Church to the Jews.

§5.1 The Church and Judaism

Explaining Luke's understanding of the Church in relation to the Jews is not straightforward, for he appears to present conflicting evidence. On the one hand, we have to take into account both Luke's censure of Judaism as well as his pro-Gentile attitudes. In his Gospel, for example, Luke has Jesus denounce the Pharisees for tithing while neglecting justice and the love of God, and for loving the best seats in the synagogue and salutations in the market place (Luke 11:42–44). The scribes also are attacked because they load people with burdens and build tombs to prophets whom their ancestors killed (11:45–47). Jesus goes on to warn the disciples of the hypocrisy of the Pharisees (12:2) and later he calls them lovers of money (16:14). In a parable he pokes fun at a pompous Pharisee praying in the temple while exalting a humble Jewish tax collector at prayer (18:9–14). Also there are harsh sayings such as the direction to leave the dead to bury the dead (9:60). This would have been seen not only as a slight on the command to honour one's parents (Exod. 20:12) and in conflict with the tradition that dealing with the dead was a higher priority than reciting

52

the Shema (*m. Ber.* 3.1a), but also contrary to all ancient sensibilities that saw the burial of the dead as a religious duty.[1]

In Acts the Jews are also heavily denounced or depicted as the villains. Peter says to his audience in Jerusalem that they had crucified and killed Jesus (Acts 2:23). The priests, captain of the temple and the Sadducees arrested Peter and John because they were annoyed at the apostles teaching the people and proclaiming in Jesus the resurrection of the dead (4:1–3). In particular, Stephen's speech stands out for its anti-Jewish sentiments. The venom is clearest in the closing words:

> You stiff-necked people, uncircumcised in heart and ears, you always resist the Holy Spirit. As your fathers did, so do you. Which of the prophets did not your fathers persecute? And they killed those who announced beforehand the coming of the Righteousness One, whom you have now betrayed and murdered. (7:51–52)

Further, through his characters, Luke is critical of dietary laws (10:15), of rules against table fellowship (11:2–10) and of the need for Gentile Christians to be circumcised (15:1–35).

Moreover, on closer examination, Luke's censure of the Jews increases as his narrative progresses. We can see this in Luke's portrayal of Paul in his mission as progressively having to turn from the Jews to the Gentiles. At first Paul is depicted as reluctant to do this. For, when Paul spoke to the Jews in Pisidian Antioch on his first trip out of Syrian Antioch he says: 'It was necessary that the word of God should be spoken first to you. Since you thrust it from you, and judge yourselves unworthy of eternal life, behold we turn to the Gentiles' (Acts 13:46). Then, at Corinth, when the Jews opposed and reviled Paul he replies in frustration: 'Your blood be upon your heads! I am innocent. From now on I will go to the Gentiles' (18:6). The climax of this theme comes at the end of Acts when, on disagreeing with Paul, the Jews in Rome leave him. Paul makes a statement which concludes: 'Let it be known to you then that this salvation of God has been sent to the Gentiles; they will listen' (28:28). So, a theme alluded to in Simeon's song (Luke 2:34), clarified in Jesus' rejection at Nazareth (4:28–30) and exemplified in the betrayal and crucifixion (22:1—23:46), is carried through apparently to explain the rejection of the gospel by most Jews and the reception of it by the Gentiles (Acts 28:28–31).

Commensurate with this, we need to keep in mind that, reading between the lines of Luke-Acts, we find hints that the Church Luke has in mind has, in some way, been cut off from the Jews. Perhaps this is echoed in Jesus' saying: 'Blessed are you when men hate you, and when they exclude you and revile you, and cast out your name as evil, on account of the Son of Man!' (Luke 6:22). The same situation may also be reflected in the story of those hearing Jesus in the synagogue being filled with anger and rising up to put

---

[1] Cf. *1 En.* 98.13; 2 Macc. 5:10; Josephus, *Ant.* 10.97; *J.W.* 2.465; 3.377; 4.317, 384–85.

him out of the city (4:28–29). Also, on a number of occasions Jewish opposition means that Paul has to leave the synagogue and even the city.[2] The break between the Jews and the Church, as Luke probably sees it, is put most dramatically and sharply in the ending of Luke-Acts. Paul has failed to be understood by the leaders and great numbers of Jews in Rome. It is after quoting Isaiah against them that, as we have just noted, salvation is said to be sent to the Gentiles and that they will listen (Acts 28:28).

If we allowed all this evidence to stand on its own we might conclude that Luke thought that all Jews were perverse. However, we have to take into account Luke's pro-Jewish material. For example, in the early chapters of Luke there is an emphasis on the Jewishness of Jesus seen in his genealogy and through the ritual prescriptions in the Law being performed by his parents, as well as in depicting the young Jesus in the temple.[3] Also, Luke's Gospel depicts the Law as good and of ongoing significance for his readers. Thus, Jesus does not raise one law above another by offering a summary of the Law in the one command to love.[4] Furthermore, in the disputes about the Sabbath, Luke is concerned to show that Jesus acted in complete accord with the Law.[5]

This favourable portrait of the Jews extends to Acts. In Jerusalem there are three thousand, then a further five thousand converts until it is said 'many thousands' of Jews had joined the new movement including 'a great many priests'.[6] The members of the new movement are faithful to the Jewish Law and traditions. The decision at the Jerusalem council, that the Gentiles should 'abstain from what has been sacrificed to idols and from blood and from what is strangled and from fornication' (Acts 15:29, cf. 20), is pro-Jewish; the apostles and Paul attend the temple[7] and Paul is even depicted as undertaking a temporary Nazarite vow (Acts 18:18; cf. Num. 6:1–21). Then, from Acts 22 onwards, Paul remains defended as a loyal, Law-abiding Jew. Luke's positive attitude to the Jews goes so far as to exonerate them from direct responsibility for Jesus' death.[8] Even Judas acted because Satan had entered him (Luke 22:3).

There are, then, two major streams of thought to keep in mind in trying to discover Luke's view of the Church in relation to the Jews. Not only are Luke's writings the most pro-Jewish – which includes showing the early Christians as loyal and faithful Jews – they are also the most anti-Jewish in the New Testament, increasing as Luke's narrative progresses. As the narrative develops, portraits of Jewish piety are replaced by sketches of hostility, leaving the negative view of the Jews to remain the strongest.

---

[2] Acts 13:50; 17:10, 17; 18:7; 19:9.
[3] Luke 2:21, 22, 24, 39, 41–52; 3:23–38.
[4] Cf. Luke 10:27–28; and Mark 12:30–31.
[5] Luke 6:1–11; 13:10–17; 14:1–6.
[6] Acts 2:41; 4:4; 6:7; 21:20.
[7] Luke 24:53; Acts 2:46; 3:3; 5:21, 42; 21:26.
[8] Acts 3:17; 13:27. Luke 23:34 was probably added after publication, for it is absent from a variety of early texts; e.g. P[75], codices Vaticanus and Bezae.

Before we can suggest what view of the Church Luke may have that enables him to hold these two strands in tension – with the negative becoming progressively predominant – we have to attend to two further pieces of evidence. First, Luke occasionally calls his readers 'Israel'. In the Infancy Narrative, in particular, salvation is said to come to 'Israel'.[9] Further, Luke insists that the group of twelve apostles must be maintained, conveying the idea that 'Israel' continues in the story of the Church (Acts 1:15–26). This is characterized in Luke's description of the post-Easter community of followers of Jesus. What was expected for Israel – a kingdom, twelve leaders, the Spirit, growth, fear of the Lord, mighty works, material well-being, for example – had come to the early community of the followers of Jesus. This suggests that Luke saw the Church as the new or renewed Israel.

Yet, second, Luke describes the life and mission of the Church as focused on the synagogue, where there are sometimes said to be both Jews and Gentiles (Acts 14:1; 18:4). Paul is said to go to the synagogues to find believers.[10] Also, believers are in the audience when Apollos speaks in the Ephesian synagogue (18:26). Further, even though Paul is advertised as the missionary to the Gentiles,[11] his activities are focused on the synagogues,[12] even when he is reaching Gentiles.[13] Indeed, Paul is rarely seen on mission outside a synagogue setting.[14]

In the light of Luke seeing the Church as the new or renewed Israel, and the importance for him of the synagogue, two particularly interesting scenarios provide insight into how Luke probably views the relationship between the Church and the Jews. One is the story involving Paul arguing in the synagogue at Corinth. After the Jews opposed and reviled Paul, presumably with Crispus (the official of the synagogue who had become a believer), Luke says Paul left the synagogue and went to the house of a God-fearer, Titius Justus (Acts 18:7–8). Luke also says the household of Crispus, as well as many Corinthians became believers (18:8). Another scenario, though with less detail, involves Paul and the synagogue at Ephesus. Luke says that, 'When some stubbornly refused to believe and spoke evil of the Way before the congregation, he left them, taking the disciples with him, and argued daily in the lecture hall of Tyrannus' (19:9). These scenarios can reasonably be described as splits in the synagogues, with the believers forming their own synagogues.

---

[9] Luke 1:54, 68, cf. 33, 69. Also, in numerous passages, Luke introduces the word 'people' into the material as those hearing the message of Jesus. In Acts the followers of Jesus are called 'a people for his (God's) name' (Acts 15:14; see also 18:10). The significance of this is that Luke is probably dependent on the Greek Old Testament where the 'people' are those God saves and leads (e.g. Zech. 2:11).

[10] Acts 9:2; 22:19; 26:11.

[11] Acts 9:15; 13:47; 14:27; 15:3, 7, 12; 21:19; 22:21; 26:17, 20, 23; 28:28. Cf. 13:46, 48; 18:6.

[12] Acts 9:20; 13:5, 14, 43; 14:1; 17:1, 10, 17; 18:4, 7, 19, 26; 19:8; 22:19; 24:12; 26:11.

[13] Acts 13:44–48; 14:1–2; 18:4.

[14] Acts 14:8–18; 17:17, 22–34. Although Acts 16:13 does not contain the word synagogue, the (place of) 'prayer' (*proseuchē*), if not a synagogue, as it was sometimes called (e.g. Philo, *Flaccus* 41; Josephus, *Life* 277, 280, 293; *Ag. Ap.* 2:10), is a Jewish place of prayer.

In drawing conclusions about Luke's view of the relationship between the Church and the Jews we have to keep in mind his increasing censure of the Jews who reject the good news associated with Jesus and his giving the impression of the followers of Jesus, in some way, being cut off from Judaism. Yet, we also have to note that Luke emphasizes the Jewishness and faithfulness to the Law of his key characters and that he calls his readers Israel and sees the promises of God as fulfilled in the people following Jesus. It is not simply that the Church, portrayed as having sprung from Jewish roots and inherited all the blessings of God, is now cut off from or independent of the Jews. For the Church is still pictured as functioning within the context of the synagogues, and Paul rarely speaks only to Gentiles. Indeed, only once are Gentiles said to be converted outside a Jewish environment or a synagogue. At the conclusion of Paul's speech at Athens 'some of them joined him and became believers, including Dionysius the Areopagite and a woman named Damaris, and others with them' (Acts 17:34).

The view and scenario that best fits the evidence is that Luke sees the Church as having realized all the hopes (and even the name) of Israel and, in being increasingly rejected by the Jews, is in the process of breaking off to form its own synagogues as the continuing people of God. That the Church in Luke's time is no further advanced than this in its evolution in relation to Judaism is shown in him having no formal, consistent title for the Church. Thus the term 'people' is still used of the Jews,[15] with only a couple of examples where it may refer to those who constitute the Church (cf. Acts 15:14; 18:10).

The Church is then, in Luke's view, on the cusp of turning its missionary efforts fully to the Gentiles, an objective Luke justifies, applauds and sets out to encourage (note Acts 28:28; cf. 26:17). With the synagogue being of such significance in Acts we turn briefly to examine this institution to bring some detail to how Luke would have viewed the life and function of the Church.

§5.2 A synagogue?

From the discovery of an inscription that was on the so-called Theodotian synagogue (*CIJ* II 1404), as well as from Acts 6:9 (the synagogue of the Freedmen) and later rabbinic writings,[16] we have good but limited evidence that there were synagogues and synagogue buildings in Jerusalem before the destruction of the city in 70 CE, particularly for Jews of the Diaspora. If it is Luke's voice that is reflected in the 'we'-passages in Acts (see ch. 1, n. 13) he may have been to Jerusalem (Acts 21:17) and seen the followers of Jesus functioning as a synagogue. That Luke thought of the first post-Easter followers of Jesus as a distinct group of Jews, with their own synagogue, is suggested early in Acts where he says the group totalled 120 persons (1:15; see §2.1).

---

[15] E.g. Acts 4:8, 10; 10:2, 22; 13:17, 24; 21:28; 26:17, 23; 28:17.
[16] See *t. Meg.* 2.6, 12, 17; *y. Meg.* 3.1.III D.

In any case, Luke's undoubted knowledge of synagogues will have been informed by the Diaspora where, as I have just argued, he depicts the followers of Jesus beginning to form their own synagogues.

It seems that there was a centrally located synagogue in virtually all Jewish communities. However, only a small number of synagogues are known from archaeological and literary evidence. For example, a Bordeaux pilgrim in 333 CE reported only one remaining of seven synagogues in Jerusalem.[17] Along with the significance of the home for Jews and Christians,[18] this suggests that many if not most synagogue meetings – including for the followers of Jesus – took place in homes or buildings that had been private dwellings (*m. Ned.* 9.2). This would be particularly true for the smaller semi-public synagogues of sectarian Jews such as the Essenes and perhaps the followers of Jesus.

We can expect that what took place in synagogues would vary geographically, for example, prayer perhaps being more significant for those in the Diaspora with limited access to the temple. Indeed, some synagogues were known as 'prayer houses'.[19] Also, semi-public synagogues, such as those of the Essenes, with their partial separation from society, probably had a greater interest in issues of purity.[20] In any case, worship likely involved praise to God, confession, blessings, prayers – including singing,[21] which was a striking aspect of Essene worship,[22] as well as a sacred communal meal (4Q504 1–2.7.4). The practice of reading the Torah, along with its competent exposition by a leader or elder (Philo, *Hypoth.* 7.13; cf. *Moses* 2.215–16) appears to have been widespread,[23] including not least among the synagogues known to Luke (Luke 4:20–21; Acts 13:15).

Although worship was particularly, and perhaps for some only, associated with the Sabbath,[24] a synagogue also had a civic or community function. For example, the Jewish historian, Flavius Josephus (*c.*37–*c.*100 CE) says that at Tiberias there was 'a meeting of everyone in the prayer house' (*Life* 277), probably called by the town and synagogue leader.[25] The leader also had the authority to determine who could attend the meeting (*Life* 294) and could ask all the people to leave the room so the council could deliberate (*Life* 300). The agenda of this particular meeting focused on the military leadership of Josephus; the only worship mentioned was probably preliminary private prayers (*Life* 295). Josephus also describes further synagogue meetings that began

---

[17] 'Itinerarium Burdigalense,' *Corpus Christianorum* (Series Latina) 175 (1965): 592.6–7 (page 16).
[18] E.g. Rom. 16:5; 1 Cor. 14:16; 16:19; Philem. 2.
[19] See *CIJ* II.1440; Josephus, *Life* 277; Philo, *Flaccus* 41; 45; 47; 48; 49; 53; 122; *Embassy* 132; 134; 137; 138; 148; 152; 156; 157; 165; 191; 346; 371.
[20] E.g. Josephus, *J.W.* 2.129, 150; CD-A 12.21–22.
[21] See the titles to Pss. 54; 55; 61; cf. 84:8; also Philo, *Contempl. Life* 29.
[22] See Philo, *Contempl. Life* 29. For singing in a Christian setting see 1 Cor. 14:15, 26.
[23] See Philo, *Good Person* 81–82. Cf. Philo, *Contempl. Life* 28. Cf. CD 20.10–13.
[24] E.g. *LAB* 11.8; Philo, *Embassy* 156; *Good Person* 81.
[25] See Josephus, *Life* 66–67, 134, 271, 294.

at seven in the morning over the next two days, at which anyone could speak;[26] one of the meetings being for a public fast (*Life* 290). Generally, a synagogue meeting seemed to be, if not all day (*Ag. Ap.* 1.209; Philo, *Hypoth.* 7.13), then in the afternoon (*m. Meg.* 3.6). However, this particular meeting, on a Sabbath morning, finished in time for the midday meal (Josephus, *Life* 297).

Religious aspects may have dominated Sabbath meetings but, in so far as the slender evidence permits us to conclude, it is likely that public synagogues were used primarily for community activities, including on the Sabbath: fasts, communal meals (Philo, *Good Person* 86; Josephus, *Ant.* 14:214–15), and political and council meetings. The description Josephus gives of a weekday meeting both confirms the relatively limited worship or liturgy, as well as the religious and the communal aspects of a synagogue overlapping.[27]

The synagogue was also likely to have been the focus of charitable activity and, probably, also healing. Essenes appointed one of their members in each city to provide clothing and other necessities for travellers.[28] Much later, the great orator and bishop of Constantinople, John Chrysostom (*c.*347–407 CE) lamented that Christians sought healing in the synagogues (*Adv. Jud.* 1.6.2; 8.6.6). Not only did Jews have a reputation for healing,[29] but there is also possibly a link between prayers for the sick and the synagogue in the Tosefta (*t. Shabb.* 16.22). In short, with Luke depicting the early Christians teaching and evangelizing in synagogues, and beginning to form their own, the general description we are able to reconstruct of them helps us see how Luke understood the Church.

§5.3 A sect?

We are also able to see how Luke understood the Church, including its relation to the Jews, from some of his specific terms for it. When Paul was before Felix, the procurator of Judea, Luke says Paul was accused by Tertullus, an attorney, of being 'a ringleader of the sect (*hairesis*) of the Nazarenes' (Acts 24:5). In his defence Paul says: 'I admit to you, that according to the Way, which they call a sect (*hairesis*), I worship the God of our Fathers' (24:14).[30] In the repetition here of the word 'sect', Luke reinforces this description of the followers of Jesus. Also, through Paul's voice, Luke tells his readers that the name at least some Christians used for themselves was 'the Way'.[31] Then, when Paul arrives in Rome, the Jewish leaders tell him the 'sect' (*hairesis*) he belongs to is everywhere spoken against (28:22). The point of interest for us

---

[26] Josephus, *Life* 280; cf. 133; also Mark 1:1–5.
[27] There is just a hint in Josephus, *J.W.* 2:287 that the synagogue may have been used as a bank, as it was in the Diaspora.
[28] Josephus, *J.W.* 2:125; cf. e.g. *t. Terumot* 1.10; *t. B. Bat.* 8;14; *b. Shabb.* 150a.
[29] E.g. Tobit 8:3; *Jub.* 10.10–14; Josephus, *Ant.* 8.44–48; *J.W.* 2.136; Philo, *Contempl. Life* 2; John Chrysostom, *Adv. Jud.* 8.5.6; 8.8.7–9.
[30] *Hairesis* in the NT: Acts 5:17; 15:5; 24:5, 14; 26:5; 28:22; 1 Cor. 11:19; Gal. 5:20; 2 Pet. 2:1.
[31] Acts 9:2; [18:25, 26]; 19:9, 23; 22:4; 24:14, 22. See §5.4 below.

is that, even though the term sect is seen to have its origin in enquirers and detractors, Luke does not deny but accepts and even emphasizes that Christianity is known as a sect.

From this it might seem reasonable to conclude that, for Luke, the Church is to be considered an unorthodox party of Judaism. However, while the term may have pejorative connotations for us, such overtones in relation to the Church only came to the fore after the New Testament period.[32]

However, in Luke's time, although society accepted and was undergirded by commonly held basic principles, there was expected to be diverse expressions of those principles. Important expressions of this diversity were the hundreds of Greek philosophical schools – Cynics, Epicureans, Pythagoreans and Stoics, for example – some having only a handful of members. From a Jewish perspective, Josephus discusses the Pharisees, the Sadducees, the Essenes, and Judas the Galilean's freedom revolutionaries (*J.W.* 2.118), calling them sects and comparing them with their Greek counterparts, the philosophical schools.[33] In doing so he was not describing the Jewish sects as aberrant but as part of the very fabric of Judaism, and probably attempting to bring to the expressions of Judaism the respectability accorded the Greek schools or sects.

In that Luke also describes the Pharisees and Sadducees as sects[34] we can suppose that, in using the word 'sect' of the followers of Jesus, Luke had similar motives: portraying them as a respectable school of thought or legitimate, perhaps even influential,[35] expression of Judaism. In this, Luke is reinforcing for readers the view that they – Jews, Greeks and God-fearers following Jesus – are at least a legitimate expression of God's purposes for and promises to his people. And we have already seen that he takes this view further in claiming the name of Israel for the Church (see ch. 5, n. 9; and §1.3.4).

§5.4 'The Way'

The conclusion that Luke was portraying the Church as a legitimate expression of Israel has to be refined when we take into account his use of 'the

---

[32] See, e.g. Ign. *Eph.* 6.2; *Trall.* 6.1; Justin, *Dial.* 62.3; 80.4; *1 Apol.* 26.8. Paul uses *haireseis* in the sense of 'factions' in Gal. 5:22. In 1 Cor. 11:19 he may be using *schismata* ('divisions') and *haireseis* ('sects' or 'factions') synonymously. More likely, he is using *haireseis* in the LXX and classic Greek sense of 'preference' or 'choice', as does Josephus (*J.W.* 6.352; 7.326; *Ant.* 1.169; 6.71, 91; 7.321, 322). See also 2 Pet. 2:1.

[33] Josephus, *J.W.* 2.122, 137, 142, 162; *Ant.* 13.171, 288, 293; 20.199; *Life* 10, 12, 191, 197. Cf. Tertullian's description of Christianity in his *Apol.* 36–39.

[34] On the Pharisees: Acts 15:5; 25:5; cf. Josephus, *J.W.* 2.162; *Ant.* 13.171, 288; *Life* 12, 191, 197. On the Sadducees: Acts 5:17; cf. Josephus, *Ant.* 13.171, 293; 20.199. Given the similarity between these diverse schools and those in the Jewish milieu, it was probably the Greek schools which served, in a general way, as catalysts for the formation of the Jewish groups or sects.

[35] On the great influence of the small number of Pharisees and Sadducees see Josephus, *J.W.* 2.163, 165.

Way' for the followers of Jesus.[36] That Luke takes this to be a designation Christians used of themselves is clearest where he has Paul say, 'I admit to you, that according to the Way, which they call a sect, I worship the God of our ancestors' (Acts 24:14).

Luke gives the impression that 'the Way' was widely applied, first using it for followers of Jesus in Acts 9:2. Saul asked the high priest for letters to the synagogues at Damascus, 'so that if he found any belonging to the Way (*tēs hodou*) he could arrest them'. Then, in 19:9 some in the synagogue at Corinth were 'speaking evil of the Way'. Similarly, in 19:23, at Ephesus 'there arose no little stir concerning the Way', and at 22:4 Paul is reported as saying that he 'persecuted this Way to the death'. In 24:22 (cf. 24:14) Luke says that Felix in Caesarea had 'a rather accurate knowledge of the Way'. This absolute, unqualified use of the word in the New Testament is unique to Acts, although the use of *hodos* in Mark suggests the term may have been used early of the Christian life.[37] The likelihood that this term pre-dates Luke is also suggested in its appearance in passages that may depend on sources originating from Paul.[38]

There are hints that, for Luke, 'the Way' was associated with faithfulness to Jewish traditions. For, in a context where Paul is defending his faithfulness to Jewish traditions (Acts 24:10–21), Luke connects 'the Way' with the 'ancestral' (*patrōos*) God of the Jews (24:14, cited above). In turn, the three times Luke uses the word 'ancestral' it is in the context of Paul defending his faithfulness to the Jewish traditions.[39] These hints that 'the Way' referred to the Christians' faithfulness to the traditions of Israel become unavoidable when we see its use in another group of the period.

In view of Acts 18:25–26, where the Christian life or message is described more fully as 'the Way of the Lord [or God]', it is most probable that Luke was using 'the Way' as a contracted form of the larger phrase. Thereby he provides us with further access to his understanding of the term. That is, light is likely to be shed on Luke's use of the term in noting that the people represented by the Dead Sea Scrolls also described their life together as a 'way' (*derek*). This was a term they also associated with 'the way of God'. Part of the clearest text reads: 'And when these become a community in Israel . . . they are to be segregated from within the dwelling of the men of sin to walk in the desert in order to open there his way (*derek*). As it is written, "In the desert prepare the way (*derek*) of [Yahweh]"'.[40] Of particular interest to us, the text goes on: 'This (i.e. way) is the study of the Law' (1QS 8.12–14).[41]

---

[36] As a title for the followers of Jesus see Acts 9:2; (18:25, 26?); 19:9, 23; 22:4; 24:14, 22.

[37] See Mark 10:46, 52; cf. 10:17, 32.

[38] For Paul's use of *hodos* ('road' or 'way') for the Christian life see 1 Cor. 4:17.

[39] Acts 22:3; 24:14; 28:17.

[40] Cf. Isa. 40:3. For 'the way of the Lord' or similar phrases in Qumran see 1QS 18.13, 25, 26; CD 20.18.

[41] See also 1QS 9.17–18; CD 1.13; cf. 2.6; 1QS 4.22; 8.10, 18, 21; 9.5, 9, 21; 10.21; 11.11; 1QM 14.7; 1Q28a 1.28.

Here 'way' is being used to describe people who gave particular attention to the Law and – importantly for our present concerns – have separated themselves from the mainstream of God's people. Notably, this separation was not assumed always to be physical detachment from society, for some Qumran scrolls reflect members living in the towns and villages.[42]

In sharing with the Qumran people both their use of 'the Way' as a description of people faithful to Jewish traditions and their interest in the quotation from Isaiah 40:3 (Luke 1:76; 3:4–6), as well as what we have seen in his use of the word 'sect', we can reasonably suppose that the hint is confirmed that Luke held the view that the members of his community were marked out from the mainstream of society as the true expression of God's expectations of and promises to his people. Thus, in Luke's use of the term 'Way', we are taken beyond the notion of the Church as a 'sect' – what others could agree was a legitimate expression of Israel living faithfully in accordance with the Law. Rather, as we saw in his general portrayal of Jews and Gentiles (§5.1), in the use of 'the Way' the Church is being portrayed as the true and faithful expression of Israel. This leads us to another word Luke used in describing the Church.

§5.5 *Ekklēsia*

Although, as we are about to see, *ekklēsia* was used to carry the idea of the Israelites gathered, this word opens up other dimensions of Luke's view of the Church.[43] In the Greek world, including for Luke, *ekklēsia* was used of any meeting or gathering.[44] It was also used of an assembly of a political body, as well as a crowd or unruly gathering of people,[45] as it is in Acts 19:39 and 41. In the Greek Old Testament *ekklēsia* was used to designate any group of people gathered for secular or religious purposes.[46] Thus it is quite natural for Luke to use *ekklēsia* to refer to a local gathering of Christians.[47] And, not surprisingly, in Acts 7:38 Luke uses *ekklēsia* of the Israelites gathered in the wilderness (also Heb. 2:12; cf. Josephus, *Ant.* 4.309). Among Luke's uses of *ekklēsia* there are two important features in relation to our interests.

The first feature to note about *ekklēsia* is the implications of the answer to the question whether or not Luke wrote 'church' or 'churches' in Acts 9:31: 'the church [or churches] throughout Judea, Galilee and Samaria [all?] had peace'. The issue at stake is whether Luke had in mind a single, universal

---

[42] Esp. 4Q265; 11Q19; and 1Q28a.
[43] For *ekklēsia* in Luke-Acts see Acts 5:11; 7:38; 8:1, 3; 9:31; 11:22, 26; 12:1, 5; 13:1; 14:23, 27; 15:3, 4, 22, 41; 16:5; 18:22; 19:32, 39, 40; 20:17, 28.
[44] See Acts 19:32, 40 (41); and, e.g. 1 Macc. 3:13; Ecclus. 26:5.
[45] Josephus, *Ant.* 12.164; 19.332; *Life* 268.
[46] Cf. Deut. 4:10; 9:10; 18:16; 31:30; 1 Kgs 8:14.
[47] Acts 5:11; 8:1, 3; 9:31; 11:22, 26; 12:1, 5; 13:1; 14:23, 27; 15:3, 4, 22, 41; 16:5; 18:22; 20:17 and 28.

Church distributed throughout various localities or whether he wrote of the various churches in their areas.

In favour of the widely accepted singular reading ('Church') is the reliability of the texts which support it – the majority of all texts.[48] However, this use of 'church' to represent either a region of churches or the universal Church would be unique in Luke's writing. While this is not impossible, when Luke wants to write of groups of Christians in a number of places he uses the plural 'churches' (Acts 15:41; 16:5). More likely, then, Luke used the plural 'churches' here in Acts 9:31, which also has significant textual support (as in Codex Bezae), and the plural can be expected here (cf. 15:41; 16:5). The change to the singular would have taken place when a Christian copyist, perhaps as early as the end of the first century, noting the words *kath holēs*, ('throughout the whole') next to the word church, and knowing the phrase *he katholikē ekklēsia* ('the catholic church'), changed churches to the singular (cf. Ignatius, *Smyrn.* 8).

In short, this verse (Acts 9:31) is consistent with Luke's use of 'church' elsewhere as a local gathering of the followers of Jesus. Thus, although Luke's narrative conveys the idea that he considered the spreading numbers of followers of Jesus all belonged to the one movement that originated in the ministry of Jesus and expanded from Jerusalem, he did not use the word 'church' in the singular to express this idea.

A second feature to note concerning Luke's use of *ekklēsia* is in Acts 20:28. Paul says to the elders at Ephesus: 'Take heed to yourselves and to all the flock, in which the Holy Spirit has made you overseers to care for the Church of God which he obtained through the blood of his own.' The intent of the phrase 'through the blood of his own' and the conflicting evidence from the manuscripts mean that we cannot be certain what Luke wrote or had in mind. It could be that the word 'son' is missing from the end of the verse which Luke meant to read, 'through the blood of his own son'. This would avoid the idea of God's blood being involved. However, 'through the blood of his own' is most likely to be original for it is well supported in the manuscripts[49] and, in Luke's world, 'own' (*idios*) was a term of endearment for near relatives (e.g. John 1:41). It could be that Luke wrote the 'church of the Lord', that is, Jesus (P[74] and Codex Alexandrinus) instead of 'the church of God' (codices Sinaiticus and Vaticanus). This also would keep the idea of God's blood from view. However, on a number of grounds – that the more difficult reading is likely to be the original, that nowhere does the phrase 'the church of the Lord' occur in the New Testament, and that 'the church of God' occurs eleven times in the Pauline corpus,[50] and here it occurs in a speech by Paul – Luke probably wrote 'the church of God'. Even though this does not fit so

---

[48] See, e.g. P[74], codices Sinaiticus, Vaticanus and Ephraemi.

[49] See, e.g. P[74] and codices Sinaiticus, Alexandrinus, Vaticanus, Ephraemi, Bezae and Basiliensis.

[50] 1 Cor. 1:2; 10:32; 11:16, 22; 15:9; 2 Cor. 1:1; Gal. 1:13; 1 Thess. 2:14; 2 Thess. 1:4; see also 1 Tim. 3:5, 15.

easily with the mention of 'the blood of his own' at the end of the verse, and as imprecisely expressed as this may now appear, Luke is representing the view that the death of Jesus was the giving of God's life.

An important aspect of this verse for understanding Luke's view of the Church is that it is said to be 'obtained' or 'bought' (*peripoieō*) through 'his own blood'. Even though this idea is well known in Paul's writing,[51] it is rare in Luke (Luke 22:19–20). Luke associates salvation primarily with the resurrection and Ascension (Acts 2:32–38; 10:34–43); the atoning significance of the death of Jesus is not emphasized. Nevertheless, in that Luke does not repudiate what he reports in his story of Paul, part of Luke's view of the Church is that it came into being not because people met together, but on the basis of the death of Jesus. The verse under discussion here (20:28) is also important in telling us about Luke's view of ministry in the Church. We will take this up later when we deal with Luke's view of leadership in the Church (§12.2).

§5.6 A household

What we have discussed so far has helped us principally in gaining insight into Luke's broader understanding of the Church in his wider world. To gain insight into his understanding of the local church we can note that, on a number of occasions, the local groups of followers of Jesus met in private homes. At Caesarea the new followers of Jesus probably met in the home of Cornelius.[52] Luke probably understands that, in Philippi, they met in the home of Lydia (Acts 16:15, 40) and the gaoler (16:31–34). In Corinth they met next door to the synagogue in the house of Titius Justus (18:8). Even in Jerusalem Luke portrays the followers of Jesus meeting in each others' homes (2:46), including the house of Mary, the mother of John Mark (12:12).

In Luke's society the household was accepted as a semi-independent socio-economic and political unit under the control of the householder. Thus, the household was a microcosm of society (cf. Matt. 12:25). With the benefit of family connections, wealthy householders could command the control of large numbers of other households and people. A household would consist of members of the family, servants, labourers, tenants, and dependent business people. Economically, religiously, socially and personally these people were dependent on the householder who in turn had a measure of legal responsibility for his people. So, with the apparent frequent conversion of whole households and the focus of the local church in a house, Luke portrays the Church not as a collection of individuals in a city, but as people belonging to a basic social unit of care and responsibility that affected every aspect of life. Individual converts could join these households and, in turn, these households provided a secure base for mission work.

---

[51] Rom. 5:18; 11:12–15; 2 Cor. 5:14, 19.
[52] Acts 10:1–2, 24; 11:14.

However, we cannot conclude from this that Luke would go on to describe the Church as a family in our understanding of the word. Rather, the notion of the Church functioning as a household, like that of a synagogue, provides Luke with a model of the Church that we would describe as an association or as an institution rather than as a family.

§5.7 In sum . . .

In this chapter we have tried to describe Luke's view of the Church within the context of the world of Luke and his readers. From one perspective we have seen that the followers of Jesus were encouraged to see themselves as a legitimate expression (or sect) of Judaism. However, in so far as the Christians' claim that Jesus was Messiah was rejected by the majority of the Jews, Christians were also to see that their practical separation from Judaism was part of the expression of being the new Israel − the people of God, receiving all the blessing God promised his people. The consciousness of this independence may account for the 'temple' not being used to describe the Christians. Yet, that this consciousness of an independent existence was still developing seems evident in Luke not settling on a particular name for the followers of Jesus, yet giving the impression that the title 'the Way' was widely used. Locally, the Christians belonged to groups of caring followers of Jesus whose corporate life was focused in homes, households and synagogues.

We now turn from the fundamentals of the origin and purpose of the Church to Luke's theme of the Spirit and the Church. This, it turns out, will add further detail to the view of the Church that is emerging from Luke's writings.

6

Luke's Pentecosts

There is no doubt that the story of the coming of the Spirit on the day of
Pentecost is of profound importance to Luke and his view of the Church;
with its setting (Jerusalem) and timing (Pentecost), and its arresting beginning (Acts 2:1), it takes a commanding position at the head of the body of
his second volume (2:1–13). Moreover, all the followers of Jesus are involved
(1:14–15; 2:1, 4) and it is testified by two witnesses.[1] Luke also offers a commentary on it (2:14–36) and refers back to it as a model or template for later
followers of Jesus (10:47; 11:15–16). The effect is to elevate the story to a
significance in his narrative that rivals Easter.

However, the Acts 2 story presents us with a puzzle. If, as Luke portrays
it, the coming of the Spirit on the day of Pentecost was such a significant
event – arguably on a level with the significance of the resurrection – why
has no other New Testament writer told us about it? An examination of
this and other stories in Acts, and other documents in the New Testament,
reveals an interesting solution to this puzzle. Importantly, for the purpose of
this chapter, this also helps increase our understanding of Luke's view of the
coming of the Spirit in relation to the Church.

§6.1 A Jerusalem Pentecost?

A first reading of Acts 2 suggests that the Spirit was given in Jerusalem on
the day of Pentecost after Easter when all the followers of Jesus were gathered in the temple. In particular, Luke says in Acts 2:1–4:

> When the day of Pentecost had come, they were all together in one place.
> And suddenly from heaven there came a sound like the rush of a violent wind,
> and it filled the entire house where they were sitting. Divided tongues, as of
> fire, appeared among them, and a tongue rested on each of them. All of them
> were filled with the Holy Spirit and began to speak in other languages, as the
> Spirit gave them ability.

At least in Luke's tradition, the 'house' (*oikos*, Acts 2:2) would probably have
been understood as a domestic dwelling, not the temple. For the otherwise
implied setting is the upstairs room (1:13), and the text says they are seated

---

[1] That is, John the Baptist (Luke 3:16) and Jesus (Acts 11:16 and, probably, 1:4–5). The widely
accepted principle of two witnesses in Jewish circles stems from Deut. 19:15: Cf. e.g. Matt. 18:16;
John 8:17; 1 Tim. 5:19; Josephus, *Ant.* 4.219; (cf. 1.209; *Ag. Ap.* 2.218, 290); Philo, *Spec. Laws*
4.53; *m. Sotah* 1.1; *m. Sanh.* 3.6; 5.2; *t. Sanh.* 1.3.

(2:2), as they would be in a home or a synagogue meeting. However, through an awkward insertion in Acts 1:15, all one hundred and twenty followers of Jesus are involved (cf. 2:1), and then three thousand respond to Peter's message (2:41). While it is not impossible to imagine three thousand people being involved in the response, in the light of Roman sensitivity to large crowds gathering and such a crowd hearing sufficiently to be able to respond to Peter's message it is probable that Luke is responsible for that figure. In any case, his readers would then likely take the 'house' (*oikos*) setting to be the temple precinct rather than a domestic dwelling (cf. 2:46). In a story reverberating with echoes of the Old Testament (see below), Luke did not need to change 'house' to 'temple', for in other places he has used 'house' for the temple when dealing with Old Testament themes.[2]

Not only has Luke relocated the story to the temple – the anticipated origin of eschatological salvation (Luke 24:49–53) – questions are also to be raised about the reference to Pentecost. He has already used the phrase 'in the fulfilment of the day' in a sentence probably of his own creation,[3] and the phrase itself,[4] as well as the word 'fulfil' are especially Lukan.[5] It is highly likely then that the date of Pentecost has been provided by Luke. If this is correct – and the discussion that follows supports this – Luke has created the idea that the Spirit was given not just to the apostles but to all the followers of Jesus when they were gathered in the temple on the particular day of Pentecost.

Through these simple changes – involving the entire group of followers of Jesus, relocating the story to the temple, with its crowds as an audience, and providing Pentecost as the date – Luke has enhanced and drawn attention to what had been a more modest story. Indeed, casting an eye across the New Testament we see that there are a number of stories and references concerning post-Easter experiences of the followers of Jesus that may not have been much different from the Acts 2 story in Luke's tradition.

§6.2 Post-Easter experiences

Of particular interest is Paul, our earliest known Christian writer, who conveys a tradition about a number of post-Easter events. In 1 Corinthians 15:5–8 he mentions a series of six resurrection appearances saying that

> [Jesus] appeared [first] to Cephas, then [second] to the twelve. Then he appeared [third] to more than five hundred brothers and sisters at one time, most of

---

[2] Luke 6:4; 11:51; 19:46; Acts 7:47–49.
[3] Luke 9:51; cf. Matt. 19:1–2; Mark 10:1.
[4] A similar phrase, using *pimplēmi* ('fill'), is found in Luke 1:23; 2:6, 21, 22; 21:22.
[5] For *pimplēmi* ('fill') see Luke 1:15, 23, 41, 57, 67; 2:6, 21, 22; 4:28; 5:7, 26; 6:11; 21:22; Acts 2:4; 3:10; 4:8, 31; 5:17; 9:17; 13:9, 45; 19:29. Otherwise, in the NT the word is found only in Matt. 22:10 and 27:48. In the NT *sumplēroō* ('fill completely') occurs only in Luke 8:23; 9:51; and Acts 2:1.

whom are still alive, though some have died. Then he appeared [fourth] to James, then [fifth] to all the apostles. Last of all, as to one untimely born, he appeared also [sixth] to me.

Paul does not say when any of these appearances took place, though at least those not involving him were soon after, yet independent of, the resurrection (1 Cor. 15:4–5).

It is possible that the Pentecost story, at least in the more modest form in Luke's tradition, is reflected in Paul mentioning that Jesus appeared to the twelve (1 Cor. 15:5). However, there is nothing in what Paul says to suggest that he knew or thought of it, or any of the other appearances, in a way that Luke narrates Acts 2.

To begin with, if Paul thought any of the appearances had taken place on the day of Pentecost we would expect him to mention it since Pentecost was considered a celebration of the giving of the Law (e.g. *Jub.* 6.17) and, arguably, he had found in Christ and the Spirit a new law (cf. Rom. 8:2; Gal. 6:2). However, Paul does not show any interest in the particular date of any of the appearances. Further, with a strong attachment to Jerusalem[6] it is notable that Paul says nothing about the city being the location of any post-Easter experiences, even though a story of an appearance to James, the leader in Jerusalem, could be expected to have been originally set there. Moreover, Paul associates the post-Easter experiences with the risen Jesus, not with the Spirit. A theologian so deeply interested in the Spirit and the ecstatic (e.g. 1 Cor. 12:1–14:40; Gal. 3:2–5) is most likely to relate a collective post-Easter, Spirit-focused and ecstasy inducing event resembling Acts 2, if he knew it.

Turning to the second Gospel we see, on the one hand, that Mark has a special interest in Galilee,[7] assigning it the place of revelation during the ministry of Jesus,[8] as well as the place of post-Easter revelation for the followers of Jesus.[9] Notably, before the passion, Mark has Jesus say to the disciples: 'after I am raised up, I will go before you to Galilee' (14:28). Later this saying is reflected by a young man in white at the empty tomb saying, 'he is going ahead of you to Galilee' (16:7). On the other hand, for Mark, Jerusalem is the origin of Jesus' opponents and the place where he is rejected and suffers.[10]

Regardless of whether or not Mark is responsible for locating post-Easter experiences in Galilee, the point for us is that, in offering an alternative location to Luke's concentration on Jerusalem, along with what we have seen of Paul's lack of interest in date and location, he decreases our confidence in the historical reliability of Luke's focus on the city. Further,

---

[6] E.g. Rom. 15:25–26, 31; 1 Cor. 16:3; Gal. 1:18; 2:1–2.
[7] See, e.g. Mark 14:28; 15:41; 16:7; and the next note (n. 8) below.
[8] Mark 1:9, 14, 28, 39; 3:7; 7:31; 9:30.
[9] Mark 14:28; 15:41; 16:7.
[10] See Mark 3:22; 7:1; 10:32, 33; 11:1, 11, 15, 27; 15:41.

Mark, our earliest Gospel, also gives no hint of knowing of a post-Easter Spirit-focused event of the significance and date that is reflected in Acts 2. With this in mind we can see that, while Luke recognizes the existence of Christians in Galilee (Acts 9:31), he suppresses references to the area[11] – even having Jesus tell his followers to stay in Jerusalem (Luke 24:49; Acts 1:4) – and highlights the significance of Jerusalem as the geographical source of early Christianity.[12]

In this discussion we can leave aside Matthew, for the Galilean locations of his major post-Easter stories (Matt. 28:16–20) are probably dependent on Mark, offering us no independent information.[13] Nevertheless, it can be said that Matthew offers no support for Luke's focus on Jerusalem. Similarly, the Fourth Gospel is possibly dependent on Luke for both the Jerusalem location and even that of Galilee for the post-Easter experiences of the disciples.[14] However, it is notable that the Fourth Evangelist, who, arguably, knows both Acts as well as the Gospel of Luke, has brought the giving of the Spirit into the same day as the resurrection (Luke 24:36–40/John 20:19–23). Thus the Fourth Gospel interweaves, if not equates, post-Easter resurrection appearance and Spirit experience.

From this we can reasonably conclude that the Fourth Evangelist rejects both the tradition of the coming of the Spirit on a scale that Luke reports and also that it took place 50 days later. Thus, even though the presence and power of the Holy Spirit in the lives of the followers of Jesus were important to the writer of the Fourth Gospel (John 14–15; 20:19–23), he did not consider the giving of the Spirit to be either on a level with the significance of the Easter story or as dramatic as Luke described the event to be.

An obvious and important point to make in concluding is that, with the possible exception of the Fourth Evangelist, other New Testament writers report resurrection appearances of Jesus rather than Acts 2-like experiences of the Spirit. Also, the results of our discussion diminish our confidence that there was circulating in early Christianity a single story of the coming of the Spirit in Jerusalem on the day of Pentecost involving all the followers of Jesus and evoking the massive response Luke relates in Acts 2. Therefore, rather than a single story of a Spirit-focused and ecstasy inducing story that is located in Jerusalem, and that took place on the day of Pentecost, it is reasonable to suppose that early Christianity knew of a number of stories of *comings* of the Spirit or appearances of Jesus, with settings of various times and places. Indeed, turning to Acts we find Luke reports other comings of the Spirit that also may imply yet more.

---

[11] Luke 22:28–34; 24:6.

[12] Acts 8:1. See also Acts 8:14–17; 9:26–30; 11:1–18, 22–30; 15:6–35.

[13] Cf. Matt. 28:7 and Mark 16:7, as well as Matt. 28:10 and Mark 16:7.

[14] Cf. John 20:19–29 (probably to be taken as set in Jerusalem as the doors are said to be locked in fear of the Jews, 20:19) and Luke 24:36–49, as well as John 21:1–14 and Luke 5:1–11 (possibly, as is frequently suggested, a post-Easter appearance which, to preserve the Jerusalem focus of the post-Easter period, Luke has taken up at this point in his narrative).

§6.3 Luke's Pentecosts

First, in Acts 4:23–31 the story of a prayer meeting ends with the comment: 'When they had prayed, the place in which they were gathered together was shaken; and they were all filled with the Holy Spirit and spoke the word of God with boldness' (Acts 4:31). This could be a variant of the Pentecost story of the coming of the Spirit: some of the same characters are involved, notably Peter and John, and both groups are said to be together or united. Also, when the group had prayed, it is said, as it was in 2:4, that their being filled with the Holy Spirit resulted in speaking. However, there are significant differences between the two stories: the presence of the prayer in this story and the response to the coming of the Spirit is not said to be the normally unintelligible speech as in the Pentecost story but preaching boldly in public. This probably means we cannot suppose they are variants of the same story.

On a first reading it could appear that Luke has created this (Acts 4:23–31) story *ex nihilo*: the story forms the climax of the narrative that began with Peter and John entering the temple (3:1) and it involves prayer (see ch. 8, n. 18), as well as using 'to make' (*poiein*) to refer to God as creator,[15] all themes important to Luke. A more careful reading suggests otherwise. Luke's use of 'son' or 'child' (*pais*, 4:27) for Jesus, a designation he only uses in relation to the Palestinian church,[16] and the mention of Herod and Pilate, likely to have come from a Palestinian tradition, suggest that Luke was using Palestinian traditions in constructing this story. In turn, this means that Luke is conveying a tradition indicating that the Spirit came on more than one occasion in Palestine to the early post-Easter followers of Jesus. This is con-firmed in other stories in Acts.

Second, in Acts 8:4–25 there is a story of the coming of the Spirit on the Samaritans in Samaria. The apostles are said to come down from Jerusalem and pray and lay-on their hands that they might receive the Holy Spirit (Acts 8:15). There is little detail in the story concerning the coming of the Spirit, though the narrative leads the reader to assume there was significant tangible response so that Simon the Sorcerer, so-called, was visibly or audibly aware of and impressed with what happened (8:18–19).

Third, in Acts 9:10–25 Luke tells of the Lord speaking to Ananias in a vision (Acts 9:10–16) and of Paul being filled with the Holy Spirit in Damascus (9:17). In that Luke does not follow his habit of linking the coming of the Spirit with Jerusalem,[17] it is reasonable to suppose that he is conveying the idea that there had been a separate coming of the Spirit at Damascus. Apart from what is said to happen to Paul, Luke supplies no details of the Spirit's coming. However, because Luke portrays Paul as sufficiently concerned about synagogues (plural) harbouring those 'who belonged to the Way' (9:2) to make

---

[15] In the NT only Mark 10:6; Acts 4:24; 14:15; 17:24 and 26 use *poiein* in relation to God as creator.

[16] Acts 3:13, 26; 4:27, 30.

[17] E.g. Acts 8:15; 10:5, 47; 11:15.

a journey to Damascus, he conveys the impression that the number of believers there was significant.

Fourth, in Acts 10:1–48 Luke relates the consequence of Peter's speech in the house of Cornelius in Caesarea. He says that, while Peter was still speaking, 'the Holy Spirit fell on all who heard the word' (Acts 10:44) and, as a result, they spoke in tongues and praised God (10:44–47). Luke clearly intends his readers to see this as similar to the Acts 2 story. There is key vocabulary common to both stories,[18] Peter says that the Holy Spirit fell on the Gentiles as in Jerusalem (10:47; 11:15), and Luke refers the saying that 'John baptized with water, but you shall be baptized in the Holy Spirit' to this story (11:16) as well as to the Acts 2 story (1:5). Once again, this shows that Luke understood that there was more than one coming of the Spirit.

Fifth to consider is Apollos in Acts 18:24–28. Although he most probably had no contact with Jerusalem – for he knew only the baptism of John (Acts 18:25) – Luke describes him as being 'fervent in spirit' (*zeōn tō pneumati*, 18:25). This is unlikely to be mere human enthusiasm. Not only can Luke use the word 'spirit' on its own to refer to the Holy Spirit (6:3, 5) but also, with Luke's interest in the ecstatic expression of the Spirit, without any qualification here, he is probably referring to an obvious manifestation of the Spirit in Apollos when he spoke. With Luke telling us that Apollos was a native of Alexandria it is reasonable to suppose that there may have been another and independent outpouring of the Spirit in that city.

Finally, in Acts 19:1–7 Luke has yet another story of the coming of the Spirit. Luke says that in Ephesus Paul found some disciples and asked, 'Did you receive the Holy Spirit when you believed?' (Acts 19:2). Not ever having heard that there was a Holy Spirit, on Paul's encouragement they were baptized in the name of the Lord Jesus. Luke says that, 'when Paul had laid his hands upon them, the Holy Spirit came on them; and they spoke with tongues and prophesied' (19:6). Again, there is significant vocabulary common to Acts 2[19] as well as, again, the contrast between the baptism of John and the coming of the Holy Spirit (11:16; 19:4). Speaking in tongues and prophecy (see 2:17) are also common to both stories. Yet, as can be extrapolated from the probable coming of the Spirit on disciples at Damascus, there is no suggestion here of a dependency on Jerusalem.

§6.4 So far . . .

Two things seem reasonable to conclude so far from this chapter. First, from other writers in the New Testament, as well as from Luke, there is good evidence that there was not one but there were many stories circulating in

---

[18] Cf. 'Spirit' (*pneuma*) or with 'Holy' (*hagios*, 2:4, 17, 18, 33, 38/10:44, 45, 47); 'tongue' speaking (*glōssa*, Acts 2:4/10:46); 'nation' (*ethnos*, 2:5/10:45); 'amaze' (*existēmi*, 2:7, 12/10:45); 'pour out' (*ekcheō*, 2:17, 18, 33/10:45); 'receive' (*lambanō*, 2:33/10:47) and 'gift' (*dōrea*, 2:38/10:45).

[19] Cf. 'Spirit' (*pneuma*) or with 'Holy' (*hagios*, Acts 2:4, 17, 18, 33, 38/19:6); 'tongue' speaking (*glōssa*, 2:4/19:6) and 'prophesy' (*prophēteuō*, 2:18/19:6).

early Christianity concerning post-Easter experiences of Jesus or the Spirit. Some of these stories were probably set in Jerusalem, others were without settings or were located elsewhere. Although they may have arisen close to Easter, the precise dating of them was not important.

Second, Luke has taken one of these stories and rewritten it to involve all the followers of Jesus at one time (Acts 1:14; 2:1). He gives the story a temple setting, dates it at Pentecost and suggests it had a dramatic impact on a large number of outside observers.[20] He also conveys the idea that at least one other coming of the Spirit was similar to it (10:47; 11:17).

Why Luke has undertaken such rewriting, and what significance he gives to his Pentecost story, is now our concern. In any case, we already have the answer to the puzzle as to why no other New Testament writer tells us of such a story; it is Luke's creation. Before we discuss Luke's intentions in the Pentecost story we need to set out what he says happened.

§6.5 What happened?

It needs to be stressed that we are not seeking to describe what happened but what Luke wants to portray to his readers about the day of Pentecost. After introducing the story of the coming of the Spirit on the day of Pentecost (Acts 2:1), Luke says:

> And suddenly from heaven there came a sound like a rush of a violent wind, and it filled the entire house where they were sitting. Divided tongues, as of fire, appeared among them, and tongues rested on each of them. All of them were filled with the Holy Spirit and began to speak in other languages, as the Spirit gave them ability. (2:2–4)

Already, in a number of ways, Luke has declared his hand in relation to what he thought was involved in the coming of the Spirit.

§6.5.1 A communal vision

Luke says that 'a sound came from heaven *like* the rush of a mighty wind' and 'there appeared to them tongues *as* of fire' (Acts 2:2). In the two words, 'like' and 'as' (*hōsper* and *hōsei*), Luke is probably telling his readers that the coming of the Spirit was a communal vision in which the gathered Christians heard something like wind and saw something like small flames of fire. Luke leaves his readers in no doubt about his view on the origin of this communal vision; he says the sound had come from heaven. The heavenly origin of the vision is reinforced not only by specifying that it was the *Holy* Spirit filling those gathered but also by saying that the vision involved a 'mighty rush of wind'. As wind was thought to accompany the presence of God,[21] this image would have brought to mind God's powerful and mysterious

---

20 See §6.1 above, and Acts 2:5–13, 37–41.
21 See 2 Sam. 22:16; Job 37:10; Ezek. 13:13.

activity in the Old Testament.[22] The symbol 'fire' would have reminded Luke's readers of the tangible, awesome presence of the pure holy God in the theophany on Mount Sinai (Exod. 19:18). We shall take up this point in a moment.

§6.5.2 The Holy Spirit filled all the followers of Jesus

Luke considers that what happened was more than a visionary experience. He says 'all of them were filled with the Holy Spirit' (Acts 2:4). Luke uses this same word 'filled' (*pimplēmi*) of a person filled by the Spirit and speaking boldly in intimidating circumstances. That is, Peter speaks boldly to the members of the Sanhedrin when he is filled with the Spirit (4:8) and, after praying, Peter and John and those with them are filled with the Spirit and said to speak the word of God with boldness (4:31).

What Luke meant by being 'filled' (*pimplēmi*) can be seen when we take into account that Luke also writes of people being 'filled' with anger (Luke 4:28), fear (5:26), fury (6:11), wonder and amazement (Acts 3:10), jealousy (5:17; 13:45), confusion (19:29), and of fish filling boats to the point of sinking (Luke 5:7). From this we can see that, for Luke, being filled with the Holy Spirit would have meant to be overcome, overwhelmed or consumed by God's Spirit in a way that dominated the feelings or emotions and controlled the activity of the person. Quite often, according to Luke, the result was inspired speaking of some kind,[23] but also included performing miracles.[24] It is notable that Luke not only says that 'all' (*pas*, 2:1) the followers of Jesus were present on the day of Pentecost (2:1) but also that 'all' – apostles and the crowd of believers (cf. 1:14–15) – were filled with the Spirit (2:4); none were excluded from this filling (cf. 2:17–18).

A careful reading of Luke indicates that he considered being filled with the Spirit more than an ecstatic experience. Notably, those chosen to wait on tables are described as 'men of good standing, full (*plērēs*) of the Spirit and of wisdom' (Acts 6:3, cf. 5, 8) and Barnabas is described as 'a good man, full (*plērēs*) of the Holy Spirit and of faith' (11:24). Interestingly, Luke can also use *plērēs* to describe Elymas the magician as being 'full' of all deceit and villainy, and a man as 'full' of leprosy (Luke 5:12). In their contexts, these uses of the adjective *plērēs* ('filled' or 'full') show that Luke considered being filled with the Spirit to mean not only a passing moment that brought about ecstatic behaviour or miraculous results but could also be a permanent and identifiable aspect of a person's character.

---

[22] E.g. Ps. 147:18; Isa. 40:24; Ezek. 37:9–14; see also Eccl. 43:16, 20.

[23] Luke 1:41–42, 67; Acts 2:4; 4:8, 31; 9:17; 13:9.

[24] E.g. for Jesus being 'filled' see Luke 4:1 ('full', *plērēs*), 14 ('in the power of the Spirit', *en tē dunamei tou pneumatos*), cf. 18 ('spirit of the Lord upon me', *pneuma kuriou ep eme*); Acts 10:38 (*echrisen . . . pneumati hagiō*, 'anointed . . . [with] Holy Spirit'). For Stephen see Acts 6:8; 7:55. For Philip see Acts 6:3; 8:6–7. For Paul see, e.g. Acts 9:17; 14:1–4.

§6.5.3 They 'began to speak in other tongues' – Acts 2:4

Luke says that Jews from every nation under the sun heard the disciples speak in their own language (Acts 2:5–6, 11). Theories abound as to what Luke meant by this. It could be that he thought the tongues or languages were new ways of interpreting the Old Testament, perhaps with wild enthusiasm on the part of the disciples. But, there is no support for this view in what Luke wrote. Psychological explanations have also been offered. For example, perhaps in rapport with the disciples' ecstatic, yet unintelligible utterances about the wonderful works of God, Luke assumed the minds of the hearers were sparked off in sympathy. Again, plausible though this theory may be, it is not supported by what Luke says.

Further, it could be that, for Luke, the miracle was not in the nature of the speaking but in the act of hearing. But, Luke uses the plural 'languages' (*glōssais*) – *glōssa* being the normal word for speech or language.[25] That is, Luke is saying that there is more than one language involved in the speaking, made all the more likely with his saying they were 'other' languages.[26] Moreover, the speaking is said to be generated by the Spirit (Acts 2:4), an unnecessary statement if he thought there was nothing unusual or miraculous about the speaking. Thus, Luke is probably saying that a number of other or foreign languages were being spoken.[27]

Therefore, the view best fitting the text is that Luke considers that, in being overcome or consumed by God's Spirit, the disciples between them spoke a number of other or foreign languages unknown to them. Yet – without interpretation – their speech was intelligible to the hearers from different language groups (Acts 2:8, 11).

What was heard was the disciples 'speaking about God's deeds of power' (Acts 2:11). Luke does not consider this an evangelistic endeavour, for of those who heard it 'All were amazed and perplexed, saying to one another, "What does this mean?"'. Rather, as comparable to what is found in other literature concerning the impact of the coming of the Spirit,[28] and taking into account the parallel in Acts 10:46, Luke probably intends his readers to understand the disciples were praising God.

Thus, for Luke, the miracle is not in the hearing, but in the speaking. In the light of such phenomena – xenoglossy or xenolalia – being reported in contemporary Pentecostalism and the charismatic movement, for example, such an explanation of Luke's intention is quite reasonable. In passing we can note that this idea of tongues is different from that found in Paul's letters. The latter were unintelligible without an interpreter[29] and, perhaps, thought to be languages of the spirit world (cf. 1 Cor. 13:1; 14:1).

---

[25] See, e.g. Philo, *Moses* 2.40; Josephus, *Ant.* 10.8. Cf. Rom. 14:11; Phil. 2:11. Except in Isa. 29:24; 32:4, where it means stammering, in the LXX *glōssa* always refers to a human language.

[26] *Heterais* ('other', plural), see Ecclus. Prologue 22; 1 Cor. 14:21.

[27] Acts 2:4, 8, 11.

[28] See *Testament of Job* 48.1—50.3 and, later than the time of Luke see *Tg. Ps.-J.* on 1 Sam. 10:6; 19:20–23.

[29] See 1 Cor. 14:6–19, 28; cf. 12:10, 30.

§6.5.4 In summary, and beyond

In the Acts 2 story Luke is conveying the idea that on the day of Pentecost all the gathered followers of Jesus experienced a communal vision which involved hearing a sound like wind and seeing tongues like fire. In this visionary experience from God, the Holy Spirit overcame, filled or overwhelmed the disciples causing them to speak in languages unknown to them but comprehensible to others. Luke implies that the ensuing speech, in its source, its boldness and perhaps in its spontaneity, would not have been possible without a filling of the Spirit.

Beyond Acts 2, Luke uses other stories to reinforce his views on what was important in the coming of the Spirit. In Acts 4:31 Luke says the coming of the Spirit is accompanied by a shaking of the place where the followers of Jesus were meeting. In Acts 8:4–25 the coming of the Holy Spirit on the Samaritans is said to be preceded by their accepting the word of God (8:14) and also involved the laying-on of hands. As in the Acts 2 story, this coming was, in some way, visible, for Luke says that Simon saw that the Holy Spirit had been received (8:18). In 9:10–25, a story later adapted (22:6–16) and abbreviated (26:12–18), Ananias lays hands on Paul to be filled with the Spirit 'and immediately something like scales fell from his eyes, and his sight was restored' (9:18). Luke goes on to say that, to the amazement of all who heard him, Paul 'began to proclaim Jesus in the synagogues' (9:20, cf. 21). In Acts 10:1–48 it is said to be while Peter was speaking that the Holy Spirit fell on those listening. The evidence or confirmation Luke reports is that 'they heard them speaking in tongues and extolling God' (10:46). Luke explicitly says that this coming of the Spirit was reminiscent of the Pentecostal coming (10:47; 11:15). In Acts 18:25 the Spirit is related to the zeal or enthusiasm of the speech of Apollos. Finally, in 19:1–7, Luke says of 'disciples' at Ephesus; 'When Paul had laid his hands on them, the Holy Spirit came upon them, and they spoke in tongues and prophesied' (19:6).

In the ways the Pentecost story is reflected in similar stories, what Luke seeks to convey as essential to him in the coming of the Spirit is clarified. He confirms that he considers the coming of the Spirit involved some tangible expression or manifestation – sometimes including healing, or speaking in tongues – that would otherwise not be expected. Also, the coming of the Spirit both prompted and enabled bold proclamation of the good news as well as significant faith response. At this point we begin to open up the issue of the significance Luke gives to the coming of the Spirit, particularly at Pentecost.

§6.6 The significance of Pentecost

To clear the way for seeing as clearly as possible the significance that Luke invests in his story of the Pentecostal coming, one persistent and popular view needs to be set aside.

§6.6.1 The birth of the Church

It is common to take Acts 2 as Luke's story of the birth of the Church. A parallel is drawn between the birth or conception of Jesus and the birth of the Church. The description of the Pentecost experience of the Church, which mentions the 'coming' of the Spirit and the reception of 'power' (Acts 1:8), and the angel's message to Mary, 'The Holy Spirit will come upon you, and the power of the Most High will overshadow you' (Luke 1:35), are seen to be parallels.

However, we have already seen that Luke most probably sees the conception or birth of the Church in Jesus' call of the twelve apostles (Luke 6:12–16; §2.4 above). In any case, a closer parallel to the story of Pentecost is to be found in Luke's story of the baptism of Jesus (3:21–22). Both stories are of the Spirit's coming from heaven (3:21; Acts 2:2). Both stories describe a visionary experience; in the case of Jesus the 'Spirit descended upon him in bodily form, as a dove' (Luke 3:22), and in the case of the disciples 'a sound came from heaven like the rush of a mighty wind' and there appeared 'tongues as of fire' (Acts 2:2–3). Both experiences of the Spirit – at the Jordan and at Pentecost – are characterized as receiving power (Luke 4:14; Acts 1:8) and are linked with the notion of baptism (Luke 3:21; Acts 1:5). The result of both experiences is also said to be the same. Jesus is subsequently said to be full of the Holy Spirit and led by the Spirit (Luke 4:1). Then, in Acts 2:4, the disciples are also said to be filled with the Holy Spirit and enabled by the Spirit, in their case, to speak in tongues. Further, Jesus begins his ministry by explaining; 'The Spirit of the Lord is upon me' (Luke 4:18), as expected by Isaiah 61:1, and Peter explains the disciples' experience as a realization of Joel's expectation, 'I will pour out my Spirit on all flesh' (Acts 2:17).

From this we can see that Luke does not parallel the coming of the Spirit at Pentecost with the birth or conception of Jesus but with his empowering with the Spirit for his ministry at his baptism. Thus, to repeat, the coming of the Spirit is not the birth of the Church for Luke, but its empowerment for mission (see §2.4 above). We are now in a position to see more clearly what meaning Luke wants his readers to see in his Pentecost story.

§6.6.2 The coming of the Spirit is an eschatological event

So important is this perspective for Luke that he draws attention to it in a number of ways. First, in repeating that Jerusalem is to be the location of the coming of the Spirit (Luke 24:49b; Acts 1:4), Luke signals to his readers that the eschatological salvation expected to arise out of the royal city of God's people has arrived.[30]

This is reinforced, second, in reply to a question of the disciples, 'Lord, is this the time when you will restore the kingdom of Israel?' (Acts 1:6), Luke

---

[30] See esp. Luke 2:25, 38; 9:31, 51, 53; 13:22, 33; 17:11; 18:31; 19:11, 28; 24:13, 18, 33, 47, 52–53; Acts 1:4, 8, 12, 19; 2:5, 14; 4:16; 5:16; 6:7; 10:39; 13:27, 31.

has Jesus use a 'not . . . but' (*ou . . . alla*, 1:7–8) construction. The negative implication of this answer is that Luke redirects attention away not only from the issue of the timing of the restoration of Israel, but also from the timing of the coming of the Spirit. The positive implication of Jesus' answer is that the coming of the Spirit is the eschatological restoration of the kingdom of Israel (cf. 1:8). This eschatological perspective is maintained in Peter's speech after the gift of the Spirit where a quotation from Joel 2:28 is changed from 'it shall come to pass afterward' to 'in the last days it shall be' (2:17). Thus, in the Spirit-filled and empowered life of the followers of Jesus, Luke says Israel is restored.

Yet, the age of the Church is not to be taken up with a political or nationalistic agenda. Rather, the Church is to be preoccupied with the universal mission of being Jesus' witnesses (Acts 1:8). So important does this theme appear to be in Luke, as well as being in contrast with modern interpretations of the mission of the Church, that we will look more closely at his view of the mission of the Church towards the end of our study (Chapter 13).

Second, another signal Luke gives that his Pentecostal narrative is of eschatological significance is in Jesus saying that the apostles are to wait in Jerusalem for 'the promise of the Father' (Acts 1:4). At one level, this is probably to be taken as the promise about to be voiced by Jesus (also Luke 24:49; Acts 2:33, 39). At another level, readers would almost certainly be prompted to recall eschatological comings of the Spirit promised in the Old Testament.[31] Moreover, elsewhere Luke uses the word 'promise' (*epangelia*) to designate the covenant between God and his people through Abraham.[32] This is clearest in Acts 2:39 where the promise of the Spirit 'to you and to your children' is an obvious echo of the covenant with Abraham (Gen. 17:7–10). Thus, the coming of the Spirit fulfils the widely held[33] promise to Abraham that the age had come when all nations would be blessed.[34] Thus, Luke's covenantal language also draws attention to the coming of the Spirit ushering in a new era.

Third, the eschatological significance of the coming of the Spirit is signalled in the introduction to the story. He begins: 'And in the fulfilment of the day . . .' (Acts 2:1). Echoing Old Testament terminology[35] he has also used in talking of the Messiah being born (Luke 2:6), and of the time when Jesus set his face to Jerusalem where he was to die and rise (9:51), Luke speaks of the coming of the Spirit as one of the key events in the history of God's activity in the world.

Fourth, that, for Luke, the coming of the Spirit on the day of Pentecost marked a new beginning is clear because, up until then, in the tradition of

---

[31] See Isa. 32:15; Ezek 36:26–27; 39:29; Joel 2:28–32.

[32] Acts 2:39; 7:17; 13:23, 32; 26:6.

[33] See, e.g. Tobit 13:11; Ecclus. 36:11–17; *1 En.* 48.4; *4 Ezra* 6.26; *2 Bar.* 68.5; Philo, *Rewards* 164–72; *Moses* 2.43–44 and later, cf. *Testament of Simeon* 7.2; *Testament of Levi* 18.2–9; *Testament of Judah* 24.6; 25.5; *Testament of Zebulon* 9.8; *Testament of Benjamin* 10.5–10.

[34] Gen. 12:3; 22:18; Acts 3:25. Cf. also note 40 below.

[35] See Gen. 25:24; Lev. 8:33; Jer. 25:12.

the Old Testament, apart from Jesus,[36] only John the Baptist and his parents are said to be filled with the Holy Spirit.[37] Notably, the followers of Jesus are not included. Luke shows consistency on this point in Luke 11:13 where the Father's gift of the Holy Spirit to the disciples is put in the future – 'shall give' (*dōsei*; see Acts 2:33). Further, the saying about blasphemy against the Holy Spirit not being forgiven is placed in the post-Easter context of the followers of Jesus being arrested and brought before the synagogue and rulers and authorities (see Luke 12:8–12 and Acts 6:10).

This point leads us to note, fifth, that the expectation of John the Baptist, that Jesus would baptize in the Holy Spirit and fire (Luke 3:16), is not realized in the period of the Gospel but on the day of Pentecost when the Spirit is poured out 'on all flesh' (*epi pasan sarka*, Acts 2:17, cf. 21). A number of times Luke makes a point of saying that 'all' the followers of Jesus were involved: in the preparation for the coming of the Spirit 'all' (probably 120 of them, 1:15) are said to be praying (1:14); on the day of Pentecost they are 'all' said to be assembled (2:1) and 'all' are filled with the Spirit (2:4). Further, the Spirit is promised to each of (*hekastos humōn*, 'each of you') the converts in Peter's audience (2:37–41). Thus, the coming of the Spirit, and the associated ecstatic experiences which are described in Acts 2 are not, at least in Luke's mind, for the twelve or for a few followers of Jesus but for all the disciples. In this we have yet further evidence that, for Luke, the coming of the Spirit marked the beginning of a new era, an era not so much of the Church as of the Spirit.

Sixth, when we compare Luke's Acts 2 story with passages written a few years earlier by Philo, Luke's focus on the epochal characteristic of the Spirit is seen even more sharply. In *The Decalogue* 32–33 Philo describes the giving of the Law:

> I should suppose that God wrought on this occasion a miracle of a truly holy kind by bidding an invisible sound to be created in the air more marvellous than all instruments and fitted with perfect harmonies, not soulless, not yet composed of body and soul like a living creature, but a rational soul full of clearness and distinctness, which giving shape and tension to the air and changing it to flaming fire, sounded forth like the breath through a trumpet an articulate voice so loud it appeared to be equally audible to the farthest as well as the nearest.

A little later Philo says that,

> from the midst of the fire that streamed from heaven there sounded forth to their utter amazement a voice, for the flame became articulate speech in the language familiar to the audience, and so clearly and distinctly were the words formed by it that they seemed to see rather than hear them. (*Decalogue* 46)

Given this shared language and imagery between Luke's description of the coming of the Spirit and Philo's description of the giving of the Law, it is

---

[36] Luke 3:21–22; 4:1, 14, 17; Acts 10:38.
[37] Luke 1:15, 41, 67; 7:26–27; see also 1:35; 2:25–27.

reasonable to suppose that Luke considered the pouring out of the Spirit as the giving of a new law, and as significant as the giving of the Mosaic Law.[38] Notwithstanding, Luke provides plenty of evidence that he considers the Mosaic Law remains valid for the people of God.[39]

Finally, the list of peoples 'from every nation under heaven' (Acts 2:5) also draws attention to the eschatological significance Luke gives to his story. Old Testament writers, as well as others in the time of Luke, expected that, in the last days, Jews scattered over the world and all the nations would return to Jerusalem to enter into a new and everlasting covenant and find salvation.[40] Luke implies that this eschatological gathering of nations has taken place in the Pentecostal coming of the Spirit. This implication is further reinforced in an interesting way.

It is hard to avoid concluding that Luke wants his readers to see Pentecost as the reversal of Babel. The influence on Luke of the Genesis 11:1–9 story, including its vocabulary, is considerable. In Genesis the whole earth (Gen. 11:1) is the backdrop to the story, and in Acts Jews from 'every nation under heaven' are involved (Acts 2:5). In Genesis those fearing being scattered (*diaspeirō*) seek to make a name for themselves (Gen. 11:4). However, in Acts those who are eventually scattered (*diaspeirō*, Acts 8:1, 4) proclaim the word; and the name being proclaimed is Jesus.[41] In Genesis the Lord confused (*sugcheō*, Gen. 11:7, 9) the language (*glōssa*, 11:7) of all the earth (11:9). In contrast, in Acts, on hearing the languages, the people from every nation were confused (*sugcheō*, Acts 2:6). In Genesis the confused people cannot hear or understand (*akouō*, Gen. 11:7) each (*hekatos*) other's speech (*phōnē*, 11:7). Yet, in Acts confused people are each (*hekatos*) able to hear or understand (*akouō*) the sound (*phōnē*, Acts 2:6) of the speaking. In Genesis the Lord separates (*diaspeirō*, Gen. 11:4) the nations, destroying the unity of one language (11:1). However, in Acts the divided tongues (*diamerizomenai glōssai*, Acts 2:3) bring a common hearing (2:6).

In echoing this story, Luke has reversed both the use of the images as well as its storyline. What Luke seems to be conveying to his readers is that, while at Babel God destroys self-seeking unity by incomprehensible tongues which led to scattering, at Pentecost, through tongues that can be understood, God's Spirit brings unity and, in selfless scattering, the word is proclaimed.

In this section we have been able to see Luke's intention in creating the story of the Pentecostal coming of the Spirit: to establish and elucidate that the coming of the Spirit was the anticipated eschatological event, one of the pivotal

---

[38] The evidence is slight – e.g. the cloud (Exod. 19:9, 13, 16; Acts 1:9), the mountain (Exod. 19:2, 3, 12, 13, 14, 16, 20; Acts 1:12), the witnesses (Exod. 20:18–21; Acts 1:6, 12) and the position of the story before the promulgation of the Law), but it may have been Luke's intention for the Ascension story in Acts to mirror Moses ascending the mountain to receive the Law.

[39] E.g. Acts 1—7; 10:13–16, 28; 11:3; 15:1–35; 16:3; 18:18, 21; 20:16; 21:18–28; 23:6; 24:17; 26:5.

[40] Among the many passages see, e.g. Isa. 2:2–3; 25:6–8; 60; Jer. 3:17; 50:5; Hag. 2:6–9; Zech. 8:22; and, outside the Old Testament, Tobit 13:(9)–11; 14:5–7; *1 En.* 90.28–33; *Sib. Or.* 3.703–31.

[41] E.g. Acts 2:21, 38; 8:12.

moments in the history of God's activity in the world. In doing so we have already see that, even though Luke considered the coming of the Spirit to be the promised covenant restoring the people of God – Israel, its purpose was not political or national. Rather, it was missional and universal. Not surprisingly, Luke's story involved tangible manifestations of the powerful presence of God.

§6.7 The implications of the coming of the Spirit

Being aware of the eschatological orientation of his story, and the new state of affairs that it implies, we are sensitive to the development of the practical implications of the coming of the Spirit that Luke weaves into his narrative.

§6.7.1 A new era and relationship with God is inaugurated

Besides the coming of the Spirit itself marking the inauguration of a new era, Luke's narrative provides a couple of further pointers that a new dimension in God's relationship with his people had been inaugurated. First, though variously dated,[42] by Luke's time the day-long Feast of Weeks was fixed in the third month of the year, 50 days after the first day of the Passover,[43] and regularly called the Feast of Pentecost.[44] What was originally a celebration of the beginning of harvest (Exod. 23:16; 34:22) had become a celebration of the giving of the Law at Sinai and was associated with the renewal of the covenant made with Moses.[45] Further, for the Qumran community, the Feast of Pentecost was also the occasion when new members were admitted (1QS 1–3). This point, most probably clear to Luke's readers, ought not be lost in noting that, in Acts, the first new members were admitted to the group of followers of Jesus on the day of Pentecost (Acts 2:41). Along with the Spirit being called the promise or covenant of the Father (see above), this reinforces the probability that, in dating it on Pentecost, Luke is signalling that the coming of the Spirit was to be understood as the inauguration of a new covenant or Spirit-based relationship between God and his people.

Also, one of the associated phenomena Luke describes of the coming of the Spirit is fire: 'Divided tongues, as of fire, appeared among them, and a tongue rested on each of them' (Acts 2:3). Luke undoubtedly intends his readers to recall the prophecy of John the Baptist: 'He will baptize you with the Holy Spirit and with fire' (Luke 3:16). It is unlikely Luke is thinking that there is a twofold baptism, a gracious filling for the righteous and a consuming fire for others. For, in Luke 3:16 John is addressing a single group of people (using 'all', *pas*) and predicts a single baptism: 'He will baptize you with (or 'in', *en*) the Holy Spirit and fire', the 'in' referring to both components. Further, in the context of Luke's narrative, John is addressing the

---

[42] See Lev. 23:15–21 (cf. Num. 28:26–31) and *m. Menahot* 10.3; *m. Hagigah* 2.4.

[43] See Philo, *Spec. Laws* 2.162, 176; Josephus, *Ant.* 3.250–52; *J.W.* 2.42–43.

[44] See Tobit 2:1; 2 Macc. 12:31–32; Philo, *Decalogue* 160; *Spec. Laws* 2.176; Josephus, *Ant.* 3.248–53; 13.252; 14.337; 17.254; *J.W.* 1.253; 2.42; 6.299.

[45] *Jub.* 1.5; 6.11, 17; 15.1–24.

same people who sought his baptism and who were expected to experience the Pentecostal baptism (Luke 3:16). Moreover, in Acts 2, the fire falls not on some but on all followers of Jesus (Acts 2:1).

A baptism that involves fire could be assumed to involve an element of destructive judgement. Indeed, a passage in *The Community Rule* from the Dead Sea Scrolls confirms that this is how Luke's readers are likely to have understood the mention of fire: 'God will then purify every human deed by his truth; He will refine the human frame for himself . . . He will cleanse him of all wicked deeds with the Holy Spirit; like purifying waters he will shed upon him the spirit of truth (to cleanse him).'[46]

With such a remarkable combination of the images of 'refining' (fire),[47] 'Spirit' and 'water' in this Qumran scroll, it is reasonable to suppose that Luke and his readers would have been influenced by a similar mix of ideas so that, for them, the baptism of fire at Pentecost meant the eschatological coming of God's refining and purifying Spirit in bringing forgiveness to his people (see Acts 2:38).

§6.7.2 The disciples are transformed

It is popularly held that it was the experience of the resurrection appearances that transformed the disciples into confident and powerful witnesses. Luke conveys a different understanding. On the one hand, being told of the resurrection, he says of the apostles: 'these words seemed to them an idle tale, and they did not believe them' (Luke 24:11). Peter is neither said to believe nor to rejoice, but to be 'amazed at what had happened' (24:12).[48] Further, towards the end of the Gospel, after depicting the disciples as not encouraged by reports of the resurrection (24:21–24), Luke sums up in his description of the eleven: 'in their joy they were disbelieving' (24:41).

On the other hand, quite early in his Gospel, in contemplating the work of the Messiah, Luke looks forward not to the cross or resurrection but to the baptism with the Holy Spirit (Luke 3:15–17). Even the glimpse of joy at the very end of the Gospel (24:52–53) is connected not with reflections on the resurrection, but with returning to Jerusalem to wait for the promise of the Father to be 'clothed with power from on high' (24:49; cf. Acts 1:4). Then, immediately after the coming of the Spirit, Peter's speech is punctuated with expressions of confidence (2:14–39). Also, at the end of the Pentecost narrative the description of life among the believers includes the line that they 'ate their food with glad and generous hearts, praising God' (2:46–47).

---

[46] 1QS 4.20–21. See also 3.7–9; 1QH[a] 16.12.

[47] Although 'refine', can refer to washing with water (Job 36:27) or straining (Isa. 25:6) to purify, it is generally associated with refining with fire in the Dead Sea Scrolls (1QS 4.20; 1QH[a] 6.3; 13.16; 14.8; 4Q177 10–11.1; see also 4Q177 29.3; 4Q511 35.2; cf. 1 Chr. 28:18; 29:4; Job 28:1; Ps. 12:7; Mal. 3:3).

[48] It is difficult to decide whether or not Luke is responsible for Luke 24:12 for, although this verse is omitted in some important texts (e.g. Codex Bezae and many Old Latin witnesses), it is found in the majority of texts, including P[75] (*c.* 200 CE), which contains the earliest extant copy of Luke.

Further, the group of followers filled with the Spirit is said to engender fear in observers (2:43), to stand fearless before judges (4:5–22) and to preach the word of God boldly (4:31). Clearly, for Luke, it was not the resurrection but the coming of the Spirit that transformed the followers of Jesus. This leads to the next point.

§6.7.3 The followers of Jesus receive power

Early in Acts Luke has Jesus say, 'you will receive power when the Holy Spirit has come upon you' (1:8). In other places Luke maintains this close association, even identification of power and the Holy Spirit.[49] This is an idea on a direct line with Old Testament writers who associated the idea of power with God and his activities[50] and is also shared by other New Testament writers; Mark 14:62 and Matthew 26:64 actually have 'the Power' (*hē dunamis*) as a name for God.

Up until the beginning of Acts, apart from Mary (Luke 1:35), Jesus is the bearer of the 'power' (*dunamis*) of the Holy Spirit in Luke's story. After being baptized, Jesus returned from the Jordan, full of the Holy Spirit (Luke 4:1). After the temptations, Jesus returned 'in the power of the Spirit' (4:14). After an exorcism, an amazed audience says that, 'with authority and power he commands the unclean spirits, and they come out' (4:36). In the introduction to a healing story it is said that 'the power of the Lord was with him to heal' (5:17). Then, summarizing Jesus' ministry, Luke says, 'God anointed Jesus of Nazareth with the Holy Spirit and with power he went about doing good and healing all that were oppressed by the devil, for God was with him' (Acts 10:38).

In two places Luke depicts Jesus as dispensing power to others. There is the story of the woman who was healed when she touched Jesus. He says, 'Someone touched me for I perceive that power has gone out from me' (Luke 8:46). In sending out the twelve to proclaim the kingdom of God and to heal, Jesus is said to give them 'power and authority over all demons and to cure disease' (9:1). This ministry takes place among the surrounding villages (9:6). Foreshadowing worldwide mission of the followers of Jesus (see Chapter 13 below), the mission of the seventy-two also involves using power (cf. 10:9, 13, 17–19). What is foreshadowed here is realized in Acts 2 where the power is said to come from being filled with the Spirit and to be for worldwide mission (Acts 1:8b; cf. Luke 24:47–49). Before exploring that theme further we need to take into account the commentary Luke gives on what he broadly terms as the coming of power.

Peter's speech (Acts 2:14–36), an interpretation of the Pentecostal coming of the Spirit, focuses on God's vindication of Jesus in the light of the dawning of the eschaton (2:22–36). However, in the first section of the speech, through citing Joel 2:28–32, Luke sets out the immediate implications of the

---

[49] See Acts 1:8; 6:3, 8; 10:38.
[50] See, e.g. Deut. 3:24; 1 Chr. 29:10–12; 2 Chr. 20:6; Pss. 21:13; 59:16; 68:32–35.

coming of the Spirit for those involved (2:16–21). Two themes dominate the quotation, the coming of prophecy and of portents and signs. First, the importance of the coming of prophecy is seen in Luke adding the words 'and they shall prophesy' to Joel 2:29. Second, in Joel 2:30, the portents are cosmological events in the expected new age. However, Luke transforms these into the miracles of the followers of Jesus that can now take place. Luke introduces the word 'signs' to his quotation (Joel 2:30/Acts 2:19) which he immediately goes on in this story to use, not only for the miracles of Jesus (2:22) but also for those of his followers (2:43) in their mission.[51] Once again we are led to a further point.

§6.7.4 The Spirit was given for mission

A superficial reading of Acts could lead to the conclusion that the coming of the Holy Spirit was to bring ecstatic experience to the followers of Jesus or an ability for them to perform wonders. However, for Luke the coming of the Spirit was primarily associated, or even synonymous, with a call to mission, not with the ecstatic. Indeed, the interchange between Peter and Simon the magician makes clear that the focus or purpose of the Spirit's coming was not the associated physical manifestations (cf. Acts 8:19).

Already, in Luke's Gospel, Jesus has been portrayed as modelling Spirit-empowerment, which is closely related to and gives rise to mission. Jesus' inaugural teaching tour, along with the example of a sermon in the Nazareth synagogue in which his agenda for mission is set out (Luke 4:16–21), arises out of him being 'filled with the power of the Spirit' (4:14; cf. 3:22). This is so much part of Luke's thinking that even the mission of John the Baptist is closely related to him being filled with the Spirit (cf. 1:15 and 16).

At the end of the Gospel, the first promise of the Spirit to the apostles and other followers of Jesus is linked with the capacity to witness concerning the suffering and resurrection of Jesus and the preaching of forgiveness 'to all nations' (Luke 24:47–49). Then the very two-part structure of Luke's work, with the second part headed by the Pentecostal coming of the Spirit, followed by many stories of the mission of the Church, inextricably ties the coming of the Spirit to the inauguration and possible fulfilment of mission.

The second promise of the Spirit also makes specific that the coming of the Spirit is for the purpose of witnessing (Acts 1:8). Luke immediately illustrates this in his Pentecost story, for, after being filled with the Holy Spirit, Peter gives witness to Jesus, especially to his resurrection (2:32). Another clear illustration of the Spirit coming for the purpose of mission is the Acts 4 prayer meeting. It ends with those present being filled with the Spirit, which, in turn, led to those gathered speaking 'the word of God with boldness' (4:31) rather than being confined to ecstatic experience. Equally clear is Paul being

---

[51] See also Acts 2:19, 43; 4:16, 22, 30; 5:12; 6:8; 8:6, 13; 14:3; 15:12. The only other use of 'sign' in Acts is 7:36 of the redemptive signs of the Exodus.

portrayed as proclaiming Jesus in the synagogues after being filled with the Spirit (9:17–20).

In view of contemporary tendencies against the view, it is important to reiterate that, for Luke, the 'power' for mission involved in the coming of the Spirit was not confined to producing an ability to talk even boldly about Jesus but included a capacity to perform mighty acts or miracles. So important is this theme in relation to mission in Luke-Acts that we will return to it later (Chapter 13). Also, in view of what we have already said about Luke's purpose and the genre of his writing meaning that he is prescribing as much as describing (§1.3 above), we will take up the implications of this in our final chapter.

§6.8 Conclusion

The puzzle as to why no other New Testament writer has told us about the Pentecostal coming of the Spirit – an event Luke narrates as rivalling the significance of the resurrection – is solved in seeing that Luke is responsible for the story as we have it.

It seems highly probable that a number of stories of sightings of Jesus, or experiences of the Spirit, circulated among early Christians. Luke took one of these stories which, if it did not already have a location, he fixed in Jerusalem; he involved not only the twelve, but all the followers of Jesus, dated it on the Pentecost after Easter, and included a massive public response to the ecstatic event. Along with recasting his Christian tradition about the coming of the Spirit, with its geographically widespread post-Easter experiences, into one dominated by a Pentecostal coming of the Spirit, Luke has elevated the significance of the coming of the Spirit not only to rival but to surpass that of the resurrection story. The coming of the Spirit on the day of Pentecost is, for Luke, the eschatological event that marks the beginning of the new age.

In a communal vision, which involved all the followers of Jesus being filled with the Spirit and being able to receive forgiveness, a Spirit-based relationship with God had been inaugurated. This brought not simply an ecstatic experience, but also a boldness and power for prophesying and performing miracles in order to carry out a universal mission of witnessing to the resurrection.

While those involved in the Pentecostal coming of the Spirit were already followers of Jesus, Luke's stories of later comings of the Spirit were the means for others also to be initiated. Thus we turn now to investigate Luke's understanding of the relationships between the coming of the Spirit, speaking in tongues and water baptism, issues that have proved sensitive and divisive, particularly in the twentieth century with the revival of Pentecostalism. We will see that at least some of Luke's views appear clear.

7

The Spirit, tongues and baptism

Here we enter the arena of a lively debate in the contemporary Church: how to describe the relationship between believing, the coming of the Spirit, tongues and baptism – in water as well as in the Spirit. Here we will ask Luke a number of questions. What is the place of the coming of the Spirit in becoming a Christian? Is tongues the initial evidence for the presence of the Spirit? Does water baptism confer the Spirit or Spirit baptism? Is water baptism required for becoming a Christian? Obviously, we are not the first and will not be the last to traverse this highly disputed territory. But we need to survey the area in order to bring it within view of our subject of the Church in Luke-Acts.

It is to be repeated that we are trying to understand these issues from a Lukan perspective. In doing so there are a number of passages to consider. However, it will neither be possible nor necessary for us to deal in full with every passage, but only with those aspects of them that help us answer our particular questions of Luke. In view of the evidence that will emerge, some of our conclusions will need to be held lightly, others more firmly than some may wish. We begin with a verse that has already been part of our discussion (see §6.3, 6.6.1, 6.6.2 above).

§7.1 Pentecost: the mark of Spirit baptism – Acts 1:5

[F]or John baptized with water, but you shall be baptized with the Holy Spirit not many days from now.

This statement is obviously significant to Luke for he has also used it in his Gospel to prefigure the Acts 2 narrative.[1] It is repeated in, as well as applied to, the story of the conversion of Cornelius (Acts 11:16). An important conclusion Luke's readers would have reached from this statement is that, whereas once the baptism of John in water was a mark of repentance and forgiveness of sins (Luke 3:3), now the baptism of the Spirit is the mark of repentance and forgiveness. This ultimate indicative function of the Spirit will also be reflected in Acts 2:38 (see §7.3 and 7.7 below).

These three occasions are the only times Luke uses the phrase 'baptism in the Spirit';[2] he does not use the phrase in his stories of the coming of the Spirit.

---

[1] Luke 3:16; cf. §6.3, 6.2 above.
[2] Luke 3:16; Acts 1:5; 11:16.

Whatever else this may mean it probably shows that it was not his preferred term for describing the coming of the Spirit, though one he took to be interchangeable with the idea of the Spirit coming upon (Acts 1:8) or filling[3] or falling on[4] or being poured out on[5] or received by[6] or being given to people.[7]

§7.2 Pentecost: Spirit baptism and tongues – Acts 2:4

All of them were filled with the Holy Spirit and began to speak in other languages, as the Spirit gave them ability.

In the use of 'all' (*pas*) Luke clearly thinks that not just the apostles were filled with the Spirit or spoke in tongues; it was for all the followers of Jesus (cf. Acts 1:15; 2:1), and all spoke in tongues. The most natural reading is that Luke is taking the ability to speak in tongues to be the result and, by implication, evidence of being filled 'with' (*en*, 'in') the Spirit.

Luke makes no mention of water baptism here. Water baptism is unlikely to be assumed, for it is mentioned in every other story we will discuss. It could be that the followers of Jesus are to be considered in the same position as Apollos who had received the Spirit and the baptism of John (Acts 18:24–29; see §7.11 below). More likely, those at Pentecost described as being the initial, unique group would make baptism anachronistic. Also, if, as we are about to see, baptism is closely related to coming to believe, this group of followers of Jesus could be described as believers since their acceptance of Jesus' call in Luke 6:13.

§7.3 Pentecost: a programmatic statement? – Acts 2:38, 41

'Repent, and be baptized everyone of you in the name of Jesus Christ so that your sins may be forgiven; and you shall receive the gift of the Holy Spirit' . . . So those who welcomed his message were baptized.

In that the phrase 'in the name of' (*epi tō onomati*) is Semitic in origin (*bshm*), with its idea of calling on or worshipping God,[8] repentance and baptism are carried out on the basis of trust or faith in Jesus Christ. There is, then, a conditional relationship between the repentance and baptism, on the one hand, and the forgiveness of sins, on the other hand; repentance and baptism in the name of Jesus are said to be 'so that' (*eis*, 'to') or for the purpose of sins being forgiven. However, the Holy Spirit is said to be a gift.[9] Further, in using 'and'

---

[3] Acts 2:4; 4:31; 9:17.
[4] Acts 8:16; 10:44; 11:15.
[5] Acts 2:17, 18, 33; 10:45.
[6] Acts 1:8; 2:33; 8:15, 17, 19; 10:47; 19:2.
[7] Acts 5:32; 11:17; 15:8.
[8] E.g. Gen. 4:26; 12:8; 13:4; 1 Kgs 18:24; Ps. 116:17; Zeph. 3:9; Zech. 13:9. Cf. Ps. 105:1; Isa. 12:4; 41:25; 44:5.
[9] Acts 8:20; 10:45; 11:17.

(*kai*) to explain the relationship between repentance, baptism and forgiveness, and the coming of the Spirit, Luke signals what will be illustrated later: the Spirit is in the gift (and timing) of God, not the natural outcome or consequence of baptism.[10]

This verse is significant as it is the only place in Acts where the ideas – repentance, water baptism, faith, forgiveness and the gift of the Holy Spirit – are all closely related. Having these terms together early in Acts, and being placed in a strategic position at the end of Peter's first sermon, it is reasonable to think that Luke intends his readers to see this verse as programmatic, both for the way a person is to respond to the message as well as for the consequences.

Also significant is Luke's description of the response of Peter's audience: 'those who welcomed his message were baptized' (Acts 2:41). Taking 'welcome' (*apodechomai*) to mean 'approve' or 'accept', as it does in other places for Luke,[11] as well as for other writers of the period,[12] welcoming the message is equivalent to believing it. The reader could, therefore, be expected to assume that the welcoming (or believing) and being baptized was shorthand for the longer description by Peter of repentance, water baptism, faith, forgiveness and the gift of the Spirit (2:38). As we proceed we will see increasing reason to take this view on this and other descriptions of conversion.

In considering the role of water baptism in the initiation process in Acts 2:38 we note that 'be baptized' is in the passive (*baptisthētō*)[13] rather than active voice ('were baptized', *ebaptisthēsan*, cf. 2:41). Even though people are commanded to be baptized, it is not something the person does, but something done to them by other followers of Jesus. Thus, the role of baptism in the initiation process is evident: baptism is submitted to, or undertaken, as a means of joining and being accepted or acknowledged by the existing followers of Jesus. This is clear from 2:41 – 'So those who welcomed his message were baptized, and there were added that day about three thousand souls' – where baptism is the indication that the three thousand have joined, it is assumed, the followers of Jesus.

From this programmatic statement it seems that Luke is portraying the relationship between water baptism and the coming of the Spirit in terms of repentance (by the respondents) and baptism (by the community) being preparatory to the gift of the Spirit (by God). If the point is not too subtle, the Spirit is given not on the condition but as a consequence of repentance and baptism. Or, to put it another way, readers are seeing that the Spirit indicates

---

[10] Cf. Acts 9:17–18; 10:43–48.

[11] In the NT, only Luke uses the term: Luke 8:40; 9:11; Acts 2:41; 18:27; 21:17; 24:3; 28:30.

[12] Note 3 Macc. 3:17; 4 Macc. 3:20; Josephus, *Ant.* 9.176; 16.378. See also Philo, *Abraham* 90; Justin, *Dial* 8.3; Diogenes Laertius, *Lives* 8.2.

[13] In referring to a person being baptized the word baptism is, save for Acts 22:16, always in the passive (something done for the person) – Acts 2:38, 41; 8:12, 13, 16, 36; 9:18; 10:47, 48; 11:16; 16:15, 33; 18:8; 19:3, 5. In 22:16 the Greek is in the middle voice which means Paul permitted himself to be baptized.

repentance, and baptism in water. Nothing is said here about the place of tongues, even though the narrative leads the reader to assume that the Spirit came on those who responded to Peter's message (Acts 2:38, 41).

§7.4 Samaritans: baptism and belief – Acts 8:12, 14–16

[W]hen they believed Philip as he preached the good news . . . they were baptized.

Now when the apostles heard that Samaria had received the word of God, they sent to them Peter and John, who came down and prayed for them that they might receive the Holy Spirit; for it had not yet fallen on any of them, but they had only been baptized in the name of the Lord Jesus. Then Peter and John laid their hands on them, and they received the Holy Spirit.

The second passage here is fraught with puzzles and difficulties. Nevertheless, it is helpful in showing Luke's view of the relationship between water baptism and receiving the Holy Spirit. The most obvious conclusion to draw is that the water baptism in the name of the Lord Jesus was not the same as baptism in the Spirit and did not confer the Holy Spirit on the Samaritans. That they had not received the Holy Spirit, even though they had been baptized in water, is a point immediately stressed by Luke (Acts 8:15–17).

It is unlikely that the Spirit had not been given because of incorrect belief. Philip's message is not portrayed as defective; as do others in Acts, he preaches 'the word'.[14] Philip proclaims 'the Christ' (or Messiah, Acts 8:5), otherwise shorthand for the gospel[15] and his 'good news about the kingdom of God and the name of Jesus' (8:12) is the same as Paul's (28:31). In addition, neither Philip's message nor his ministry are corrected by Peter and John (8:14–25).

Also, it is unlikely that the coming of the Holy Spirit is delayed for the edification of the apostles so that witnessing the coming of the Spirit contributes towards their 'conversion' to the idea that 'God shows no partiality' (Acts 10:34). On the one hand, Luke associated the Samaritans with the Jews not the Gentiles (see §13.3 below). On the other hand, Peter and John ('they', 8:25) are depicted as having the same message as Philip,[16] as they had before this story.[17]

It could be that the Holy Spirit had not been given because apostles from Jerusalem were required to impart the Spirit. Yet Luke goes straight on to depict Philip (not one of the twelve) being involved in the conversion of the Ethiopian eunuch, whose faith or conversion is not questioned (Acts 8:26–40). Also, Luke obviously considered the church at Antioch to be authentic

---

[14] Acts 8:4; cf. 2:41; 6:2; 8:14.
[15] Cf. Acts 9:22; 17:3; 18:5, 28; 26:23.
[16] Acts 8:4, 5, 12, 14, 25.
[17] On the message as *logos* see Acts 2:41; 6:2, 4; 4:4; and on *Christos* see 2:36, 38; 3:6, 18, 20; 4:10, 26; 5:42.

and to be Spirit filled for, even though, on hearing of a great number turning to the Lord there, the church at Jerusalem sent Barnabas (also not one of the twelve) to Antioch. He is said to do nothing other than 'exhort them all to remain faithful to the Lord' (11:23). Further, the Holy Spirit came on the Ephesians with only the involvement of Paul (19:1–7), who is obviously not one of the twelve.

Yet, it does seem that a connection with the Jerusalem apostolate is important to Luke. Although Philip is not part of the group of apostles, he is one of the seven in the Jerusalem community (Acts 6:5; 8:4–5). Not only is Barnabas strongly associated with Jerusalem before this point in the story,[18] but also both he and Paul are accorded the status of an apostle alongside the twelve in Jerusalem.[19] The importance of the Jerusalem connection in this story is probably reinforced with Peter and John – specifically said to be from Jerusalem (8:14) – laying hands on the Samaritans to receive the Spirit (cf. 6:6).

Again there is no mention of speaking in tongues by those receiving the Spirit. To suggest that it is implied in Luke saying that Simon saw that the Spirit was given through the laying-on of hands runs ahead of the evidence we have to hand and is not at all convincing. There is no doubt that Luke thought there was external evidence of the Spirit's coming (Acts 8:18). However, it could equally have been a falling down or expressions of heightened joy, or some signs of spiritual drunkenness (cf. 2:13; Eph. 5:18).

§7.5 The Ethiopian: water baptism as response – Acts 8:36, 38

[T]hey came to some water, and the eunuch said, 'See, here is water! What is to prevent my being baptized?' . . . And they both went down into the water, Philip and the eunuch, and he baptized him.

Luke does not mention the laying-on of hands, nor the coming of the Spirit, nor are tongues mentioned. A first reading would suggest, therefore, that baptism in water was all that was required for conversion including, perhaps, the coming of the Spirit. However, exactly the same question about what can prevent water baptism is asked by Peter following the gift of the Holy Spirit being poured on Cornelius and those with him (Acts 10:47). It is possible, then, that Luke thinks that the Holy Spirit has been poured on the Ethiopian eunuch. In any case, Luke betrays no criticism of the eunuch's belief or conversion. For Luke, therefore, baptism is the eunuch's response to hearing and, the reader assumes, believing in the message about Jesus.

There is only very limited support in the manuscripts for the text of Acts 8:37 being part of what Luke wrote: 'And Philip said, "If you believe with

---

[18] Acts 4:36–37; 9:27; 11:22.
[19] Acts 14:4, 14; §2.5.3 above.

all your heart, you may." And he replied, "I believe that Jesus Christ is the Son of God".[20] Nevertheless, even though it is unlikely to be from Luke's hand, this insertion does spell out what is implicit in the text.

From this passage we can also see most clearly that it is not the connection with an apostle that is important to Luke. Rather, Philip's origins (Acts 6:5; 8:4–5) and the eunuch having visited Jerusalem are sufficient to tie his salvation to the tradition. Interestingly, the eunuch is not portrayed by Luke as thereafter involved with or indissolubly bound to any aspect of the organized or institutional church community; he is depicted as being alone as he goes on his way. Yet the reader can be assured of his salvation because he is connected with the church at Jerusalem, as well as in being described as going on his way rejoicing (8:39).

§7.6 Paul: Spirit-filled, then baptized – Acts 9:17–18

In this, the first of three stories of Paul's conversion, Luke says that, laying his hands on him, Ananias says,

> 'Brother Saul, the Lord Jesus, who appeared to you on your way here, has sent me so that you may regain your sight and be filled with the Holy Spirit!' And immediately something like scales fell from his eyes, and his sight was restored. Then he got up and was baptized.

That Luke wished Paul to be seen as exercising faith could be seen in him being portrayed as obedient to the voice in the vision and to the instructions of Ananias. More obviously, since the only element in the narrative between the promise of the Spirit and Paul's response is the falling of scales from his eyes and their healing, a reader would reasonably assume that Luke thinks Paul being filled with the Spirit was concurrent with the restoration of his sight.[21] There is no indication Luke wished to convey the idea that Paul spoke in tongues when he was filled with the Holy Spirit. There is no doubt, though, that with the scales and the healing Luke considered the process of Paul's conversion an obviously tangible experience.

Uncharacteristically, in this story God's action of filling Paul with the Holy Spirit precedes water baptism by the followers of Jesus.[22] As will be more clearly illustrated in the story of Cornelius (see §7.7 below), Luke is probably signalling that the reluctance of the followers of Jesus (here Ananias, Acts 9:13–16) to accept a new member is overtaken and overruled by God's acceptance and call of Paul.

Once again, as the word 'baptism' (*ebaptisthē*) is in the passive, it seems Luke understands that the baptism in water is given to Paul as a response to

---

[20] Acts 8:37 is found in, e.g. the eighth-century Codex Basiliensis, though omitted from, e.g. P[45], perhaps from the first half of the third century, and the Vulgate, Syriac and Coptic translations.

[21] On the receiving of sight as a metaphor for salvation see §13.3.1.3.

[22] Cf. Acts 2:38; 8:12, 14–16; 19:1–7.

his being filled with the Spirit. This story also shows that Luke did not think that only one of the twelve apostles could administer baptism or authenticate the conversion. Ananias was not an apostle, though he probably baptized Paul (Acts 9:18) as well as, perhaps, the other disciples of Jesus at Damascus (9:19). Yet, as we have seen (§2.5.3), through Paul's eventual elevation to the apostolate Luke's readers will take Paul to be tied into the Jerusalem church traditions. In any case, the statement that the Lord Jesus 'has sent me' (9:17) will already establish the authenticity of Paul's relationship to the work of Jesus in this volume.

§7.7 Cornelius: belief, the Spirit, then water baptism – Acts 10:44–48

[T]he Holy Spirit fell upon all who heard the word . . . the gift of the Holy Spirit had been poured out even on the Gentiles, for they heard them speaking in tongues and extolling God. Then Peter said, 'Can anyone withhold the water for baptizing these people who have received the Holy Spirit just as we have?' So he ordered them to be baptized in the name of Jesus Christ.

Although it is not mentioned, Luke's readers would have understood repentance to have been involved not only in the mention of forgiveness[23] but also in Cornelius being described as generous (Acts 10:2; cf. Luke 3:11). Notably, the point at which Luke says the Holy Spirit fell on the household of Cornelius was as Peter was speaking about the forgiveness of sins received by those who believe (Acts 10:43). This conveys the idea that Luke thinks Cornelius and those with him believed and were forgiven. Thus, the Holy Spirit is given as the household of Cornelius 'hears' (*akouontas*, present, active participle, 'those hearing') or responds by believing in Jesus. Luke articulates this view in having Peter say in 15:8: 'And God who knows the heart bore witness to them, giving them the Holy Spirit'. In turn, the evidence that they had been given the Holy Spirit was not something deduced from what they believed or had done in water baptism – that had not yet taken place – but their speaking in tongues and praising God (10:46).

For the first time since Acts 2, Luke mentions tongues: 'the Holy Spirit had been poured out even on the Gentiles, for [*gar*] they heard them speaking in tongues and extolling God'. Tongues, along with praising God, are portrayed as the evidences for the Holy Spirit falling on the Gentiles.[24] It is unlikely that Luke intends the praising of God to be the speaking in tongues, as it was in Acts 2:4, 11. The natural reading of the passage under discussion, as well as of 19:6 where tongues and prophecy are mentioned together, is that tongues is one of the expressions of the Spirit's activity. This is a reasonable

---

[23] Cf. Luke 3:3; 24:47; Acts 2:38; 5:31.

[24] Without any hints from Luke to the contrary, readers are likely to assume this is the same kind of speaking in tongues as in Acts 2:4 (xenoglossy or xenolalia), not mentioning interpretation, though here there is no indication whether or not it was understood. See §6.5.3 above.

reading for there seems to be evidence in Acts that Luke did not think tongues was the only form of ecstatic speech.[25]

As we have not so far seen Luke display any consistent interest in linking tongues with the coming of the Spirit it is reasonable to conclude that Luke is not generally interested in making a close and indissoluble connection between tongues and the coming of the Spirit. In that tongues in this story of Cornelius comes in a narrative that Luke is tying back to Acts 2, his interest in the tongues episode is probably to strengthen the parallel between the coming of the Spirit on the Jews and on these God-fearers. In any case, Luke continues to establish another pattern: the coming of the Spirit was obvious to observers.

In the light of the programmatic statement in Acts 2:38, the coming of the Spirit here before water baptism reinforces the point of Peter's vision that God shows no partiality (Acts 10:34) and that he is overriding any reluctance of the Church in accepting the Gentiles. Notwithstanding, water baptism remained a response to what God was already doing and could not be withheld. Baptism could not be withheld, probably, in the sense of not being able to deny the believers the outward ceremony which marked them as being just as much followers of Jesus as those in Jerusalem who had experienced the day of Pentecost (see 11:17). Also, once again, Peter recalls the saying about the difference between John's baptism and that of the Spirit (cf. 1:5). Luke is able to reinforce the point that, while the water baptism of John marked repentance, now the Spirit's baptism is the mark of repentance and forgiveness, both of which Christian baptism acknowledges (see §§8.1 and 3).

This is the first of four stories in which households are said to become believers,[26] fuelling the debate as to whether or not babies and small children were among those baptized. We will leave our conclusions until we have taken into account all four stories. Here we note that, with the Holy Spirit falling on 'all who heard', and that they are said to speak in tongues and extol God, it is more likely that only those of responsible age were thought to be involved.

§7.8 Lydia: faith, then baptism as communal acceptance – Acts 16:14–15

> The Lord opened her [Lydia's] heart to listen eagerly to what was said by Paul. When she and her household were baptized, she urged us, saying, 'If you have judged me to be faithful to the Lord, come and stay at my home.'

Whether Lydia is a single woman, a divorcee, a widow, a married woman or even owner of the home, we do not know. Whether there were children in the household, we cannot tell. If she was divorced it is likely the children

---

[25] Acts 2:14; 4:8, 31; 7:55; 11:28; 13:2, 10–11, 52.
[26] Acts 10:44–48; 16:14–15, 30–33; 18:8.

would have been living with the father.[27] However, if she was a widow she may have had children with her.[28] In short this passage is of little help in making any decisions about the baptism of babies or small children.

'Baptism' – again in the passive (*ebaptisthē*) – is clearly both the response to what the Lord had done for Lydia as well as, from what she says about being judged faithful, the way the other followers of Jesus signified that she was accepted by or was one of them. It goes without saying that neither tongues nor the coming of the Spirit is mentioned.

§7.9 The Philippian gaoler: belief, then water baptism – Acts 16:30–33

'Sirs, what must I do to be saved?' They [Paul and Silas] answered, 'Believe on the Lord Jesus, and you will be saved, you and your household.' They spoke the word of the Lord to him and to all who were in his house. At the same hour of the night he took them, and washed their wounds; then he and his entire family were baptized without delay.

Once again, baptism in water is portrayed as linked to, yet following, belief. Nothing is said about the coming of the Spirit or tongues. If anything, the tangible evidence of belief is the gaoler's joy (Acts 16:34) and especially the hospitality he offered Paul and Silas (16:33–34). The hospitality (cf. Josephus, *Ant.* 18.232), as well as their removal from confinement – described as the required sentence (Acts 16:23–24) – could have constituted a punishable act,[29] thus showing the level of the man's new faith.

Whether or not children were involved in the 'entire' (*holos*) household being baptized we will leave to the discussion at the end of this chapter (§7.13 below). Nevertheless, we can note that Paul and Silas are said to have spoken the word of the Lord to the gaoler's household, giving the impression that they, like the gaoler, believed on the Lord Jesus before being baptized (Acts 16:31–32). In any case, what is clear is that, as Luke tells it, not just the head of the household was baptized. We find a similar perspective in the next passage.

§7.10 Crispus: belief, then water baptism – Acts 18:8

Crispus, the official of the synagogue, became a believer in the Lord, together with all his household; and many of the Corinthians who heard Paul became believers and were baptized.

---

[27] Cf. Cicero, *Topics* 19; Tacitus, *Ann.* 2.86; Dio Cassius, *Hist.* 48.44.5; Paulus, *Sententiae* 2.24.

[28] Cf. Plutarch, *Sulla* 6.10–12; *Antony* 9.1–2; 10.3; 31.1–3; Cicero, *In Defence of Cluentius* 11–12, 14, 21–23, 25–28, 30–31, 33, 35, 40, 165, 179.

[29] The so-called Western text (e.g. Codex Bezae, Old Latin) may be evidence of this if its addition of the comment that the gaoler 'secured the rest' (*tous loipous asphalisamenos*) was meant to ameliorate his error.

Although not said directly, Luke is probably implying that this leading Jew in Corinth was baptized. Again, we have sufficient information to see that water baptism – in the passive, as we would expect (see ch. 7, n. 13) – follows as a response to belief. There is mention neither of the Spirit nor of tongues.

In considering the possibility of babies being baptized, we can take into account that even though the 'entire' (holos, cf. Acts 16:3) household is baptized, not just the head, they, on 'hearing believed' (akouontes episteuon, cf. 10:44–48). This is not a description that would naturally include children. We will need to take into account other stories before drawing any conclusions.

§7.11 The Ephesians: John's baptism, belief, water baptism, then the Spirit – Acts 19:1–7

> Paul passed through the interior regions and came to Ephesus, where he found some disciples. He said to them, 'Did you receive the Holy Spirit when you became believers?' They replied, 'No, we have not even heard that there is a Holy Spirit.' Then he said, 'Into what then were you baptized?' They answered, 'Into John's baptism.' Paul said, 'John baptized with the baptism of repentance, telling the people to believe in the one who was to come after him, that is, in Jesus.' On hearing this, they were baptized in the name of the Lord Jesus. When Paul laid his hands on them, the Holy Spirit came upon them, and they spoke in tongues and prophesied – altogether there were about twelve of them.

What Luke says here about water baptism and the reception of the Spirit is better understood if the story is taken together with the previous, similar, story about Apollos (Acts 18:24–28). Apollos is described as eloquent, well versed in the Scriptures, and having been instructed in the way of the Lord, speaking accurately the things of Jesus. The one criticism made of him was that he knew only the baptism of John (18:25). Similarly, the Ephesians in this story know only of John's baptism. Priscilla and Aquila are said to correct Apollos (18:26). However, they are not said to rebaptize him; but the Ephesians are baptized again.

The difference between Apollos and the Ephesian disciples is probably that Apollos had already received the Holy Spirit. The Ephesians say that they had never even heard that there was a Holy Spirit (Acts 19:2). That Luke thought Apollos had received the Holy Spirit is, as we have seen, probably indicated in describing him as 'fervent in Spirit' (18:25; see §6.3 above). Also, this phrase used for Apollos recalls Luke's description of those who could not withstand the wisdom 'and spirit' (kai tō pneumati) in which Stephen spoke.[30] Further, Paul uses a similar phrase of Christians (tō pneumati zeontes, Rom. 12:11). Therefore, if we are reading Luke correctly, and the Ephesians had not received

---

[30] Acts 6:10; cf. 6:3; 19:21; 20:22.

the Holy Spirit, they are not properly or fully Christians and, unlike Apollos, the baptism of John was of no consequence.

That Luke does not think they are fully Christian is shown not only in the need for the Ephesians to undergo the complete process of initiation into the group of followers of Jesus, but also probably by the way he initially describes them (Acts 19:1). Luke describes them as 'disciples'. For Luke, 'disciple' is usually equivalent to 'Christian'. He uses the word to refer to Christians in a particular place (e.g. 6:7; 9:19), and when describing a section of the Christians he either says 'some' of the disciples (21:16) or specifies that they were Paul's disciples (9:25). However, when describing the Ephesians as disciples, this is the only time in the whole of his writings that Luke does not use the definite article with 'disciple'. Luke may be signalling that the Ephesians were not true disciples or Christians. Further confirmation of this is that when Paul goes on to teach the Ephesians he says that John told people to go on and believe in Jesus, as if the Ephesians had not done so (19:4). The impression left on the reader is that the Ephesians do go on and believe, for they are baptized in water. Then Paul lays hands on them and the Holy Spirit comes upon them and they spoke in tongues and prophesied. It could be concluded from this that Luke thought the laying-on of hands was a part of baptism. However, from the evidence we have, it is not until the third century, and then only occasionally, that the laying-on of hands may have been tied with the coming of the Spirit at baptism (see Tertullian, *Bap.* 8).

As with that of the Spirit coming to Cornelius, in this story Luke's narrative carries considerable detail. It is unlikely that this detail is required because it is a foundational account through which Christianity is introduced into another region or group of people, for the story of the first conversion in Europe, that of Lydia (Acts 16:13–15), is very brief. More likely, it is Luke's interest in establishing the reception of the Spirit as critical for being a disciple that has motivated his writing in such detail.

§7.12 Paul: water baptism, forgiveness and faith – Acts 22:13–14, 16

Luke's third story of Paul's conversion will not need to concern us, for it has been cast even more firmly as an appearance-call story. It describes nothing about what happened to Paul, save that he was told: 'But get up and stand on your feet' (Acts 26:16). However, here in the second story Luke has Paul recount his Damascus road experience in which Ananias says to him,

> 'Brother Saul, regain your sight!' In that very hour I regained my sight and saw him. Then he said, 'The God of our ancestors has chosen you to know his will, to see the Righteous One and to hear his own voice . . . And now why do you wait? Rise and be baptized and wash away your sins calling on his name.'

The question, in colloquial Greek, 'And now why do you wait?' (*kai nun ti melleis*) recalls Peter's question after the coming of the Spirit on Cornelius.[31] Here, the confident basis of the question is Paul being chosen by God, knowing him and seeing the Righteous One. Thus, if Luke assumes his readers have in mind what he said in the first telling of Paul's conversion where Paul is healed and filled with the Spirit, the initiative that God takes in this story, and in the intimacy that he relates to a person, would be taken to amount to the same thing.

Paul's response involves an act of faith. Calling on a person's name was an expression of trust in the person named.[32] For example, Paul is said to trust his future to the emperor by calling on or appealing to Caesar.[33] How baptism and sins being washed away are related is not clear. It could be they are thought to take place at the same time or that baptism symbolizes the washing away of sins. In any case, both are dependent on faith: 'calling on his name'. Thus, if we were to argue that baptism washes away sins we could only do so on the basis that it was dependent on faith.

§7.13 Discussion and conclusions

In the light of debates in the contemporary Church, we have been passing under review evidence that might help us understand Luke's perspective on the relationship between believing, the coming of the Spirit, speaking in tongues and baptism, both in water and the Spirit. In particular we have been interested in knowing how Luke would answer a number of questions. What is the place of the coming of the Spirit in becoming a Christian? Is tongues the initial evidence for being filled with the Spirit? Does water baptism confer the Spirit or Spirit baptism? Also, is water baptism necessary for salvation? In turn, questions about the role of water baptism raise further questions about infant baptism. The following, rather necessarily lengthy conclusions contribute to answering these questions.

§7.13.1 Baptism in the Spirit

One matter can be cleared up right away. Although not his preferred term, but one found in his tradition, 'baptism in the Spirit' is a way of describing the initial coming of the Spirit. Moreover, from what we have established earlier we have to add here that Luke does not consider there to be one coming or filling of the Spirit (see Chapter 6 above). Luke portrays followers of Jesus repeatedly or characteristically, if not always, filled with the Spirit.

---

[31] Acts 10:47; 11:17; cf. 8:36.
[32] See Acts 2:21; 9:14, 21; 15:17.
[33] Acts 25:11, 12, 25; 26:32; 28:19.

§7.13.2 Aspects of initiation

Our difficulty in answering the questions we are putting to Luke is in the small amount of relevant information in most of his conversion stories. This information can be readily seen when displayed in chart form. In the table opposite, the title of each story is a list of key aspects or elements in the order they appear in the narrative.

From this chart it is easy to see that most information is given in two stories in particular: Peter's sermon on the day of Pentecost, including its response (Acts 2:38, 41), and the coming of the Spirit on Cornelius and his household (10:43–48). In the case of the Samaritans, the coming of the Spirit and some visible response is also included along with belief and baptism in water (8:12, 14–16). There is also reasonable detail in the story of the initiation of the Ephesians (19:1–7), detail given, it was suggested, not to tell a conversion story of a new group of people but because Luke was taking time to correct error. What is notable is that all four stories mention four elements: belief, baptism in water, the coming of the Spirit and speaking in tongues or obvious response.

Most of the other stories have been reduced to mentioning only belief (in some form) and water baptism. The obvious conclusion to draw from this is that Luke expects his readers to see these stories as shorthand accounts in which all the other elements can be assumed. Thus, although the response of some to Peter's sermon on the day of Pentecost is only said to be welcoming his message and being baptized (Acts 2:41), it would make nonsense of Luke's narrative if readers were not to assume this was the shorthand description of the response to what Peter had just said: 'Repent, and be baptized everyone of you in the name of Jesus Christ so that your sins may be forgiven; and you shall receive the gift of the Holy Spirit' (2:38). Then, in the story of the Ephesian disciples, when Luke needed to correct belief and clarify the point that without the Spirit a person could not be seen as a Christian, he returns to giving a more detailed story. He once again mentions belief, water baptism, the Spirit coming, tongues, as well as prophecy. In short, we can almost certainly take the less detailed narratives to be sketches in outline of a fuller view that Luke's readers are expected to assume is required for becoming a Christian. What is important is what Luke maintains in his abbreviated stories: belief, then community affirmation and acceptance or integration in baptism.

In just two stories – the first story of Paul's conversion and also Cornelius and his household – we have seen that the person is filled with the Spirit before water baptism. Also, in each case Luke uses considerable space in his narrative to give detail to the reluctance of the existing followers of Jesus to accept the new members. In God's acceptance overtaking and therefore overruling human hesitancy Luke is making clear that, against expectations, the persons involved – Paul, the once-persecuting Jew, and the Gentiles – are to be accepted by the followers of Jesus, including his readers.

Table: Initiation stories in Acts
Key elements in narrative order

Pentecost 2:4	Peter's sermon 2:38	Response to Peter 2:41	Samaritans 8:12, 14–16	Eunuch 8:36	Paul 9:17–18	Cornelius 10:43–48	Lydia 16:14–15	Gaoler 16:30–33	Crispus 18:8	Ephesians 19:1–7	Paul 22:16
Spirit baptism tongues	belief repentance water baptism belief forgiveness	belief water baptism	belief water baptism Spirit baptism obvious response	belief? water baptism	belief? Spirit baptism sight restored water baptism	belief forgiveness Spirit baptism tongues and praise water baptism	belief water baptism	belief water baptism	belief water baptism	belief water baptism Spirit baptism tongues and prophecy	belief? water baptism

If, in the four more detailed stories, Luke is giving a more complete description of what he understands by becoming a Christian then the term conversion is inadequate for what he thinks takes place. In these stories Luke is describing more than a turning; repentance is only one aspect in what he sees as an initiation scenario that involves repentance, belief, baptism in water and the gift of the Spirit.[34]

In these conclusions we can see how Luke would answer the question on the relationship between becoming a Christian and the coming of the Spirit. He would not say that they are equivalent but that, along with belief, repentance and water baptism, the Spirit's coming is one of the components involved in the initiation of a person into the followers of Jesus (Acts 2:38, 41). More specifically, to repeat what became obvious from Peter's appeal at Pentecost: repentance (by the respondents) and baptism (by the community) in preparation for the gift of the Spirit (by God) enables a person to become one of the followers of Jesus or part of the Church.

§7.13.3 Tongues as initial evidence?

If the four detailed stories of initiation best describe Luke's understanding of Christian initiation, can we take it that he thought speaking in tongues was integral to, or even the initial evidence of, receiving the Spirit? In favour of a positive answer is that, in the obvious intent to cast the story of Cornelius as a parallel to the Pentecostal coming of the Spirit to show that the Gentiles had also received the Spirit (Acts 10:47; 11:17), Luke includes speaking in tongues in both stories (2:4; 10:46). And, in his other longer story of the initiation of the Ephesian disciples, tongues is also mentioned (19:6).

Yet, in Peter's call at the end of his Pentecost sermon, and in the response to it, there is no mention of tongues. At a point in the narrative where readers might expect those who joined the group on the day of Pentecost to be described as having the same experience of tongues, they are not. Instead, in both Peter's quoting from the Old Testament to explain the coming of the Spirit and in the aftermath of the three thousand being added, it is prophecy, visions, dreams, portents, salvation (Acts 2:17–21), involvement in the group and signs and wonders (2:42–47) that Luke describes as the result of the coming of the Spirit. Also, in the story of the Spirit coming on the Samaritans no particular manifestation is mentioned, only the implication that it was obvious (8:18). Further, in the first story of Paul's conversion or call, the obvious results of the Spirit's coming were something like scales falling from his eyes and his sight being restored (9:18). In the case of Cornelius and his household there was not only speaking in tongues but also extolling God (10:46); in the case of the Ephesians, prophecy accompanied the tongues (19:6).

The most obvious conclusion to draw from this is that Luke did not think speaking in tongues was the initial evidence of the coming of the Spirit. Those

---

[34] In Acts the verb 'repent' (*metanoeō*) is found in 2:38; 3:19; 8:22; 17:30; 26:20; the noun 'repentance' (*metanoia*) is in 5:31; 11:18; 13:24; 19:4; 20:21; 26:20.

who wish to argue that tongues is the initial evidence for being filled with the Spirit will have to look elsewhere. Luke is not interested in making a close and indissoluble connection between tongues and the coming of the Spirit. Rather, he wants to establish for his readers that the Spirit's coming was unavoidably obvious to bystanders, and this evidence involved ecstatic or supernatural manifestations, sometimes including tongues.

§7.13.4 The Spirit and water baptism

Another question on which we have sought Luke's view is, does water baptism confer the Spirit or Spirit baptism? In short, no. In the case of the Samaritans Luke made it clear that they had not received the Holy Spirit, even though they had been baptized in water (Acts 8:15–17). The reader could only conclude that water baptism in the name of the Lord Jesus was not the same as and did not confer the Holy Spirit. The story of the Ethiopian eunuch only mentions water baptism, so it might be concluded that this was all that was necessary to bring about conversion. However, a closer reading showed that water baptism was a response to an already changed person. Moreover, taking into account that Luke's longer stories of initiation are to be assumed in reading his shorter ones, the same conclusion is reached: it is inconceivable that he would consider baptism in water to confer the Spirit. In fact, if our reading of the story of the Ethiopian is correct, baptism is never said to be the sole aspect or required response to affect initiation or conversion. Luke never identifies water baptism and the baptism of the Spirit, nor can it be said the baptism in water causes God to give his Spirit.

§7.13.5 The necessity of water baptism

Still to be answered is the question we are putting to Luke: is water baptism necessary for conversion or salvation? This question arises because baptism in water features in every initiation story, at least after the Pentecostal coming of the Spirit on the one hundred and twenty. This apparent lacuna we explained was probably because Luke is describing the situation of the apostles and first followers of Jesus as unique and preparatory for what was ahead in his narrative. Yet, from Luke's perspective it seems baptism is thereafter necessary for conversion. This is not because baptism alone saves but because, on the one hand, it was the action to which a person was able to submit indicating a faith response. On the other hand, we noted that 'be baptized' (*baptistheto*) is in the passive so that in baptism a person was submitting to acceptance by the existing community of followers of Jesus. Thus, for Luke, baptism is necessary in that belonging to the group of followers of Jesus or Christians is fundamental to becoming and being a Christian.

Luke's views can probably be summarized by saying that, whereas once the water baptism of John had been a symbol of a person's repentance, since Pentecost the coming or baptism of the Holy Spirit is evidence of repentance and trust. In turn, water baptism in the name of Jesus symbolized both the repentance, as well as integration into the Church.

§7.13.6 Infant baptism?

On whether or not children below responsible age should be baptized there have been centuries of long, painful and divisive debates. Of course, in constructing a contemporary theology of baptism there will be sources to consider besides Luke–Acts. Nevertheless, in Luke's four stories involving the baptism of households, we have found no direct evidence to help decide whether or not he would have thought this included baptizing babies.

However, an indirect approach probably allows us to draw a reasonably secure conclusion. To begin with, it is probable Luke held the long-standing view, widely shared across the Hellenistic world, that children were marginal to society and did not 'count'[35] so that he would not have taken them in to consideration even when describing a 'complete' (*holos*, Acts 18:8) household. Also, Paul, a hero of Luke's, is unlikely to have baptized children, for in 1 Corinthians 7:14 Paul assumes the cleanliness of the believer's children is determined by the parent, an unlikely statement if the children had been baptized. Further, it is not until the turn of the second and third centuries that we have the first clear reference to the baptism of babies.[36] Added to these points, moreover, the aspects or 'events' of initiation (repentance, belief, baptism in water and baptism in the Spirit) are so closely related in Luke's understanding – with his consistent emphasis on believing – that the baptism of babies would probably be incomprehensible for him.

§7.14 So far . . .

As well as sketching the background to Luke–Acts, so far, we have done two things. We have attempted to describe some of the basic aspects of Luke's view of the origin, nature and purpose of the Church. Then, as the Spirit dominates the opening section of Acts after the introduction, we have tried to describe and understand the coming of the Spirit to the followers of Jesus through Luke's eyes. Since the corporate life of the followers of Jesus as well as attacks on its well-being feature so prominently, especially in the early chapters of Acts where his narrative is set in Jerusalem,[37] we need to turn to examine Luke's portrait of the life of the Church after, and in the light of, the coming of the Spirit.

---

[35] On the often minor interest in or low view of children see, e.g. Cicero, *Tusculan Disputations* 1.93–94; *Letters to Atticus* 10.18; Plutarch, *Num.* 12.2; Seneca, *Letters* 99.1, 14; Josephus, *Ag. Ap.* 2.204; cf. Clement of Alexandria, *Christ the Educator* 1.5, 6.

[36] See *The Apostolic Tradition* 21.4–5 (late second century?); Tertullian, *Bap.* 18 (turn of the second and third centuries); Cyprian, *Letters* 64.2 (mid-third century); Origen, *Hom. Lev.* 8.3; *Comm. Rom.* 5.9 (mid-third century). For earlier possible hints see Irenaeus, *Haer.* 2.22.4; *Fragment* 34 (late second century).

[37] E.g. Acts 2:43–47; 4:32–37; 5:12–16; 6:1–6.

8

Problems in the early Church

The call for the twenty-first-century Church to emulate the Church or churches of Acts seems to assume that Luke portrays a triumphant, trouble-free Church. Yet, even a superficial reader of Acts must admit to the narrative including reports of significant problems in the churches Luke portrays, not least in his beloved Jerusalem. Indeed, from the space given to particular issues, as well as reading between the lines, it appears that Luke wanted to address a number of major issues that would interest his readers.

The Church of the twenty-first century, growing in culturally hostile environments, is likely to suffer great persecution, so it is of note that the first and most widely reported problem encountered by the followers of Jesus in Luke's narrative is that of persecution. There are also the problems of the tension between the Hellenists and Hebrews, as well as between the rich and the poor. On an initial reading of Luke and Acts the role and care of women does not seem to be a problem for Luke or his readers. However, from what we know of the station of women in the ancient world, and from the amount of attention Luke gives the motif, it can be supposed that he was addressing a significant issue for his audience. Setting out how Luke describes these problems, as well as how he sees they should be understood, managed or solved, is the focus of this chapter. Another problem, a failure in mission, which probably eclipses all of these problems, will be dealt with separately in Chapter 13.

§8.1 Persecution

Given its early and sustained appearance in his work and the space Luke dedicated to this theme, it is reasonable to assume that persecution was important in what he wanted to say about the life of the Church. At the beginning of the Gospel the topic is introduced in Simeon's otherwise joyous song about the coming salvation and his blessing of the holy family (Luke 2:29–35). Simeon says that the child is destined 'to be a sign that will be opposed' (2:34). That the opposition will be from his own people is presaged in Jesus being said to be the falling and rising of many in Israel (cf. 12:51–53; Isa. 8:14–15). Also, echoing Old Testament passages,[1] Simeon says to Mary, 'a sword will pierce through your own soul also', telling not only of the anguish Mary will suffer over her son's rejection but also of his death (Luke

---

[1] Cf. Pss. 22:20; 37:15; Zech. 12:10; 13:7.

2:35). Then, throughout his Gospel, Luke portrays Jesus predicting his fate,[2] suffering rejection (e.g. 4:28–29; 9:52–56) and eventual death (23:44–48).

Luke also begins to develop the theme of the suffering of the followers of Jesus. The clearest statement in the Gospel about suffering and persecution is in 21:12–19. Luke says that before 'the end' there will be persecution. Jesus says, 'They will lay their hands on you and persecute you, delivering you up to the synagogues and prisons, and you will be brought before kings and governors for my name's sake' (21:12). Readers are warned that family and friends will hand over followers of Jesus to be put to death (21:16) by both Jews and Gentiles (12:12). However, Luke ameliorates Mark's statement 'children will rise against parents and have them put to death' with the limitation 'and they will put some of you to death', suggesting that the suffering is by no means all-pervasive (Mark 13:21/Luke 21:16).

Turning to Acts we find a litany of stories of suffering and persecution. Peter and John are arrested and taken before the Jewish Sanhedrin (4:1–22); the apostles are imprisoned (5:18); persecution in Jerusalem scatters all disciples but the apostles, and Saul ravages the Church (8:1–3); Herod lays 'violent hands' on some who belonged to the Church and then kills James by the sword (12:1–2). To this list should be added the stories scattered through Acts of the persecution or imprisonments of Peter and John, Silas, Barnabas and Paul and, notably, the martyrdom of Stephen, the archetypal suffering-follower of Jesus.

From this catalogue of suffering and persecution, which we have noted was foreshadowed in the words of Jesus and can be seen exemplified in Luke's heroes, it is reasonable to suppose that Luke's readers were suffering in similar ways and that the period between Easter and 'the end' was, for Luke, the period of 'the Church under stress'. In dealing with this almost pervasive theme of suffering and persecution Luke unfolds a number of themes providing sources of understanding and encouragement for his readers.

§8.1.1 Persecution and suffering are part of God's order for his messengers

In casting Simeon's speech in the form of prophecy, and echoing the Old Testament, Luke indicates that the impending sufferings of Jesus and his mother are part of God's foreknowledge and economy.[3] The same end is served in sayings about Jesus' suffering being prophesied (Luke 18:31) or fulfilling Scripture,[4] or being in line with the way God's Old Testament messengers are treated.[5] Similarly, in a number of places, Luke portrays Jesus suffering rejection (e.g. 4:28–29; 9:52–56) and predicting his own demise in terms of

---

[2] Luke 9:22, 44; 17:25; 18:31–33.
[3] Luke 2:29–35: cf. Gen. 15:15; 46:30; Job 19:27; 42:5; Pss. 67:3; 98:2–3; Isa. 8:14; 40:5; 42:6; 46:13; 49:6, 9; Dan. 11:41.
[4] Luke 18:31–34; 22:37; 24:25–27, 44.
[5] Luke 4:24; 6:22–23; 9:9; 11:49; 13:33–34; 20:9–17.

it being 'a necessity' (*dei*) or ordained by God.[6] The intimate involvement of God in Jesus' death is also signalled in the series of divine passives relating to his 'destiny' (2:34), his being 'handed over' (9:44) and his work being 'finished'.[7]

As Jesus predicted his own suffering so he predicts that of his followers, showing their persecution also to be part of God's economy in that it also fulfils prophecy (Luke 12:11–12; 21:12–19). The rejection that was experienced by the Old Testament prophets, and by Jesus, Luke also shows to be the experience of the followers of Jesus[8] as they also are being sent out on mission as 'lambs into the midst of wolves' (10:3).

Concomitantly, Luke develops the theme that suffering is an inherent and necessary part of being a follower of Jesus (cf. Luke 6:22), particularly in its missionary aspects. Indeed, in Acts 9:15–16 Luke treats 'bring my name' as a synonym for 'suffer for my name'. Also, in Luke's Gospel, Jesus says, 'Blessed are you when people hate you, and when they exclude you, revile you, and defame you on account of the Son of Man.'[9] Thus, 'following' is connected with bearing a cross (9:23; 14:27) and exemplified in Simon of Cyrene (23:26). This leads to another theme Luke develops in relation to that of persecution.

§8.1.2 The encouragement and example of Jesus

Luke's major theme in relation to the suffering of Christians is the encouragement and example of Jesus. This motif is developed not only through Jesus' prediction of the suffering of his followers (12:4–12; 21:12–19) but also the specific encouragement his teaching contains. For example, Jesus says, 'By your endurance you will gain your souls' (2:19). Later in the narrative Jesus says, 'do not worry . . . the Holy Spirit will teach you' (12:11–12). Later still he says, 'I will give you words and a wisdom that none of your opponents will be able to withstand or contradict' (21:15). The switch in subject here between the Holy Spirit (12:12) and Jesus (21:15) would have signalled to the readers that their experience of encouragement from the Spirit was from Jesus, the one who had experienced and taught about suffering. Luke also has Jesus say, 'not a hair of your head will perish' (21:18). In the face of some of the tragic stories in Acts, and probably their own experience of persecution, this promise would have been interpreted, at least in part, eschatologically. This perspective is supported earlier in Luke where he has Jesus say that his disciples need not fear those who kill the body for they can do no more than that (12:4).

A significant aspect of the encouragement from Jesus comes in teaching on loving one's enemies (Luke 6:22–23, 27–36). For example, Jesus says, 'Love

---

[6] Luke 9:22; 17:25; 24:7, 44.
[7] Acts 13:32; cf. 18:31. See also 20:28.
[8] Acts 4:18, 23–31; 5:18, 40; 7:51–53, 58–60; 8:1; 9:2, 23–24; 12:2–4; 13:50; 14:5, 19; 16:22–23; 17:5–9, 13; 18:12–17; 19:23–41; 20:19; 21:30–32; 22:4–5; 23:12–14; 24:2–9; 26:10; 28:16.
[9] Luke 6:22; cf. 21:12, 17.

your enemies, do good to those who hate you, bless those who curse you, pray for those who abuse you' (6:27–28). This we see Luke including in his Acts narrative in the prayer in Acts 4:24–30. A similar encouragement from Jesus comes in his teaching on perseverance in the face of 'trials' or 'afflictions' (*peirasmos*, see 22:28; Acts 20:19). For example in the parable of the sower, some are said to hear the word and receive it with joy, but in a period of 'testing' (*peirasmos*) fall away (Luke 8:13) rather than 'endure' (*hupomenē*, 8:15). Those who share the trials of Jesus will receive from and share with him a kingdom (22:28–29). Or, those who endure or persevere are told will gain their lives (21:19) which, from 9:24–25, has more to do with eternal security than present safety (cf. 12:8–10). Thus Jesus teaches his disciples to pray that they will not succumb in the time of trial (11:4), which they faced with him on the Mount of Olives (22:40, 46).

Peter is cast as one who does not endure in the face of persecution (Luke 22:31–34, 54–62), though early in Acts he is the first (2:14; cf. 32) and major witness to Jesus. The story of Stephen provides a graphic example of endurance in the face of persecution (7:54—8:1) and, later in Acts, Paul succeeds where Peter initially did not, in being ready 'to die in Jerusalem for the name of the Lord Jesus' (21:13; cf. 20:19).

Besides the models in his stories and the direct words of encouragement, Luke's readers could also be expected to take encouragement from the parallels between Jesus' predictions in the Gospel and the narratives of suffering in Acts, most obvious in comparing Luke 12:4–12 and 21:12–19 with Acts 4:1–31 and 5:17–42. For example, as predicted (Luke 21:11, 12), the followers of Jesus are arrested,[10] are brought before synagogues, rulers and authorities (21:11; Acts 4:5–6); in difficult circumstances the Holy Spirit aids speaking;[11] they are put in prison;[12] and opponents are not able to 'withstand' the followers of Jesus (Luke 21:15; Acts 4:14).

That Luke intends his readers to find encouragement in the example of Jesus' suffering is apparent in the parallels he draws. For example, both Jesus and his followers face the same opponents;[13] the support of the crowd inhibits action against Jesus as well as his followers;[14] the authority of both Jesus and his followers is questioned (Luke 20:2; Acts 4:7); Psalm 118:22 is used to interpret the experience of the rejection of both Jesus and his disciples (Luke 20:17; Acts 4:11); the phrase 'laid hands' is used of both Jesus and his followers being arrested;[15] the authorities are said to 'come upon' (Luke

---

[10] Acts 4:3; 5:18; cf. 21:1, 27.
[11] Luke 12:12; 21:12; Acts 4:8.
[12] Luke 21:12; Acts 5:19, 22, 25.
[13] The scribes (Luke 19:47; 20:1, 19, 39, 46; 22:2, 66; 23:10; Acts 4:5), the chief priests (Luke 19:47; 20:1, 19; 22:2, 4, 50, 52, 54, 66; 23:4, 10, 13; 24:20; Acts 4:6, 23; 5:17, 21, 24, 27), elders (Luke 20:1; 22:52; Acts 4:5, 8, 23), the Sadducees (Luke 20:27; Acts 4:1; 5:17), temple police (Luke 22:4, 52; Acts 4:1; 5:24, 26), the leaders (Luke 23:13, 35; 24:20; Acts 4:5, 8, 26), and the Sanhedrin (Luke 22:66; Acts 4:15; 5:21, 27, 34, 41).
[14] Luke 19:48; 20:6, 19, 26; 22:2; Acts 5:26.
[15] Luke 20:19; Acts 4:3; 5:18.

20:1; Acts 4:1) both Jesus and his followers while they are speaking; and both Jesus and his followers are beaten (Luke 22:63; Acts 5:40).

These parallels between Jesus and his followers find their apotheosis in the parallel between the suffering of Jesus and Stephen. Parallels include the unjust trials, the mockings, the prophetic style of their messages in the face of death, the final prayer offering their spirits to the Father and to the Lord Jesus, as well as the prayers of forgiveness for their respective persecutors (see Acts 6:8—8:1). In that we have already noted some of the parallels between Luke's portraits of Jesus and Paul (Chapter 4), all we need to recall here is that, in his portrait of Paul and the persecution he faced, Luke appears to be echoing the suffering of Jesus as a model for Paul and, hence, associating Paul with Jesus: each seized by a gang, each being struck, each tried four times, the crowd shouting to each, 'Away with him', and each of them, three times, being deemed innocent.

Not only is Luke blurring the distinction between the era of Jesus and his post-Easter followers (see §3.3 above) but also readers would find encouragement in their suffering not being unique but shared by their predecessors, notably their scriptural as well as more recent heroes, including Jesus. In turn, this leads to another theme Luke promotes in the face of his readers suffering persecution.

§8.1.3 Suffering and success

For Luke there is a symbiotic relationship between suffering and mission success, between death and the spread of the gospel. In his narrative the perpetrators intend persecution to put a stop to the spread of the movement and its message. For example, in discussion, the assembled rulers, elders and scribes in Jerusalem, along 'with Annas the high priest, Caiaphas, John, and Alexander, and all who were of the high priestly family' (Acts 4:6), are said to want to stop the movement spreading (4:17). To that end, they order and threaten Peter and John 'not to speak or teach at all in the name of Jesus' (4:18). Also, the narratological implications of Saul 'breathing threats and murder against the disciples of the Lord' (9:1) and going to synagogues in Damascus with letters from the high priest are to stamp out the spreading sect. However, Luke plots his story to show that the persecution was counterproductive, playing into the hands of God. Most notably, a severe persecution against the Church said to begin in Jerusalem on the day of Stephen's death caused followers of Jesus to be scattered,[16] though not to the detriment of God's work. Instead, Philip went to Samaria proclaiming the Messiah (8:5), others travelled as far as Phoenicia, Cyprus and Antioch (11:19). Then, throughout Acts, the same pattern recurs.[17]

In these examples of their predecessors, and especially in the stories of the deaths of Jesus and Stephen, Luke's readers can see that suffering and death

---

[16] Acts 8:1, 4; 11:19.
[17] See Acts 13:50–51; 14:5–6, 19–22; 16:39–40; 17:5–10, 13–15; 20:1–3.

open the way for others to enter into salvation. The death of Jesus, followed by the resurrection and Ascension, made it possible for the power and direction of the Holy Spirit to be given. Then, the death of Stephen opened up the way for the mission of the Church to go beyond Jerusalem. In turn, the readers are likely to conclude that their own suffering and death can pave the way for others to experience salvation.

Luke does not tell of the death of Paul, though, as we have seen, he gives ample clues to his readers that it has taken place (Acts 20:17–38; cf. §3.2.3 above). It may be, then, that Luke ended his story on such a positive note and did not tell the story of Paul's death so that he could show his readers more sharply that Paul's suffering and perseverance made it possible for them to believe (28:31). By implication, their own suffering, perseverance and even martyrdom will make it possible for others to believe. Besides these more theoretical considerations – persecution and suffering are part of God's economy from his messengers, the encouragement and example of Jesus, and the symbiotic relationship between suffering and mission success – Luke's narrative offers his readers pragmatic help in other themes that he cultivates and associates with suffering.

§8.1.4 Prayer

Considering no more than his vocabulary, Luke has greater interest in prayer, especially in relation to Jesus, than any of the Gospel writers.[18] In relation to the issue of persecution and suffering we can note that Jesus is depicted as praying, not only at times of spiritual revelation (e.g. Luke 3:21–22; 9:28–32) and at important points in his ministry (5:16; 6:12), but also in times of crisis and suffering. For example, there is a possibility that Luke wished to imply that Jesus was praying the first time he faced opposition, when he was in the desert being tempted by the devil (4:2). For, although the genealogy of Jesus (3:23–38) interrupts the narrative to affirm him as the Son of God (3:38), readers can infer that Jesus is being depicted as praying immediately before his temptation (cf. 3:21; and 4:1–2). Also, Luke says that Jesus did not eat during the time of his temptation, and prayer and fasting were closely associated in the early Church.[19] More obviously, Luke says that Jesus had prayed for Simon that, as Satan has demanded to sift him like wheat, his faith would not fail and that he would be able to strengthen his brothers (22:31–32).

---

[18] E.g. considering only one word, Luke uses the verb *proseuchomai* ('pray') 35 times, 19 times in his Gospel (Luke 1:10; 3:21; 5:16; 6:12, 28; 9:18, 28, 29; 11:1 [twice], 2; 18:1, 10, 11; 20:47; 22:40, 41, [44?], 46) and 16 times in Acts (1:24; 6:6; 8:15; 9:11, 40; 10:9, 30; 11:5; 12:12; 13:3; 14:23; 16:25; 20:36; 21:5; 22:17; 28:8), whereas it occurs 15 times in Matt. (5:44; 6:5 [twice], 6 [twice], 7, 9; 14:23; 19:13; 24:20; 26:36, 39, 41, 42, 44) and 10 times in Mark (1:35; 6:46; 11:24, 25; 12:40; 13:18; 14:32, 35, 38, 39). In a similar size corpus, Paul uses *proseuchomai* 17 times (Rom. 8:26; 1 Cor. 11:4, 5, 13; 14:13, 14 [twice], 15 [twice]; Phil. 1:9; Col. 1:3, 9; 4:3; 1 Thess. 5:17, 25; 2 Thess. 1:11; 3:1; also see Eph. 6:18 and 1 Tim. 2:8).

[19] The association between prayer and fasting is especially obvious in the changes made by later copyists to Mark 9:29 and Acts 10:30 to include mention of both fasting and prayer. See also Luke 2:37; Acts 13:3; and 14:23.

Then, on the Mount of Olives, Jesus tells the disciples to pray so that they will not enter into or succumb to temptation (22:40) and he himself prays (22:41–42). Thus, Jesus prays about his impending death and just before his arrest (22:41–46). He also prays as he hangs on the cross; in a loud cry he commits his spirit into the hands of his Father (23:46).[20]

In Acts we see that, following their first experience of opposition – in which Peter and John had been held in custody overnight and questioned by the Sanhedrin – the followers of Jesus responded by praying. Notably, the prayer is neither for revenge on their persecutors nor for deliverance from suffering. Rather, they pray for the ability to speak the Lord's word boldly in the face of opposition (Acts 4:27, 30), as they already have been doing (2:29; 4:13). Further, they ask that their bold speaking be accompanied by God's activity in healing and in signs and wonders in the name of Jesus. Their prayer is answered dramatically, a point we will return to shortly. Boldness remains a recurrent theme in relation to the followers of Jesus facing persecution. For example, as well as being mentioned of Peter (2:29) and Peter and John (4:13), it is said to characterize the ministry of Paul before uncertain Christians in Jerusalem (9:27–28) and his speaking in the Ephesian synagogue before stubborn and disbelieving Jews (19:8), as well as his defence before Festus.[21]

In short, Luke draws his readers' attention to this view of the proper response to suffering and persecution. It is not to be a desire to escape or for revenge on the oppressors but, like Jesus before them, his followers are to remain faithful to the Lord, praying for and, in being filled with the Holy Spirit, receiving boldness in the face of painful opposition. This theme found early expression in the Lord's Prayer, for, as we have seen, the petition not to be led into or succumb to temptation is a request not to be found unfaithful.[22]

Further, in showing prayer to be appropriate in times of persecution in the face of death, Stephen is depicted as in a prayerful trance (Acts 7:55–60). Consistent with the prayer in Acts 4:24–30, Stephen is portrayed not as asking to be delivered from the situation, but as boldly faithful to God as Jesus was in his suffering and death. When Peter was arrested and kept in prison by Herod 'earnest prayer for him was made to God by the Church' (12:5, 12). While in prison, 'about midnight Paul and Silas were praying and singing hymns to God' (16:25). Once again, in both of these instances, it is notable that revengeful prayer is missing. The emphasis is on the faithfulness of Jesus' followers in the face of suffering and opposition from the same sources as Jesus.

§8.1.5 God is tangibly present

We have seen in Luke's Gospel that, for those facing persecution, Jesus promises both his help (Luke 21:15) and that of the Holy Spirit (12:11–12). Jesus

---

[20] The verse, 'Then Jesus said, "Father, forgive them; for they do not know what they are doing"' (Luke 23:34) is not found in important early texts. See ch. 5, n. 8.

[21] Acts 26:26; see also 13:46; 14:3; 18:26.

[22] For Luke's use of 'temptation' (*peirasmos*) as it relates to the idea of falling from faithfulness see Luke 4:13; 8:13; 22:28, 40, 46; Acts 20:19.

goes so far as to say, 'not a hair of your head will perish' (21:18). The serious-
ness with which Luke wishes his readers to take these promises is seen in some
of his dramatic rescue stories in Acts relating to persecution. For example, in
a fit of jealousy the Sadducees had arrested the apostles and put them in the
common prison in Jerusalem. However, at night an angel of the Lord is said
to have opened the prison doors and led them out (Acts 5:17–21). Also, Luke
says that on Saul's way to Damascus to arrest men or women belonging to the
Way, Jesus appeared to him and transformed him into a chosen instrument
(9:1–22). Then Peter, who had been imprisoned by Herod, was unchained by
an earthquake and led to freedom by an angel (12:6–11). Similarly, at Philippi
Paul and Silas were released from prison by an earthquake (16:25–27).

For these stories to have any credibility as encouragement, Luke and his
readers would have shared the view that this kind of tangible intervention
by God remained a real possibility. Yet Luke is no triumphalist. As we noted
at the beginning of this section, he also includes stories with tragic endings,
as in the case of Stephen, James and, probably, Paul. Yet, while Luke and his
readers may have expected God's tangible presence to be experienced not
only in dramatic rescues in the darkest hours but also in the gift of bold action
and speech to persevere in faith and mission, they were confident that, even
in death, they would be in Paradise with Jesus (Luke 23:42–43; cf. Acts 7:55–56).
Moreover, at least Luke was confident that the mission of the followers of
Jesus would be unhindered – if not enhanced – in the face of the most severe
persecution. Thus, from Luke's perspective, God does not remove his servants
from the world of persecution and the pain of serving him. Rather, God will
rescue, empower or eschatologically reward the followers of Jesus as they remain
faithful, enduring persecution. In the light of such a perspective, it is not surprising that Luke develops the theme of joy.

§8.1.6 The Church is to be characterized by joy

Luke was not the first Christian to draw attention to the importance of joy
in the Christian life. Paul, before him in his early writings, shows that
he considers joy to be part of the very fabric of Christian living: 'become
imitators of us and of the Lord', he says, 'for you received the word in much
affliction, with joy (*chara*) inspired by the Holy Spirit' (1 Thess. 1:6). However, with Luke, we reach a high point in the description of the Church as
characterized by joy. Throughout Luke and Acts different expressions for
joy are found – some of them are either unique to Luke or rarely used elsewhere in the New Testament: 'to give freely', 'gladness', 'be glad', 'to praise',
'to gladden' and 'leap for joy'.[23] None of these words is used by the other
Synoptic Gospel writers.

---

[23] The data are as follows: 'to give freely' (*charizomai*, Luke 7:21, 42; Acts 3:14; 25:11; 27:24);
'gladness' (*agalliasis*, Luke 1:14, 44; Acts 2:46); 'be glad' (*agalliaō*, Luke 1:47; 10:21; Acts 2:26);
'to praise' (*ainein*, Luke 2:13, 20; 19:37; 24:53; Acts 2:47; 3:8, 9); 'to gladden' (*euphrainein*, Luke
12:19; 15:23, 24, 29, 32; 16:19; Acts 2:26; 7:41); and 'leap for joy' (*skirtaō*, Luke 1:41, 44; 6:23).

Reading through the Gospel we see that, initially, the coming of Jesus is met with joy. When Elizabeth meets Mary, the unborn John the Baptist leaps for joy in her womb (Luke 1:44). Mary responds by saying that her spirit 'rejoices' in God her Saviour (1:47). Then, like Jesus, to be involved in mission is a joy: the seventy-two returned from their mission with joy and are taught that their names are written in heaven (10:17, 20). Repentance and accepting the invitation to salvation are the basis of joy according to the three parables of the lost sheep, coin and son (15:3–32) and the story of Zacchaeus (19:1–10). The crowd of disciples also rejoices over the triumphal entry of Jesus into Jerusalem (19:37). In fact, the first part of Luke's work ends not with sadness on Jesus' departure but on a joyous note. Finally, he says that, having been commissioned for mission, promised the Spirit, blessed by Jesus and having worshipped him, the disciples returned to Jerusalem with great joy from the scene of the Ascension and were continually in the temple blessing God (24:49–53).

Joy is also one of the characteristics of the picture Luke gives of the Church in the early part of Acts. There is a great list of events and occasions related to joy. For example, on the day of Pentecost Peter, citing Psalm 16:8–11, spoke of the resurrection and the resultant gladness and joy (Acts 2:24–28), and the first Christians are said to eat together in gladness (*agalliasis*, 2:46). On leaving the Jewish council the apostles rejoiced that they had been counted worthy to suffer dishonour for the name of Jesus (5:41). There was much joy in Samaria as a result of Philip's ministry of preaching, healing and exorcism (8:8) and the converted eunuch went on his way rejoicing after being baptized (8:39). Likewise, the Gentiles rejoice to hear that Paul's message applies to them and they are said to be filled not only with the Holy Spirit but also with joy (13:48, 52). Then, the reports of Paul and Barnabas concerning their successful mission gave great joy to the brethren (15:3) and the converted Philippian gaoler rejoices with his household that he believed in God (16:34).

Further, Luke makes an interesting connection between food and joy. For example, the lost son returns to a joyous feast (Luke 15:23–24) and Zacchaeus is said to rejoice in being able to entertain Jesus (19:6). In the parable of the rich fool the man expects to be able to eat and rejoice in the future (12:19) and the rich man at whose gate Lazarus begged ate joyously or sumptuously every day (16:19). In Acts, Luke also links food and joy in having Paul and Barnabas describe God satisfying their hearers' hearts with food and gladness (Acts 14:17; cf. §8.4.4 below).

There is then, through both parts of Luke's work, a clear note of joyful exultation. In fact, unless we take seriously Luke's portrait of the Church as victorious and joyously confident in its life and mission, we will have failed to grasp an essential element in Luke's message to his readers about God's intended character of the Church, not least in the face of persecution. We turn now to note another important characteristic of the Church: the imperative of community and the series of threats to its function that Luke addresses.

§8.2 The imperative of community

In the story of the election of Judas' replacement we noted that the person needed not only to have been with Jesus but also to have been a member of the group around him (Acts 1:22–23; see §2.5.3). Not only does this enable Luke to stretch his initial definition of an apostle to include others besides those specifically appointed by Jesus, it also implies a communal dimension to being an apostle. Apostleship was not summed up in being called by Jesus or even mirroring and maintaining his ministry; it included being part of a group. Thus, for Luke, at the very core of the Church – its DNA – is the notion that the Church is not a collection of individuals related to Jesus but a community around him and of which he is a part.

Throughout the first few chapters of Acts there are intimations that Luke saw the idea of community as integral to the Church. For example, he describes the followers of Jesus being devoted to activities that have a community dimension: prayer (Acts 1:14), the apostles' teaching, fellowship and breaking bread (2:42; see §9.5 below). The point is also made in his generous use of words for 'together' (see §2.1 above).

There is further support in seeing the corporate nature of the Church as fundamental to Luke in his use of the term 'brothers' (*adelphoi*) in Acts to describe the group of followers of Jesus.[24] Already, in his Gospel Luke has used the term for the followers of Jesus.[25]

To a twenty-first-century reader it might be assumed that Luke was conveying the idea that the Church is a family. Indeed, in Luke 8:21 Jesus talks about his 'mother and brothers' (cf. e.g. Josephus, *Ant.* 11.300). However, in Luke's time *adelphoi* was also used for the members of a party, sect or religious society (e.g. Josephus, *J.W.* 2:122). And, in view of what we have seen of Luke's use of the idea of a sect to convey some of his understanding of the Church (see §5.3), and his using 'brother' or 'brethren' of fellow Israelites, it is likely that calling followers of Jesus 'brothers' is an expression of Luke's mindset that the followers of Jesus are members of the same close-knit religious community (see Luke 8:21), be they Jews (e.g. Acts 2:37), Hellenists (6:3) or Greeks (e.g. 15:1, 23).

In attending to specific threats to the unity of the community Luke deals with four faultlines in his narrative: the Jew and Gentile racial division; the sociological divides between rich and poor and high and low; the damage of dishonesty and selfishness; and the divide between Hebrews and Hellenists. Each of these requires our attention.

§8.3 The Church: Jews or Gentiles or both?

Taking into account all his writings, one of the greatest challenges Luke addresses is the inclusion of the Gentiles among the followers of Jesus (esp. Acts

---

[24] E.g. Acts 2:37; 6:3; 10:23; 11:1; 15:1; 16:2; 17:6; 18:18; 21:7; 28:15.
[25] Most obviously, see Luke 6:41, 42; 8:19–21; 17:3; 22:32.

10:1—11:18). Luke's interest in the cultural diversity of the Church is considerable, perhaps, because of his own experience. For in what may be his home church, Luke says that Jewish Christians at Antioch had been converted by (presumably Jewish) Christians from Jerusalem (11:19). However, some of those from Jerusalem, originally from Cyprus and Cyrene and, therefore, probably Greek speaking, spoke to the Hellenists or Greek-speaking Gentiles (11:20). Readers can assume many of these Greek-speaking Gentiles were converted for, when Paul and Barnabas are said to return from southern Galatia and Pamphylia, they tell as news that a door of faith was being opened to the Gentiles (14:27). But, at this stage, there is no suggestion of dissension between these groups. Eventually, however, into this bed of cultural diversity certain individuals from Judea – perhaps Pharisees who had become Christians (cf. 15:5) – came and sowed their teaching that salvation was contingent on being circumcised (14:26–15:1).

The enormity of the problem as Luke sees it can be gauged by the amount of space he devotes to the problem.[26] So deep did Luke see the dispute between Paul and Barnabas and the teachers from Jerusalem that it could not be resolved without sending a delegation back to Jerusalem (Acts 15:2–4). There, Peter mediates between the predominately Greek-speaking Jewish Christians from Antioch and believers in Jerusalem 'who belonged to the sect of the Pharisees' (15:5).

Luke's solution to the problem of Gentiles becoming and being part of the Church is not to do as we find in Paul: offer a direct theological defence of the inclusion of the Gentiles (e.g. Rom. 1—4; 9—11). Rather, first, consistent with the nature of his writing, Luke uses his narrative to underscore the universal nature of salvation and the mission of the Church (cf. §4.1.1 above). Characters early in his Gospel talk of the universality of God's salvation. For example, the aged Simeon praises God saying, 'my eyes have seen your salvation . . . a light for revelation to the Gentiles' (Luke 2:30, 32). And in his opening address in the synagogue at Nazareth, Jesus forecasts that his ministry will reach outside Israel (4:24–27). Readers see this in the story of the centurion's slave being healed (7:1–10). However, this universality is only a foretaste of what is anticipated to be the future work of the Church.[27]

Second, Luke's strategy is dominated by his view that God has taken the practical initiative and saved the Gentiles who, in turn, are to be accepted. Not only is this clear from what we have just seen from his Gospel, but it also becomes plain in Acts. On associating with Gentile believers, Peter is criticized by his fellow Jews (Acts 11:2). On hearing Peter's report of the coming of the Spirit on the household of Cornelius, however, his compatriots conclude, 'Then God has given even to the Gentiles the repentance that leads to life' (11:18). Indeed, Luke portrays God taking the initiative, in that 'While Peter was still speaking, the Holy Spirit fell upon all who heard the word' (10:44).

---

[26] See, esp. Acts 10:1–11:18; 15:1–35; 21:17–26.
[27] Cf. Luke 10:1–12, 17–20; 13:28–29; 14:15–24; 24:47–48.

Third, part of the initiative that Luke portrays God as taking is that he has prepared the followers of Jesus through visions for the mission to the Gentiles. Thus, the coming of the Spirit on Cornelius and his household is prefaced by the story of a vision Peter has, making the point through a heavenly voice that, 'What God has made clean, you must not call profane' (Acts 10:15; cf. 10:11). Then, through his narrative sequence, with the story of Cornelius following immediately, Luke applies this assertion of cleanliness to the Gentiles (cf. 10:17). Variations of this theme of the initiative of God in saving the Gentiles in Acts are seen also, for example, in having Jesus say at the end of the Gospel, 'that repentance and forgiveness of sins is to be proclaimed in his name to all nations, beginning from Jerusalem' (Luke 24:47).

Fourth, Luke brings Scripture into play to support his view that God has taken the initiative in establishing the universal nature of the Church and its mission. On the day of Pentecost, it is Scripture that Peter cites to explain that the Spirit is being poured out on 'all flesh' and that 'everyone who calls on the name of the Lord shall be saved'.[28] As only Jews have so far received the Spirit (Acts 2:1–4), Luke's use of Scripture becomes predictive, though only for what has taken place among the Gentiles in his narrative (cf. §§10.2 and 3 below). More generally, God's universal sovereignty is also seen in other citations of Scripture. For example, Stephen's speech uses Isaiah 66:1–2 to establish the point that God is not confined to things the Jews have constructed, but that heaven is God's throne and the whole earth his footstool (Acts 7:49–50).

Finally, Luke shows his readers how this unity is worked out in practice. Luke says that, in practical terms, unity is maintained by Jews continuing to live according to the law (Acts 21:17–26) and the Gentiles only being asked to 'abstain from what has been sacrificed to idols and from blood and from what is strangled and from fornication' (21:25). As well as the profound problem of the inclusion of the Gentiles into the Church, there are other challenges that Luke's readers appear to be facing.

§8.4 Rich and poor, high and low

Among Luke's readers there were probably both the rich and the poor. There is a tell-tale sign of the rich among Luke's readers in the way he relates the story of the so-called rich young ruler (Luke 18:18–30). In Mark, on hearing that he must sell all he has and give to the poor, the man goes away sorrowful (Mark 10:22). However, Luke omits the detail of the man going away, leaving the reader to suppose that such a person could become a follower of Jesus and be among Luke's readers (Luke 18:23). Then, other stories such as the parable of the rich fool (12:16–21) and the parable of the rich man and Lazarus (16:19–31) – both unique to Luke – would have their best impact if there were wealthy people among Luke's readership to

---

[28] Acts 2:17/Joel 2:28; Acts 2:21/Joel 2:32; cf. §10.2 below. See also Acts 4:12 for the universal implication of the Ps. 118:22 citation in Acts 4:11.

heed the warnings. The story of Zacchaeus, also unique to Luke, again probably reflects the existence of wealthy folk in Luke's audience who had been generous to the poor (19:1–10).

Not only were there the wealthy but also, from the cumulative impact of a number of stories, including that of the rich young ruler, there were probably Christians of high social standing among those expected to read Luke-Acts. The story of the centurion that Luke took up from Q (Luke 7:1–10) is probably an indication of this. The same is probably true of the story of the centurion at the cross who declared Jesus to be 'innocent' or 'just' (*dikaios*, 23:47/Mark 15:39). In Acts it is a centurion, Cornelius, who is portrayed as opening the way for Gentiles to become Christians (Acts 11:18). As a centurion (or sergeant in contemporary terms), Cornelius would have been a soldier who had served with distinction. He would have been well travelled and well paid. That his household and family were with him (10:1) means that Cornelius was either garrisoned there for some time or had retired, in which case, he would have belonged to the upper echelons of society. In any case, he would have been a person of considerable standing in society with whom Luke's readers could identify.[29]

Acts 13:1 also tells of a person of high social standing being in the church at Antioch. Manaen, one of the prophets and teachers, is said to be a *suntrophos* ('foster-brother'), that is, brought up in court with, or at least courtier of, Herod Antipas.[30] Similarly, Luke 8:2–3 mentions some women (including Joanna, the wife of Chuza, Herod's steward) providing for Jesus and the disciples out of their means. These references probably reflect Luke considering that there were Christians of means as well as high standing, including those connected with royalty, among his readership who would relate to these stories.

In contrast, the presence of the poor in Luke's readership is strongly suggested by his parable of the great feast (Luke 14:15–24). After the first round of invitations from the householder had been refused, in anger, he told his servant to 'Go out at once into the streets and lanes of the town and bring in the poor, the crippled and the blind and the lame' (14:21). A similar list occurs in the opening programmatic statement of Jesus' ministry (4:18) as well as those John the Baptist is told are helped by Jesus' ministry (7:21; see also 6:20–21). The parable of the friend asking for three loaves of bread at midnight, depicting a poor person unexpectedly having to entertain, also leads us to assume that there are such people in Luke's readership (11:5–8). Further, Luke's discussion of the community of goods and the daily distribution in the Jerusalem church is best explained if he considered himself addressing both rich and poor readers (see §13.3).

That there were significant difficulties between the rich and poor, and high and low readers, seems clear from stories we have just mentioned: the community of goods and the daily distribution of goods. Also, the encouragement

---

[29] See, e.g. Tacitus, *Ann.* 2.65; 13.9; 15.5; *The Histories* 2.58.
[30] See MM 614 (*suntrophos*) and LJS 1729 (*suntropheō*).

we have noted that the poor receive from Jesus, as well as the criticism Luke has of the wealthy, have their greatest impact if there was obvious and un-resolved tension between the rich and poor, and the high and low among the readership.[31] A number of themes in Luke–Acts would help Luke's reader see his perspective on this issue.

§8.4.1 The foolishness of wealth

The criticism of the rich is not only indicative of probable tension between rich and poor among Luke's readers but it is also likely to be part of his solution to the problem. For example, the parable of the so-called rich fool who died before realizing his material aspirations is told as a warning against greed and seeing life consisting in having many possessions (Luke 12:13–21, esp. 15). Also, appended to the wedding banquet parable (14:7–11) Luke has Jesus say that invitations to meals should not be to those able to repay the host but to 'the poor, the crippled, the lame and the blind' (14:13). The con-clusion is drawn that the host will be blessed by repayment at the resurrec-tion of the righteous (14:14).

§8.4.2 The blessing of poverty

Another of Luke's contributions to solving the problem of the social rifts among his readership is to highlight the blessedness of being poor. Early in his story, Luke has Mary rejoicing in the Lord because he had noticed her despite her low estate or poverty (Luke 1:48). In the light of this God has put down the mighty and exalted the lowly or 'poor' (*tapeinos*, 1:52).[32] Then, the mention of the newly born Jesus being laid in a manger[33] may indicate that Luke thought he was born in poverty. On presenting him at the temple, his parents are said to make the offering of two birds (2:24), the offering of the poor (Lev. 12:8). In this Luke more clearly draws attention to his view of the economic circumstances of Jesus' birth and upbringing.

In giving his reader his perspective on poverty and social standing, Luke has Jesus say that one of the prices of being a follower of Jesus is to be leaving a house or a wife or a brother or a parent or children (Luke 18:29). Mark says that the reward is to receive a hundred times what has been left – includ-ing houses and land (Mark 10:30). Not so in Luke's version of the story. The specific material benefits of being a follower of Jesus are played down. The followers of Jesus are simply told they will get much more in this time and eternal life in the age to come (Luke 18:30).

In the Old Testament the poor were originally those who were lacking in material resources (Deut. 15:4, 11). But poverty came to mean not only the downtrodden (Amos 2:6; 8:4) and those who can only look to God for help (Ps. 10:2; Amos 5:12b), but also all those who await salvation (see further

---

[31] Luke 1:52–53; 6:24–26; 12:13–21; 14:7–14; 16:19–31.
[32] See James 1:9–10 where the 'lowly' (*tapeinos*) are contrasted with the 'rich' (*plousios*). Cf. Luke 1:52–53.
[33] Luke 2:7, 12, 16.

§13.3.1.1 below). So, in Luke's first beatitude the poor who are blessed are those, unlike the rich fool (Luke 12:16–21), who do not trust in their own resources. Rather, they are those who turn to God for the salvation they have awaited. Also, being materially poor need not concern followers of Jesus for, just as God feeds ravens who have no storehouses (12:24) and clothes plants that do not work (12:27–28), God will clothe and care for them. In fact, says Jesus, 'Sell your possessions, give alms; provide yourselves with purses that do not grow old, with a treasure in heaven that does not fail, where no thief approaches and no moth destroys' (12:33). And, Jesus concludes this teaching on the blessings of being materially poor, 'For where your treasury is, there will your heart be also' (12:34).

§8.4.3 The cost of wealth

The other side of the coin of the blessing of being poor is the cost of being wealthy. The very first 'woe' is addressed to the rich. 'Woe to you who are rich', Jesus says, 'for you have received your reward' (Luke 6:24). Also, Luke includes some strong teaching of Jesus against wealth and materialism. For example, 'watch and beware of all covetousness; for a man's life does not consist in the abundance of his possessions' (12:15). 'Life is more than food, and the body more than clothing' (12:23). Jesus is said to warn that it was not possible to serve both God and wealth (16:13). Not surprisingly then, Jesus is said to tell the rich ruler to sell all he had and distribute it to the poor (18:22). And, as we will see in the next section, in the new community of Jesus' followers in Acts, Barnabas sells a field and gives the money to the apostles. Thus, for Luke, a key to the solution of the division between the rich and the poor is not only the need to share possessions but to understand the blessing of being poor – and the cost of being wealthy.

§8.4.4 Hospitality

Another solution to the problem of the apparent rift between rich and poor, high and low, and between Hebrews and Hellenists (see §8.6 below), is Luke's emphasis on the theme of hospitality or table fellowship. In Luke's world, hospitality – the sharing of a meal – was the expression of friendship. Well before Luke's time, Plato had discussed meals as a way of making friends rather than enemies (Plato, *Laws* 671c–72a). Writing in the same period as Luke, Plutarch said, 'A guest comes to share not only meat, wine, and dessert, but conversation, fun, and amiability that leads to friendship' (*Table Talk* 660b). Like Luke in his Gospel (14:7–14), Plutarch abhors the practice of seating guests at meals according to status because that works against table fellowship (also Pliny, *Letters* 2.6; and Martial, *Epigrams* 3.60).

That hospitality is a symbol of Christian unity for Luke seems clear when we see the way he has emphasized that Jesus accepted the hospitality of the socially unacceptable and was himself, on occasions, host at meals of his followers (see above). For example, Jesus accepted an invitation to eat with Zacchaeus the tax collector (Luke 19:1–10) and was the host at a meal in

Emmaus (24:28–35). Then, in Acts, the issue of unity and the need to accept Gentiles into the Church are also highlighted through the theme of table fellowship. Thus, Peter goes to help Cornelius join the followers of Jesus after he understands that Jewish followers may accept the hospitality of Gentiles (Acts 10:28–29). Peter then stays with Cornelius for some days (10:48). Also, Paul and his companions accept the hospitality of Lydia (16:14–15) and the Philippian gaoler (16:34), for example (cf. §8.3 above).

Being familiar with the Old Testament, Luke's readers would have discerned further ideas from his emphasis on table fellowship. In the Old Testament the end time was expected to be like a banquet. Isaiah 25:6 says that, 'On this mountain the Lord will prepare for all peoples a banquet of rich food, a banquet of fine wine, of fat things full of marrow.' More particularly, the Messiah was expected to bring happiness among the poor and the afflicted who would be part of his banquet community. Isaiah 55:1–3 addresses the poor: 'you that have no money, come, buy and eat! Come, buy wine and milk without money and without price.'[34]

It is not surprising then that Luke depicts Jesus (the Messiah) feasting with what his opponents see as undesirables: tax collectors and sinners (Luke 5:27–32; 15:1–2). Nor is it surprising that a feast or banquet is used to portray the end time (14:16–24). The focus of this parable is that it is only the poor, maimed, blind and lame who are ready to accept the householder's servant's invitation to the great feast (14:21). In developing the banquet theme Luke contrasts earthly feasting with the heavenly banquet. Jesus says, that those who are hungry now are blessed for they shall be satisfied, and woe to those who are full now, for they shall be hungry (6:21, 25). Also, the rich man, clothed in purple and fine linen feasted sumptuously every day while Lazarus wanted to be fed from what fell from the rich man's table. After death, it is implied, the roles have been reversed (16:19–31).

The table fellowship theme is also pressed into service to address problems relating to social status. For example, Luke's account of the Last Supper at which Jesus is the host (Luke 22:1–38) contains a reinforcement of the earlier teaching of Jesus about his followers not seeking personal prestige and status (22:24–27).

In coming to Acts, it is wholly in line with Luke's banquet theme in the face of breaches of community that, in his description of the Church after the first intake of new believers, he says that they devoted themselves not only to the apostles' teaching and the prayers but also to the fellowship and to the breaking of bread (Acts 2:42). Then he says, 'day by day they were in the temple together and breaking bread in their homes, they partook of food with glad and generous hearts' (2:46). We turn now to the first breach of community in Luke's portrait of the followers of Jesus, which involves severe repercussions for the culprits.

---

[34] See also Exod. 24:9–11; Deut. 12:5–7; Lev. 7:11, 15; 22:29–30; Pss. 22:26; 23:5; 78:24–9; Isa. 65:13–14; Zeph. 1:7; Song 5:1. See also §13.3 below.

§8.5 The damage of dishonesty and selfishness

In describing the Jerusalem community as together (Acts 2:46) or united (4:32), Luke twice says the followers of Jesus held their property in common, and that goods were distributed according to need (2:44–45; and 4:32, 35), so that 'there was not a needy person among them' (4:34). The importance for Luke of this materially united community is shown in that it is part of a description that echoes the Shema (Deut. 5:4–5). There, the aspects of heart, soul and might – which in Luke's time could also mean property[35] – sum up the all-encompassing responsibilities of the people of God.

The story of what is portrayed as the first fissure in the Jerusalem community is a violation of the principle of common ownership (Acts 4:32—5:11). The breach of the community is in Ananias secretly withholding from the apostles some of the proceeds of a property sale (5:1–2). The tragedy of the breach is heightened in that it is reported immediately following Luke's example of Barnabas, one of the lead characters in Acts, selling a field and bringing the entire proceeds to the apostles (4:37).

Luke's resolution of the error involves Peter uncovering the crime – perhaps informed by the Holy Spirit (cf. Acts 5:3) – and in the sudden death of both Ananias and Sapphira, his wife and accomplice (5:5–10). Luke ends his story by saying that 'great fear' or 'great awe' (*phobos megas*) seized those who heard it.[36] By this, Luke means not simply that a miracle had taken place, nor that the appropriate response was trembling or an emotional one. Rather, portraying God as active in the story,[37] the fear of God is implied. Linked with Luke's heavy dependence on the Old Testament, where there is an association of fear of God with understanding and submitting to his will,[38] this probably conveyed to his readers God's endorsement of the unity around the sharing of property.

An underlying assumption required of the reader of this story is that without the sharing of property and the redistribution of funds there would have been needy persons in the community (cf. Acts 4:34). This is confirmed in the next faultline in the Jerusalem church that is part of Luke's narrative.

§8.6 A further breach of community:
Hebrews and Hellenists

The first breach of the community involved only one couple and was immediately, if drastically, resolved. The second breach, a cultural one, is related as touching the whole community and having a long-term impact on the Church.

Luke famously depicts the Jerusalem community as comprising not only people of different economic and social positions but also of different cultures.

---

[35] CD 9.11; 12.10; cf. Ecclus. 7:30.
[36] Acts 5:11; cf. 5:5. For Luke's use of *phobos* ('fear') see Luke 1:12, 65; 5:26; 7:16; 21:26; Acts 2:43; 9:31; 19:17; and for 'great' (*megas*) fear also see Luke 2:9; 8:37; Acts 5:5, 11.
[37] Acts 5:3, 4, 9.
[38] E.g. esp. Deut. 4:10; 6:13; 10:12, 20; 13:5.

Barnabas, a Levite, is said to be a native of Cyprus (Acts 4:36). Nicolaus, listed among the seven appointed to serve table, is said to be a proselyte from Antioch (6:5), probably implying that all the others listed were born Jews. However, Luke probably intends those listed to be understood as Hellenists. For, though Greek names were used by Palestinian Jews (cf. 1:23) – some of Jesus' disciples carried Greek names (Andrew, Philip and Bartholomew, cf. 1:13) – the proselyte Nicolaus would have been understood to be a Hellenist, and all the others listed have Greek names.

It is in the story where this list appears that Luke narrates the second breach of community: Hellenists complain against the Hebrews that their widows were being neglected in the daily distribution of charity (Acts 6:1–6), perhaps taking up the familiar local method of relief.[39] The meaning of the two terms, Hebrews and Hellenists, and the nature of this dispute are not immediately obvious, for Luke has introduced the two parties without notice or explanation. The Hebrews[40] can probably only be defined over against the 'Hellenists' (*hellēnistai*). Notwithstanding, the meaning of the term and the identity of the Hellenists are difficult to determine, not least because the term is only used in the New Testament in Acts, the earliest known occurrence of the word.[41]

Given that Luke tells the story of Cornelius as the entry of the Gentiles into the Church,[42] it is most probable that he considers the Hellenists to be Jews not Greeks. Indeed, the word itself and later sources suggest the expression was used of those who took up living as Greeks and spoke the language well.[43] In Acts 9:29 Hellenists are simply Greek-speaking Jews, and in 11:20[44] Greek-speaking Gentiles. The context of 6:1–6 suggests Luke understands them to be Jews who had taken up Greek culture, subsequently became Christians and who may have been natives of Palestine, or have emigrated to Palestine. Nicolaus, being the only one identified from another place, Antioch, is probably, therefore, the exception.

As Luke places the Hebrews over against these Hellenists or Greek-cultured Jewish Christians (cf. Philo, *Confusion* 129), he is probably thinking of them not as Jews in general but as traditional or conservative Jews, most probably natives of Palestine, whose obvious cultural marker was Hebrew or Aramaic, generally thought to be the language of everyday life.[45] In other words, Luke probably intends portraying Hellenistic Jewish Christians (cultural outsiders)

---

[39] Cf. *m. Pe'ah* 8.7; *t. B. Meṣi'a* 3.9; *b. B. Bat.* 8a–b; *B. Meṣi'a* 38a.

[40] In the NT *hebraioi* ('Hebrews') occurs only here and in 2 Cor. 11:22; and Phil. 3:5 (twice, once in the singular).

[41] Acts 6:1; 9:29; 11:20. Thereafter, the earliest reference to the *hellēnistai* ('Hellenists') is found in the second half of the fourth century in Bishop Ammon of Egypt, *Letter* 7.8.

[42] Acts 10:45; 11:1, 18.

[43] See, e.g. Sextus Empiricus, *Adversus Mathematicos* 1.246; Chrysostom, *Homily* 14 (on Acts 6:1) and 21 (on Acts 9:29).

[44] The likely reading of Acts 11:20 uses the word *hellēnistai* ('Hellenists'), as in, e.g. codices Vaticanus, Bezae and Basiliensis, rather than *hellēnes* ('Greeks'), as in, e.g. P[74] and Codex Sinaiticus.

[45] Cf. e.g. *Sib. Or.* 3.69; 2 Macc. 7:31; 11:13; 15:37; 4 Macc. 4:11; 8:2; 9:6, 18; 17:9.

as unhappy with the more traditional Palestinian Jews because their widows were being neglected in the daily distribution of charity.

The solution in Luke's narrative to this cultural clash breaching community is to create a division of labour. The apostles are affirmed in giving attention to 'the word of God' or preaching (Acts 6:2; cf. Luke 1:2), as well as to the regular hours of Jewish prayer (Acts 6:4, see §6.6 above): nothing must divert the attention of the apostles – the Church in microcosm – from its essential focus. However, to solve the problem seven people are chosen to 'serve tables' or to see that the widows among the Hellenists are not neglected. Thus, Luke sees the solution to the breach of community to be the appointment of leaders from among those complaining to see their people receive attention.

The widows here are incidental characters in relation to the main theme of this story. Nevertheless, widows are a special interest in Luke's Gospel.[46] He emphasizes that they, a disadvantaged group, are no less than others the recipients of salvation.[47] In Acts, besides the story we have been discussing, Luke also shows an interest in the care of widows in the community of followers of Jesus (Acts 9:39). This leads us to a subject of particular interest to twenty-first-century readers of Luke-Acts.

§8.7 Women

The views on women among Luke's readers are likely to have been diverse. Reflecting Jewish tradition, Rabbi Eliezar is reported to have said that for a man to teach his daughter the Law was as if to teach her lechery (*m. Sotah* 3.4). This expresses the view that women were to be classed among the Gentiles, slaves and children.[48] Yet, another tradition says a man could set up his wife as a shopkeeper or appoint her a guardian (*m. Ketubbot* 9.4) and her testimony, in some cases, was as valid as that of a man's (2.5–7; *m. Sotah* 9.8). Although, historically, Greek and Roman cultures had low views of women (e.g. Xenophon, *The Economist* 7–10), by the time Luke was writing, more liberal attitudes were also evident (e.g. Plutarch, *Tiberius* 1.4; *Gaius* 19.1–3). Against this background, the way Luke writes about women probably indicates that he considered his readers – along with others in their world – were facing the issue of the place and care of women.

It is not easy to understand Luke's intention in what he says about women, though it is obvious he places special emphasis on them. In the first two chapters it is Elizabeth and Mary, rather than Zechariah and Joseph, their husbands, who are the centre of attention. It is these women, rather than their

---

[46] Luke mentions widows in Luke 2:37; 4:25, 26; 7:12; 18:3, 5; 20:47; 21:2, 3; Acts 6:1; 9:39, 41. Otherwise in the NT 'widow' is only at Matt. 23:13 (in some texts); Mark 12:40, 42, 43; 1 Cor. 7:8; 1 Tim. 5:3 (twice), 4, 5, 9, 11, 16 (twice); James 1:27; Rev. 18:7.

[47] Luke 2:37; 4:25–26; 7:11–17; 18:1–8; 20:47; 21:1–4.

[48] E.g. *m. Ber.* 3.3; *m. Sukkah* 2.8; *m. B. Meṣi'a* 1.5.

husbands, who hear first of the coming of Jesus, who are praised by the angels and who prophesy.[49] In particular, in being described as the Lord's 'servant' (Luke 1:38, 48) and obedient to his word, Mary is portrayed as an ideal disciple, a position from which she never falters (8:19–21) and which Luke later reaffirms (Acts 1:14).

Then, in a series of male–female parallels – Zechariah and Elizabeth (Luke 1:11–20, 26–38), Simeon and Anna (or Hannah, now a widow, 2:25–38), Simon the Pharisee and the woman who was a sinner (7:36–50), Ananias and Sapphira (Acts 5:1–11) and Priscilla and Aquila (18:24–28), for example – Luke maintains the importance of women in his narrative. This pairing may also reflect a heightening prestige of marriage, begun by the reforms of Augustus, which Luke sees as an opportunity to use for his own purposes.[50]

In his ministry Jesus is portrayed as associating with, as well as offering forgiveness to, a 'sinful woman' (Luke 7:36–50). He is also shown accompanied not only by the twelve but also by women, as he proclaimed the good news of the kingdom of God (8:1–3). Two of these women, Mary Magdalene and Joanna are mentioned again, saying they could not find the body, a report the apostles incorrectly took to be an unbelievable, idle tale (24:10–11). In another story unique to Luke, a woman cries out, 'Blessed is the womb that bore you and the breasts that you sucked.' However, Jesus is said to reply that the greater blessedness was to hear and keep the word of God (11:27–28). The story of Jesus' visit to Mary and Martha, also unique to Luke's Gospel, carries the same view: sitting at the Lord's feet and listening to his teaching was important and implies women should not be denied discipleship (10:38–42).

This emphasis on women suggests that Luke may have considered his readers resistant to the view that women were legitimate recipients of the benefits of salvation and could be accepted as followers of Jesus, no less than were the men. It may also be that Luke supposed his readers were neglecting widow believers.

Over against these problems Luke offers some emphases as correctives. We have just seen that Luke emphasizes the place of women as recipients of the message and the subject of praise from an angel from God. Women, along with the twelve, accompanied Jesus through his ministry (Luke 8:1–3; 23:55; Acts 1:14) and, represented in the pattern of Mary, are faithful disciples. In the passion narrative, Luke tells his readers that it is the women who were the last to leave the cross and the first to arrive at the tomb.[51] Even though in society the witness of a woman might be rejected – the report of the women regarding the empty tomb (Luke 24:11) – their witness to the empty tomb proves to be correct and valuable (24:11, 22–24).

However, Luke does not include women among the twelve. This cannot be, as we will see, because he wishes to exclude women from leadership. Nor

---

[49] Luke 1:28, 30, 41–45, 46–55.
[50] See *Corpus Inscriptionum Latinarum* 6.32323.57; also Horace, *Odes* 4.5; Propertius, *Poems* 3.12; 4.3.
[51] Luke 23:49, 55—24:3, 10.

can it be that women cannot be witnesses of the resurrection, for he affirms this role of women (Luke 24:24). Rather, women are probably excluded from the twelve because the twelve are intended to stand in a symbolic relationship to the twelve male patriarchs (cf. 22:30; Acts 26:7). Nevertheless, Luke wishes to give women a place in the life and ministry of the Church. It is possible that Luke goes to such lengths to include women simply because the twelve did not include women.

In his second volume Luke continues to depict women as having a significant place among the followers of Jesus. In the first list of the followers in Acts 1:14 the women are mentioned. Later, in using the rare feminine form of 'disciple' (*mathētria*), Tabitha is accorded the status of a disciple (Acts 9:36).[52]

The importance of the place of women is seen in Peter's speech on the day of Pentecost. The prophecy from Joel 2:28–32 is taken up and applied to the coming of the Spirit to the followers of Jesus: 'your sons and your daughters shall prophesy . . . yes, and on my menservants and my maidservants in those days I will pour out my Spirit' (Acts 2:17, 18). In this manifesto for the new society of God's people, both men and women are equal recipients of the prophetic Spirit. In the third cameo of life in the earliest group of followers in Jerusalem Luke says that the growing number of believers included 'both men and women' (5:14). In turn, Saul is said to drag off men and women and commit them to prison (8:3; 9:2). In Acts 17:34 Luke mentions a woman convert by name – Damaris – and in 17:4 and 17 leading women became believers. It seems that Luke wants to emphasize that women, including leading women of society, have a legitimate place among the followers of Jesus.

Luke goes further to give women strategic roles in the picture of the churches in Acts. Mary, the Mother of John Mark, appears as a wealthy widow. She has a maid, Rhoda, and a home large enough in which many people can gather to pray (Acts 12:12). In other words, Mary probably hosted a church in her home. We can note in passing the use of the masculine for 'many' (*hikanoi*, 12:12) did not mean that Luke thought he was depicting meetings of only men. In contrast, in the story of Lydia, set in Philippi (16:11–15), Paul and his companions visit what Luke depicts as an all-women prayer meeting (16:13). Luke goes on to say that Lydia became the leader of a church in her household, or at least was the host to a church (16:15, 40).

In the light of this, it is not surprising that Luke affirms women as teachers in his portrait of Aquila and his wife Priscilla.[53] Having introduced her (Acts 18:2), thereafter her name is listed first when Luke mentions the couple.[54] While it was not unusual in Jewish and Christian circles to mention the wife first, it could be that Luke cites her first because, in his mind, Priscilla

---

[52] *Mathētria* ('disciple') occurs only here (Acts 9:36) in the NT and in earlier literature only in Anonymus Photii, *Fragmenta* 237.16; Brotinus, *Testimonia*, Fragment 1.10; Posidonius, Fragment 78.99; 114.88; Diodorus Siculus, *Hist.* 2.52.8.

[53] Acts 18:1–3, 18, 24–26.

[54] Acts 18:18, 26; see also Rom. 16:3; 2 Tim. 4:19.

had more prominence in the Church or was (also?) of higher social standing than Aquila. Be that as it may, Luke depicts her, as well as her husband, teaching Apollos. This fact seems to be more important to Luke than what was taught, which is not mentioned. Nevertheless, we can gather that Apollos was probably at least taught about baptism (18:25) and the messianic interpretation of the Scriptures (18:28).

Another role in which Luke portrays women in the Church is as prophetesses. At Caesarea, Philip the evangelist is said to have four daughters who prophesied (Acts 21:9). From what Luke says about prophets (see Chapter 11 below) we can assume that Luke thought these prophetesses exercised a leadership role in their church. Luke says that these prophetesses were unmarried (*parthenos*, 'virgin'). The only other prophetess in Luke's writings – Anna, the daughter of Phanuel (Luke 2:36) – is also unmarried (*chēra*, 'widow'). This prompts us to note that most of the significant women in Acts are either widows or never married. What was potentially a position of disadvantage and neglect, God had invested with value.

Over against this positive role and the place for women we need to take into account what can be detected as Luke's hesitation in relation to women and prophecy. In Mark 14:3–8 a woman who anoints Jesus' head with oil acts as a prophet in declaring Jesus' death and messiahship. But, when Luke tells the story the element of prophecy is exchanged for one of repentance and loving gratitude (Luke 7:36–50). Further, often, women who speak are corrected by Jesus: the woman who blesses Jesus' mother (11:27–28), the women who weep for Jesus (23:27–28) as well as Martha (10:41–42) are all corrected. Most interesting is this latter case of Mary and Martha (10:38–42). In verse 40, Luke says Martha was 'distracted with much serving (*diakonia*)'. It is hardly possible to avoid the idea that, in this word, Luke is implying that Martha is being distracted by 'much ministry'. Indeed, in Acts, the word 'ministry' is used only of men.[55]

Then, in Acts, despite the quotation from Joel 2:28–29 affirming the place of women in prophecy (Acts 2:17–18), Luke gives no examples apart from mentioning Philip's daughters being prophetesses (21:9). The one example he gives of a woman prophesying – the mantic girl at Philippi – is condemned as demonic (16:16–18). In the light of all the positive things that Luke says about the place of women in the Church this anomalous material is difficult to interpret. It is not that he is avoiding or forbidding women's role in ministry; the Joel prophecy and the daughters of Philip tell against that. Rather, it could be that Luke remains reflective of the times in which he lives. While women, along with men, are recipients of salvation, he may need to be circumspect in the light of criticisms that women in spiritual leadership signals overtones of magic and disorder. It could also be, taking into account the story of Mary and Martha, that Luke considers that some women in his readership are being distracted with too much involvement in ministry. In any

---

[55] E.g. Acts 6:1; 11:29; 12:25.

case, it is reasonable to conjecture Luke considered an issue in the wider Church to which he was writing was that women, along with men, were legitimate benefactors of salvation, and were to be accorded full status and care as followers of Jesus.

§8.8 Conclusion

There may be some problems in the early Church that, if he knew about them, Luke could be accused of passing over. For example, what Paul says in Galatians about the fundamental rift between himself and Peter gets scant, if any, treatment (cf. Acts 15:1–35). However, it cannot be said that Luke is a triumphalist, portraying the Church as problem free and, in every enterprise, successful. Indeed, we have by no means exhausted Luke's allusions to possible problems he addresses among his readership; there is the dispute between Paul and Barnabas (15:36–41) and the problem of false teaching (20:28–30). However, these issues appear minor in relation to his view of the Church compared with those we have discussed.

From the space he gives them, we have seen that Luke pays particular attention to the problem of persecution and, over against his view of the imperative of community, he gives attention to the problem of rich and poor, high and low being in the Church; the damage to the life of the community caused by dishonesty and selfishness; the cultural tensions exhibited in the disagreement between the Hebrews and the Hellenists; and the place or role and care of women.

In the face of these considerable difficulties, Luke not only provides material in the teaching of Jesus, and constructs his narrative so that his characters provide models for his readers, but also emphasizes positive themes in relation to the difficulties he addresses: the example and encouragement of Jesus, the importance of shared activity, the pursuit of unity (particularly through hospitality and the sharing of possessions), and the blessedness of being poor and the cost of being wealthy, for example. Not least in the face of difficulties, early in this chapter we noted that Luke also proposes that joyful fellowship should characterize the Church, and he also affirms the importance and role of women. In our examination of various aspects of the Church as Luke portrays it, we turn to examine what he has to say about worship.

9

Worship

What is Christian worship? How should it be understood and what should take place in Christian worship? What part does the Eucharist or Lord's Supper play in worship and how important is it for the life of the Church? Would Luke, for example, support the still-popular view of John Calvin (1509–64) that the Church is to be found 'Wherever we see the Word of God purely preached and heard, and the sacraments administered according to Christ's institutes' (*Institutes*, 4.1.9)? What would Luke make of the view that the Eucharist is an instrument of invisible grace or that the Church is a community gathered around the sacrament and the word of God?

With questions such as these in mind, the purpose of this chapter is to describe Luke's understanding of Christian worship – the distinctively religious features or aspects associated with the corporate gatherings of Christians. In doing this we have to keep in mind that Luke and his readers were conscious that their emerging religious traditions and experiences had recent roots in a religion where there were three focal points of worship life: the Jerusalem temple, the synagogue and the home. Indeed, he depicts the followers of Jesus involved in all three, including for worship, or at least what appear to be aspects of it. The synagogue has already been seen to shape what Luke wants to say about the fundamentals of the Church (see §5.2 above). This will continue to be evident in relation to worship. We will also see the significance of private homes in Luke's understanding of worship among the followers of Jesus. In view of the temple providing the setting for the first scene in the Gospel (Luke 1:5–23) and Jerusalem being the setting of Luke's story of the early days of the Church (e.g. Acts 1:4), it is not surprising that his portrait of the Church in Jerusalem is nuanced by and drawn in the shadow of the temple; and his narrative never really moves far from it (cf. 21:15, 26).

§9.1 The temple

Although there was some Jewish criticism of the temple,[1] the building and the institutions were widely revered, even by Jews in the Diaspora. It is reported that they gladly paid their annual temple tax.[2] The temple was the centre of attention not only for the festivals – especially the Passover (Josephus, *Ant.* 17.214) when the city was crowded with tens of thousands of visitors – but

---

[1] Cf. *Sib. Or.* 4.24–30 and also the hints by Philo, *Good Person* 75; *Abraham* 89–93.
[2] See Exod. 30:13; Neh. 10:32; Josephus, *J.W.* 7.218; Philo, *Spec. Laws* 1.133, 141–44.

also for daily attendance (Exod. 29:38–42; Num. 28:2–8), notably the twice-daily Tamid or whole offering service. Although much of our information comes from after the destruction of the temple, it is likely that early each day priests prepared for the morning sacrifice. Then, in front of the Court of the Priests, the priests placed parts of the lamb on the fire along with a mixture of flour and olive oil, and poured wine around the altar as a libation, all paid for by the temple tax (Josephus, *Ant.* 3.237). During these activities the Levites sang the Psalm appointed for the day (*m. Tamid* 7.4) and played stringed instruments; two priests played trumpets (2 Chr. 29:26–28), and the people prostrated themselves, then the singers continued (Ecclus. 50:17; *m. Tamid* 7.3). Individuals were then able to bring sacrifices until just before the second daily sacrifice later in the afternoon (*m. Pesaḥim* 5.1; cf. Lev. 12). On the Sabbath the burnt offerings were doubled,[3] on feast days the sacrifices were further increased (Num. 28:16–31). As this schedule suggests, and as Luke reflects – even if exaggerated (Acts 4:1–4), the temple was a place bustling with people attending corporate worship and conducting business required for offering sacrifices (cf. Mark 11:15), as well as being present for individual worship or piety (cf. Acts 21:26), or meetings with priests (cf. Mark 1:44).

Luke's portrayal of the post-Easter followers of Jesus in Jerusalem participating in the life and routine of the temple is both considerable and significant. He ends his Gospel by saying that the post-Easter followers of Jesus 'were continually in the temple blessing God' (Luke 24:53).[4] In his summary of the life of the Church in Jerusalem Luke says that the followers of Jesus attended the temple 'daily' (*kath' hēmeran*, Acts 2:46; cf. §5.1 above). Peter and John are depicted as going to the temple – probably for the second daily sacrifice (3:1), and the group met there daily (2:46; 5:12), almost certainly to pray and praise,[5] as well as to receive visions (22:17). Luke also uses the temple as a venue for preaching and teaching (4:1–4; 5:20–21). Somewhat later in his narrative, Luke says that Paul visited the temple in relation to the end of a period of personal purification (Num. 6:9–12; *m. Nazir* 6.6) and to offer individual sacrifice (Acts 21:26).

Luke's readers are seeing that a high regard for the temple and its worship – also expressed early in the Gospel stories of Zechariah and Elizabeth, Joseph and Mary, Simeon and Anna (Luke 1:5—2:52) – is at the root and was part of early Christian worship. Even though most of his readers would never experience worship in the Jerusalem temple, they are to know that their worship traditions have their roots and also explanations in that worship. That is, their worship is informed by the joyous worship traditions that are associated with focusing on God's sacrifice-based forgiveness.

---

[3] Num. 28:9–10; Philo, *Spec. Laws* 1.170; Josephus, *Ant.* 3.237.
[4] In the light of the early chapters of Acts, readers are likely to have detected some hyperbole in this statement (cf. Acts 2:25; 10:2; 24:16).
[5] See Luke 24:53; cf. 1:10; 2:27–32, 36–38; 18:10–14; 19:46.

Moreover, second, in the final words of the Gospel, Luke has provided this tradition with a re-interpretive key, giving Christian worship its focus and motivation. The very last words of the Gospel depict Jesus' followers 'continually in the temple blessing God' because they were motivated by seeing the risen Jesus, perhaps as their high priest,[6] who is also the focus of their worship (Luke 24:52–53). When Luke's characters 'bless' or 'worship' (*eulogeō*) God it is in relation to his gift of salvation,[7] so readers would most likely take this worship to be in response to salvation. Also, from what would have been taken to be a portrait of salvation-based joy, Luke's readers would be reminded that the joy that marked the Tamid service is now to be found in the people whose worship in relation to God's salvation is focused on the risen Jesus. Yet, it is not that Luke wanted to portray Christian worship as divorced from Jewish worship. On the contrary.

§9.2 Maintaining Jewish ways of worship – Acts 1:12–14

The first reference to prayer in Acts turns out to be a piece with the general conclusion that Luke considered involvement in Jewish worship to be important for early Christians and their understanding of worship. Following his story of the Ascension, Luke says the eleven returned to Jerusalem and went to 'the upper room' (*to huperōon*) where they were staying (Acts 1:12–13). The upper storey of a large oriental house was often used by the learned as a place to gather to pray and study (Dan. 6:11; Acts 20:8). These rooms were also rented out or used for guests (Luke 22:11; Acts 9:36). So, it is not surprising that Luke should depict the group of Jesus' disciples gathering in such a place. Luke then gives a description of their activities, not necessarily confined to what happened in that room, but probably intended to include it: 'All these were constantly devoting themselves to prayer' (1:14).

What Luke is conveying about worship in this summary statement picturing the eleven praying is probably dependent on his use of the term 'the prayer' (*tē proseuchē*, singular with an article). Luke could intend *tē proseuchē* to refer to prayer generally (as for Jesus in Luke 6:12), perhaps in the upper room, as Origen thought (*Cels.* 8.2). However, since the term is also used for a place of prayer in Acts 16:16 (cf. 16:13), as it was for Jews – especially for a synagogue (see ch. 5, n. 14) – it is likely that Luke is referring to the Jewish statutory public prayers, including the particular times of prayer, part of the essence and great treasure of being a Jew (e.g. *m. Ber.* 4.1–9.5).

These statutory prayers he portrays the followers of Jesus attending to in their homes (cf. Acts 10:9, 30),[8] perhaps in the synagogues (cf. 22:19), and

---

[6] Luke 24:50; cf. Lev. 9:22; Ecclus. 50:20–22. If Jesus is depicted as their high priest, it is a theme in which Luke shows little interest.

[7] See Luke 1:42, 64; 2:28; 13:35; 19:38; cf. Acts 3:26; otherwise in Luke-Acts see Luke 2:34; 6:28; 9:16; 24:30, 50, 51, 53.

[8] The noon prayer time may have been kept by particularly devout Jews. See Ps. 55:17; Dan. 6:10; cf. *Did.* 8.3.

certainly in the temple (see the previous section). There is some support for this view in the prayer being described as 'constant' or 'devoted' (*proskartereō*),[9] for Luke's phrase is remarkably close to a first-century Greek inscription concerning a slave who is freed with the condition of 'constantly (*proskarterein*) attending the place of prayer' (cf. MM 548).

Therefore, along with noting the reference to prayer coming in this first summary of the activities of the post-Easter followers of Jesus, it is reasonable to suppose that Luke saw constant prayer or devotion to the Jewish prayer times and places as particularly important in his portrayal of the corporate life of the early followers of Jesus. In that these prayer times – including before and after meals – were of the utmost value and significance in Jewish self-identification, along with what we have noted about what he says in relation to the temple, this has the effect of portraying the eleven (and the other followers of Jesus) not only as devout and faithful people of God but also, in particular, as maintaining Jewish ways of worship.

§9.3 Prayer and community meetings – Acts 1:15–26

The story following that of the gathering in the upper room is of a meeting that focuses on the election of Matthias (Acts 1:15–26). We have already noted that the number of one hundred and twenty present (1:15) suggests that Luke probably understood it at least as a synagogue-type meeting if not as the followers of Jesus having their own synagogue. This is confirmed when we note the parallels with the synagogue meetings described by Josephus (*Life* 276–303) – the leader of the community (Peter) taking charge,[10] the opportunity for the community to participate in the meeting, and the meeting dealing with issues of appointing leadership. Although, in Acts, this is a business meeting, not intended for worship, Luke says that prayer was involved for the election of Matthias. Josephus also describes prayer as involved in a synagogue meeting in that it began with 'formalities [or readings] and prayers' (*Life* 295). In other words, Luke describes a community or synagogue-type meeting in which an aspect of worship (i.e. prayer) plays a part.

Already it seems that Luke's descriptions of Christian gatherings are informed by what would have taken place in the synagogues. Therefore, it is reasonable to extrapolate that he would have understood Christian meetings to involve reading the Torah and the prophets, exposition of the readings, singing, praying, public fasts, all under the direction of the leaders.[11] However, we should not suppose that mundane matters were excluded. At least from our perspective, Luke himself has the sacred and secular involved in

---

[9] Acts 1:14; see also 2:42; 6:4; cf. 2:46.
[10] See Josephus, *Life* 66, 67, 134, 294, 271.
[11] See 2 Macc. 8:27; 4Q504 1–2.7.4; CD 20.10, 13; Philo, *Embassy* 156; *Good Person* 81–82; *Contempl. Life* 28–29; *Hypoth.* 7.13; *LAB* 11.8; Josephus, *Life* 277, 280, 295.

Christian meetings, as in the story of the election of Matthias (cf. Josephus, *Life* 280, 295).

§9.4 Pentecost – Acts 2:1–4

An obvious conclusion to draw from Luke saying, 'When the day of Pentecost had come, they were all together in one place' (Acts 2:1) is that Luke is depicting the followers of Jesus gathering like other groups of Jews, such as the Essenes (cf. 1QS 2.19–25), to celebrate the annual day-long feast of Weeks or Pentecost.[12] In this particular case, so far as the Dead Sea Scrolls can be expected to reflect what was understood to take place in the celebrations – not only among those living at Qumran but also for those in the towns and cities (cf. CD 7.6–9) – the followers of Jesus would have been involved in saying 'Amen' to their leaders reciting the loving kindness of God. They would also be confessing sin, asking God to give wisdom and knowledge, for example, and to be merciful to those gathered. Although the gathered worship of the Essenes involved cursing their enemies (1QS 1.16–2.25), Luke is unlikely to think this fitting of Christians, for his portrait of the Christians' response to their enemies is one of tolerance (e.g. Acts 4:29–30).

We should not suppose that all the prayers would have been written or memorized (cf. Josephus, *J.W.* 2.128). At least some Jews encouraged considerable free expression in prayer (cf. *m. Ber.* 4.4; *'Abot* 2.13), particularly in personal prayers.[13] In so far as this conjecture reflects what Luke had in mind, he is portraying the followers of Jesus involved in Jewish worship, celebrating the renewal of the covenant. In turn, the followers of Jesus are, once again, depicted as faithful Jews in their worship. Also, contributing to a pattern that we shall see Luke developing, we note that worship was thought to involve an encounter – in this case a dramatic encounter – with the Spirit of God.

§9.5 A summary of activity – Acts 2:42

A key passage in contributing to our understanding of Luke's view of worship among the followers of Jesus is Acts 2:42–47. In particular, verse 42 could be taken as describing the sequence of an early Christian service that involved the Eucharist: 'They devoted themselves to the apostles' teaching and fellowship, to the breaking of bread and the prayers.' However, at least from what we know from a slightly later period, we would not expect the prayers to follow the breaking of bread in such a service (cf. *Did.* 9–10). Also, in a list of singular items the plural 'the prayers' (*tais proseuchais*) is a puzzle. In any case, in his summaries, of which this passage is one, Luke is attempting to

---

[12] Lev. 23:15–21; Num. 28:26–31; Deut. 16:9. Cf. *Jub.* 6.17–31; Tobit 2:1; 2 Macc. 12:31–32; Josephus, *Ant.* 3.252; *J.W.* 1.253.
[13] Cf. Additions to Esther (C) 14:3–19; *1 En.* 84.5–6; and Josephus, *Ant.* 14.24.

depict the life of the early Christians in general rather than their worship (Acts 4:32–35; 5:12–16). Therefore, doubt is raised that Luke is attempting to describe the liturgy of a worship event. Notwithstanding, an examination of each item of Christian activity in this verse contributes to our understanding of Luke's view of worship.

The first item is 'the apostles' teaching'. For Luke, the apostles are the twelve appointed by Jesus (Luke 6:13–16), reconstituted after the loss of Judas (Acts 1:15–26), and expanded to include Paul and Barnabas (14:4, 14). We have already noted that Luke implies that the whole of his second volume continues the activity and teaching of Jesus (1:1; see Chapter 3 above). In turn, it is the apostles who are the characters in the narrative giving the clearest expression of that continuity. The apostles' role of providing this link between the life of Jesus and the life of the Church is seen early in Acts where Jesus' departure takes place 'after giving instructions through the Holy Spirit to the apostles whom he had chosen' (1:2), and then in their replicating Jesus' ministry of miracles and teaching.[14] The teaching role is seen as of particular importance in Acts 6:2–4 where the apostles determined to devote themselves 'to serving the word' (6:4) rather than tables.

Yet, in mentioning the apostles' teaching in the summary in Acts 2:42, Luke probably did not intend to convey the idea that the apostles were handing on a formal set of teaching or instructions, nor that this was taking place in a worship setting. For the apostles' proclamation generally is called teaching (cf. Acts 5:28), as is speaking or preaching to the proconsul, Sergius Paulus (13:12). In turn, while this activity could have taken place in the setting of a meeting, Luke does not give the impression that it was restricted to Christian gatherings (cf. 20:20).

The second item in the list of activities of the new members of the community is 'fellowship' (*koinōnia*, Acts 2:42). This is the only occasion Luke uses the word. Therefore, we have little information from him to determine its meaning. Looking at the use of *koinōnia* in the remainder of the New Testament it is used principally of a close relationship, association or sharing in common with others, something or someone, especially Christ.[15] Also, in the New Testament, on three (perhaps four) occasions *koinōnia* is used of sharing with, or contributing to, those in need.[16] If the former meaning of *koinōnia* – having to do with relationships – is intended in Acts 2:42 then Luke is probably conveying the idea that Christians met together for the benefit of close association. Alternatively, however, we should probably take Luke to be using *koinōnia* to denote Christians contributing to the material needs of each other, for when Luke uses the associated word, *koinos* ('common'), in this section,

---

[14] See, e.g. Acts 2:14, 22, 43; 3:12; 4:33; 5:12, 20, 25.
[15] 1 Cor. 1:9; 10:16; 2 Cor. 6:14; 13:13; Gal. 2:9; Phil. 1:5; 2:1; 3:10; Philem. 6; 1 John 1:3, 6, 7.
[16] Rom. 15:26; 2 Cor. 8:4; 9:13; see also Heb. 13:16. Cf. Aristotle, *Ethics* 8.9; Diogenes Laertius, *Lives* 10.11.

it refers to the sharing of material possessions (2:44; 4:32); and, notably, this is a major theme in the immediate context (2:45), as well as in his story of the Jerusalem church as a whole (4:32–5:11). As we just noted in relation to the apostles' teaching, Luke does not give the impression that this charitable activity was confined to the gatherings, though, with the possibility that synagogues were the focus of charitable work (see §5.2 above), and that he saw the synagogues as a venue for healing,[17] it is likely that Luke saw the Christian gatherings as involving distributing goods to the poor.

The third element of Acts 2:42 is 'the breaking of bread'. To what does this refer? In a potentially liturgical setting, we need to ask if Luke intended it to refer to the celebration of the Last Supper. Compared with Paul's description of such a meal (1 Cor. 11:23–26), in Acts wine is not mentioned,[18] nor is there mention of any so-called 'words of institution', nor does there seem to be any reflection on the theological significance of the meals as in Paul's comments (10:15–22; 11:23–34). In order to explain these differences it could be that there were two different religious meals celebrated by the early Christians. One – reflected in Acts – was the joyful love feasts that continued the tradition of the post-resurrection meals of Jesus and his followers. The other meal – reflected in Paul's writings – was a rehearsal of the Passover meal held by Jesus and his disciples in the upper room before the crucifixion. However, such theories are unnecessary and do not take sufficiently into account the background of the term 'breaking bread'.

Even though Luke just possibly uses the term 'breaking bread' for a meal (cf. Acts 20:7), and by early in the second century Christians were using it to refer to the whole meal (Ign., *Eph.* 20.2; cf. *Did.* 14.1), in a Jewish setting the term referred only to the act of breaking bread and the accompanying blessing at the beginning of a meal (cf. *b. Ber.* 46a; *Shabb.* 117b). Notably, in his three other uses of the term, Luke has preserved this distinction. In his Acts 2:43–47 cameo of the Jerusalem church that immediately follows the verse which we are examining (2:42) the distinction is possible in his saying, 'they broke bread at home and ate their food with glad and generous hearts' (2:46). In any case, the distinction is obvious in Acts 27:35–36. During the storm at sea Paul urges those on board to eat. 'After he had said this, he took bread; and giving thanks to God in the presence of all, he broke it and began to eat. Then all of them were encouraged and took food for themselves.' Similarly, in the story of Paul's farewell visit to Troas, Luke says, 'Then Paul went upstairs, and after he had broken bread and eaten, he continued to converse with them until dawn' (20:11). Although in these three cases the breaking of bread is arguably distinct from eating the meal proper, in no case does it appear that a celebration of the Last Supper is in mind. This is particularly obvious in

---

[17] See Luke 4:31–37; 6:6–11; 13:10–17.

[18] It is notable that the Western text (e.g. Codex Bezae) does not have Luke 22:19b–20: 'which is given for you. And he did the same with the cup after supper, saying, "This cup that is poured out for you is the new covenant in my blood"'. Cf. 1 Cor. 10:16; *Did.* 9.2–3.

27:35–36, where non-Christians are part of the ensuing meal. This conclusion is not overturned by an examination of what Luke says in his Gospel.

In the Emmaus story Jesus is said to be recognized when 'he took bread, blessed and broke it, and gave it to them' (Luke 24:30). The previous time Luke portrays Jesus breaking bread is in the story of the Last Supper (22:19). The most natural explanation is that the way Jesus is assumed to interpret the breaking of the bread in the Emmaus story caused his followers to recall the Last Supper. However, Cleopas and his companion were not at the Last Supper (see 22:14). Therefore, it is more likely that Luke intends to give the impression that Jesus' habit of breaking bread and praying at the beginning of a meal was generally recognizable; and he has given an earlier example in the story of the feeding of the five thousand (9:16).

Therefore, it seems right to conclude that, by the term 'breaking bread', Luke is referring not to the Last Supper but to the Jewish act, including prayers, that began, yet was distinct from, the meal proper. From Luke's perspective, therefore, every meal in which the followers of Jesus participated after Easter was now a joyous recollection of meals they shared before Easter.

The fourth item in the list of early Church activities in Acts 2:42 is 'the prayers'. Grammatically, the two items, 'the breaking of bread and the prayers', are tied together and slightly separated from the two preceeding items. Given that the Jewish act of breaking bread involved a blessing (*b. Ber.* 46b), it is possible that the reference to prayer here refers to the blessing associated with the breaking of bread. However, in other places Luke does not identify the breaking of bread in this way. More notably, the term, 'the prayers' (*tais proseuchais*, plural with the article), is similar to the reference to prayer in Acts 1:14 (*tē proseuchē*, singular with the article), which we have argued is a reference to the followers of Jesus being faithful to the appointed times of Jewish prayer. That Luke is generally intent on portraying the followers of Jesus as devoted to the Jewish prayer times is confirmed not only when we take into account the reference to Peter and John 'going up to the temple at the hour of prayer, the ninth', to be part of the worshipping crowd[19] but also when we note the mention of the twelve as devoting themselves to prayer (*tē proseuchē*, Acts 6:4). Therefore, those who have joined the group are portrayed here in this summary (2:42) as taking up the same devotion to Jewish prayers as the eleven and the other followers of Jesus mentioned in Acts 1:14.

The end result of our discussion of the list of items in Acts 2:42 is that it is neither a liturgy nor even, in itself, a list of aspects or items of worship. Nevertheless, the list still sheds light on Luke's view of worship. The verse corroborates what we can assume from Luke seeing the synagogue as a model for early Christian meetings. That is, although not confined to them, the apostles' teaching was seen to be part of the meetings. Also, in that

---

[19] Acts 3:1; cf. 2:46; 5:12.

synagogues were considered an important place for catering for the needs of the poor, and that fellowship or sharing of material possessions is mentioned here, it is reasonable to suppose that Luke took meetings to involve distributing goods to the poor. However, surprisingly, and perhaps disturbingly for some, we have not seen evidence here that Luke thought a celebration of the Last Supper was part of worship. From what Luke says about 'breaking bread' it would seem that every meal would be a reminder of both the meals the disciples shared with Jesus throughout their time together as well as the final time they ate together.

§9.6 A summary – Acts 2:43–47

In pursuing our interest in Luke's view of worship, we have already seen that this summary of activities in the Jerusalem church that follows Acts 2:42 expresses Luke's interest in daily temple attendance and the breaking of bread, the latter probably as a reminder of the joyous meals shared with Jesus before Easter. There are two further aspects of this summary to note. First is the mention of 'praising God' (2:47) for, initially, it could be taken to refer to worship. However, on closer examination of his other uses of the idea of praising God,[20] we see that Luke is more likely to be describing the general characteristics of the followers of Jesus than their meetings. This perspective makes most sense of the comment 'having the good will of all the people' attached to mention of praising God (2:47), for the character of the people rather than their meetings are likely to be thought to engender good will.

Second to be noted is that, here, at the end of the story of Pentecost, Luke says that 'daily' (*kath' hēmeran*) they were 'at home' (*kat' oikon*, Acts 2:46). In this phrase, *kat' oikon*, Luke is unlikely to mean that all the Christians – just said to be over three thousand (2:41; cf. 1:15) – met daily in the same house in Jerusalem, but that they met in separate homes.[21] The other similar reference to meeting in homes says, 'And every day in the temple and at home (*kat' oikon*) they did not cease teaching and preaching Jesus as the Christ' (5:42). Not only does this reinforce the importance of the temple as a place of Christian meeting and activity, homes are established as the other focal point of Christian communal activity.[22] Later in Acts, when mentioning the Christians meeting in Jerusalem, Luke says that they had gathered to pray in the home of Mary, the mother of John Mark (12:12, cf. 25). Thus, for Luke, while any or all the homes of the followers of Jesus were meeting places, this home may have been thought by him to be a focal point of the church in Jerusalem.

---

[20] Luke 19:37; Acts 2:47; 3:8, 9.

[21] Although the article is not required in a prepositional phrase, to indicate a single house Luke is more likely to have written *kata ton oikon*. Also, in having *kat' oikous* ('in houses'), Codex Bezae has taken the Christians to be meeting in a number of homes.

[22] Acts 2:2, 46; 5:42; 8:3; 20:20; cf. 16:15.

§9.7 A prayer meeting – Acts 4:23–31

Evidence that Luke saw prayer as an important part of the meetings of the followers of Jesus comes at the end of the story of Peter and John's release from prison. Those hearing their report 'raised their voices together to God' (Acts 4:24). There follows the longest prayer text in Acts.[23] The prayer opens with 'Sovereign Lord' (*despota*). As this is a term found in liturgical settings at the end of the century[24] and as the prayer is based on a *pesher* (Aramaic, 'interpretation') of Psalm 22:1–2, in a style similar to that found in Qumran (cf. 4Q171, 173), it is reasonable to suppose that Luke is reflecting a liturgical prayer or style of prayer known to him.

What is also notable in relation to our interest in Luke's view of Christian worship is that he finishes the story by saying that, 'When they had prayed, the place in which they were gathered together was shaken; and they were all filled with the Holy Spirit and spoke the word of God with boldness' (Luke 4:31). In that the prayer included a request 'to speak your word with all boldness' (4:29), Luke would invariably intend the answer that is given in this verse to refer not to bold preaching in the meeting but to a more general boldness in their witness. Also, the grammatical tense of the answer – 'they spoke (*elaloun*, imperfect) the word' – also implies a protracted activity (4:31).

Equally interesting for what Luke thought happened at a meeting of followers of Jesus is the idea of a place shaking in response to the presence of God (Acts 4:31). In the call story of Isaiah the pivots on the thresholds of the temple are said to shake, not at the voice or presence of God but at the voices of the heavenly beings calling out in worship to God (Isa. 6:4). Nearer to the time of Luke, in 2 Esdras 6:14 there is the warning that on hearing a heavenly voice the ground may shake and then, 'While he spoke to me, little by little the place where I was standing began to rock to and fro.'[25] From this we are bound to conclude that Luke thought that a meeting of followers of Jesus could, as in the story of Pentecost (cf. Acts 2:2–3), involve an experience of God that could be described in terms of a tangible presence.

§9.8 Outside Jerusalem

That Luke considers that the Christians outside Jerusalem were part of the life of the local synagogues is shown by the way he depicts the Christians at Damascus as active members of the synagogue, for the synagogue is where Paul is supposed to be able to find followers of Jesus (see ch. 5, n. 10).

---

[23] Acts 4:24–30; cf. 1:24–25; 7:59–60.
[24] Cf. e.g. *Did.* 10.3; *1 Clem.* 59.4; 60.3; 61:1, 2.
[25] 2 Esd. 6:29; cf. Virgil, *Aeneid* 3.88–91; Ovid, *Metamorphoses* 9.782–84; 15.669–72. Also, see Exod. (Hebrew text) 19:18.

From what we know about synagogues we can deduce something of what Luke would have considered to be the worship life of the early Christians. Some synagogues, such as the synagogues of the Freedmen (Acts 6:9) and the Theodotian synagogue in Jerusalem, as well as those of the Essenes scattered across Palestine – particularly those maintaining celibacy (cf. Josephus, *J.W.* 2.160–61), were only semi-public and only of limited general appeal. However, the public synagogues that were centrally located and sometimes the only large building in a town – which were seen by all as the focus of the life of the Jewish community[26] – attracted involvement from across the Jewish community, including those who became followers of Jesus.

Given that, in the ancient world, it was not possible to distinguish religious and social spheres of life, we can expect these functions to coexist in the synagogue. Indeed, we have seen this in Luke describing synagogue-type meetings that involve both religious and non-religious aspects. Nevertheless, in so far as our limited evidence permits us to conclude, it is likely that public synagogues were used primarily for community activities, including on the Sabbath, for fasts, communal meals and political and council meetings, at which, probably, anyone could speak (see §5.2 above).

The religious aspects of a synagogue meeting – limited to the reading of the Torah and the prophets and their interpretation, and also worship or prayers (said or sung) – may have dominated the Sabbath meetings.[27] However, the description Josephus gives of a weekday meeting, beginning with 'formalities [or readings] and prayers' (Josephus, *Life* 295, see above), both confirms the relatively limited liturgy as well as the overlap of the religious and the communal aspects of the use of a synagogue.

From this we can suppose that it is likely that Luke thought that the early Christians not only met in homes (see above) but also joined in the meetings and worship aspects of the local synagogues, including taking opportunities to speak publicly about Jesus. For example, Luke says that having been converted on the way to Damascus, Saul does not arrest the Christians in the synagogues but, 'in the synagogues immediately he proclaimed Jesus, saying, "He is the Son of God"' (Acts 9:20). The first activity reported of the newly commissioned missionaries from Antioch is to proclaim the word of God in the synagogues of the Jews in Cyprus (13:1–6). In Pisidian Antioch, after the reading of the law and the prophets, Paul is invited to speak (13:14–16). As the Christians are leaving they are begged to return on the next Sabbath. Luke says that on the next Sabbath almost the whole city gathered to hear the word of God (13:42–44)! Then, on other occasions, the Christians are depicted as using the synagogues as a forum to speak about Jesus.[28]

---

[26] Cf. Philo, *Embassy* 132–35; Josephus, *Ant.* 19.299–310; *J.W.* 2.289.

[27] Cf. the Theodotus inscription (*CIJ* II 1404); Luke 4:16–17; Acts 13:14–15; 15:21.

[28] Acts 14:1; 17:1–2, 10, 17; 18:4, 19, 26; 19:8; 24:12.

§9.9 A leaders' meeting? – Acts 13:1–3

In Acts 13:2 it is said that while the prophets and teachers at Antioch 'were worshiping (*leitourgountōn*) the Lord and fasting, the Holy Spirit said, "Set apart for me Barnabas and Saul"'. It is not immediately obvious precisely what Luke means by the verb 'worship' (*leitourgeō*). Only twenty or thirty years later, also possibly in relation to Antioch, the Didachist describes the work or ministry (*leiturgeō*) of the bishops and deacons as the ministry (*leiturgia*) of the prophets and teachers (*Did.* 15.1).[29] While this is a general description of the work of key figures, in Acts, Luke's narrative reads most naturally as a meeting of five prophets and teachers. There is no mention of the wider group of Christians, nor is there any need to presuppose their presence, for we know from Josephus that leaders of a community could meet alone in a synagogue setting (cf. *Life* 300).

If we take into account the next verse (Acts 13:3; cf. Luke 2:37), where Luke says that the commissioning of Barnabas and Saul involved 'fasting and praying', we might conclude that he thought worship denoted prayer. For here fasting is linked with prayer as fasting has just been linked with worship so that prayer and worship could be taken as synonymous. However, in the commissioning of Barnabas and Saul Luke is probably not describing the same worship and fasting scene of the previous verse. Rather, not only does the nature of the narrative itself suggest that a lapse of time is to be assumed between the two individuals being identified by the Holy Spirit and being sent out, but also the use of *tote* ('then') – which suggests a sequence of events[30] – implies at least a subsequent scene in the narrative. Further suggesting that Luke intended to describe a separate scene in the phrase 'prayer and fasting' is his use later of the phrase as a key element in the commissioning of leaders in 14:23.

In understanding what Luke meant by 'worship' we can note that, in the Greco-Roman world, the *leitourgeō* family of words was used not only for political or general service to people[31] but also for cultic activity, including that concerning the Jerusalem temple.[32] In the Greek Old Testament the word was used primarily for the service of the priests and Levites in the temple.[33] But these last uses are of only indirect help here. More helpful, and from the

---

[29] That the *Didache* may come from Antioch is suggested by the mention of cereal crops growing on hills (*Did.* 9.4), the lack of running water (7.2), the relative wealth of the community (13), the number of visitors (11) and Christians coming in to join the community (12), along with the Jewish elements (1–6), and a concern for the needs of Gentiles (6:2–3; 7; 9:5).

[30] In Acts 1:12; 4:8; 5:26; 6:11; 7:4; 8:17; 10:46, 48; 13:3, 12; 15:22; 17:14; 21:13, 26, 33; 23:3; 25:12; 26:1; 27:21, 32; 28:1.

[31] E.g. Xenophon, *Memorabilia* 2.7.6; Josephus, *J.W.* 1.488; cf. Rom. 15:27; *P. Oxyrhynchus* 1413.17.

[32] E.g. Josephus, *J.W.* 2.321, 409; 5.231; 13.55; 20.218.

[33] E.g. Exod. 28:35; Num. 8:22; 2 Chr. 5:14; 13:10; 35:3; Joel 1:13; 2:17; Judith 4:14; cf. Luke 1:23. See also Philo, *Worse* 63; 66; *Drunkenness* 2; *Flight* 93; *Moses* 2.152; *Spec. Laws* 1.82, 113, 242.

same period as Luke, is Philo who can use the word metaphorically in saying that the mind is able to minister to God.[34] Also, from the same period, the writer of the Wisdom of Solomon uses *leiturgia* to mean, or at least include, prayer and incense unrelated to the temple (Wisd. 18:21). In this we see the term worship being used where, in referring to a mental attitude and activities such as prayers, the functions associated with the temple are carried out in other places and in other ways. Indeed, the second century (CE) translation by Theodotion of Ephesus of Daniel 7:10 uses *leitourgeō* for the angels worshipping God.

Thus, although Luke's use of the word 'worship' in Acts 13:2 could be taken to mean prayer, it probably includes the sense of speaking to or praising or worshipping God rather than simply, if at all, petitioning God. We have no evidence to say more – for example, that Luke had in mind a celebration of the Last Supper. Indeed, not only does the mention of a fast most likely exclude this, but it also adds to our understanding of what Luke probably had in mind using the word 'worship'.

In the ancient world, fasting was associated with vows (e.g. Tobit 7:12), grief (e.g. 1 Sam. 31:13; 2 Sam. 1:11–12), remorse,[35] and was an expression of virtue[36] and intensity of prayer (e.g. 2 Sam. 12:15–16) and was expected to repel evil spirits.[37] Fasting was also undertaken to facilitate a relationship with the divine, so that abstention was thought to increase receptivity to revelations.[38] For example, fasting was part of the preparation for those sleeping in a temple to receive oracles.[39] Notably, in the Old Testament, Daniel is described as fasting in preparation for his encounters with God in visions[40] and Moses is said to fast during his time with, and while receiving the commandments from, the Lord (Exod. 34:28; Deut. 9:9). Since we have seen that Luke understood worship to involve an encounter with God, it should not surprise us that he describes fasting as part of worship.

In short, from what we can glean from Acts 13:1–3, Luke is probably describing two meetings of prophets and teachers, perhaps the leaders of the church at Antioch. In the first meeting it was a fast that involved prayers of worship. During the initial gathering that Luke describes, the Holy Spirit was understood to call for two of their number to be sent off on mission. How this is communicated to the group is not said. In view of examples of the Spirit speaking directly to a person, as in Acts 8:29 concerning Philip joining the eunuch's chariot, Luke probably thought that the Spirit spoke to one of the

---

[34] Philo, *The Heir* 84: *ho gar nous . . . leitourgei theō* ('For the mind . . . ministering to God').

[35] E.g. 1 Kgs 21:27; Neh. 9:1–2; *Pss. Sol.* 3.8; *4 Ezra* 10.4; *As. Mos.* 9.5–7.

[36] E.g. Ezra 8:21; Ps. 69:10; *Testament of Joseph* 3.4–5; 4.8; 10.1; cf. Philo, *Spec. Laws* 2.197.

[37] Plutarch, *Is. Os.* 361; *Obs.* 417c; *Pseudo-Clementine Homilies* 9, 10.

[38] E.g. Cicero, *Div.* 1.51.115; Iamblicus, *The Mysteries*, III.11. Cf. 2 Chr. 20:1–4; Tertullian, *On the Soul* 48.

[39] Cf. Strabo, *Geography* 14.1.44; Philostratus, *Life of Apollonius* 2.37.

[40] Dan. 9:3; 10:2–3, 12.

five present (see also Acts 10:19; 16:6–7). In relation to our interest in Luke's view of worship we need to note that he thought that worship could involve a tangible or anthropomorphic encounter with the Spirit. A subsequent meeting involved fasting and prayer in relation to the commissioning of Barnabas and Saul. This emerging picture is congruent with what Josephus tells us about a series of synagogue meetings in Tiberias, at least one of which was called as part of a public fast (*Life* 290). Josephus gives the impression that the meetings began with some formalities or readings and prayers that might have been carried out silently and privately (*Life* 295; see also Philo, *Contempl. Life* 27).

§9.10 Sunday worship? – Acts 20:7–13

A question that arises from being part of the Church in the twenty-first century is, does Luke portray the Church as meeting on Sundays for worship? On the one hand, Jews met together in synagogues or in homes on the Sabbath,[41] and some Christians continued to observe Jewish laws.[42] On the other hand, Paul's suggesting that the Corinthians put aside money on the first day of the week for him to collect may imply that some early Christians were meeting on Sundays.[43]

The story in which Eutychus is taken away alive after having fallen from the third storey and been taken up as dead, could be set within a Sunday worship event. We have already had cause to mention Acts 20:7 in connection with the breaking of bread (§9.5). Here we can enquire what further light this verse may shed on Luke's view of worship. It cannot be concluded that the meeting (probably of believers, cf. Acts 20:2) said to take place on 'the first day of the week' is, for Luke, a distinctive Sunday worship event, for this is the only time Luke mentions this phrase and it seems to have no particular significance. We have already arrived at the conclusion that Luke is not intending to depict a Eucharistic service. In turn, he is not attempting to depict Paul first preaching and then the Christians (alone) celebrating the Eucharist after the restored Eutychus and others had left. Rather, there is no particular liturgical significance to anything in this story; Luke is simply telling a story of an evening gathering at the end of a seven-day stay in Troas in which Paul was involved in discussing (*dialegomai*, 20:7, 9) or conversing (*homileteō*, 20:11) rather than preaching. In short, Luke seems to have no particular interest in the followers of Jesus meeting on Sunday, the first day of the week.

---

[41] See, e.g. 4Q400–407; 4Q503; 4Q504 1–2.7.4; 11Q17; *LAB.* 11.8; Philo, *Good Person* 81–82; *Embassy* 156.

[42] See Justin, *Dial.* 47; Irenaeus, *Haer.* 7.26.2; Epiphanius, *Refutation of all Heresies* 29.7.

[43] 1 Cor. 16:1–3; cf. Rev. 1:10; *Barn.* 15.

§9.11 Conclusion

Our task has not been to reconstruct the worship life of the historical early Christian community or communities that may be reflected in Luke's writings. Rather, our task has been to read off from his text some of the key features of Luke's view of worship: what is worship, what should take place in a worship meeting and what part the Eucharist or Lord's Supper should play in worship and the life of the Church?

The strongest impression Luke has left on his readers is that he does not consider that the followers of Jesus were, at least initially, isolated from the worship life of the (other) Jews. Rather, in his narrative, the followers of Jesus were faithful and thoroughly committed Jews in their prayer habits, in worshipping as devout Jews and, in so far as they were able, in being part of the twice-daily Tamid services in the temple. So important is the temple to Luke that he has it remain a focal point of worship even for Paul the traveller.

Moreover, Luke's promotion of the faithfulness of Christians to Jewish worship is also seen in his portrayal of Christian meetings as synagogue-like. In particular, from the way Luke describes a gathering of Christians in an upper room as a synagogue-type meeting (Acts 1:15–26), it is clear that Luke considered the Christians were also worshipping as part of their own functioning synagogue or, subsequently, had a number of synagogues in Jerusalem in homes and, further abroad, in both homes and in the public synagogues. Thus, Luke sees Christian worship not simply as taking its rise from Jewish traditions but as continuing to remain faithful to Jewish ways. This is true not only in Jerusalem but also for Christians further afield, reminding the readers that they are the true Israel.

In the story of Pentecost, Luke gives us his only example of Christians meeting for the express purpose of worship. Though we have no direct evidence, so far as Luke gives the impression they were Jews meeting to celebrate the Feast of Weeks, he probably intended to convey the view that those gathered would be saying 'Amen!' to the recitation of God's love, confessing their sins and asking God for wisdom, knowledge and mercy.

Otherwise, Luke portrays distinctively religious activities as only a part of the reason for meetings that could have been called to resolve leadership or charity issues, to hear reports of activities, distribute aid to the poor, eat together, plan for mission work or commission missionaries. From the little we know of synagogue meetings we can suppose that on the festivals or the Sabbath religious aspects dominated: the reading from the Torah and prophets and their interpretation – which almost certainly would have involved a particularly Christian interpretation (cf. Acts 8:30–35) – as well as worship or prayers (memorized or extemporary) that were said or sung. Healing and fasting may also have taken place (cf. 13:2).

In that, on more than one occasion, Luke depicts a worship event as involving what could be described as dramatic encounters with God in which he was experienced as tangibly present, this is clearly an important aspect of Luke's understanding of worship in which God was thought either to fill them with his Spirit or to give them direction.

The most striking result of this discussion of Luke's view of worship is that he does not portray the Christians as celebrating the Last Supper. Instead, through the rubric of 'breaking bread' and his description of their meals (Acts 2:47), he depicts them as joyously remembering all the meals shared with Jesus before Easter. We have no evidence in Luke's writings, therefore, to support the view that he saw the Eucharist as an instrument of invisible grace or that the Church gathered around the sacrament or that the Church actualizes itself in the sacrament. However, we will see that the Church embodies Jesus and serves God in its mission of universal salvation, so Luke would probably assent to the idea that the Church itself is a sacrament.

Also, to say that, for Luke, the Church gathered around the word of God as an explanation of its origin and purpose is misleading. While the Church is depicted as giving attention to the word of the apostles, it is the call of Jesus that began and gathered the Church. Further, the idea of the Church gathering around the word also does not do justice to Luke at a practical level. Luke depicts the Church gathering around or having other focal points – worship, fasting, prayer, debate, listening to reports, for example; and although the handing on of the word by the apostles was important to Luke, he gave no impression that this was confined to meetings. The profound differences between how Luke saw the Church and how we may see it is carried further as we turn to discuss the place of Scripture in the Church.

10

Scripture and knowing God

It is the conviction of large sections of the contemporary Church that the Bible (and, for some, the Bible alone) is to be a source of knowledge of God and guidance for the Church and its members. It is the purpose of this and the next chapter to see how far this approach is reflected by Luke in his writings and, if the evidence demands it, suggest an approach to the Bible in relation to theology and faith that may be more attuned to the most prolific writer in the New Testament. In the next chapter we shall be discussing the place of experience in, what can broadly be termed, knowing God. Here we begin by exploring Luke's view of his Scriptures, particularly in Acts where we could anticipate his views to be most obvious on how he might expect his readers to relate to and use their Scripture. In the concluding discussion we will see that Luke's Gospel shows Jesus using Scripture in a way that becomes more obvious in Acts.

§10.1 Luke and Scripture

The importance early Christians placed on their Scriptures – generally the Septuagint – is almost everywhere evident in the New Testament. For example, depending on the distinction one makes between quotations and allusions, in fifty to sixty places in Romans Paul cites the Old Testament. Also, even if it could not be agreed that the book of Revelation explicitly quotes Scripture, it almost constantly echoes the Old Testament and has some clear allusions to it.[1] Luke cites the Septuagint or, sometimes, a similar text, around twenty-five times in his Gospel and about forty times in Acts. In addition, like his contemporaries, Luke not only alludes to Scriptures but also plunders its vocabulary and imitates its style.

Also like his contemporaries, Luke uses his Scriptures in a number of different ways. For example, Old Testament characters are portrayed as analogues for Jesus (e.g. Luke 9:54/2 Kgs 1:10–12) and texts are used as proof of the divine aspect of, or involvement in, an event;[2] other passages function as prophecy. The use of the Old Testament as prophecy involves Luke showing that Jesus fulfils Scripture (e.g. Luke 4:21) and that the salvation coming in Jesus had

---

[1] See Rev. 1:7 (Dan. 7:13 and Zech. 12:10); 2:26–27 (Ps. 2:8–9, LXX) 3:7 (Isa. 22:22); 3:19 (Prov. 3:12); 4:8 (Isa. 6:3); 6:16 (Hos. 10:8); 9:20 (Dan. 5:23); 10:6 (Exod. 20:11); 13:7 (Dan. 7:21); 14:7 (Exod. 20:11).

[2] E.g. Acts 2:14–21/Joel 2:28–32 (3:1–5 in the Hebrew text).

a universal reach (Luke 3:4−6/Isa. 40:3−5). The Old Testament is also used by Luke to show that not only is Jesus predicted by and part of the biblical story (Acts 4:11/Ps. 118:22) but so also is the universal mission of the Church. As we shall see, at the end of his Gospel Luke has Jesus say, 'it is written, that the Messiah is to suffer and to rise from the dead on the third day, and that repentance and forgiveness of sins is to be proclaimed in his name to all nations, beginning in Jerusalem' (Luke 24:46−47).

However, even though overlap can be expected, the focus of this part of our study is not on the function of Scripture in Luke's text (how he uses it in constructing his narrative) but on what role he thought what has come to be called the Old Testament had in the life of the Church, his readers. In other words, we are neither enquiring about the way Old Testament quotations advance his narrative, nor is it our aim to draw attention to how Luke considers the Old Testament to contribute to his Christology or even his ecclesiology. We are also not particularly interested in what Luke says concerning Jesus or the early Christian community through applying the Old Testament to them. Rather, we want to know how Luke expected his readers to relate to and use their Scriptures. That this is a reasonable question to put to the text of Acts, in particular, will become apparent as we proceed.

In our discussion we shall leave aside Luke's many allusions to the Old Testament. Not only would this require more space than is available here but also we cannot be sure of the significance of the allusions. Luke may be assuming that the ancient text is, or should be, part of the warp and weft of his readers' minds or it may be that we are only seeing that he readily expressed himself in the vocabulary and concepts of the Old Testament and did not require it of his audience. Therefore, to place our considerations on more certain ground we shall give our attention to the overt discussion of the Scriptures and the direct quotations from the Old Testament that are found in Acts − places where Luke uses whole phrases or sentences that can also be found in his Scriptures.

§10.2 Old Testament quotations

In the body of his Gospel, compared to Acts, Luke has relatively few quotations from the Old Testament.[3] Yet, the Gospel's introduction is permeated by Old Testament vocabulary as well as carrying allusions to and quotations of the ancient text.[4] Through this, readers are led to think that what is about to be related has its origin and explanation in the Old Testament, and that Jesus is inextricably and intimately tied to the people of God.[5] Then, in the conclusion of the Gospel, although no text is quoted, again the Old Testament provides the backdrop as well as subject matter of much of the narrative.[6]

---

[3] See Luke 7:22, 27; 8:10; 10:27; 13:35; 18:20; 19:38; 20:17, 28, 42–43.
[4] Notably, see Luke 1:46–55, 68–79; 2:14, 29–32; 3:4–6; 4:1–30.
[5] Luke 2:21–38, 41–52; 3:23–38.
[6] See Luke 24:21, 25–28, 32, 44–47.

This proximity of the ancient text to the surface of the narrative enables Luke to affirm the connection between the Scriptures and a number of aspects of Jesus: his identity (particularly his Jewishness, see ch. 5, n. 3) and his ministry,[7] his humanity,[8] his suffering as Messiah[9] and his resurrection.[10] Luke is also able to adumbrate the coming of the Spirit being foretold by Scripture ('the promise of the Father')[11] and to interpret the impending narrative of the mission of the Church to all the nations in terms of the Old Testament (Luke 24:47), an important factor to keep in mind as we turn to the quotations in Acts.

§10.2.1 Acts 1:16–20

In the story of the replacement of Judas, the speech Peter makes initiates the election of Matthias. He says, 'Friends, the scripture (*tēn graphēn*, singular) had to be (*dei*) fulfilled, which the Holy Spirit through David foretold concerning Judas' (Acts 1:16). 'Scripture' is probably not a reference to any particular passage (e.g. Ps. 41:9), including those which follow. Rather, being in the singular and with the citation of two passages, 'Scripture' probably refers to its predictive function in general.

After describing the fate of Judas, Peter says, 'For it has been written . . .' (Acts 1:20) and cites Psalm 69:25 (LXX, 68:26): 'Let his home become desolate, and let there be no one to live in it.' From this it would seem that, as well as having a predictive function, Luke is showing that he thinks that Scripture is to be used among the followers of Jesus to make sense of events in which God's hand is to be confirmed, despite their initially discouraging nature. Luke then cites Psalm 109:8, 'Let another take his position of overseer.' Luke uses this citation to justify the election of Matthias. In this Luke is portraying the followers of Jesus using Scripture as a guide or, perhaps, to justify their actions and only indirectly as a predictor of events.

§10.2.2 Acts 2:17–35

The Old Testament citations here are those threaded through Peter's Pentecost sermon. In this part of Luke's narrative he has a story of the followers of Jesus acting in such a way that, even though Luke's readers are told they are filled with the Holy Spirit (Acts 2:4), observers in the story say that they are under the influence of alcohol (2:13). In the ensuing speech by Peter Luke has him explain that they are not drunk. Instead, citing Joel 2:28–32, Peter says that what has happened is God pouring out his Spirit in the last days. In this way,

---

[7] See Luke 24:27, cf. 44; cf. e.g. 1:28–37, 46–55, 68–79; 2:29–32; 3:4; 4:17–19; 7:22; 20:17–18.
[8] Luke 2:6–12; 4:2, 16–23; 7:13; 10:21; 13:10–17, 34; 15:1–2; 18:15–17; 19:41, 45–46; 22:39–46; 23:46; 24:39.
[9] Luke 24:46; cf. 18:31–33; Acts 8:32–35; (Isa. 53:7–8). See also Luke 24:26; Acts 3:18; 17:3; 26:22.
[10] Luke 24:46. See also Luke 18:33 and below on Acts 2:17–35 and 13:33–37.
[11] Luke 24:49. See below on Acts 2:17–35.

what was unclear in the Old Testament is now made explicit (cf. Num. 11:29). Also, although Joel is taken to be predictive, Luke has Peter use the text to explain and make sense of what the followers of Jesus had already experienced and, it is reasonable to assume, readers have also experienced and need an explanation showing that it is of God.

Similarly, in the next quotation from the Old Testament Luke uses Psalm 16:8–11. Again, while having a predictive aspect, Luke's real interest in the Psalm is that he is able to use it to confirm God's involvement in Jesus' ministry, death and resurrection. For, having set out Jesus' life, he begins the quotation by saying, 'For David says concerning him . . .' (Acts 2:25). However, the next citation is clearly predictive. Luke says that since David was a prophet he knew that God would put one of his descendants on the throne.[12] Luke then cites Psalm 16:10 (LXX, 15:10) as foreseeing (*prooraō*) the resurrection.

The final Old Testament passage Luke uses in Peter's speech is Psalm 110:1 (LXX, 109:1), extensively cited by early Christians.[13] Luke's argument is that, as David remains dead, the Ascension talked about by him in the Psalm must be of the Messiah rather than himself (Acts 2:29, 31). Again, this is a predictive use of the text, though Luke is also showing how a puzzling text is elucidated by the subsequent events of Jesus' life.

§10.2.3 Acts 3:13–25

A proximate citation of Exodus 3:6 and 15 occurs in Peter's speech in Luke's narrative of Peter and John healing a lame man at the gate of the Jerusalem temple. Luke does not draw attention to the passage as a quotation; rather, Scripture provides Luke with vocabulary to describe the God of whom Jesus was the servant: 'The God of Abraham, the God of Isaac, and the God of Jacob, the God of our ancestors' (Acts 3:13). For this description to assume its full force in establishing the God of Jesus, Luke would have expected his readers to recognize its origin. In turn, we can suppose that Luke expected that the concepts and vocabulary of their Scriptures were active and working parts of the theological speculations of his readers.

§10.2.4 Acts 4:11

Once again Luke cites Psalm 118:22 (LXX 117:22; cf. Luke 20:17), as do others before and after him.[14] Again an Old Testament citation comes in a speech. Peter is explaining that it has been by the name of Jesus that the man by the Gate Beautiful has been healed. With some modifications, Luke cites

---

[12] Acts 2:30. See 2 Sam. 7:12–14; Ps. 132:11.

[13] In the NT see Matt. 22:44; 26:64; Mark 12:36; 14:62; 16:19; Luke 20:42–43; 22:69; Acts 2:34–35; 5:31; 7:55–56; Rom. 8:34; 1 Cor. 15:25; Eph. 1:20; 2:6; Col. 3:1; Heb. 1:3, 13; 8:1; 10:12–13; 12:2; 1 Pet. 3:22; Rev. 3:21; and also, e.g. *1 Clem.* 36.5–6; Pol. *Phil.* 2.1; *Barn.* 12.10; Justin, *Dial.* 32.2, 3, 6; 35.6; 56.14; 83:1, 2; 127.5; *1 Apol.* 40.7; 45.2; Tertullian, *Marc.* 3.7.5; 4.41:4; 5.9.6; 5.17.6; Irenaeus, *Haer.* 2.28.7; 3.6.1; 3.10.6; 3.12.2; 3.16.3; 4.33.11.

[14] See Mark 12:10–11/Matt. 21:42; 1 Pet. 2:4, 7; and, e.g. *Barn.* 6.4; Irenaeus, *Haer.* 3.12.4; 4.33.1; and Justin, *Dial.* 126.1.

the Psalm as being explained by the events associated with Jesus that he has just outlined: 'This is "the stone that was despised by you, the builders; it has become the cornerstone"' (Acts 4:11). Notably, it is probably Luke who changes the Septuagint's word 'rejected' or 'passed over' (*apodokimazō*) to 'despised' (*exoutheneō*).[15] The despising – what might be taken to have been done in ignorance – becomes an act of contempt, an understandable alteration in Luke's narrative concerning conflict between the followers of Jesus and religious authorities. The addition 'by you', also perhaps by Luke,[16] further sharpens the criticism of the 'builders', a term used at the time for religious leaders.[17] As with other citations, while this one is presumed to have a predictive function, the events Luke narrates are also taken to clarify the obscure in the text.

§10.2.5 Acts 4:24–26

Having described the first bout of persecution of the followers of Jesus, Luke's conclusion to the story of Peter and John in the temple (cf. Acts 3:1) is dominated by a prayer that draws attention to the themes of God's sovereignty and the boldness of the followers of Jesus. Again the scriptural quotations come in a speech, this time a prayer. Luke's quotation of Scripture (Ps. 2:1–2) is not so much for its predictive value (though it has that) as to help make sense of what had happened to Peter and John. That is, the antagonism of Herod, Pilate and the Gentiles is described in Scripture; even in the suffering God has been sovereign.

§10.2.6 Acts 7:2–53

The retelling of the biblical story in Stephen's speech, the longest speech in Acts, is peppered with allusions to and quotations from the Old Testament.[18]

---

[15] In the Gospels and Acts *exoutheneō* ('despise') occurs only at Luke 18:9; 23:11; Acts 4:11 (in the remainder of the NT, see also, Rom. 14:3, 10; 1 Cor. 1:28; 6:4; 16:11; 2 Cor. 10:10; Gal. 4:14; 1 Thess. 5:20). In both occurrences in his Gospel it is likely that Luke is responsible for the word; Luke 18:9 is a seam between two parables and 23:11 is from a trial scene that could have been created by Luke.

[16] That Luke, rather than his tradition, is responsible for changes to Scripture can be seen when he cites and changes Scripture from his Jesus tradition: Luke 7:22/Matt. 11:5 (where Luke drops two occurrences of *kai* ['and']); Luke 7:27/Matt. 11:10 (where he drops *egō* ['I']) Luke 8:10/Mark 4:12/Matt. 13:13 (where Luke has probably synthesized his two sources); Luke 9:35/Mark 9:7 (where he has exchanged *agapētos* ['beloved'] for *eklelegmenos* ['chosen']); Luke 10:15/Matt. 11:23 (where Luke has *tou* ['the'] before *hadou* ['Hades']); Luke 10:27/Mark 12:31/Matt. 22:39 (where Luke has probably composed this verse with his eye not only on Mark and Q but also on the order of material in Deut. 6:5); Luke 18:20/Mark 10:19 (where, again, Luke has an eye on Mark as well as the LXX [MS B; cf. Philo, *Decalogue* 51]); Luke 19:38/Mark 11:9 (Luke adds 'the king'); Luke 19:45/Mark 11:17 (Luke has dropped 'for all the nations'); Luke 20:28/Mark 12:19 (Luke smooths out Mark); Luke 22:69/Mark 14:62 (Luke's changes include dropping reference to Dan. 7:13 and making clear Mark's circumlocution for God); and Luke 23:34/Mark 15:24 (Luke recasts the verse).

[17] CD 4.12, 19; 1QpHab 10.5–13.

[18] Acts 7:3 (Gen. 12:1), 5 (Gen. 48:4), 6 (Gen. 15:3), 7 (Gen. 15:14; Exod. 3:12), 14 (Gen. 46:27), 18 (Exod. 1:8), 27–29 (Exod. 2:13–15), 32 (Exod. 3:6), 35 (Exod. 2:14); 7:33–34 (Exod. 3:5, 7, 8, 10), 37 (Deut. 18:15), 40 (Exod. 32:1), 42–43 (Amos 5:25–27), 49–50 (Isa. 66:1–2).

Luke is not the first (nor the last) to rehearse the biblical story or, more accurately, the story of God's people: *Jubilees*, Philo, Josephus and Pseudo-Philo all took their turn in recasting the biblical narrative for the benefit of their readers. In particular, by recasting the Old Testament, the *Genesis Apocryphon* and the *Damascus Document* (cf. CD 2.14–6.11) from Qumran helped the Essenes justify their claim that the biblical story reached its apotheosis in them.

In his turn, Luke retells the biblical story through Stephen's speech using particularly the characters of Abraham (Acts 7:2–8) and Joseph (7:9–16), though Moses dominates the passage (7:17–44) and Solomon appears briefly (7:47). Moses is not only a parallel or type of Jesus – both visit their people,[19] both are powerful in word and deed (Luke 24:19; Acts 7:22) and both are rejected[20] – but also, in Moses being rejected a second time, Luke is probably using him to show that the persecution of the followers of Jesus is a second rejection of God's messengers. For, in the climax of Stephen's speech the audience is accused of 'opposing' (*antipiptete*, present tense) not Jesus but the Holy Spirit (Acts 7:51, cf. 53).

Luke also depicts much of the mighty acts of the biblical story as taking place outside the land and apart from the temple (Acts 7:48–50). Therefore, he is able to justify the mission of the Church outside Judea, and prepare his readers for the narrative of the spread of the gospel beyond Jerusalem (8:1b–3).

Thus, the biblical story reaches its climax in focusing not only on the tragic rejection of Jesus (Acts 7:52) who is, in fact, now seated at the right hand of God (7:55–56) but also on his followers (7:51–53). With the use of the Old Testament, Luke has been able to uphold the legitimacy of the claim of the followers of Jesus that, despite profound opposition (from God's people!), they are God's glory or presence and prophets bringing salvation to his people – and the Gentiles. In short, for Luke, his readers are to find their story – including their Gentile mission – in the story of their Scriptures.

§10.2.7 Acts 8:32–33

Luke identifies Isaiah as the passage being read aloud by the Ethiopian.[21] Back at the end of his Gospel, through a statement of the risen Jesus – 'Oh, how foolish you are, and how slow of heart to believe all that the prophets have declared!' (24:25) – Luke recognized the difficulty Jesus' followers have in interpreting his rejection and suffering in terms of promised salvation in Scripture. Luke goes on to say that Jesus 'interpreted to them the things about himself in all the scriptures' (24:27, cf. 44–49). Here, in Acts, having the eunuch not able to understand the text unless someone guides him (8:31), Luke once more signals to his readers that the text does not self-evidently suggest salvation took place in the events reported of Jesus. Notably, having Philip explain

---

[19] Luke 1:68, 78; 7:16; Acts 7:23.

[20] Acts 7:25, 35, 39, 52.

[21] Acts 8:30; see 8:32–33; and Isa. 53:7–8. Although silent reading was practised in antiquity, audible reading appears to have been more common. See, e.g. Livy, *History* 6.25.9; Augustine, *Confessions* 6.3; *Pirke Aboth* 6.5.

what is, admittedly, an obscure Old Testament text in terms of the good news about Jesus (8:35), Luke establishes an interpretive reciprocity between Scripture and the Jesus events, each elucidating and explaining the other.

Moreover, although, after Philip's proclamation of the good news about Jesus, the eunuch was in a position to respond by asking for baptism (Acts 8:36), Luke implies for the reader that the good news of Jesus that found its beginning in Isaiah 53:7–8 also included Philip's – the Church's – application or proclamation of it. Thus, Luke establishes a reciprocity of understanding not only between the text and the events associated with Jesus but also between the text and the proclamation of the same. In other words, Luke would be expecting his readers to be able to see in the ancient writings not only God's salvation in the Jesus events but also their mission, and also that this mission brought clarity to otherwise unclear texts.

§10.2.8 Acts 13:16–52

In this sermon by Paul in the synagogue at Pisidian Antioch there are a number of citations of the Old Testament,[22] clear references to its characters (esp. Acts 13:17–22), as well as allusions to the text (13:29, 32). Not surprisingly, from what we have seen so far, the Scriptures are viewed as promises or prophecies that have been fulfilled, particularly in the resurrection of Jesus (13:32–35, 41). Once again, the Old Testament is used to provide the inalienable prehistory of the Jesus story in order to show that, in him, 'God has brought to Israel a Saviour' (13:23). However, yet again, there is the strong theme of the recognition that it is initially difficult to align the Old Testament with Christian claims about Jesus and what happened to him. This is most obvious in Paul saying, 'the residents of Jerusalem and their leaders did not recognize him or understand the words of the prophets' (13:26).

Given that a number of Luke's characters in Acts, including Paul, are modelled on Jesus, Luke is probably typical of ancient writers in wishing to employ biographical example as a pedagogical device.[23] In turn, we can expect that Luke would anticipate his readers seeing Paul's use of the Old Testament in the synagogue sermon as a model for their use. That is, in their debates with fellow Jews, Christians could be expected to find in their Scriptures the prehistory and promise of God's salvation in Jesus, as well as the raw material for their message about him. Also, because Paul's final use of a text (Acts 13:41/Hab. 1:5) is in the form of a warning to his hearers, Luke's readers might also be expected to find in the sacred text the vehicle for warning fellow Jews.

Luke says that 'the next Sabbath almost the whole city [of Pisidian Antioch] gathered to hear the word of the Lord' (Acts 13:44). But, rejection

---

22 Acts 13:22/Ps. 89:20; Acts 13:33/Ps. 2:7; Acts 13:34/Isa. 55:3; Acts 13:35/Ps. 16:10; Acts 13:41/Hab. 1:5; Acts 13:47/Isa. 49:6.

23 Heb. 11:4–40; 13:7; *1 Clem.* 9–12; 17–18; 55; Pol. *Phil.* 8–9; Isocrates, *To Demonicus* 9–12; Pliny, *Letters* 8.13; Plutarch, *Demetrius* 1.4–6; Seneca, *Letters* 6.5–7. See also the discussion and data cited in §1.3 above.

by the Jews caused Paul to say that he and his companions were now turning to the Gentiles, 'For so the Lord has commanded us' (13:47). He then
cites Isaiah 49:6, 'I have set you to be a light for the Gentiles, so that you
may bring salvation to the ends of the earth.' In having Paul say that the Lord
'has commanded us', Luke may have wished his readers to recall the beginning of Acts for, the only other time Luke uses *entellomai* (to give orders or
instructions) in Acts is in 1:2 where it is Jesus who does the instructing of
the apostles.[24] Perhaps, then, Luke intends his readers to elide the commands
of Jesus with what they find in Scripture. In any case, both Jesus and
Scripture command the mission to the Gentiles (cf. Acts 1:8). Further, assuming his readers noted that Isaiah 49:6 is also echoed in Luke 2:32, where it
is applied to Jesus, they are also, once again, likely to draw the conclusion
(from Scripture) that their mission to the Gentiles was a realization of Jesus'
mission to the Gentiles.

§10.2.9 Acts 15:13–21

Here in Luke's narrative, the apostles and elders at Jerusalem are meeting to
decide whether or not Gentiles need to be circumcised and keep the law to
become part of the Church. In the vision that heads the story of the inclusion of the Gentiles (Acts 10:9–16), Peter resists the unclean foods on the
basis of general allusions to the Old Testament (cf. Lev. 11:1–47; Deut.
14:3–20). He even alludes to the Old Testament in his protest (cf. Ezek.
4:13–14). However, at least as this point, Luke does not – he cannot – offer
any texts to counter Peter's particular views. Instead, God's voice is seen
to trump Peter's scriptural position; and the vision of God's intervention
becomes the interpretive key for God taking the initiative in including the
Gentiles in the people of God.

However, here in Acts 15, Luke is able to use Scripture in relation to the
more general problem of the inclusion of the Gentiles. Luke says that, after
much debate, Peter told the group that his going to the Gentiles and God
giving them the Holy Spirit 'just as he did to us' (Acts 15:8) meant that no
distinction was being made between Jews and Gentiles: 'all will be saved through
the grace of the Lord Jesus' (15:11). Then, on hearing a report from Barnabas
and Paul about the Gentiles becoming believers, Luke has James make a
summary speech quoting mainly Amos 9:11–12, but also citing phrases from
Jeremiah 12:15 and Isaiah 45:21.

It could be that Luke understood the rebuilding of the dwelling of David
(Acts 15:16/Amos 9:11) that James cites to refer to the conversion of Israel,
the Jews, as the necessary precursor to the influx of the Gentiles. This is
highly unlikely, for Luke has already adopted the view that the Gentile mission
had begun, not least on the basis of the Jews rejecting the word of God (Acts
13:46; cf. 28:28). More likely, as Christological considerations govern the use

---

[24] Luke otherwise uses *entellomai* only in Luke 4:10.

147

of many of Luke's quotations from the Old Testament,[25] the rebuilding of the dwelling of David refers not even to the Church or the disciples (that comes in the next verse) but to the coming of the Messiah, as the Qumran people had also understood Amos 9:11 (4Q174 1.11–13).

Thus, notably for us, the Old Testament quotations are introduced as agreeing with (*sumphōneō*, Acts 15:15) what has already been shown to Simon Peter in a vision (10:9–16, 28) and to Paul through Ananias (9:15–16), to have taken place in Caesarea (10:44–48) and other locations (14:1–28), and then detailed here in this report to the followers of Jesus in Jerusalem. That there are no texts used back in chapter 10 is not because Luke did not think the problem could be solved without reference to the text, but because it is not until chapter 15, where the texts are used, that the narrative brings the problem to a head and is finally addressed using Scripture.

The Old Testament is used to show that the inclusion of the Gentiles among the people of God, which has already taken place, is supported by Scripture. Luke is likely to assume, then, that in their questioning of the mission to, and the place of, the Gentiles among the followers of Jesus, the sacred writings of his readers would yield positive support. They are also most likely to conclude that experience of God's initiative is to be privileged over the text, at least as they have known that experience.

§10.2.10 Acts 23:5

Luke says that on hearing the order that he should be struck on the mouth during his defence before the Sanhedrin, Paul says to the high priest, 'God will strike you, you whitewashed wall' (Acts 23:3). Having been told he has insulted God's high priest (23:4), Paul says that he did not realize he was the high priest, 'for it is written, "You shall not speak evil of a leader of your people"' (23:5), quoting Exodus 22:28 (LXX 22:27) – 'leader' being changed to the singular to suit the occasion.

At the level of historicity, this scenario raises a string of questions: how could Paul not have known it was the high priest who had ordered him to be struck; was his eyesight poor, or, unknown to Paul, had there been a change of high priest; did he assume that under Roman law there was no functioning high priest; or, just perhaps, was there irony in Paul's excuse? We cannot be sure. In any case, what is important for us to note is that the citation of the Old Testament shows not only that Luke thought that Paul, his hero, was a law-abiding Jew but also, in particular, that Scripture could be used to

---

[25] Acts 2:25–28/Ps. 16:8–11; Acts 2:30/Ps. 132:11; Acts 2:31/Ps. 16:10; Acts 2:34–35/Ps. 110:1; Acts 3:13/Exod. 3:6, 15; Acts 3:22/Deut. 18:15–16; Acts 3:23/Deut. 18:19; Lev. 23:29; Acts 3:25/Gen. 22:18; 26:4; Acts 4:11/Ps. 118:22; Acts 4:24–26/Pss. 146:6; 2:1; Acts 7:37/Deut. 18:15; Acts 8:22–33/Isa. 53:7–8; Acts 13:22/Ps. 89:21/1 Sam. 13:14; Acts 13:33/Ps. 2:7; Acts 13:34/Isa. 55:3; Acts 13:35/Ps. 16:10; and Acts 15:16–17/Amos 9:11–12. This is not to deny that God often, though not always (cf. Acts 2:31; 8:32–33), is the subject of the quotations (see 2:17; 7:42–43, 49–50; 13:33, 34, 35, 41, 47; 15:16–17). Luke also has the Holy Spirit as the speaker in the Old Testament quotations (see 4:25; 28:25).

determine behaviour. Paul is a model for his readers, so we can take it that Luke would expect the Church to use the Old Testament to determine behaviour.

§10.2.11 Acts 28:26–27

At the close of his second volume Luke portrays Paul under house arrest in Rome, visited by great numbers of Jews (Acts 28:24). Luke says Paul testified to the kingdom of God and tried to convince his visitors about Jesus from the Law and the Prophets. In response to the disbelief of some, Paul says that the Holy Spirit was right, and cites Isaiah 6:9–10 about people listening and not understanding, and looking but not perceiving (cf. Matt. 13:14–15).

Like others before him,[26] as well as after,[27] Luke found this passage useful in helping his readers interpret not only the lack of understanding that Jesus faced (Luke 8:10) but also their own rejection by Jews: failure to respond to God's messenger was inherent in the message itself. In the global structure of Luke's two-volume work, standing in its conclusion, this passage, notably, from Isaiah's call to mission, provides the readers with the rationale not only for their lack of success with Jews but also, in particular, the impetus for the Gentile mission. Indeed, readers are likely to pick up the parallel between this passage, their own inherent call to Gentile mission, and that of Paul's in 9:15, beginning with 'Go . . .' (to the Gentiles).[28] Moreover, Luke goes on immediately in the final sentence of Acts to portray Paul welcoming 'all who came to him' (Acts 28:30), presumably the Gentiles (cf. 28:28).

In the narrative structure of this particular story, once again there is an admission by Luke that it is not immediately obvious that the message of the Church about Jesus and the kingdom of God is found in the Old Testament (also see above on Acts 8:32). Once again, in that Paul, the hero of the latter half of Luke's second volume, is probably to be emulated by the readers (see §3.2.3 above), it is reasonable to suppose that Luke assumed his readers would, with his help, find in the Old Testament the rationale for Jewish opposition as well as the motivation for the Gentile mission. Just as Jesus and then Paul were rejected by the Jews, and the message taken to the Gentiles, so the readers can be assumed to understand their own experience of rejection and then impulse for the Gentile mission with its inevitable success. In turn, Luke can expect his readers to see that their mission is a continuation of the stories of the Old Testament prophets and of Jesus. In this portrait of Paul they, further, can see the justification for leaving the Jews for a Gentile mission (28:26–28).

§10.3 Discussion and conclusions

Although there may be many other matters of interest arising from Luke's use of the Old Testament, here we have confined ourselves to answering the

---

[26] Mark 4:12; Rom. 11:8; cf. Matt. 14—15.
[27] John 12:40; and, e.g. Justin, *Dial.* 12.2; 33.1; 69.4; Tertullian, *Apol.* 21.17; *Marc.* 3.6.5, 6; 4.19.2; 4.31.4; 5.11.9; *To the Heathen* 2.1.3; *On the Resurrection* 33.2.
[28] *Poreuou* in Acts 9:15 and *poreuthēti* in 28:26.

question, how did Luke expect his readers to relate to and use their Scriptures? Being less certain how readers could be expected to respond to his echoing the Old Testament, we have given attention only to Luke's overt discussion of the Scriptures and his direct quotations in his second volume where, with a post-Easter setting, like his readers, we could expect more obvious answers to our questions.

To begin with, from what we have seen, Luke was deeply familiar with his Scriptures and is likely to have expected the concepts and vocabulary of the Old Testament to be an active part of his readers' intellectual creativity. Over against later and ongoing tendencies and temptations in the Church to dispense with the Old Testament,[29] Luke maintains that the Scriptures are of continuing relevance for Christians.

However, he would not have anticipated his readers finding the ancient texts self-evidently reflecting either the Jesus story or the significance he claimed to give it.[30] A number of times Luke signals an admission that the Christian interpretation of Scripture will not be immediately obvious to his readers. But, having established or confirmed the place and voice of Jesus in Scripture, he probably anticipates his readers being able to see not only the place of Jesus in the Old Testament but also that the commands of Jesus and the commands of Scripture are to be taken as one and the same.

Second, not only does Luke expect his readers to find the Old Testament Christologically rich but also to mine it for ecclesiological self-understanding. In the light of what he has written in relation to the texts, Luke probably expects his readers to use the Old Testament to find their place (and plight) in the biblical story. Part of this place in biblical history includes the identity of the Christians as well as their realization or actualization of Jesus' mission to the Gentiles. In particular, as Luke uses his heroes as models for his readers, he can be taken to presume they will find in the Scriptures the raw material of their message.

Third, an interesting observation to be made from this exercise is that all but one of the Old Testament quotations (Acts 8:32–33) occur in speeches.[31] There is nothing about the speeches that suggests Luke thought scriptural interpretation was a particular prophetic gift or act. For there is little indication that such utterances came as a result of any special inspiration by the Holy Spirit. Rather, in view of all those involved in the Pentecost narrative being filled with the Spirit (2:4) and, one of them, Peter standing up 'with the eleven' (2:14) to give a speech that involved scriptural interpretation, Luke's readers will assume all followers of Jesus can be involved in such utterances (cf. 6:5; 7:55). Moreover, in view of Spirit-inspired Scripture (e.g. 1:16) being part of the fabric of the mind of both Luke and his characters, there is further

---

[29] See the hint in 1 Tim. 1:8 and, notably, the attitudes to the OT by the heretic Marcion of Sinope (died *c*.160). See Irenaeus, *Haer.* 1.27.2; Tertullian, *Against Heretics* 37–38; *Marc.* 1.19; 4.1–2.

[30] See the discussion above in §10.2, especially on Acts 4:11; 7:2–53; and 8:32–33.

[31] In the Gospel of Luke 4:18–19; 7:22; 13:35; 19:38; 20:17, 28, 42–43, all but 10:27 and 20:17 are on the lips of Jesus.

evidence that it is likely that he would have expected scriptural interpretation to be possible by any of his readers at any time.

In any case, citations from the Old Testament occur in speeches where the audiences are Jews and proselytes. At the same time, no speech with a Gentile audience has a quotation from the Old Testament, though the Scriptures are often echoed.[32] Perhaps the reasonable extrapolation from this is that Luke would have anticipated his readers using the Old Testament only in a Jewish context when preaching or in debates between his readers and (other) Jewish members of the synagogue about Jesus and the early Christians fulfilling Scripture.

Fourth, as we might anticipate, Luke understands Scripture to be predictive. However, in every case, we have seen that Luke was using the text to make sense of, or interpret, events and stories that had already taken place. He does not relate the Old Testament text to events that might take place in the future. In other words, nowhere have we seen evidence that Luke would have expected his readers to see still-future events predicted in the Old Testament texts, not even the Parousia. Confidence in the Parousia – Christ's reappearance in glory at the consummation of the age – is secured by the resurrection, not by a text (Acts 17:31). Even Acts 2:19–21, which cites Joel 2:30–32 concerning portents in the heavens above and signs on the earth below, as well as the sun being darkened, is not associated with the future. Instead, the text is firmly linked with what had already taken place in the coming of Jesus and, even more recently, in the coming of the Spirit.

There is a potential exception to this non-predictive use of the Old Testament in Luke's Gospel. After some sympathetic Pharisees warn him against Herod, Jesus laments over Jerusalem and says, 'You will not see me until the time comes when you say, "Blessed is the one who comes in the name of the Lord"' (Luke 13:35). This refers not to the final apocalyptic coming of Jesus but to his entry into Jerusalem (see 19:38). Rather than being a predictive prophecy of a still-future event it is warning in the form of an ambiguous prophecy of the response to his completed work in Jerusalem (cf. 13:33). It will be fulfilled – the benefits of Jesus' competed work will be recognized – by either observers or participants.

Fifth, even though the Scriptures may have been very important, *Luke thought that Christians were first and essentially people of the Spirit. They were not, primarily, people of the book. What they were and experienced had not arisen through the contemplation of a text or the theological or ethical application of it to their theology or lives. Rather, what the readers were, and had experienced, had come about through their response to the reported coming of Jesus and, particularly, their own experience of the Spirit's coming.*

Thus, Luke's use of the Old Testament makes a strong case that readers could be expected to turn to the text alone not to determine who they were but to make sense of their history and already existing experience of the Spirit.

---

[32] See Acts 14:15–17; 17:22–31; 20:18–35; 22:1, 3–21; 24:10–21; 25:8, 10–11; 26:2–23, 25–27, 29; 27:21–26.

Looking back to the Gospel we see Jesus quoting from the Old Testament as he interprets his ministry or mission[33] and response to it (Luke 8:10). Jesus also explains John the Baptist in terms of Old Testament expectations (7:27; cf. Exod. 23:20). Thus, Jesus, Luke's preeminent model for his readers, also finds the explication of his story, his mission and his situation in Scriptures.

Notwithstanding, we have to keep in mind Acts 1:20 where Psalm 69:25 (LXX, 68:26) is used to guide or, perhaps, justify the election of Matthias. Also, in having Paul regret his abuse of the high priest in the light of Exodus 22:28, Luke shows he thought that Scripture could be used to determine behaviour (Acts 23:5). In that this scene is part of the portrait of one of his heroes, who is otherwise shown to be a law-abiding Jew, there is reason to suppose that he would see his readers doing the same thing. Again, in his Gospel, Luke has Jesus in conversations with a lawyer[34] and a certain ruler[35] using the Old Testament as a measure of behaviour.

Sixth, for Luke's readers, Scripture was to be taken as much as explaining as determining what happened. We saw that Luke established a reciprocity of understanding between the ancient texts, on the one hand, and traditions about Jesus and the coming of the Spirit, on the other hand. Luke also drew his readers' attention to the reciprocal hermeneutic between the texts and their own existence, along with the nature of their mission, including the suffering, rejection and persecution involved. This not only gave the readers the potential to see their existence as having its place in the biblical story, but also helped them see that seemingly discouraging stories and events, including the failure of the mission to the Jews as well as the necessity and success of the Gentile mission, could be read in the Scriptures.

This hermeneutical reciprocity between ancient text and contemporary experience is also seen in the way Luke puts Scripture on the lips of Jesus and his interlocutors. In response to the Sadducees, Jesus reinterprets Moses' teaching on a widow marrying her late husband's brother in the light of the experience of the new eschatological situation (Luke 20:28; cf. Deut. 25:5–10). Again, this reciprocity is seen in the way Psalm 110:1 is reinterpreted by Jesus. He acknowledges the text speaking of the Messiah defeating his enemies while asserting that the Messiah is more than a descendant of David (Luke 20:42–43).

For Luke's readers, the Christian life was to proceed not from studies of the text but in using the text to understand what God had done or was doing; Scripture explained what had happened and had been experienced. Nevertheless, what had happened or had been experienced also explained Scripture. Yet, although the relationship between the text and event (including experience) was reciprocal, it was event (including experience) that was primary; the text was interpretive.

---

[33] Luke 4:18–19 (cf. Isa. 58:6; 61:1); Luke 7:22 (cf. Isa. 26:19; 35:5; 61:1); Luke 13:35; 19:38; and 20:17 (cf. Ps. 118:26; Zech. 9:9).
[34] Luke 10:27; cf. Lev. 19:18; Deut. 6:5.
[35] Luke 18:20; cf. Exod. 20:12–16; Deut. 5:16–20.

11

Experience and knowing God

The place we have seen Luke give to experience alongside Scripture in faith and theological speculation obliges us to broaden the discussion to understand more fully how he would have seen his readers gaining guidance from, and knowledge of, God. In fact, Luke's second volume is heavily laden with story after story of his characters being guided or taught not by a book or by reflecting on history or tradition but by taking into account present or recent (sometimes numinous) experiences. In one passage particularly (Acts 15), Luke gives an example of how the human and the divine intersect in seeking to know God. Before we draw attention to this material and attempt to understand its implication for Luke's readers, there is an interpretive key to be recalled.

§11.1 Jesus and guidance

It is clear Luke understood that Jesus' coming and ministry fulfilled ancient prophecy – as much by clarifying it as being predicted by it. In turn, the Old Testament could also be taken as confirming God's involvement in the Jesus event and also in his conception of the Church. Notwithstanding, Luke takes Jesus not simply as having a historic role in the origins of the Church but also as having an ongoing function in informing and guiding the Church. This point – an important interpretive key to Acts – is clear from the opening of the book.

We have already had cause to note that Luke begins part two of his writings saying that, in his first book, he had dealt with 'all that Jesus began to do and teach' (Acts 1:1; see Chapter 3 above). In that Luke is collapsing the distinction between Jesus before and after Easter, readers could be expected to assume that in the ensuing narrative Jesus would be depicted as continuing his activities and teaching.

Indeed, Luke quite directly portrays Jesus as continuing to be involved with his followers after Easter. For example, in the Gospel Jesus – the one coming after John – is said to be the one who will baptize with the Holy Spirit and with fire (Luke 3:16), a story that takes place in Acts 2. As we have seen, just as Luke portrays Jesus as choosing the twelve apostles (6:13), so he is active in choosing the successor to Judas, this time through the mechanism of casting of lots (Acts 1:15–26). Further, just as Jesus directed the mission of his followers before Easter[1] so he also directs the mission of his later

---

[1] Acts 9:1–6, 10; 10:1–21.

followers (9:5–6; 22:18). Concomitantly, 'the Lord' who speaks to and directs Ananias would most likely be taken by the readers to be the Lord (Jesus) of Saul's experience (9:10–16, esp. 16). Moreover, in Luke introducing the idea that it is Jesus who sends or baptizes with the Spirit[2] he shows that Jesus – now risen – was still understood to be actively involved in the life of his followers. In that the experience of the Spirit is the experience of the activity of Jesus, we are led to the subject of this chapter.

Initially, however, we also have to take into account that the interpretive key of Acts 1:1 is also likely to lead readers to assume not only that Jesus would remain an active character in the narrative but also that what Jesus taught in the first volume would remain relevant for the narrative world of the second volume. This is confirmed in the first sketch of the life of the post-Easter group of followers of Jesus. Luke says the group of new followers of Jesus devoted themselves to the apostles' teaching (Acts 2:42). Readers could be expected to assume that Jesus' teaching would be handed on, or at least reflected, in this activity because these are those who had been with Jesus for his entire ministry (1:21–22) and are frequently depicted as the audience of his teaching.[3]

In other places key characters in Acts are depicted as handing on what was known about Jesus.[4] Paul, Barnabas and Apollos are portrayed as teachers who could be expected to do this. For example, it is said that Barnabas took Saul to Antioch and remained there for a whole year teaching a large company of people (Acts 11:26). And in the last verse of Acts the last activity of Paul mentioned is teaching: 'teaching about the Lord Jesus Christ with all boldness and without hindrance' (28:31).[5]

Yet, it has to be conceded, Luke does not seem to envisage that his readers would simply regurgitate the sayings of Jesus to find guidance in life and thought. For it cannot be maintained that it was the teaching, or teaching alone, that Luke thought was critical to be handed on. Nowhere does Luke explicitly portray any of his characters doing so. Instead, in the speeches, we hear only about the existence of Jesus rather than even summaries of his teaching. It cannot be, therefore, that Luke thought the post-Easter followers of Jesus were mere custodians of a body of teaching handed down from Jesus. Rather, can it not be supposed that Luke saw the ongoing activity of Jesus not (only?) in the replication of his teaching but (also?) in his followers being directed by him and, in modelling him, embodying him in their teaching and activity that is directed by the Spirit? In other words, to take seriously what Luke says in the first sentence of his second volume, could it not be that everything Luke relates in Acts is to be read as the teaching (and

---

[2] See Luke 24:49; Acts 1:4–5; 2:33; cf. Luke 3:16.
[3] See, e.g. Luke 6:17; 8:1, 9; 9:18; 10:1–2; 11:1–2; 12:22; 16:1; 17:1, 22; 18:31; 20:45; 22:14–15; 24:36, 44.
[4] Acts 4:2, 18; 5:21, 25, 28, 42.
[5] See also Acts 15:35; 18:11, 25; 20:20; 21:21, 28; and, perhaps, 13:1.

activity) of Jesus? What is described is prescribed. Therefore, we now take up the point that Luke understood that post-Easter followers of Jesus could be guided by the experience of the Spirit, whom Jesus sent.

§11.2 Ongoing experience of the numinous

There are a number of ways in which, according to Luke, the Holy Spirit is able to guide and direct the followers of Jesus in their actions and beliefs.

§11.2.1 Inspired eloquence

Having established – particularly at the end of the Gospel and early in Acts – that the activity of the Spirit can also be taken to involve, or overlap with, that of Jesus (cf. ch. 11, n. 2), Luke goes on to establish an overlap between the activity of the Spirit and the activity of the followers of Jesus. Just as Jesus was empowered (Luke 3:22) and directed by the Spirit in the face of adversity (4:1), as well as in knowing what to say (4:18), so his followers would also be guided by the Spirit. Luke has Jesus say that the Holy Spirit will teach his followers what to say when they are brought before the synagogues and the rulers and the authorities (12:11–12). This guidance is clearly important, for Luke also has Jesus say that, in the face of persecution and before authorities, 'I will give you a mouth and wisdom, which none of your adversaries will be able to withstand or contradict' (21:15).

This kind of empowering and guidance by the Holy Spirit is illustrated in Luke's second volume. For example, when Peter and John have been brought before the Sanhedrin, Luke says, 'Peter, filled with the Holy Spirit, said to them . . .' (Acts 4:8). Also, Stephen, said to be full of grace and power, is confronted by members of the synagogue of the Freedmen: 'But they could not withstand the wisdom and the Spirit with which he spoke' (6:10).[6] Thus, in situations in which Christians might otherwise be tongue-tied and helpless, Luke says the Holy Spirit is able to bring help through inspired eloquence.

§11.2.2 Dreams and visions

In the ancient world dreams and visions (often taken as interchangeable; Num. 12:6; Acts 2:17) were seen as a source of divine communication.[7] Apart from the book of Revelation, there are more dreams, visions and appearances in Acts than in the whole of the rest of the New Testament put together. Obviously Luke considered them very important, and he explicitly attributes them to the Holy Spirit (Acts 2:17). However, Jesus, perhaps because he, like Moses, heard directly from God, did not need dreams. For example, in the Transfiguration story Luke highlights Mosaic features of Jesus (Luke 9:28–32; cf. Num. 12:6, 8).

---

[6] Cf. Acts 4:25–31; 5:29–32; and also 18:9–10; 27:23–24.
[7] E.g. *Jub.* 32; Josephus, *Life* 208–210; *J.W.* 3.350–51; Diogenes Laertius, *Lives* 8.32.

The dreams and visions in Acts do not reveal the future, as we might expect from Old Testament examples or from the book of Revelation.[8] Instead, Luke uses these phenomena in two ways. The first way is as part of his five narratives that involve new mission initiatives. In the first such narrative Stephen gazes into heaven and sees the glory of God (Acts 7:55). In that only Stephen and the readers are privy to the vision (the characters simply hear what Stephen reports, 7:55–57), only the readers know that Stephen has had a similar experience to that just reported of Abraham when he was told to leave his country and go to the land that would be shown him (7:2–3). In this the readers are being shown that it is God who, using visions – here in conjunction with Scripture – has initiated the mission beyond Jerusalem (8:2). In the remaining stories of new mission initiatives, it is Luke's individual characters who are more directly involved in being guided through the experience of visions.

In the second story of missionary initiative, what is probably to be taken as a long visionary experience, Philip is told by an angel to converse with an Ethiopian who had been to Jerusalem to worship and was reading the prophet Isaiah (Acts 8:26–40). Although only Philip could be said to have had a visionary or trance experience, it is clear that, in the visit to Jerusalem and in the reading of Scripture, Luke's readers would see the eunuch as being prepared for the encounter with Philip. In a third story, the Lord (Jesus) is said to appear not only to Paul (9:3–9) in his call to the Gentiles (9:15), but also to Ananias (9:10–19). Fourth, Luke tells the story of Cornelius being directed by an angel in a vision to send for Peter (10:1–8) who, the next day, through a 'trance' (*ekstasis*), understands that God shows no partiality (10:9–48, esp. 34).

Like that concerning Philip and the Ethiopian, the fifth story of missionary initiative also has only one vision. Paul is said to have a 'vision' (*horama*) at night of a Macedonian man standing, pleading, 'Come over to Macedonia and help us' (Acts 16:9). Yet, the night vision – probably intended to be taken as a dream – is said to involve not a heavenly figure but a representative of those to whom Paul is being called. As in the previous two stories, there is the same impact on the reader: through visions God is seen to be both directing the missionary as well as having prepared those to whom the missionary goes. In other words, for Luke, at both the global level (as illustrated by the story of Stephen), as well as at the level of individual experience, Luke conveys the view that God uses visionary experience to direct the mission of the Church. In the latter stories God is portrayed as both directing the individual messengers as well as preparing those receiving his messengers.

It is notable that Luke sees dreams and visions as sufficient in themselves to warrant new initiatives in mission, without always requiring legitimation from Scripture. Only in the story of Stephen and the mission going beyond

---

[8] E.g. Dan. 4:19–27; Rev. 4:1; though see Acts 2:17.

Jerusalem is Scripture used to build a case. Even in the third telling of Paul's call to mission, Scripture is not used to legitimate the mission. Instead, Scripture is the content of his message (Acts 26:22; cf. 9:22). And, if in the fifth story (where the vision of the Macedonian convinced them that 'God had called us to proclaim the good news to them') there is an echo of Joel 2:32, its purpose is not to confirm the vision but, given the programmatic use of Joel in Acts 2, to signal the nature of the good news.

Besides directing the mission of the Church, the other way Luke uses visions in Acts is to show that God warns and encourages his messengers in difficult situations. In Acts 18:9–10, one night Paul is told by the Lord in a 'vision' (*horama*) that he is not to be afraid of speaking. Paul is similarly encouraged in Acts 23:11 (cf. 27:23–24). Both of these experiences are probably to be understood as dreams. Interestingly, neither the dreams nor the visions are thought to need interpretation; the content of the vision or dream is immediately apparent either to the readers (as in the case of Stephen's vision) or to the characters in the stories. Finally, in relation to dreams and visions one thing bears repeating: Luke is writing with the expectation that his heroes would be emulated by his readers, thus it can be supposed that he would have anticipated Spirit-inspired visions and dreams to remain essential in guiding his readers, both in their activities as well as their beliefs, particularly about mission and in times of difficulty.

§11.2.3 Prophecy

In Luke's narrative, prophets – men as well as women (Acts 21:9) – are another way God, through the Holy Spirit (cf. 2:17), is thought to guide the early Church. To begin with, we note that on the day of Pentecost all, not just some of, the followers of Jesus are portrayed as involved in being filled with the Holy Spirit (2:4). Although not directly equated with prophecy, through the quotation from Joel, readers are led to assume that what has happened to all the followers of Jesus on the day of Pentecost is an example of an expectation that the activities of the Holy Spirit include prophesying for all, as well as seeing visions and dreaming dreams (2:17–18). Similarly, where Luke says that when Paul laid his hands on the 12 Ephesians and the Holy Spirit came on them and they spoke in tongues and prophesied, the entire group of twelve is involved (19:6). In the light of these two stories it seems Luke assumes that, on being filled with the Spirit, every believer has the ability to prophesy – as well as speak in tongues, see visions and dream dreams.

Nevertheless, Luke depicts prophecy as associated with a few individuals in particular. He tells of some prophets, including Agabus, visiting Antioch from the Jerusalem church (Acts 11:27–28; see also 21:10). Clearly Luke sees these as exercising a travelling ministry. However, in that Paul and Barnabas are also said to be prophets based in Antioch (13:1), Luke would not have thought travelling prophets were based only in Jerusalem or that only Jerusalem had such a ministry wider than its own city. Luke depicts other prophets as residing in Antioch rather than travelling (13:1; see also 19:6). Thus, some prophets were probably thought to remain in the one church.

§11.2.4 The guidance of prophecy

There are other passages in Acts showing how Luke thought prophets guided and directed the followers of Jesus. First, prophets had the task of predicting the future. For example, along with the symbolic action of tying his own hands and feet with Paul's belt Agabus says, 'So shall the Jews at Jerusalem bind the man who owns this belt and deliver him into the hands of the Gentiles' (Acts 21:11). This predictive prophecy was not fulfilled in so many words. Paul was, in fact, rescued from the Jews by the Romans (23:12–35), though the Jews could be seen to be responsible for Paul ending up in the hands of the Gentiles (28:17).

Second, the role of prophet includes or overlaps with that of teacher, as in Acts 13:1. Luke says that 'there were prophets and teachers' in the church in Antioch. From this passage and the list of names which follow (Barnabas, Simon-Niger, Lucius of Cyrene, Manaen and Saul), it is not immediately clear whether some were prophets and some were teachers, or if all five were both prophets and teachers. However, it is most probable that the five fulfilled both roles: (a) the list of names is most naturally taken in parallel with both titles; (b) in other places Luke shows Barnabas and Paul in both roles;[9] (c) this (Acts 13:1) is the only place in Acts where Luke uses the word 'teacher'[10] so that it is not surprising that, early in Acts, the function of teaching is carried out not by a separate group but by apostles (2:42); (d) the Vulgate or Latin translation (fourth century) and Codex Bezae (fourth to sixth centuries) take the roles to be fulfilled by the same people; and (e) the *Didache* (late first or early second century) has individuals performing both functions (*Did.* 15.1).

Third, for Luke, encouragement is also an important role of a prophet and could be taken to be part of the way he thought Christians were guided. Barnabas, whom we have just noted is listed among the prophets and teachers at Antioch (Acts 13:1–2) and introduced as having a name meaning 'son of encouragement' (4:36), is said to encourage the disciples to continue in the faith (14:21–22). Judas and Silas, who were also prophets, were charged with the task of communicating the decisions of the Jerusalem council and are said to have encouraged the Christians with many words and strengthened them (15:32; see also 16:40).

It may be possible to deduce at least one way Luke thought people were encouraged by prophecy. In Acts 2 the speaking in tongues is explained as prophecy (Acts 2:17–18). This prophesying is said to be heard in terms of reports about 'the mighty works of God' (2:11). Thus, at least one form of

---

[9] E.g. Acts 11:26; 14:22; 15:35.
[10] 'Teacher' (*didaskaloi*) is in the plural. Luke uses 'teacher' many time of Jesus in his Gospel (Luke 3:12; 7:40; 8:49; 9:38; 10:25; 11:45; 12:13; 18:18; 19:39; 20:21, 28, 39; 21:7; 22:11), and the plural of the teachers in the temple (Luke 2:46).

prophecy that encouraged Christians was probably a rehearsal of the mighty deeds of God in the Scriptures, and perhaps also of what God had done in Jesus (see 10:38).

A fourth aspect of how Luke saw prophets guiding the Church is in his likely understanding of them as leading or respected people in their churches. This seems clear from the case of Judas and Silas. They are members of the Jerusalem church and Luke calls them 'leading men'.[11] That is, in being highly influential they would have had the privilege of exercising their roles from a position of innate respect.

As well as these functions of prophets or prophecy – predicting the future, teaching, encouraging and being highly influential – also to be considered is that of declaring God's judgement. Acts 13:10–11 might be cited (Paul's rebuke of Elymas the magician) as well as 28:25–29 (Paul's indictment of the Jews in Rome). Acts 5:1–10; and 8:20–24 could also be noted, where Peter informs Ananias and Sapphira, and Simon the magician of God's judgement. However, while this aspect of prophecy is familiar in the Old Testament,[12] Luke does not directly associate it with the prophets he portrays. Only at one point in Acts is speaking words of judgement possibly linked with a prophetic role. Following his identification as a prophet in Acts 13:1, Saul is related as delivering words of judgement to Elymas the magician (Acts 13:10–11). Thus, while the same person (Paul) may have been involved in prophecy, the different roles Paul plays in the two separate stories suggests that it is unlikely Luke associated prophets or prophecy with delivering words of judgement.

§11.2.5 Testing prophecy

It remains to draw attention to one further aspect of Luke's portrayal of prophets and prophecy. In writing to the Corinthians, Paul said that when prophets spoke in a gathering, others were to weigh or 'test' (*diakrinein*) what was said (1 Cor. 14:29). Luke gives no such injunction or its equivalent. It could be that, twenty or thirty years after Paul, in the relatively developed Church of Luke's time, prophets were operating within a more structured and less charismatic Church than known by Paul. However, what we have already seen – and what we have just noted about the lack of precision over the roles of a prophet and the function being (at least potentially) open to all – suggests that Luke's understanding of the Church remained fundamentally charismatic. Indeed, there are two places where the testing of prophecy might be in view.

First, Luke says that, while the Christians at Antioch were praying to the Lord and fasting, the Holy Spirit said to them, 'Set apart for me Barnabas and Saul for the work to which I have called them' (Acts 13:2). It is reasonable to assume that this took place through one of the prophets being prompted by the Spirit to speak. In turn, the other Christians might be understood to have confirmed what was proposed to be from the Lord for they

---

[11] *Andras hēgoumenous*, Acts 15:22; see §12.1.2 below.
[12] E.g. Isa. 3:13–15; Jer. 1:13–14; 4:5–6; Ezek. 4:1–17.

are said to have fasted, prayed and laid hands on Barnabas and Saul before sending them out (13:3).

Second, it could be argued that, when Agabus delivered his prophecy, accompanied by the visual aid of Paul's belt, Luke is assuming that the prophecy is weighed or tested by Paul in that, even though there was truth in it, he rejects it (Acts 21:10–14). From these two cases, where prophecy can only be inferred to have been tested, the lack of overt reference to testing suggests that, for Luke, the evaluation of prophecy was not the pressing issue that it had been for Paul, even though his view of the Church remained fundamentally charismatic. Before drawing our conclusions we need to take into account an example of how Luke understood the relationship between the divine and the human in knowing God.

§11.3 The divine and the human

An obvious point in Luke's narrative where human experience and knowing God intersect is in the story of the Jerusalem council (Acts 15; see also 13:3–4). The issue said to be facing the council was whether or not it was 'necessary for them [the Gentiles] to be circumcised and ordered to keep the law of Moses' (15:5). The council concludes with a letter being issued to Antioch communicating the decision not to burden the Gentiles with more than the essentials for good relations – eating together – between Gentiles and more conservative Jews: abstaining from what has been sacrificed to idols, from blood, from what has been strangled and from fornication.[13]

Towards the end of the letter, the process or the basis of the decision is summed up in the line, 'it has seemed to the Holy Spirit and to us' (Acts 15:28).[14] Here Luke is suggesting the divine and the human have, in some way, been working in concert or in parallel to produce the decision of the council. An examination of the council narrative may reveal what Luke understands by this. Does he mean, for example, the leader decided or the disciples voted or they had a quiet inner assurance of the rightness of the decision? Or, are the human and divine elements in the decision to be understood differently?

Luke's narrative of the meeting involves a number of elements. At the beginning of the meeting there was, according to the text, 'much debate' among the apostles and elders (Acts 15:6). Then, Peter stood up to give an extended report (15:7–11) that God testified to the Gentiles by 'giving them the Holy Spirit, just as he did to us' (15:8). As in a few other places in the New Testament,[15] here 'testify' or 'witness' (*martureō*) means to guarantee something. In this case the 'cleansing of their hearts by faith' (15:9) is testified or guaranteed by the reception of the Holy Spirit (15:8). In the additional

---

[13] Acts 15:20, 29. 1 Cor. 10:8; Rev. 2:14, 20 associate idolatry and sexual immorality. Cf. Wisd. 14:12.

[14] My translation; 'good', generally supplied by English translations (e.g. NRSV), is not in the Greek.

[15] Acts 13:22; Heb. 11:2, 4, 5, 39.

comment, 'just as he did to us' (15:8), Luke is referring to the coming of the Spirit on the Jewish Christians in Acts 2:4 (cf. 10:47; 11:14). The conclusion readers are to draw is that God sees no distinction between Jew and Gentile, a point already put on Peter's lips in relation to his vision preparing him to go to Cornelius (11:12). The importance of Peter's report in the narrative is seen in James later referring to it (15:14).

Next, Barnabas and Paul tell the council 'of all the signs and wonders that God had done through them among the Gentiles' (Acts 15:13). This report makes two points. On the one hand, the report of miracles is evidence of God's activity among the Gentiles. On the other hand, it is a report that these miracles were done by the hand of those arguing that it is not necessary for the Gentiles to be circumcised and keep the Law of Moses. Luke makes these points for he considers that miracles are both evidence of God's activity and his endorsement of ministry,[16] here a ministry of taking the good news to the Gentiles.

Finally, the leader, James, speaks, using thoroughly biblical language.[17] His report points out to those assembled that what Peter has said shows God has looked favourably on the Gentiles (Acts 15:14). James says this agrees with the words of the prophets, shown by Amos 9:11–12.[18] Again, what Luke's readers are to notice is that the coming of the Holy Spirit on the Gentiles has made clear that God has also – already – looked favourably on or saved them.[19] God has returned to rebuild his people to extend to and include all people, even the Gentiles (Jer. 12:15; Amos 9:11–12). Although James simply says Peter's report 'agrees with the words of the prophets' (Acts 15:15), the priority of the reports of experience becomes evident.

The priority of experience over the text is seen in that there is no collecting and weighing of different texts, some of which would be hostile to the Gentiles being placed among the people of God.[20] Instead, a passage is cited that correlates with the report of God's activity in including the Gentiles in salvation. Amos 9:11–12 is probably used because it seems to have been the focus of some debate among Jews in relation to the acceptance of the salvation of the Gentiles (cf. *Tg. Ps.-J.*).

Luke then says that, on the basis of God's activity among the Gentiles and its agreement with Scripture, James 'therefore' (*dio*, Acts 15:19) reached the 'decision' (*krinō*) that became part of the letter (cf. 15:20 and 29). The emphatic 'I' – 'Therefore *I* judge' (*dio egō krinō*, 15:19) – underlines that James and James alone reached the decision. Here James is fulfilling the same function that Peter took in the story of Pentecost: what had happened was given

---

[16] See Acts 2:22; 7:36; 10:38; 14:3.
[17] Cf. Deut. 14:2; 26:18–19; 1 Kgs 5:5.
[18] Being only a proximate rendering of the LXX, and as Acts 15:16 and 4Q174 1.1.21.2.12 use the same wording in quoting Amos 9:11 suggests Luke was using a text other than the LXX known to us.
[19] Cf. Acts 15:14; Luke 1:68; 7:15–16.
[20] E.g. Deut. 7:1–6; Joel 3:1–21; cf. *Pss. Sol.* 17.23–27.

scriptural interpretation by the leader. Congruous with this action, a leader of a synagogue was able to act on behalf of the people.[21] According to James, the Gentiles should not be troubled beyond a few restrictions related to food consumption and sexual behaviour. By implication they need neither be circumcised nor ordered to keep the Law of Moses (15:1, 5).

Beyond this decision, Luke says the apostles and the elders, with the whole church, decided (*dokeō*) to send a delegation to Antioch with a letter (Acts 15:22). This point is soon repeated in the letter itself, with the addition of the idea that the decision was 'unanimous' (*homothumadon*, 15:25). It is likely that Luke considered this decision was expressed through voting. Not only does voting seem a reasonable way a unanimous decision of a group would be expressed, but also Josephus uses *dokeō* ('decide') in a way that implies voting; he says, 'it has been decided (*edoxe*) by me and my council' (*Ant.* 16:163). Although the decision to send the letter was subsequent to James' decision it portrays the people's involvement in affirming his decision. Once again, there is a rough parallel here with the crowd's response to Peter's scriptural interpretation of the Day of Pentecost. The people by their believing and being baptized affirm Peter's view (Acts 2:37–41).

In this we are able to see that, for Luke, the phrase 'it has seemed to the Holy Spirit and to us' (Acts 15:28, see ch. 11, n. 14) did not mean, for example, that there was among those present some quiet inner assurance assumed to be from the Spirit, perhaps expressed through voting. Nor does Luke say that the Holy Spirit illuminated a scriptural text to aid decision making. Nor does Luke's narrative say there was any ecstatic speech involved. Nor, we should add, is there a unilateral or isolated decision or decree by a leader or group of leaders. Rather, on the one hand, God had taken the initiative in giving the Holy Spirit to the Gentiles and doing signs and wonders among them. On the other hand, the human aspect in the decision making is seen in the debate, the reports, the leader detecting a congruence between Scripture and the reports and, finally, in the agreement of those present to communicate the decision.

In short, Luke understood the human and the divine to be working in concert in a particular way. It was dominated by the divine (a tangible, obvious, initial activity of the Holy Spirit) with the leader recognizing and understanding this in the light of perceiving an agreement with Scripture. The role of the community was one of witnessing and, by its willingness to be involved in communication, affirming the decision. With our more democratic temper of mind we should not overplay the role of the crowd; the crowd did not vote to create the decision, the leader made the decision. The crowd played very much a secondary, even if important, role of affirming an existing decision. In this Luke has provided his readers with a methodological matrix for theological development, the implications of which we can discuss in the final chapter (see §14.6 below).

---

[21] See, Josephus, *Ant.* 4.214, 287; *m. Meg.* 3.1; *t. Meg.* 2.12; *y. Meg.* 3.2.74a.

In the light of this conclusion we need to return to take account of the story in Acts where Luke appears to depict Paul as not listening to other believers (cf. §11.2.4 above). After Agabus enacts and announces his prophecy that Paul will be bound in Jerusalem and handed over to the Gentiles (Acts 21:12), Paul refuses to listen to those urging him not to go to Jerusalem. However, the urging of the people is not in concert with what the readers have been told of Paul being 'captive to the Spirit' in going to Jerusalem (20:22; cf. 23). Thus, Paul is depicted as remaining faithful to the direction of the Holy Spirit rather than being dissuaded by the weeping (21:13).

§11.4 Conclusions

In this and the previous chapter we have been enquiring about Luke's views on how followers of Jesus gained knowledge of and guidance from God. In the last chapter we saw that, although Luke understood Scripture to be profoundly important, Christians were not people of the book, at least not in the sense that they found God in, or their initial identity through, reading sacred texts. Rather, Luke considered that Scripture explained what had already happened and been experienced. And, even though there was a reciprocal relationship between the text and event or experience, it was event or experience that was primary; the text was interpretive.

In other words, Luke is not supposing his readers should search their holy writings for direction from God. Rather, Luke would expect the followers of Jesus to turn to the Old Testament writings in an attempt to understand what they had already experienced of Jesus or of God through the Spirit.

In view of his privileging of event or experience over the text in knowing God and his guidance, in this chapter we have been enquiring about Luke's understanding of experience or event in relation to knowing God. Luke shows God directing his people through their following the example and teaching of Jesus, and through the Holy Spirit enabling inspired eloquence, providing dreams, visions and prophets to predict the future, teach, encourage and influence, though not declare God's judgement. However, the evaluation or testing of this prophecy, if even in his purview, was not the pressing matter it had been for Paul.

A point where we may have caught a glimpse of Luke's thinking on the interface between these ecstatic means of knowing God and human initiative is at the end of the story of the Jerusalem council. There, we saw the divine as dominant – tangible, obvious, initial activity of the Spirit, though only understood in concert with the human. As in Acts 2, the human element that contributed to the realization of the knowledge of God and his guidance was the leader recognizing and understanding the divine in the light of perceiving an agreement with Scripture. Also, similar to Acts 2, part of the human aspect was the role of the community witnessing and affirming the decision of the leader. The important practical implications of this for contributing to a model of the use of Scripture and a methodological matrix for theological development we will leave until the end of our study.

12

Early catholic, Protestant or charismatic?

Unfortunately, dividing lines criss-cross the contemporary Church on the subject of authority and leadership. For example, on the one hand, vast tracts of the Christian landscape are dotted with local churches independent of all outside authority, believing they are responsible to God and to God alone for their life and leadership. On the other hand, various denominations express to varying degrees the view that authority in a church is not vested or contained entirely in the local setting: the Roman Catholic Church, for example, exemplifies a high value of central governance and leadership through the pope and bishops.

Even when the Bible – frequently the work of Luke in particular – is used to construct contemporary views of the Church, leadership structures are worked out differently. So-called episcopal churches maintain a threefold order of bishops as successors to the apostles, priests as successors to the elders, and deacons as successors to the seven in Acts 6. With an eye on Luke's description of Paul, other churches take the local pastor acting alone, or along with or subordinate to a group of deacons or elders, to express the Bible's view of leadership or authority.

With Luke implicated as a contributor to this confusing picture, it is appropriate to look again at what he has to say. We need to ask whether or not his writings disclose evidence of early catholicism. This term could be used to suggest a range of things, including that Luke had exchanged fervent eschatological expectation for an institution, or that the Church denied Judaism the name Israel, keeping it for itself. As in this chapter, early catholicism could also be used to raise the question as to whether or not Luke has attempted to establish an ecclesiastical system with Jerusalem as the headquarters. We have already seen that Luke is not responsible for the idea of the twelve, though it is he who calls them apostles (see §2.3). Nevertheless, there is the issue of whether or not he holds to some form of apostolic succession.

Instead of proposing an episcopal order with the so-called threefold ministry, Luke may favour a presbyterian model with the local church, and each successive level of the wider Church, governed by an elected body. Alternatively, Luke may wish his readers to take up a more congregational or locally independent form of leadership. In view of the high profile of the Spirit in Acts, it has to be asked to what degree Luke sees the Church as charismatic: in the appointing of leaders, what is the role of the Church and what is the role of the Spirit?

It may be that we do not have to choose between all these options. Luke may wish to portray a range of views or, perhaps, a development over time in the way the Church was governed. This might enable his readers to trace the sanctioned origins of their experience of church structure. Of course, we need to be open to the possibility that none of these scenarios reflects Luke's view. We will proceed by looking, in turn, at the various models of ministry or leadership and authority that Luke appears to portray.

There is no escaping that leadership and authority are of interest to Luke. He portrays Jesus as the leader of those around him and he has two stories of disputes among the apostles about which one of them was to be regarded as the greatest (Luke 9:46–48; 22:14–27). In Acts, although Jesus is still the principal character in the narrative (Acts 1:1), it is important to Luke that the group of twelve is reconstituted before taking up leadership.[1] In turn, it is Peter, who appears to be the leader of the group,[2] who also recognizes the salvation of the Gentiles. Notwithstanding, James later seems to be the authority figure in Jerusalem, with strong evidence that Luke also sees his jurisdiction extending further afield (15:13; 21:18). Also, there are the seven who are elected to serve tables in Jerusalem (6:1–6). In this city,[3] as well as in Ephesus (20:17), and more generally (14:23), elders appear in the narrative. Paul is also shown to exercise considerable and geographically widely spread leadership responsibilities.[4] Yet, it could be that Luke has him subordinate to the leadership at Jerusalem.[5]

§12.1 Luke's models of ministry

To repeat what was said at the beginning of this study: it is not our concern to piece together a historical reconstruction of the models of authority and leadership in the earliest Christian communities. Instead, our objective is the equally hazardous one of attempting to hear what Luke intended to say to his readers about leadership and patterns of authority in the Church. In short, our task is not to recover the historical models of ministry in the early Church, but to view the model or models of ministry from Luke's perspective.

We will examine what Luke has to say about leadership in those centres where the evidence is clearest: Jerusalem, Antioch and Ephesus. Along the way we will take note of how Luke describes the relationship between Jerusalem and churches in other places. But we need to begin with a brief examination of what Luke says in his Gospel about leadership and authority among Jesus and his followers. For we have already seen that Luke places the origin of the Church in the setting of Jesus' pre-Easter ministry (§2.4 above).

---

[1] Acts 1:15–26; 2:14, 37; 4:35.
[2] Acts 1:13, 15; 2:14, 37; 5:1–11, 29; 8:14; 12:2.
[3] Acts 11:30; 15:2, 4, 6, 22, 23; 16:4; 21:18.
[4] Acts 11:30; 13:1; 14:23, 26; 15:2, 35, 36; 18:18–21; 20:1–2, 17–38.
[5] Acts 12:25; 15:2, 4, 12, 22; 16:4; 18:22–23; 21:17–26.

§12.1.1 Jesus and his followers

In Luke's Gospel those following Jesus fall into two distinct groups. In Mark the distinction is less clear, though the attentive reader is aware that there are more than the twelve, 'for there were many who followed him' (Mark 2:15; cf. 3:34–35), including Levi, not listed among the twelve (2:14–15; cf. 3:16–19), as well as some women (15:40–41). In Mark 4:10 those around Jesus, along with the twelve, are a little later all referred to as 'his disciples' (4:34). There may also be a hint of a larger group of disciples in 10:32. Here, the natural reading is of Jesus walking ahead of his followers and then calling the twelve, in particular, from the other followers.

The way in which Luke brings into focus this picture of two groups is seen in his alterations of Mark. In Mark Jesus simply calls to himself those he wanted, appointing twelve (Mark 3:13–14). Luke, however, specifies that Jesus chose the twelve from among his disciples (Luke 6:13), whom he goes on to say are a great crowd.[6] Also, Jesus not only sends out the twelve on mission but also seventy-two others whom he identifies as disciples (10:1, 23). Thus, for Luke's readers the embryonic Church comprises the twelve and the larger group of disciples (cf. 24:9), a point he confirms early in his second volume (Acts 1:12–14; and §2.1 above). Here, as we will see, we also have the same organizational structure sketched out that Luke has for the post-Easter communities: the Church led by a group in which there is a key or lead figure.

However, although the twelve are portrayed as distinct from the other disciples of Jesus they have no leadership positions or roles in relation to the wider group. Jesus exercises direct leadership over all his followers. Luke is clear that it is not until towards the end of his ministry that Jesus confers leadership responsibilities on the twelve,[7] and that leadership is to be taken up in the future (Luke 22:28–30; see §2.5.2). Even though, within the twelve, Peter, John and James are singled out as having a closer relationship with Jesus than the others,[8] this is a privilege of proximity to Jesus rather than of priority over others (22:24–27).

Nevertheless, in his Gospel, Luke shapes particularly Peter's character in preparation for his leadership role in the second volume. Peter enters the narrative as a leading figure from his days as a fisherman (Luke 5:1–11) and goes on to have a leading position in,[9] as well as to speak for, the group.[10] His tarnished image in the tradition is renewed,[11] though he remains far from perfect (esp. 22:54–62). He is given a specific call which has as its climax the charge and description of his future role: 'Do not be afraid; from

---

[6] Luke 6:17, 19; cf. 19:37–40.
[7] Cf. Philo, *Flight* 73; Josephus, *Ant.* 3.169, 220; 1QM 3.1–3; 5.1–2; 1QS 8.1; 11Q19 58.11–15.
[8] Luke 8:51; 9:28–36, 54; 22:8.
[9] Luke 5:1–11; 8:51; 24:12, 34; cf. 22:31.
[10] Luke 5:8; 6:14; 8:45; 9:20; 12:41; 18:28; cf. 9:33.
[11] Cf. Mark 8:31–33 and Luke 9:22; Mark 13:3 and Luke 21:7; Mark 14:29–31 and Luke 22:31–34.

now on you will be catching people' (5:10). Later, Peter is singled out as the subject of prayer by Jesus and told that, after recovering from his early failures, he will have the role of strengthening or giving 'support' (*stērizō*) to others (22:31–32).[12]

This strengthening or supporting role of leadership is commensurate with Luke's view of leadership as serving others,[13] a point he makes in the two Gospel passages about greatness. In the first, an argument among the disciples (Luke 9:43) prompts Jesus to use a child as a model of greatness (9:46–48). In a second paragraph, also taking its rise in a dispute among the apostles (22:14, 24), Jesus says, in contrast to the approach of the Gentiles, among his followers the greatest is the least 'and the leader one who serves' (22:26). There is a poignancy to this lesson in that the argument takes place immediately after Jesus has been speaking of his own self-giving death (22:14–23, esp. 19). In these aspects of the portrayal of Jesus and his followers, especially the twelve, readers would see that, though they were not perfect, the apostles and pre-eminently Peter had been called by Jesus to positions of leadership to be exercised after Easter. However, leadership among the followers of Jesus is not based on competitive greatness but, reflecting that of Jesus, on service or giving support or strength to the others.

§12.1.2 Ministry at Jerusalem

The picture Luke gives of the believers in Jerusalem is one of a large crowd of followers of Jesus – the twelve, women who followed Jesus, his mother and brothers, as well as other believers (Acts 1:14–15; see also Luke 8:2–3) – remaining in the city after the Ascension.[14] So important is the group of twelve among them – obvious even from the number twelve itself (see §2.5.1 above) – that Matthias is elected to restore the number after the defection of Judas (Acts 1:15–26). The importance of this group is also clear from the new followers devoting themselves to the apostles' teaching (2:42); even Peter's speaking on the day of Pentecost is done 'with the eleven' (2:14). In response to the sermon, the people speak not to Peter alone but to Peter 'and the rest of the apostles' (2:37). Though others are performing miracles – notably Stephen (6:8) and Philip (8:4–40) – the apostles are portrayed as leading the way in such activity.[15]

One of the features of Luke's description of the Jerusalem community is the holding of all things in common (Acts 2:44; 4:32). Reading between the lines, one expression of this, the charitable support of the widows, was originally the responsibility of the apostles (6:2). As Luke sees it, under the pressure of time (6:2), this Jewish practice (see ch. 8, n. 39) was being neglected. Thus

---

[12] In Judg. 16:26, 29 a house is said to 'rest' (*epistērizō*) on pillars and the Psalmist is said to 'lean' (*epistērizō*) on God since birth (Ps. 71 [LXX 70].6). Cf. Isa. 36:6.

[13] In Acts note also *epistērizō* ('strengthen') in 14:22; 15:32, 41; 18:23.

[14] Luke 24:49–53; Acts 1:4, 12–13; 8:4.

[15] Acts 2:43; 3:1–10; 5:12–15.

a group of seven is chosen to take up the role (6:3). In that Luke makes no further comment on the other material expression of the community of goods, the distribution of capital, readers would assume the apostles retained that responsibility (4:34—5:11).

Luke's readers would also have gained the impression that the group of seven was subordinate to the twelve. Even though grammatically he has the whole group pray and lay hands on the seven (Acts 6:6), it is the twelve who call and take responsibility for the meeting in which the seven are appointed (6:2), and those selected are gathered before the apostles (6:6). The assumption of the continued superiority of the apostles in Jerusalem is apparent in their remaining devoted to prayer and the ministry of the word (6:4), and staying on in Jerusalem when persecution scattered the other followers of Jesus (8:1).

Luke nowhere gives the seven a name. They are not, as convention has it, called 'deacons' (*diakonoi*) like those described in the Pastoral Epistles.[16] Luke only says they are 'to serve' (*diakonein*) in their duty, as the apostles are in theirs (Acts 6:4).

On a first reading, it seems that, alongside this twofold leadership of the apostles and the seven, Luke says an eldership eventually developed. For in Acts 11:30 he mentions elders in the Jerusalem church. However, even later, Luke only ever writes of there being a twofold leadership in the Jerusalem church: apostles and elders.[17] In 11:30, when the Antiochene church sends 'relief' or 'service' (*diakonian*) to the Christians in Judea they send it to the elders, not to the seven as could be expected (cf. Acts 6:3). Even the emergence of James as leader in place of Peter (12:17; 15:13) is probably not intended to violate the twofold form of leadership. For, even in the narrative of the Jerusalem council where James and Peter have roles, there are only two groups of leaders mentioned: elders and apostles (15:3, 22). Thus, Luke's readers are likely to assume that James – a brother of Jesus (cf. 1:14) – is being accorded the status of an apostle.[18]

It could be that Luke is using the term 'elder' only in the sense of a senior member of the community. He uses the word in this sense in his quotation of Joel when, over against 'young men' (*neaniskoi*), he mentions 'your old men (*presbuteroi*) shall dream dreams' (Acts 2:17). Even if, for its meaning, Luke is not restrained by what he finds in Joel (LXX 3:1), *presbuteroi* are more than senior members in relation to the care of the Church in that he has Paul 'appoint' (*cheirotoneō*) them to this duty (Acts 14:23). Mere seniority, therefore, does not explain their role for Luke; they are selected and appointed.

It is quite reasonable to suppose, then, that in Luke's mind the elders are none other than the seven set aside to take care of or serve the daily distribution. That, in the early part of Acts, he does not refer to them as elders

---

[16] 1 Tim. 3:8, 12; 4:6.
[17] Acts 15:2, 4, 6, 22, 23; 16:4.
[18] Cf. 1 Cor. 15:7; Gal. 1:19; see §2.5.3 above.

could simply be so that there was no confusion with the Jewish elders.[19] Further, that Luke saw some flexibility in the role of elder and that they are none other than the seven, is seen from the way he portrays them. He portrays the seven or the elders as having a wider ministry than serving tables. Philip, also called Philip the evangelist (Acts 21:8), is shown to be an evangelist and conducting miracles in Samaria,[20] Gaza (8:26), and from Azotus to Caesarea (8:40; see also 21:8). Neither is Stephen confined to serving tables for he also 'did great wonders and signs among the people'.[21] Moreover, in view of it being widely considered among the Jews that seven was the number of town leaders,[22] Luke's readers are likely to assume that the seven appointed to serve table would have a wider function that involved leadership.

Before drawing our conclusions about Luke's portrayal of leadership and authority in Jerusalem we can note that he says there was a group of prophets there (Acts 11:27; cf. 21:10). At the end of the narrative of the Jerusalem council Luke says that along with those sent to Antioch with the letter were Judas and Silas whom he refers to as prophets (15:32) and 'leading men' (*andras hēgoumenous*, 15:22). It is not clear from Luke what part they may have played in the leadership at Jerusalem. However, the use of the term *hēgoumenoi* ('leaders') at the time suggests they may have been the most highly regarded or significant of the leadership or elders.[23]

Therefore, we can conclude that, from Luke's perspective, leadership and authority in the earliest community in Jerusalem had three components. As a group, with a lead figure, perhaps best described as *primus inter pares*, the twelve provided the early leadership. Under the pressure of being unable to fulfil all their responsibilities, this group was quickly supplemented with the appointment of the seven. Whatever the historical reality, Luke also refers to these as the elders who are not only involved in decision making but also share in the same evangelistic activities as the apostles. Either through evolution or, more likely, through Luke conforming the leadership to reflect what he knew in his own time, by the Jerusalem council, the triadic leadership (lead figure, apostles and elders) is now dyadic: a single leader with the apostles and elders acting as one group. James assumes the key leadership role in place of Peter, perhaps because he was the Lord's brother; Luke has no interest in explaining why or the details through which this took place.

§12.1.3 Ministry at Antioch

In Luke's story, Antioch was the most important city outside Jerusalem in the beginnings and spread of Christianity. Nicolas, one of the seven appointed in Jerusalem, was from Antioch. He was a Gentile who had become a Jew and

---

[19] Acts 4:5, 8, 23; 6:12.
[20] Acts 8:5, 6, 13.
[21] Acts 6:8; cf. 2:43; 5:12.
[22] Cf. Josephus, *Ant.* 4.214; *J.W.* 2.571; *y. Meg.* 3.74a; *b. Meg.* 26a.
[23] Thucydides, *History* 2.89.9; *Letter of Aristeas*, 14.2; Diodorus Siculus, *Hist.* 16.89.1; cf. Luke 22:26; Acts 14:12; 1 Thess. 5:13; *1 Clem.* 1.3; 21.6; Shepherd Hermas, *Vision* 3.9.7.

in turn a Christian (Acts 6:5). Luke says that it was at Antioch that the disciples were first called Christians (11:26).

In the scattering of Christians from Jerusalem as a result of Stephen's martyrdom, Luke says some travelled as far as Antioch and spoke only to the Jews (Acts 11:19). However, he also says, some Christians came to Antioch from the island of Cyprus and the north African port of Cyrene. They preached the Lord Jesus to the Greeks with great success (11:20–21). News of a large number of Greeks turning to the Lord reached the church in Jerusalem. As had happened after Philip's successful preaching in Samaria when Peter and John were sent to Samaria (8:14), someone, this time Barnabas, is sent to the new Christians (11:22). As Luke describes it, Barnabas offers no formal sanction of the Antiochenes' faith, either through the laying-on of hands or baptism in water or the Spirit. However, his rejoicing and encouraging them (11:22) signals their acceptance by a representative of the church in Jerusalem.

Luke has developed the character of Barnabas so that he becomes an appropriate delegate. Like some of those preaching to the Greeks, he also came from Cyprus (Acts 4:36). Further, Luke describes him in a similar manner to the seven in Jerusalem: a good man, full of the Holy Spirit and of faith.[24] Moreover, his portrayed submission to the apostles in laying the proceeds of a land sale at their feet (4:37) and his being known for his gift of encouragement (4:36) increases his suitability not only to sanction the growth of the Church but to deal with any possible division between Jews and Greeks.

Besides these aspects of his credentials, Luke is probably portraying Barnabas as the key person within a group of leaders at Antioch. Barnabas is the one who goes to Tarsus seeking Saul so he could join him in teaching the disciples at Antioch (Acts 11:25–26). When these two are mentioned together in relation to Antioch, Barnabas is most often named first.[25] Also, Barnabas heads the list of prophet-teachers at Antioch, with Saul mentioned last (13:1), perhaps because he was the most recent member (11:25–26).

Yet, whatever key role Barnabas may have had, his trip to Jerusalem (Acts 15:2) and his mission work (13:1–4) show that Luke was not portraying him as an indispensable leader. In any case, Barnabas was not alone in his role for he is one of five in a meeting of prophets and teachers or, probably, prophet-teachers (13:1–3; see §9.9 above). Notably, this is the group who, without any reference to Jerusalem, appoints and sends Barnabas out on mission with Saul.

Also, as well as the probable prime position of Barnabas within a group of prophet-teachers, we have to take into account that Luke emphasizes the leadership of the Holy Spirit at Antioch. He says that while the group of prophet-teachers was worshipping the Lord and fasting it was the Holy Spirit

---

[24] Acts 6:3, 5; 11:24.
[25] Acts 11:30; 12:25; 13:2, 7; 15:12, 25; see also 13:43, 46, 50; 15:2, 12, 22, 35.

who said 'set apart for me Barnabas and Saul' (13:2). Then, Luke repeats that they were sent out by the Holy Spirit (13:4) even though the remaining prophet-teachers had been involved in sending them out (13:3).

This appointment of Barnabas and Saul by the prophet-teachers in Antioch, without any recourse to Jerusalem, shows that Luke is not attempting to tie all authority to that city or to the apostles. Nevertheless, Antioch is portrayed as otherwise in deference to the Jerusalem church. Jerusalem assumed initial responsibility for the situation in Antioch. Barnabas had been sent from Jerusalem (Acts 11:22), and then prophets, including Agabus, Judas and Silas, are readily accepted from Jerusalem (11:27–28; 15:32). Relief money is sent to Jerusalem (11:29); the circumcision issue was referred to Jerusalem (15:2), and, in turn, the letter of instruction from Jerusalem was warmly received (15:31).

Thus, according to Luke, in leadership at Antioch there was a group of prophet-teachers headed by Barnabas, who also had a travelling ministry. Apart from the issue of the entrance of the Gentiles into the Church, the group was not subordinate to the leadership at Jerusalem, but led under the direction of the Spirit. Yet, there was a ready cooperation with and deference to the Jerusalem church. This structure or pattern of leadership turns out to be similar to that which Luke portrays as evolving at Jerusalem, a group in which there was a lead individual.

§12.1.4 The Ephesian ministry

Luke says that when Paul sailed into Miletus he sent word to Ephesus for the 'elders' (*presbuteroi*) to come to him (Acts 20:17). When they arrived he spoke to them saying, among other things, 'Keep watch over yourselves and over all the flock, of which the Holy Spirit has made you overseers (*episkopoi*), to shepherd (*poiminē*) the church of God' (20:28).

Those looking to justify a hierarchical church government have sought support in this verse. However, 'overseer' (*episkopos*) here is not a title but a task to 'keep watch' (*prosechō*)[26] over or pay attention to themselves and their people as would, by implication, a shepherd (Acts 20:28). Therefore, it would be a mistake to conclude that Luke had in mind a hierarchical form of church leadership as in the Pastoral letters, for example.[27] Notably, the Holy Spirit is said to 'place' (*tithēmi*) or appoint the leaders (20:28). The most natural reading of this is not that the Spirit has given them a 'gift' (*charisma*, cf. 1 Cor. 12:4) but a role. From Luke's other stories of appointing leaders, readers would assume that the choice came about through a 'concerted' effort between the divine and the human.[28]

---

[26] A word favoured by Luke. See Luke 12:1; 17:3; 20:46; 21:34; Acts 5:35; 8:6, 10, 11; 16:14; 20:28. In the remainder of the NT: Matt. 6:1; 7:15; 10:17; 16:6, 11, 12; 1 Tim. 1:4; 3:8; 4:1, 13; Titus 1:14; Heb. 2:1; 7:13; 2 Pet. 1:19.

[27] 1 Tim. 3:2; Titus 1:7; cf. 1 Pet. 2:25.

[28] Acts 1:21–25; 6:1–6; 13:1–4.

There is no suggestion that Luke thought there was any other category of ministry or leadership at Ephesus apart from elders. Nevertheless, he does portray Paul as exercising responsibility for the Ephesians and, indeed, other churches around the Mediterranean.[29] Again, this model of ministry or leadership is simple and the same as Luke has for the church at Antioch: a group of local leaders taking care of the day-to-day running of 'the flock', whose head person is a travelling missionary exercising occasional oversight. There is no evidence of the Ephesians having a responsibility to the Christians in Jerusalem. The connection with other Christians is provided in Paul. As in Antioch, the Holy Spirit is said to be involved in the appointment of leaders.

There are two aspects of Acts 14:23 that offer some confirmation that we are correctly reading Luke's understanding of leadership or ministry as two tiered. Towards the end of the narrative of Paul's so-called first missionary journey Luke says, 'after they [Paul and Barnabas] had appointed elders for them in each church, with prayer and fasting they entrusted them to the Lord in whom they had come to believe'. First, as at Antioch and Ephesus, this scenario implies a local group of elders responsible to a travelling missionary. Second, Luke gives no hint that the appointments involved any input from Jerusalem or the twelve. In view of the increasing apostolic stature of Paul (see §2.5.3 above), Luke does not need to portray any recourse beyond Paul to have these Christians firmly related to the origins of the Church. As the appointment process involves prayer and fasting, as it did at Antioch, Luke probably has in mind Paul and Barnabas being the instruments of the Spirit in making the choices (Acts 13:2).

§12.2 Qualifications and tasks for key figures

Before answering some of our questions about Luke's view of leadership – early catholic or charismatic, for example – we need to take into account how he describes the qualifications and tasks of his key figures. As we will see, being easy to set out makes them no less challenging to the contemporary Church.

Luke has two aspects to the qualification for membership of the apostolate. First, as Peter implies, not only does the person need to have been a follower of Jesus from the baptism of John until the Ascension but also, second, to have done so 'among us' (Acts 1:21–22). This was, as he has Peter say, to enable the person to 'become a witness with us to his resurrection' (1:22). However, in order to provide a bridge between the first and subsequent generations of believers, we have seen that Luke understands witnessing the resurrection also to be possible through having seen the risen Jesus, as in the case of Paul (22:6–11; cf. §2.5.3 above). In that Paul and Barnabas are also raised to membership of the apostolate (esp. 14:4, 14), it is to be noted

---

[29] See below on Acts 14:21–23. Cf. 15:36, 41; 16:4–6; 18:23.

that Luke does not have them commissioned by any or all of the twelve. It is enough for Luke to have these two relating positively to the church in Jerusalem (15:1–35).

Beyond considerations for the apostolate, Luke also sets out qualifications for his key figures in his story of the election of the seven to serve tables (Acts 6:1–6). First, in Acts 6:3 the twelve direct the group of disciples to 'select from among yourselves seven men of good standing'. The text is unclear. It could be that, rather than this being a particular qualification, the seven selected were 'well spoken of' or 'approved' in ways that Luke goes on to list (cf. 10:22). However, if Luke had in mind that being of 'good repute' was a qualification in itself,[30] he probably had in mind business matters, for the seven were being chosen for administrative tasks and were also to have wisdom (see below). In any case, the character of the seven was seen to be important.

Second, another of Luke's qualifications for leadership is to be full of the Holy Spirit.[31] We have already established that, for Luke, to be filled with the Holy Spirit is to be overcome or consumed by God's Spirit. Or, as we tried to show, Luke understood being filled with the Spirit not to be a moment in personal experience but an ongoing and identifiable quality of life (§6.5.2 above).

Third, to be full of 'wisdom' (*sophia*, Acts 6:3) was also required of the seven. From the way he uses the word in other places we gather that Luke probably thinks of 'wisdom' as special insight or worldly practical common sense. It was given by God to those close to him.[32]

Fourth, Luke does not list faith as a requirement or qualification for leadership for the seven. However, when Stephen is chosen he is described as 'a man full of faith' (*pistis*, Acts 6:5). It is unfortunate that, in English, *pistis* is generally translated 'faith' and understood as a human quality. *Pistis* would be more faithfully translated 'trust' or 'confidence' in God. This would highlight the fact that the word has to do with a person being open to God and recognizing a dependence on him. Thus, in saying Stephen was full of faith, Luke is describing one of his key characters as trusting and depending on God.

Fifth, we have already seen that Luke established early in his Acts narrative that just as prayer was an integral part of his portrait of Jesus,[33] so prayer is of profound importance to his lead characters, as well as for the group of believers (§3.1.4 above). This provides strong backlighting and reinforcement for his having Peter say that the apostles will devote themselves to prayer (Acts 6:4).

Sixth, Peter also says that the apostles will devote themselves to the service (or preaching) of the word.[34] In that, for Luke, the purpose of the Church

---

[30] Cf. Acts 16:2; 22:5, 12.
[31] Acts 6:3, 5; cf. 7:55; 11:24.
[32] Luke 2:40, 52; 7:35; 11:31, 49; 21:15; Acts 6:3, 10; 7:10, 22.
[33] Luke 3:21; 5:16; 6:12; 9:18, 28–29; 11:1–2; 22:41.
[34] Acts 6:4; cf. 6:2; Luke 1:2.

is encapsulated in the title and task of the 'apostles', these last two characteristics – prayer and service or ministry of the word – would have been notable
for the readers as important in Luke's key characters.

Seventh, and perhaps most challenging of all, Luke's key characters are,
time and again, not only commanded to perform miracles or signs and wonders, but are described as doing so. The sending out of the twelve was for
the express purpose of exercising power and authority over demons (Luke
9:1–6). The commission to the seventy-two included the command to
'heal those in it who are sick' (10:2); and they returned to report that 'even
the demons are subject to us in your name' (10:17). In Acts the first story of
individual activities of the apostles is of Peter and John going to the temple
and healing a man (Acts 3:1–10; see 5:12–15). Beyond the apostles, Luke depicts
others, Philip for example, involved in performing miracles:

> And the multitudes with one accord gave heed to what was said by Philip,
> when they heard him and saw the signs which he did. For unclean spirits came
> out of many who were possessed, crying with a loud voice; and many who
> were paralysed or lame were healed. (8:6–7)

Paul is another obvious example of this characterization of ministry involving
the miraculous.[35] It cannot be ignored that Luke is portraying his lead characters – characters intended as models for his readers – as not only speaking
about the resurrection or about forgiveness, but also performing miracles.

Eighth, for the sake of completeness, we recall here that Luke says the elders
of the church at Ephesus are charged to 'keep watch' or 'give attention' (*pros-
echein*) to themselves and their people as a shepherd would of sheep (Acts
20:28). We can add that paying attention to a flock was an Old Testament
metaphor for the way God cared for his people.[36] Thus, Luke would have
understood that to give attention to someone was to care for people as God
cares. Calling Josephus to give evidence, to oversee or keep watch was to
look after someone carefully, including investigating their well-being and
visiting them when sick (e.g. Josephus, *Ant.* 9.179). The importance of this
task is seen in Luke saying that the people the elders are to oversee are those
God has bought with blood![37]

Ninth, 'service' (*diakonia*) does not so much portray the task of leaders as
the character of leadership. Six times Luke uses the word 'service' to describe
the nature of what leaders were doing. In Acts 1:17, Peter says that Judas
was numbered among the apostles and was allotted his share in this 'service'.
Thus, the whole of the work of the apostles before and after Easter is characterized as 'service', usually translated 'ministry' or 'work' (see also Acts 1:25).
In Acts 6:4, the apostles determine to give themselves to the 'work' or 'service'

---

[35] Acts 9:17–19; 13:4–12; 14:8–18; 15:12; 16:25–26; 19:11–20; 20:7–12; 28:1–10.
[36] E.g. Ps. 23; Isa. 40:11; Ezek. 34.
[37] Although God is the subject of the phrase 'through his own blood' (*dia tou haimatos tou idiou*,
Acts 20:28), it is obviously a clumsy reference to the death of Jesus. See §5.5 above.

of preaching. The work of Barnabas and Saul – probably at Antioch – is called 'service' (12:25) and the whole of Paul's work is called 'service' (20:24; 21:19). For Luke, a leader's work is so characterized as service that it can be called service. A leader is a servant. This leads us, finally, to note again that Peter, Paul and Barnabas are described as strengthening those in the Church (see ch. 12, n. 12).

§12.3 Conclusions

Was Luke an early catholic attempting to establish an ecclesiastical system with Jerusalem as the headquarters? Or, was he a Protestant in that he advocated elected councils leading churches that were independent of each other? Or, perhaps Luke was a charismatic proposing that it was the Spirit who appointed and directed leaders. Although Luke is only one voice in the choir of the New Testament, so large is his contribution to the New Testament and so central to his purpose is the portrayal of life among the followers of Jesus after Easter that any discussion of Christian leadership that seeks input from the New Testament is bound to give considerable attention to what he has to say.

We have not been able to find any evidence that Luke was attempting to establish an ecclesiastical system with Jerusalem as the headquarters; too much in the narrative takes place without recourse to Jerusalem or the leadership there for Luke to be seen as an early catholic or even presbyterian in this sense. Yet, Luke portrays the radiation of the gospel from Jerusalem and the occasional deference of other churches to Jerusalem, including their looking to the Jerusalem leadership for decisions. This suggests Luke saw the Jerusalem church as the source of what became a self-propagating radiation. In this readers would have been able to see that their expression of Christianity was firmly rooted in, though not controlled by, the past in Jerusalem – in what God had done with his people. Luke, in this way, can be credited with being an early catholic.

That Luke understood there to be an apostolic succession of leadership could be argued from the way Jesus assigns leadership to Peter and the apostles, who, in turn, sanctioned the work of God in other places. Also, Barnabas is firmly connected with Jerusalem when he takes up leadership at Antioch. Paul's commissioning is without the direct imprimatur of any Jerusalem figure, though his acceptance by the Jerusalem church is portrayed by his introduction by Barnabas. Then Luke portrays Paul as moving among the apostles and eventually taking up the status of an apostle and being sent to Tarsus by the Christians in Jerusalem (Acts 9:26–30).

Yet, to be kept in mind, without any explanation, James replaces Peter. Additionally, without attention to Jerusalem or the leaders there, Luke has Paul and Barnabas appoint leaders in churches. Thus, if Luke is not propos-ing a formal apostolic succession, he provides his leaders with sufficient ties to Jerusalem or its leaders that a complete independence of a church from this tradition would seem not to have crossed Luke's mind.

In the appointing of leaders we have seen that Luke considers both the Holy Spirit and other leaders or followers of Jesus to be involved. Leadership was neither by appointment alone nor by charisma alone. In concert, Luke has the divine and the human realizing God's oversight of the Church. Not surprisingly, Luke's requirements for leadership involve characteristics that are not always easy to assign exclusively to a human or divine origin: to be of good standing, to be full of the Spirit, full of faith, to be wise, and to be given to prayer and the ministry of the word, for example. Then, the tasks of a leading figure are said to include strengthening or supporting others. Not surprisingly, therefore, service often describes the character of what leaders do. At least from a contemporary perspective, another surprise is that Luke understood church leaders to be people who performed miracles in conjunction with preaching the word.

Evidence that Luke considered the form of church leadership or government to have evolved is found in his portrayal of the Jerusalem church. It seems that, after a brief period of leadership by Peter and the apostles, Luke understood that the seven (or elders) formed a subsidiary leadership group, which soon reverted to acting as a single group, eventually headed by James. However, further evolution does not seem to have taken place. Thereafter, in a more Protestant style, Luke describes – and is therefore most probably advocating – leadership in the various churches as consisting of a group with an individual, *primus inter pares*, over a local body of believers. The leading individual is also portrayed as a travelling missionary, only occasionally at home in the local church, therefore the group, not an individual, provided day-to-day leadership of a church.

In short, Luke proposed that the Church was strongly central in origin (early catholic), but not formally central in oversight of other churches (congregational and charismatic); leadership of the local church was to be by a group (Protestant) with a key leader having firm ties with Jerusalem (early catholic and Protestant); appointment was by the Spirit (charismatic), yet involved other leaders or the group (early catholic and Protestant). But, to repeat, Luke would not have understood a church or church leaders independent of others. In the final chapter we will attempt to listen to what Luke might say in a contemporary conversation about church structure and leadership.

13

Mission: evangelism or social action or both?

Of all the challenges – both surprising and disturbing – that Luke offers the contemporary Church it is in the area of the nature of mission: how the Church is to enable more people to know God's love and become followers of Jesus. So large is this theme in Luke-Acts that we will not be able to do justice to all its features. Instead, the purpose of this chapter is to explore those aspects of Luke's understanding of mission running counter to usual interpretations of the nature of the mission of the Church. In doing so we will discuss Luke's understanding of the relationship between eschatology and mission, and his apparent concern over the failure of mission among his readership. The large central section of this chapter will be taken up with exploring Luke's view of mission in relation to social action before attempting to set out the main features of his understanding of the mission of the Church.

It can hardly be doubted that mission is important to Luke. Luke's first description of God is as Saviour (Luke 1:47; cf. 1:46–56). In the parables of the lost sheep, the lost coin and most movingly in the story of the lost son, God is implied to be a missionary searching for and then joyful in finding the lost (15:1–32). Further, as we will see, that Jesus is a missionary is also a point that cannot be missed. That the Church is to be a missionary is equally clear. It is presaged in Luke's Gospel: the twelve who represent the leaders of the post-Easter Church are named 'apostles' – delegates sent out on mission with full authority to represent Jesus (6:13). In the sending out of the seventy-two (10:1–12, 17–20), Luke prefigures the Church's mission to the Gentiles. In the parallels where Jesus is portrayed as the pattern for its life and ministry, the Church is cast as existing primarily for mission. For example, just as Jesus is anointed by the Spirit for a mission (3:21–22; 4:18–19), so were his followers (Acts 1:8); and both missions are directed by the Spirit.[1] The Church also preaches forgiveness of sins just as Jesus did before it.[2]

The impression on the reader that mission is the priority of the Church is even clearer and stronger in Acts. The opening of Acts is particularly significant as Luke assigns the period between the taking up of Jesus and his return as the time of the mission of the Church, a mission continuing that of Jesus

---

[1] Luke 4:1, 14, 18; Acts 10:38–42; and Acts 1:8; 4:31; 8:29, 39; 10:19; 11:12; 13:2, 4; 15:28; 16:6–7, 10; 18:21.

[2] With Acts 2:38; 5:31; 10:43; 13:38; 26:8 compare Luke 1:77; 5:17–26; 7:36–50. Further, see §3.1 above.

(Acts 1:1–11). Then, in three idealized sketches of the early community at Jerusalem, the results of mission in terms of the numerical growth of the community is important.[3] Then, echoing the mission of Jesus, through Acts there are not only further summaries that draw attention to growth,[4] but there is also story after story of Luke's characters involved in mission.

Most notable in Luke's agenda to show the Church to be a missionary society or organization is his portrait of Paul. In the third story of the commissioning of Paul, for example, the Lord Jesus says, 'I am sending you to open their eyes and turn them from darkness to light, and from the power of Satan to God, so that they may receive forgiveness of sins and a place among those who are sanctified by faith in me' (Acts 26:17–18). This sounds like, and could equally be, a description of Jesus' ministry. Indeed, the two ministries are summarized similarly.[5] Most significantly for the readers, apiece with a practice of the time, Luke leaves the ending of Acts open. He expects his readers to take up in their lives what has become Paul's story (see §3.2.3 above). Though Paul dies, he lives in their ministry; the end of his mission is the beginning of theirs – to the ends of the earth (1:8).

Some of the reasons why the theme of mission pervades and dominates Luke's two volumes are, therefore, already clear from his theology and his understanding of the ministries of Jesus, as well as from the way he portrays the key characters in his Christian tradition, especially Paul. Alongside these reasons are two others that need to be considered as also contributing to Luke's special interest in the mission of the Church. The first is Luke's eschatology. The other is his probable indictment that his readers are failing in their mission.

§13.1 Eschatology and mission

How we read Luke's eschatology has implications for how we understand his view of the Church and its mission. If the end is expected soon[6] the role of the Church would be to stay alert and ready (cf. Luke 21:25–36). An imminent end could also bring an urgency to mission (cf. Acts 2:14–36), even hastening the eschaton (3:19–21). Or, if Luke thinks the Parousia has been delayed or is to be some considerable time in the future, the role of the Church could be to prepare for the coming salvation (3:19–21). Alternatively, perhaps if the exaltation of Jesus is his return (cf. Luke 19:15; Dan. 7:13), Luke thought the eschatological event was the Ascension which, in his narrative, is the hinge about which his two volumes move. The Church, then, is the experience and expression of realized salvation. If, however, as we will see, Luke is holding together the present and future in eschatology,

---

[3] Acts 2:42–47; 4:32–37; 5:12–16. Cf. §3.2.2 above.
[4] Acts 6:7; 12:24; 19:20.
[5] Luke 4:40–1; 6:17–19; 24:46–47; Acts 5:12–16; 8:4–8.
[6] Cf. Acts 2:17; 17:31; 24:15, 25.

the Church can be seen both to experience the presence of God and still be waiting for an even greater coming of the kingdom of God.

We have already agreed that Luke was probably not teaching his readers that the return of Christ would be long delayed, nor have we seen that the 'end times' was a central issue among his reasons for writing (§1.3.4 above). For it seems clear that Luke does not have the same eschatological urgency as some Christians had before him. For example, he has added sayings of Jesus about preparing for the master's delayed return (Luke 12:35–48; cf. Mark 13:33–37). Also, in Mark, Jesus says the disciples will not die before the king-dom of God has come 'in power' (9:1). But, in Luke's more general state-ment, the disciples will simply see the kingdom before they die (Luke 9:27).

Just how long Luke thought the period of the Church would extend is not clear. On the one hand, he has material which may suggest the period would be brief. He has the saying of Jesus: 'this generation will not pass away until all these things have taken place' (Luke 21:32). However, for Luke 'this generation' probably refers generally to evil, stubborn people.[7] On the other hand, as we have just noted, he includes sayings of Jesus which imply a significant period of time, as in the parable of the delayed master.[8] Nevertheless, even this significant period is part of the end. For, since the coming of Jesus, some elements of what was expected in the 'end times' have become present realities (7:22; 11:20). Moreover, as the coming of the Spirit means the ministry of Jesus is now embodied in his followers (e.g. Acts 1:1), in its life the Church now embodies and expresses some of the hopes of the end.

Yet, the life and activity of the believers after Easter do not encompass all Luke's hopes for the 'end times'. In Acts 3:19–21, Luke has Peter say to the Jews in the temple precinct: 'Repent therefore, and turn to God so that your sins may be wiped out, so that times of refreshing may come from the presence of the Lord.' This first part of the passage probably refers to present experience: the 'times' (*kairoi*) of refreshment is plural and likely to refer to the life experienced by the believers.[9]

However, the verse clearly goes on to refer to the future: 'and that he may send the Messiah appointed for you, that is, Jesus, who must remain in heaven until the times of the restoration of all things that God announced long ago through his holy prophets' (Acts 3:20–21, my translation). All the details of this difficult statement need not detain us. However, it is unlikely that Luke has in mind the conversion of all people is to take place before the Messiah is sent, not least because the 'all things' (*pantōn*) to be restored is neuter rather than masculine. Also, although it may include Israel (cf. 1:6–7), in view of the use of 'restoration' (*apokatastasis*) in the period, 'all things' more likely refers to the whole of creation being returned to its

---

[7] Cf. Luke 11:29–32, 50–51; 16:8.
[8] Luke 12:41–48; cf. 12:38; 13:8.
[9] E.g. Acts 2:4, 38, 43–47; 4:32–35; 5:12–16.

former glory.[10] Luke is not, therefore, urging the completion of the mission of the Church to hasten the coming of the Messiah. Instead, he is expressing the view that, in responding to the message, the audience can be among those to whom the Messiah is sent when creation is restored. That is, Acts 3:19–21 shows that Luke believed the Church existed in the time between the Ascension and the consummation of all things.[11]

This is how Luke portrays the Church early in the second volume where he draws attention to the issue of the relationship between the Church and the Parousia. He introduces the question from the apostles, 'Lord, will you at this time restore the kingdom of Israel?' (Acts 1:6). For Luke's readers this would probably have been understood as a question both about the timing of the Parousia as well as its national implications. However, what is important in understanding Luke's view of the relationships between the Church and the 'end times' is Jesus' answer: 'But, you shall be my witnesses' (1:8). This means that until the consummation of history the apostles, representing the Church, are to be involved in a mission of witness.

§13.2 Failure in mission

As well as an eschatological perspective that is driving Luke's idea of mission there is another factor that probably needs to be taken into account. So important is the theme of mission in his narrative that the first readers could reasonably suspect that Luke thought they were failing in their mission. Indeed, there are some specific hints in the text to suggest not only the nature of their failure but also the solutions.

One hint of failure in mission is probably in the story of the call of the first disciples (Luke 5:1–11). Jesus has been teaching the people from a boat a little way from the shore. When he had finished he told Simon, 'Put out into the deep and let down your nets for a catch.' However, Simon replies, 'Master, we toiled all night and took nothing!' In the context of a call to mission (fishing for people, 5:10) this reply may be a foil for Luke's readers to reflect on their own failure in mission to 'catch' any people. Along with the term 'Master'[12] the remainder of the reply of Simon may also show how success in mission may come: '[A]t your word I will let down the nets' (5:5). That is, mission may come through obedience to the Master or his Spirit, as is confirmed in Acts in the mission taking place in obedience to divine direction.

Second, the failure of mission among Luke's readership may be evident in the story of the mission of the seventy-two which prefigures the mission of the Church to the world. It is headed by the saying: 'The harvest is plentiful,

---

[10] Mal. 3:24; Isa. 62:1–5; 65:17; 66:22; *1 En.* 45.4–5; 51.4; 96.3; 2 Esd. 7:75; 13:26–29; cf. Rom. 8:18–23; *As. Mos.* 10.10.

[11] Acts 1:11; 17:31; 24:25; see also 23:6; 24:15, 21; 26:6–8; 28:20.

[12] *Epistatēs* ('Master') is only used in Luke; see 5:5; 8:24, 45; 9:33, 49; 17:13.

but the labourers are few' (Luke 10:2), which readers would take as describing their post-Easter situation. The solution to the problem of too few labourers involved in mission is immediately offered: 'pray therefore the Lord of the harvest to send out labourers into his harvest' (10:2).

In Acts, this connection between prayer and mission is apparent in two related ways. On the one hand, Luke suggests that mission arises out of prayer in that Barnabas and Saul are sent out to mission 'after praying and fasting' (Acts 13:3; cf. §9.9 above). On the other hand, Luke also portrays those on mission praying. For example, after the story of the arrest and release of Peter and John, the longest prayer text in Acts reaches its climax in a request for bold speech and for accompanying signs and wonders (4:24–30). Also, when the workload of the apostles (the initial missionaries) increases they are said to affirm that they are to devote themselves 'to prayer and serving the word' (6:4).

Third, in Acts 1:6 there may be a hint of Luke considering that there was a failure in mission among his readers. The disciples ask Jesus, 'Lord, will you at this time restore the kingdom of Israel?' As Jesus' answer is that, at this time (Acts 1:6), the apostles are to receive power for witnessing when they receive the Holy Spirit (1:8), Luke is probably signalling that universal mission ought to be the focus of his readers' attention rather than eschatology and its political implications.

Fourth, in Stephen's speech (Acts 7:2—8:53) Luke is probably charging his readers with having a fortress model of mission. Although Jerusalem had fallen by the time Luke was writing, Stephen's speech makes most sense if Luke's readers – perhaps in being uncertain about the gospel that had come to them – remained preoccupied with Jerusalem as the focus of God's final triumph and were expecting the Gentiles to go to the city to enter into God's salvation (cf. Isa. 2). However, Stephen's speech points out that God spoke to his people well before sacrifices, the temple or their arrival at Jerusalem. In fact, they heard God best apart from these. While affirming the Jewish origins of the Church, through the voice of Stephen, Luke redirects the focus of mission from the temple to one that is global and directed outward. Though propelled by persecution, straight after Stephen's speech, Luke portrays all but the Jerusalem apostles going out from Jerusalem (Acts 8:1–5). For Luke, successful mission is not clinging to the past, nor to a place, nor waiting for people to come to them but in being 'scattered about preaching the word' (8:4), as exemplified preeminently in Paul. Therefore, along with his main aim to assure his readers that God's salvation has not passed them by, in these ways as well as most obviously in the open-ended conclusion to Acts, Luke urges his readers to continue Jesus' mission in their own narrative.

§13.3 Evangelism or social action or both?

If mission is important – to be the preoccupation of the Church until the return of the Messiah – yet Luke is suggesting his readers are failing in their mission, what kind of mission does he envisage for them? It is commonly urged that the Church has a two-pronged mission: evangelism and social action; preaching for faith or conversion, as well as tending to the needy in society. Having what is arguably the most accessible view of mission in the New Testament, Luke is the writer most often called on to support this idea. In this section we will test whether or not Luke has such a two-pronged view of mission. As we draw our conclusions we will need to take into account Luke's view of salvation as the realization of the powerful presence of God in an individual's present and future experience of, for example, forgiveness, eternal life, the gifts of repentance and the Spirit, as well as in various kinds of healing (see §4.1 above).

Since it is Luke's view that the Church is to be a continuation of the life and ministry of Jesus (e.g. Acts 1:1) we are obliged to begin an attempt to set out Luke's understanding of mission with a discussion of Jesus' mission in relation to social action. We will do this through a brief examination of (1) a strategic passage in Luke, (2) the Magnificat, (3) the Beatitudes, (4) Luke's Gospel ethical material, as well as taking into account (5) the nature of Jesus' ministry. Then (6), in key passages in Acts we will see that we are confronted with strong reasons to call into question any possible reliance on Luke for a two-pronged view of mission.

§13.3.1 A mission of freedom from sin and the demonic – Luke 4:16–30

The story of Jesus reading from Isaiah is rightly taken to be programmatic for Luke's understanding of the mission of Jesus as well as of the Church. This is clear at least from the position of the passage in Luke's corpus and from the passage containing the first words of Jesus, as well as from Luke's first use of *euangelizien* ('to proclaim'). This is a term he often uses to encapsulate Jesus' ministry[13] and also that of his followers.[14] The programme Luke sets out in 4:18–19 is taken from Isaiah 61:1; 58:6 and 61:2. It can be translated as follows:

> The Spirit of the Lord is upon me
> for he has anointed me.
> He has sent me to preach[15] to the poor,
> to proclaim to the captives release
> and to the blind sight,
> to send away the oppressed released,
> to proclaim the acceptable year of the Lord.

---

[13] Luke 4:43; 7:22; 8:1; 16:16; 20:1; Acts 10:36.

[14] Luke 9:6; Acts 5:42; 8:4, 12, 25, 35, 40; 11:20; 13:32; 14:7, 15, 21; 15:35; 16:10; 17:19.

[15] Many translations supply the noun *euangelion* ('gospel' or 'good news'). However, Luke avoids the noun in his Gospel and only twice uses it in Acts (15:7; 20:24). For the verb, *euangelizein* ('to evangelize' or 'to preach'; cf. 4Q521), see Matt. 11:5; Luke 1:19; 2:10; 3:18; 4:18, 43; 7:22; 8:1; 9:6; 16:16; 20:1; Acts 5:42; 8:4, 12, 25, 35, 40; 10:36; 11:20; 13:32; 14:7, 15, 21; 15:35; 16:10; 17:18.

Before examining how this passage sheds light on Luke's view of the mission of Jesus there are some preliminary matters to take into account. First, the line in Isaiah 61:1 about being sent to 'bind up (or heal, *iaomai*) the broken-hearted' is missing in Luke. This has never been adequately explained, though leaving out this phrase does enable Luke to maintain his broad-brush description of Jesus' ministry in terms of proclamation. For, as we shall see, even the mention of sight for the blind is associated with proclamation. In turn, second, the use of the technical Christian term 'to proclaim' (*kērussein*) in place of the Septuagint's 'to call' (*kalesai*) in the last line of the above quotation is readily explicable as using a word well established among Christians.[16]

Third, of all the things that Luke wants to communicate in this program-matic passage it is obviously that Jesus' mission has a divine origin. Notably, the material from Isaiah begins with a statement about the anointing of the Spirit of the Lord. Also, Luke has already used such phrases as Jesus being 'full of the Holy Spirit' and being 'led by the Spirit' (Luke 4:1, 14) and he has said that the Holy Spirit descended upon him at his baptism (3:22). These phrases show Luke wants his readers to understand that God is behind the mission of Jesus that he is about to describe.

In turning to see what this passage tells us about Luke's view of the mission of Jesus we can note that not only is this passage seen as important in encap-sulating Luke's view of mission, it is also taken as establishing socio-economic and political action as essential in the mission of Jesus and, therefore, in turn, the mission of the Church. In particular, it could be argued that the way Luke quotes Isaiah is an attempt to free the Old Testament promise from its limit-ation to the people of God. One way of testing this interpretation is to deter-mine who, according to this passage, Luke thought the 'poor', the 'captives' and the 'oppressed' represented and what he expected these beneficiaries of the ministry of Jesus to receive.

1 The 'poor' could be variously identified: the pious, the social outcasts, the economically poor, the heirs of salvation or the voluntarily poor. A way forward in establishing their identity is found when we take into account two aspects of Luke's use of the term. First, in the three cases where Luke has Jesus describe his ministry to the poor, Isaiah 61:1 is either quoted or echoed.[17] Along with his general interest in Isaiah,[18] this strongly suggests that Luke's understanding of the identity of the poor as the focus of Jesus' ministry would be elucidated through noting how the poor are under-stood in Isaiah.

---

[16] For the Christian use of the word before Luke, see Mark 1:4, 7, 14, 38, 39, 45; 3:14; 5:20; 6:12; 7:36; 13:10; 14:9; 16:15, 20; Rom. 2:21; 10:8, 14, 15; 1 Cor. 1:23; 9:27; 15:11, 12; 2 Cor. 1:19; 4:5; 11:4; Gal. 2:2; 5:11; Phil. 1:15; 1 Thess. 2:9.

[17] Luke 4:18; 6:20; 7:22.

[18] See, esp., Luke 3:4–6; 4:18–19; 19:46; 21:26; Acts 1:8; 4:24; 7:49–50; 8:32–33; 13:34, 47; 15:18; 28:26–27.

The book of Isaiah offers three broad and interrelated portraits of the poor that correspond to the three parts of the book, usually called First, Deutero- and Third Isaiah. In First Isaiah (chapters 1—39) the poor are the peasants of the pre-exilic period being squeezed off their lands by the rich and powerful.[19] In Deutero-Isaiah (chapters 40—55) the poor are the exiles in captivity.[20] Notably, in Third Isaiah (chapters 56—66), from where the quotations in Luke 4 come, the poor are not some of the people of God or even outsiders but the whole nation of humiliated and dispirited returnees in Jerusalem awaiting salvation.[21] There is a similar perspective found in the Qumran scrolls.[22] The poor are not a section of society but are the whole community – representing all Israel; the poor are all those who will be saved (1QM 13.13–16) or who revere God while waiting for salvation (CD 19.9–10; cf. Zech. 11:11) or, having endured the preliminary period of distress, are saved (4Q171 2.9–12).

This leads us to note, second, that Luke's overall use of the 'poor' reflects that of Third Isaiah. In the three occurrences of the 'poor' we have so far noted they head (Luke 4:18; 6:20) or end (7:22) the list to sum up or represent *not some* of those to whom Jesus ministers and who receive salvation. Rather, the poor represent the entire scope or all recipients of his eschatological ministry. In the parables of humility (14:12–14, esp. 13) and of the great banquet (14:15–24, esp. 21), being poor is also the lead characteristic of all the recipients of salvation in Jesus' ministry. Also, Lazarus, a representative recipient of salvation, is twice described as poor in the parable (16:20, 22), over against the person tormented in Hades who is called rich (16:21, 22). To put this point the other way around: only the poor are saved. At the same time, to be saved, the rich become poor (19:8; cf. 18:18–25).

It is reasonable to conclude, therefore, that for Luke the poor – all the benefactors of Jesus' eschatological ministry – are not to be understood as a disadvantaged section of society. Instead, the poor are the nation of Israel as a whole, suffering and subjected, waiting and expecting God to bring eschatological salvation. Again, to put this the other way around, the 'poor' is a metaphor for all those saved, misunderstood as the needy by those who see themselves not needing the salvation offered in Jesus. Of course, later in the Gospel Luke will also make reference to the socially and economically poor (see Luke 18:22; 19:8; 21:3). How these references relate to a programme of social action we will discuss below. (That Luke does not mention the poor in Acts could be because eschatological salvation is associated with the coming of Jesus; eschatological salvation has come in Jesus, the poor have been satisfied.)

---

[19] E.g. Isa. 3:14–15; 10:1–2; 25:1–5.
[20] See Isa. 41:8–20; 42:22; 49:13.
[21] See, e.g. Isa. 58:4–7; 61:3; 62:4, 8. Cf. Pss. 9:18; 68:10; Zech. 11:7, 11.
[22] See also *Pss. Sol.* 5.2, 11; 10.6; 15.1; 18.2; cf. *1 En.* 108.7.

2 The identity of the 'captives' (*aichmalōtois*) is not immediately clear. The word, occurring only here in the New Testament, was generally used in the period for prisoners of war (e.g. Josephus, *Ant.* 10.68). However, a set of fragments from Cave XI at Qumran points to the likelihood that bondage to sin (11Q13.5–7) as well as the demonic (11Q13.10–15) were also part of the contemporary understanding of captivity (see also *Testament of Dan* 5.7–13). Also, the word was soon used metaphorically by Christians.[23] Luke's particular understanding of the word can only be determined by its immediate context.

3 The phrase, 'to the blind sight', is not out of place here in what turns out to be a catalogue of metaphors for all those who are to receive salvation (Luke 4:18). Of particular note is Third Isaiah portraying those waiting for the dawn of salvation as seeking light.[24] Notably, the Targum (or Aramaic translation) of Isaiah 61:1 reads: 'say to the prisoners, be revealed to the light'. In other words, receiving sight was a recognized metaphor for receiving salvation.[25] That receiving sight is a metaphor for salvation is well within the compass of Luke's thinking as seen in Acts 26:18 where he describes salvation as opening eyes, and people turning from darkness to light (cf. Acts 9:8, 17–18). In turn, it is particularly notable that the only story of the healing of a blind person in his writings involves the person asking Jesus for salvation ('have mercy on me', Luke 18:38) and becoming a disciple (18:43); Luke gives no examples of the followers of Jesus giving sight to the blind. In other words, mention of giving sight to the blind is probably not giving notice of Jesus' healing of the physically blind (though it includes that) but is a metaphor for his whole ministry of bringing salvation. Nor can we conclude that, in emulating Jesus, Luke would expect the ministry of the Church to involve the care of the blind. That misconstrues the image and empties it of its significance. Rather, modelling Jesus' ministry, as Luke expresses it in this metaphor, the Church would exercise a ministry of salvation.

4 This is also the only time 'crush' or 'oppress' (*thrauō*) is used in the New Testament. In the period it was used for being crushed literally,[26] as well as figuratively.[27] In a few places, where the whole nation is described as being crushed or oppressed, the Septuagint uses *thrauō* to translate the Hebrew *rāṣaṣ*,[28] a word also used in the Dead Sea Scrolls of those who were oppressed spiritually (CD 13.10). It is possible, though it cannot be

---

[23] E.g. Hippolytus, *Refutation of All Heresies* 1.24.6; 10.9.3; Cyril of Jerusalem, *Procatechesis* 16.1.

[24] Isa. 58:10; 59:9–10; 60:1–3, 19–20; 62:1: Isa. 42:7 (Deutero-Isaiah) uses the same metaphor of those released from exile.

[25] Cf. e.g. Mark 10:46–52; John 9:1–41; Rom. 2:19; 2 *Clem.* 1.6; 9.2.

[26] E.g. in LXX, Exod. 15:6; Num. 17:11; *Pss. Sol.* 8.39; and, e.g. Diodorus Siculus, *Hist.* 20, 93, 2; Josephus, *Ant.* 8.390.

[27] E.g. 1 Sam. (LXX) 20:34; Judith 9:10; Josephus, *J.W.* 1.323; *Barn.* 3.3 (along with Luke 4:18 also citing Isa. 58:6).

[28] Deut. 28:33; Isa. 42:4; 58:6.

pressed – for different Greek words are involved – that Luke may also have in mind those oppressed by the devil being released. For, in Acts 10:38, Jesus is said to have healed all who were 'dominated' or 'oppressed' (*katadunasteuō*)[29] by the devil. Also, in Luke 13:16, Satan is said to have 'bound' (*deō*) a woman for eighteen years. In any case, uncertainty about Luke's use of the word 'crush' is cleared up when we turn to note that he says the oppressed are 'released'.

5 The noun 'release' or 'deliverance' (*aphesis*) is an important word for Luke[30] and his interest in it may explain the penultimate line of the quotation inserted from Isaiah 58:6, which also contains *aphesis*. This word had a wide range of meanings in the New Testament world, including release from legal obligations (Plutarch, *Alex.* 13.2) such as marriage or debt, release of political and social prisoners,[31] as well as forgiveness of sin (Diodorus Siculus, *Hist.* 20, 54, 2). Importantly, apart from this passage, every other time *aphesis* is used in Luke, as well as in the rest of the New Testament, it always refers to the forgiveness of sins. Indeed, in Peter's sermon in Acts, which is parallel to this one by Jesus (see §3.1 above), *aphesis* is also used and expressly connected with sin (Acts 2:38).

If the unqualified use of *aphesis* here (Luke 4:18) is intended to broaden the release to involve more than sin, it is probably to include sickness. For, when we consider the verb, 'release' (*aphiēmi*) we note that he says that not only sins[32] but also fevers (4:39; cf. 40–42) leave a person. Therefore, and importantly for the argument of this chapter, it is most likely that the liberty or release Luke has in mind is the forgiveness of those crushed or oppressed by sin (and perhaps by Satan) as well as – perhaps to a lesser extent – sickness, not the liberation of socio-economic and political prisoners.

6 It could be that, in the line 'to proclaim the acceptable year of the Lord', a literal jubilee is in mind (cf. Lev. 25:8–55). This would give a clear socio-political dimension to this passage. However, significantly, the Qumran literature suggests that, in the New Testament period, the expected jubilee

---

[29] Cf. Amos 4:1 where *katadunasteuō* translates *'āšaq* which is used in parallel with *rāṣaṣ*: 'who oppress (*'āšaq/katadunasteuō*) the poor, who crush (*katapateō/rāṣaṣ*) the needy'.

[30] *Aphesis* (noun): 17 times in the NT, 10 of which occur in Luke-Acts; see Matt. 26:28; Mark 1:4; 3:29; Luke 1:77; 3:3; 4:18 (twice); 24:47; Acts 2:38; 5:51; 10:43; 13:38; 26:18; Eph. 1:7; Col. 1:14; Heb. 9:22; 10:18. *Aphiēmi* (verb): 143 times in the NT, 34 of which occur in Luke-Acts; see Matt. 3:15 (twice); 4:11, 20, 22; 5:24, 40; 6:12 (twice), 14 (twice), 15 (twice); 7:4; 8:15, 22; 9:2, 5, 6; 12:31 (twice); 32 (twice); 13:30, 36; 15:14; 18:12, 21, 27, 32, 35; 19:14, 27, 29; 22:22, 25; 23:13, 23 (twice), 38; 24:2, 40, 41; 26:44, 56; 27:49, 50; Mark 1:18, 20, 31, 34; 2:5, 7, 9, 10; 3:28; 4:12, 36; 5:19, 37; 7:8, 12, 27; 8:13; 10:14, 28, 29; 11:6, 16, 25 (twice); 12:12, 19, 20, 22; 13:2, 34; 14:6, 50; 15:36, 37; Luke 4:39; 5:11, 20, 21, 23, 24; 6:42; 7:47 (twice), 48, 49; 8:51; 9:60; 10:30; 11:4 (twice); 12:10 (twice), 39; 13:8, 35; 17:3, 4, 34, 35; 18:16, 28, 29; 19:44; 21:6; 23:34; John 4:3, 28, 52; 8:29; 10:12; 11:44, 48; 12:7; 14:18, 27; 16:28, 32; 18:8; 20:23 (twice); Acts 5:38; 8:22; 14:17; Rom. 1:27; 4:7; 1 Cor. 7:11, 12, 13; Heb. 2:8; 6:1; Jas. 5:15; 1 John 1:9; 2:12; Rev. 2:4, 20; 11:9.

[31] 1 Esd. 4:62; Philo, *Names* 228; Josephus, *Ant.* 12.40; 17.185.

[32] See Luke 5:20, 21, 23, 24; 7:47, 48, 49; 11:4; 12:10; 17:3, 4; 23:34; Acts 8:22.

was not, at least for some, a literal one but the time of ultimate salvation and judgement (see 11Q13). In any case, the context of the line in Isaiah 61 makes clear that the theme of jubilary release is used to describe the coming of a time of salvation rather than a literal jubilee; this is a perspective Luke is likely to have taken up because of his dependence on this passage.

7 Finally, in quoting from Isaiah 61:2, Luke does not take up the phrase 'and the day of vengeance of our God'. In other words, not only is the positive note of grace (see Luke 4:22) maintained, but any hint of political revenge by way of the eschatological destruction of the Gentile oppressors, expected in the Messianic age, is absent here in Luke's portrait of Jesus' ministry.

Our reading of this programmatic passage has undermined the view that Luke is setting out a socio-economic or political agenda for the mission of Jesus and, consequentially, for the Church. The disadvantaged in this passage – the poor, the captives, the blind and the oppressed – are not the physically or politically needy sectors of society but are the whole of God's people awaiting salvation or release from the bruises and oppression caused by sin and, perhaps, Satan. Two other important passages in Luke require brief comment in relation to a supposed socio-economic and political agenda of the ministry of Jesus.

§13.3.2 The Magnificat – Luke 1:46b–56

This passage could be seen as Luke's call to political revolutionary action. Indeed, the Old Testament metaphor in the hymn – 'the arm of the Lord' (Luke 1:51–52) – shows that the Exodus or heavily political model of salvation provides the background to the passage (e.g. Exod. 6:1–6; cf. Deut. 3:24). However, again, in this context of a preliminary description of Jesus' ministry of salvation, the 'lowly' and 'hungry' (Luke 1:51–52) characterize not particular sections of society being saved but the whole of Israel in her desperate need of salvation.

§13.3.3 The Beatitudes – Luke 6:20–26

In the blessings addressed to the poor, hungry, weeping, hated, excluded and reviled (Luke 6:20b–22) it is, at first, reasonable to consider that Luke has a socio-political agenda. However, we have to keep in mind not only that Jesus is addressing the disciples (6:20a) but also the understanding of the 'poor' that we have seen Luke took up from the Old Testament, and is also known to us from the Qumran scrolls. That is, it is the disciples who are the 'poor', the 'hungry' and those 'weeping'; they are those who recognize their need and receive the kingdom of God. The poor are not a section of the disciples, but represent all the followers of Jesus who have been in need of God's salvation.

Now we turn to examine Luke's ethical material. For, on a prima facie reading, this material lends credence to the view that Jesus is proposing a mission that involves feeding and clothing the poor.

§13.3.4 The ethical material

According to Luke's programmatic statement in Luke 4:18–19 – and confirmed by the Magnificat (Luke 1:46b–56) as well as the Beatitudes (6:20–26) – the recipients of Jesus' mission are not sections of the society needing socio-economic and political help but are all God's people requiring his salvation. Nevertheless, the ethical material could be read differently as encouraging the followers of Jesus to social action in the world.

To begin with, an important key to interpreting Luke's ethical material is to take into account that he confines Jesus' ministry almost entirely to the people of God. We see this boundary being set in Luke's so-called great omission. The material in Mark 6:45 — 8:26, which Luke omits at Luke 9:17, is a self-contained unit depicting Jesus on a tour through Gentile territory, beginning and ending at Bethsaida, which he regarded as part of Galilee (see Luke 8:26). From hints elsewhere (e.g. 9:10/Mark 6:45), it seems he probably knew this material and has dropped it intentionally. Also, at 9:18 Luke drops the place name of Caesarea Philippi as the setting of Peter's confession (cf. Mark 8:27).

Only once does Jesus venture very briefly into Gentile territory, in the story of the exorcism of the demoniac 'in the country of the Gerasenes, which is opposite Galilee' (Luke 8:26; cf. 40). The impression is given, then, that Jesus and the disciples remain almost entirely in Galilee and that Jesus' ministry is confined almost exclusively to the Jews and the Samaritans whom, as we shall see (unlike Matthew), Luke associates with the Jews.[33] The Gentile ministry is foretold (2:32; 24:47) as well as prefigured in the Gospel,[34] but not commenced until Acts.

Luke's main purpose in concentrating on Jesus' ministry to the people of God – Jews and Samaritans – was to highlight that the mission of the post-Easter Church would include the Gentiles. However, it also has the effect of clarifying his view of the place of the ethical material in his Gospel; it is for insiders (the followers of Jesus, the new people of God) rather than for the wider world. Taken together, these two factors – Luke has Jesus' ministry focused on the people of God, and his Gospel is addressing the followers of Jesus – are key in interpreting what Luke says on wealth, poverty and social justice. That is, we can expect that the material he gives is most probably not in order to provide an agenda for the Church in relation to the world. Rather, the material is likely to be intended to provide teaching for followers of Jesus. That is, the material was designed to give guidance for their life together as it related to wealth, poverty and equitable social relations. In other words, the poor or disadvantaged are not outsiders but insiders: neglected or disadvantaged people of God. This means that, unless specifically directed otherwise (see below on Luke 3:7–14), Luke could expect his readers to take

---

[33] Luke 9:2 (contrast Matt. 10:5), 52; 10:33; 17:16; see also Acts 8:5; and below.
[34] Luke 8:26–39; 10:1–12, 17–20.

the ethical material as guiding internal relationships rather than injunctions on how to deal with those outside the community. There are a number of passages containing ethical material that we need to consider briefly to help clarify and develop an understanding of Luke's perspective on the place of social action in the mission of Jesus and the Church.

1 Luke 3:7–14 is said to be a piece of John the Baptist's ethical teaching on sharing possessions and food, on not collecting more tax than set down, as well as not extorting money. On a first reading these instructions (especially those on sharing food and clothing, Luke 3:11) could be taken as teaching readers how to go about social action in relation to out-siders. However, John is addressing insiders, the people of God, who have Abraham as their ancestor (Luke 3:8). Even the soldiers, who are not to extort money (3:14) are likely to be Jewish police protecting the Jewish tax collectors, or Jews in Herod Antipas' army (Josephus, *Ant.* 18.113), for Roman soldiers are unlikely to be interested in John's ministry.

2 Luke 6:27–38, a part of the Sermon on the Plain (Luke 6:17), contains instructions to the disciples in the hearing of the crowd (6:17, 20) on loving their enemies and doing good to those who hate them. An initial reading might suggest that followers of Jesus are being given a set of ethics to guide them in their charity work for outsiders. However, this material is not presented as the mission, or part of the mission, of the followers of Jesus. For example, the saying, 'bless those who curse you' (6:28), and the statement encouraging the giving of a second garment (6:29) are not instruc-tions concerning the content of the mission of the followers of Jesus but are more naturally taken as reactive ethics for facing outside pressure (6:30) or opposition (6:27–29, 35). In other words, these injunctions are not about the nature of the Christian mission involving giving to the poor, but are directions for the behaviour of followers of Jesus on how to live lovingly with outsiders who may be antagonistic. Indeed, as we have noted, it is the disciples (note 6:20) who are described as poor and hungry (6:20–21), not outsiders. In any case, it is to be kept in mind that the backdrop of the activity of Jesus and his followers is limited to the people of God so that all involved in the giving and receiving are 'insiders'.

3 Luke 10:25–37. The story of the so-called Good Samaritan could be seen to be confounding evidence for the theory of mission that is emerging from the work of Luke. That is, Jesus could be seen to be advocating care of outsiders as a Samaritan cared for an outsider. This turns out not to be the case.

Hatred between Jews and Samaritans fluctuated, reaching a peak when John Hyrcanus, the Hasmonean, destroyed the temple of the Samaritans on Mount Gerizim just after 129 BCE (Josephus, *Ant.* 13.255–56). However, by the time of Herod the Great, who reigned from about 37 to 4 BCE, Samaritans seemed to have been permitted access to the inner court of the temple at Jerusalem (*Ant.* 18.30). And, despite the fluctuating animosity between Jews and Samaritans, most significantly from our perspective, Josephus includes Samaria in a description of Jewish provinces, clearly regarding them as essentially Jewish (*J.W.* 3.35–58).

Luke also sees the Samaritans as insiders, albeit illegitimately ostracized. It is true that Matthew maintains the animus-based distinction between God's people and the Samaritans in the saying to the disciples going out on mission, 'On the way do not go among the Gentiles and do not go into a Samaritan town, but go instead to the lost sheep of the house of Israel' (Matt. 10:5–6). However, Luke omits this passage from his stories of the commissions for mission (Luke 9:2–5; and 10:1–20). Also, in the story of the cleansing of the ten lepers, it was the Samaritan among them who returned to thank Jesus for his healing (17:11–19). Further, although in the story of Philip Luke recognizes a distinction between Judea and Samaria (Acts 8:4–25), in Acts 1:8 ('in Jerusalem and in all Judea and Samaria and to the end of the earth') the regions of Judea and Samaria are taken together, as they are in 8:1 and in 9:31, where Galilee is mentioned as well. Thus, although in the story of the Good Samaritan Luke recognizes the antipathy between the Jews and the Samaritans, and the attempt by the Jews to exclude them, he still sees them as part of the people of God. In the story of the Good Samaritan, Luke would not be advocating or assuming the care of an outsider but the necessity of care between legitimate members of the people of God who are not at peace with each other.

4 Luke 11:41–42 is probably also to be understood as instructions on how to live lovingly with antagonistic outsiders. The passage is a saying of Jesus criticizing the Pharisees for tithing while neglecting 'justice' (*krisis*) and the love of God. In the context, the love of God is probably neglecting to express the kind of love God shows. 'Justice' (*krisis*) most probably also has to do with social relations in the community of God's people.[35] A comparable saying in this same category is Luke 20:46–47 where the disciples are warned to beware of the scribes devouring widow's houses. That is, disciples are not to act in their internal relations as do some of the Jews.

5 Luke 12:22–34. This passage on anxiety and trust has its climax in the command: 'Sell your possessions, and give alms' (Luke 12:33). Initially, this command to the disciples (12:22) could be seen as a call to be involved in social welfare. However, the purpose of this action is portrayed not in its benefit to the poor but in bringing about a dispossession of goods by the disciples and a consequent expression of trust in God. This is a common feature of Luke's treatment of the distribution of wealth, for many of the passages which refer to dispossession do not even refer to the poor or imply any particular recipients.[36] When the poor are mentioned it is probably simply because they are the obvious recipients of those

---

[35] See Matt. 12:18; 23:23/Luke 11:42.
[36] Luke 5:11, 28; 8:14; 9:3; 10:4; 12:15; 14:33; 16:13–15; 18:24–30; 21:4.

expressing their complete trust in God by divesting themselves of wealth. That is, generosity is not motivated by or related to the needs of the poor but the needs of the rich. For example, in the story of Zacchaeus, who is the focus of attention, the poor are mentioned simply to provide recipients for the main character to divest himself of wealth.[37] This understanding of social action is even clearer in 22:35 where Luke reflects on Jesus' commission for mission. Luke has Jesus ask, 'When I sent you out with no purse or bag or sandals, did you lack anything?' The disciples answer, 'Nothing!' Thus, it needs to be noted, the point of having little, as also in 12:33, is not so the poor can be fed but so there can be an expression of trust in God.

6 Luke 14:7–24 contains the parables of the marriage feast (Luke 14:7–11) and the great banquet (14:15–24), as well as what, at first sight, appear as ethical instructions on meeting the needs of the disadvantaged in society (14:12–14). However, when we take into account that Luke has deliberately confined Jesus' ministry to the people of God, the needy here are probably intended to be understood as the disadvantaged among the people of God, not those outside. In any case, once again, the plight of the disadvantaged is not Luke's main concern. For, the resulting blessing of inviting the poor, crippled, lame and blind to a banquet is not said to be in their needs being met but 'because they cannot repay you' (14:14). That is, Luke is more concerned about the principle that God includes the humble and excludes the proud in his salvation than about offering ethical advice. Thus, his mention of the needy is not to portray them as the focus of mission; they are foils to provide a way the followers of Jesus can express their humility before God (cf. 14:11).

We can now draw some conclusions from what we have noted of Luke's ethical material in relation to it being seen as possible encouragement for the followers of Jesus to be involved in social action in the wider community. Most importantly, we have seen confirmed that Luke's ethical material is to be read not only in the light of the ministry of Jesus being confined to the people of God – to insiders, but also that the disciples themselves can be termed poor or hungry. This means that all those involved in the giving and receiving are 'insiders'. For example, in the story of the Good Samaritan, the care of an outsider is not being advocated. Instead, the necessity of care between legitimate members of the people of God, who are not at peace with each other, is the concern. Also, where care of the poor is advocated it is not to provide instruction on how to go about mission but to set out the practical responses appropriate to repentance or to provide a way to express humility before, and trust in, God. If what we have advocated so far in this chapter is a reasonable reflection of Luke's perspective, we can expect his general description of Jesus' ministry to bear this out.

---

[37] Luke 19:1–10; cf. 3:11; 11:41; 12:21, 33; 16:9–12; 18:22.

§13.3.5 The nature of Jesus' ministry

In describing the Lukan ministry of Jesus, as well as noting that it was focused on insiders (see §13.3.4 above), we have to take into account a number of facets included by Luke. First to consider is Jesus' ministry of exorcism. After announcing his ministry through reading and explaining the passages from Isaiah, the first activity Jesus undertakes in Luke is casting out a demon (Luke 4:31–37). Yet, even though the first three stories of Jesus' ministry have to do with exorcism,[38] the longer introduction to the ministry of Jesus, including the quotation from Isaiah (see above on Luke 4:16–18), broadens the view of Jesus' ministry we gain from Mark. Also, unlike Mark, Luke makes an attempt to sustain the impression that exorcism as well as healing remained an important aspect of Jesus' ministry. Thus, when the disciples of John the Baptist ask if Jesus is 'he who is to come or shall we look for another?' (7:20) Luke adds the words, 'In that hour he cured many of diseases and plagues and evil spirits, and on many who were blind he bestowed sight' (7:21). This not only makes sense of John's disciples returning able to say what they had heard and seen but it also enables Luke to emphasize healing and exorcism as part of Jesus' ministry.

The little biographical statement in Luke 13:32; 'Go and tell that fox [Herod], "Behold, I cast out demons and perform cures today and tomorrow, and the third day I finish my course"', also has the effect of maintaining the high status of healing and exorcism in Luke's portrait of Jesus. The same end is served by Luke's introduction to the Sermon on the Plain where a great crowd of disciples and a great multitude of people are said to come and hear Jesus and to be healed of their diseases and to be cured of unclean spirits troubling them (Luke 6:17–18). Finally, as part of Luke's attempt to maintain healing and exorcism as an important part of Jesus' ministry is Acts 10:38 where he has Peter say Jesus 'went about doing good and healing all that were oppressed by the devil'. This not only draws attention to exorcism but the generalized reference – 'those oppressed by the devil' – suggests that the demonic is broader than 'possession' and that all sickness has a demonic dimension (see Luke 13:10–17).

Second, for Luke, Jesus is a healer. In portraying Jesus as a healer, Luke emphasizes two things in particular in relation to the mission of Jesus. One thing Luke wants to show is that Jesus' ministry was both in healing and in teaching. For example, in the story of the exorcism in the synagogue at Capernaum Mark has entwined the themes of healing and exorcism (Mark 1:21–8). However, Luke separates them so that Jesus is said, first, to teach on the sabbath and then to enter the synagogue and perform the exorcism. In turn, Luke has the crowd respond separately to each aspect of Jesus' ministry (Luke 4:31–37). Also, as a result of the cleansing of the leper Mark says the people came to Jesus from every quarter (Mark 1:45). However, when Luke

---

[38] Luke 4:31–37, 38–39, 40–41.

concludes the story he says that great multitudes gathered to hear Jesus, as well as to be healed of their infirmities (Luke 5:15). This tendency to attempt to hold in balance Jesus' healing and teaching ministry can also be seen in other stories, such as the man with the withered hand (Mark 3:1–6/Luke 6:6–11), and the setting of the Sermon on the Plain which is immediately followed by two dramatic healing miracles.[39]

Another thing Luke wanted to emphasize is that Jesus' healings give reason for belief. This view is most obvious in the story of Jesus' answer to the question asked by the disciples of John the Baptist as to whether or not Jesus was 'the coming one'. In Q, his source, John's question arises out of Jesus' teaching (Matt. 10:1—11:1). In Luke, the context of John's question is two miracles that the disciples of John report (Luke 7:1–17). Further, in the context of his reply, Luke adds that, in that hour, Jesus cured many of diseases and plagues and evil spirits, and to many that were blind he gave sight (7:21). In turn, Jesus is able to tell the disciples of John to report to their master what they have seen and heard. In other words, the miracles give reason for belief in Jesus. Similarly, the story of the healing of the ten lepers shows that gratitude to, or faith in, Jesus and praise to God are the proper responses to healing for Luke (17:11–19). When we deal with the signs and wonders in Acts (see §13.5.3 below) we will, again, see how effective miracles of healing are in turning people to trust in Jesus.

Further in this outlining of Luke's view of the mission of Jesus, Jesus is a Teacher-Preacher.[40] Mark introduced Jesus as a preacher of repentance (Mark 1:15). Not so Luke. Only later does repentance enter into view in Luke's writing (Luke 10:13). Rather, Jesus is introduced as one marking the beginning of a new era in which release from captivity, particularly of sin, is possible (4:18–19). This message is grounded on Luke's understanding that God has sent his eschatological Spirit on Jesus and is exercising his reign or sovereignty. In other words, because of God's anointing of Jesus with the Spirit, Jesus is authorized and able to preach and teach the kingdom or reign of God. For Luke, this teaching-preaching was the very reason for the coming of Jesus. At the first mention of the theme of the kingdom of God in Luke, Jesus says that he was sent for the purpose of preaching the kingdom or reign of God, at 4:43.

Luke never explains the phrase the kingdom or reign of God, though he says it is to be consummated in the future.[41] Yet, it is already present in the coming, message and ministry of the anointed Jesus. This is most clear in Jesus saying that 'today' the prophecy of Isaiah had been fulfilled (Luke 4:21). The presence of the reign of God is equally clear in Jesus' response to the questioning of the disciples of John the Baptist (7:22). Also, in 11:20 Jesus

---

[39] Mark 3:7–13/Luke 6:17–49; see also 7:1–17.
[40] That Luke does not distinguish between a teaching and preaching mission of Jesus see ch. 3, n. 3.
[41] E.g. Luke 12:35–48; 22:16, 30.

says, 'If it is by the finger of God I cast out demons, then the kingdom of God has come upon you' (my translation). Further, when asked by the Pharisees when the kingdom of God was coming, Jesus says: 'The kingdom of God is not coming with signs to be observed; nor will they say, "Lo, here it is!" or "There!" for behold, the kingdom of God is among [*entos*, or within] you' (17:20–21).

That Luke expects a profound and radical response to this presence of God's reign in the coming and teaching of Jesus is possibly evident in Luke 16:16. There Jesus is reported as saying that everyone enters the reign violently. This is a saying of uncertain meaning. Nevertheless, it could quite reasonably mean that everyone who enters into the reign of God can do so only by fulfilling the radical and demanding invitation. Also, when dealing with some of the ethical material in Luke we saw the radical demands for would-be-followers of Jesus.

This outline of Luke's view of the ministry of Jesus shows that he considers it to be one of bringing to insiders eschatological salvation – the kingdom of God, expressed in the exorcisms and healings as well as freedom from the oppression of sin that he announces. There is nothing in Luke's portrait of the ministry of Jesus to suggest he was modelling social action towards outsiders.

§13.3.6 Mission and social action in Acts

When we turn to the second part of Luke's work we see more clearly his perspective in relation to so-called social or political justice and concern for the poor among the post-Easter followers of Jesus. Already, at the end of his Gospel, Luke had made it plain that the mission of the Church was to be a witness to the resurrection as well as proclaiming repentance and forgiveness (Luke 24:47–48). Earlier in the sending out of the twelve (9:1–6) and then the seventy-two he foreshadows the mission of the Church as only curing the sick (including the demonized, 10:17–18) and saying that the kingdom of God has come near, with the expected response of repentance (10:9). In these passages, critical for understanding Luke's perspective on mission, there is no hint that social or political action of any kind is in mind. When we turn to Acts we find this understanding of mission is developed and well illustrated (e.g. Acts 2:37–42; 3:1–16).

1   Acts 1:6–8, a passage we have had cause to note a number of times, bears on the potential political aspect of Luke's view of mission. As Jesus was leaving them, the disciples are said to ask him if he is about to restore political independence to Israel: 'Lord, will you at this time restore the kingdom to Israel?' (Acts 1:6). The answer is, in effect, 'No!' The disciples are not to know or become anxious about the times and seasons regarding the end time (1:7; cf. Luke 24:21). Neither is Jesus going 'to restore the kingdom of Israel'. That is, he is not going to fulfil their political expectations, nor is he going to fulfil their narrow nationalistic hopes. Instead,

the disciples are promised the Holy Spirit for universal mission (Acts 1:8).
It is obvious from this that Luke did not think that the social condi-
tions and political institutions of the time would be immediately or directly
affected by the followers of Jesus. Instead, the political dimensions of
salvation are put in the future, beyond even the indefinite time of the
mission of the Church.

2 Acts 2:43–47; 4:32–35 and 5:12–16 are Luke's sketches of the early post-
Easter community of followers of Jesus in Jerusalem. In these three idyllic
scenes Luke depicts the followers of Jesus working out the principles
of social justice which he has set out in his Gospel (cf. Luke 3:7–14;
14:12–14). He says that 'all who believed . . . had all things in common and
they sold their possessions and goods and distributed them to all, as any
had need' (Acts 2:44–45). In the next cameo Luke says: 'no one said that
any of the things which he possessed was his own, but they had everything in common . . . There was not a needy person among them, for as
many as were possessors of land or houses sold them, and brought the
proceeds of what was sold and laid it at the apostles' feet and distribution
was made to each as any had need' (4:32, 34–35). All we need to note here
is that Luke is not portraying the followers of Jesus giving aid or applying
the principles of social justice and fairness to those outside the community.
Rather, the principles of social care are being applied to the internal life
of the community of believers.

3 Acts 3 is the story of the healing of the lame man at the temple. When
Peter and John are asked for alms it is clear and notable they do not offer
any proceeds from the community purse (Acts 2:44). From this it is
reasonable to conclude that what funds they had were for internal use
not for outsiders, despite their apparent need. Thus, Peter says 'I have no
silver or gold, but in the name of Jesus Christ of Nazareth, walk' (3:6).
At the very point Luke could have given an example of the followers of
Jesus giving alms, or sharing clothes and feeding the poor as part of their
mission; he chose instead to show the purpose of mission and the nature
of salvation to be miraculous physical healing, not giving alms.

4 In Acts 6:1–6 Luke says that the task of seeing that the widows of the
Hellenists were not neglected in the daily distribution (Acts 6:1) was given
to seven men (6:3). The precise identity of the Hebrews and the Hellenists
need not detain us (see §8.6 above). What is important to note is that
the natural reading of the passage, as well as the force of the disagreement,
requires us to assume that both groups were part of the community of believers. And the followers of Jesus distributed the common funds (2:44–45)
not to outsiders but among their own group. Thus, there is no evidence
to suggest that the seven are portrayed as caring for widows outside the
group of followers of Jesus.

5 Acts 9:36–43 is the story of the death and raising of Tabitha who had been
caring for widows. Verse 41 says that Peter presented Tabitha alive to 'the
saints and the widows'. This does not imply that they are not Christians.

In fact, it is generally assumed that the widows are part of the community of believers. The only evidence in the text from which we could infer their position in relation to the community is Luke's use of the article, 'the widows' (*hai chērai*, as in Acts 6:1). It could not be construed from this that the widows were a separate order of believers (as, perhaps, in 1 Tim. 5:3–16). Rather, Luke is probably conveying that they were a recognizable group among the believers, as in Acts 6:1 (cf. 1:14). If this is correct, again, we have an example in Acts of the community of believers doing 'good works and acts of charity' (Acts 9:36) among its own members rather than outsiders. In any case, from the lack of clarity in his writing, we can be confident that Luke does not see himself as providing a mission mandate for caring for widows outside the community.

6 In Acts 11:27–30 Luke says the disciples at Antioch determine to send funds to the brethren who lived in Judea. The very important point for our purposes is that, in the face of a predicted world-wide famine (Acts 11:28), the disciples are portrayed as ignoring the social needs of the non-believers around them. Instead, the focus of the social action is directed exclusively towards fellow Christians, albeit in another place.

§13.4 So far . . .

In the light of the contemporary conviction that the mission of the Church comprises both evangelistic and social action – alleviating social ills – it is astonishing that Luke, the New Testament writer who has provided the most detailed theology and practice of mission, offers no support for such a view. In particular, our examination of the programmatic statement in Luke 4 has cast doubt on the idea that Luke thought Jesus' mission was either socio-economic or political in nature or that it was directed to particular materially needy sections of the people of Israel. Instead, Jesus' mission is portrayed as announcing forgiveness – and, probably, release from the demonic – to the whole people of God. Thus, the poor in Luke are all the recipients of salvation; even the disciples are called poor. Further, the description of Jesus' ministry confirms that Luke sees Jesus as bringing eschatological salvation in the form of forgiveness, exorcisms and healing, not in any social action. In this we find corroborative support for our earlier conclusion that Luke sees salvation not in political or economic but in spiritual and personal terms (see esp. §4.4).

In the ethical material Luke is not providing a component of a mission mandate to the disadvantaged. Rather, on the one hand, he is outlining a community ethic for insiders. On the other hand, he portrays the poor as foils to enable the expression of repentance and total trust in God and his provision. Also, instead of being part of a mission mandate, some of the ethical material provides a reactive ethic in light of antagonism from outsiders.

In Acts, political dimensions of Jesus' ministry are pushed into a future beyond that of the Church. The mission of the Church in relation to those outside the community of believers is portrayed as continuing the preaching and healing ministry of Jesus. The care of the disadvantaged is directed solely to believers, ignoring the plight of a materially needy world.

In the face of loud contemporary voices to the contrary, we probably have to conclude that, from Luke's perspective, in our terms, mission = evangelism = proclaiming forgiveness or demonstrating the gospel in healing or exorcism, no less and no more. So-called social justice or social action is not part of Luke's theology and practice of mission. Rather, social action is directed to the Christian community. It may not be inaccurate to say that, *whereas we preach the gospel to each other on Sundays and seek to bring social justice to the world, Luke maintained that the Church should preach the gospel to the world and apply social justice within the Church.*

§13.5 The mission

One of the important implications of our discussion so far in this chapter has been to lay the ground for showing that Luke's view of the mission of Jesus and the Church is entirely salvation-healing orientated. In turn, we are now in a position to set out what seem to be the main features of Luke's understanding of the mission of the Church.

§13.5.1 Mission as witness

At the end of his Gospel, anticipating his narrative of the post-Easter community, Luke has Jesus say that his followers are 'witnesses' of these things (Luke 24:48). In the New Testament, the idea of being a witness is almost wholly restricted to Luke's writings[42] where it is always related to the resurrection.[43] Thus, the role of a witness is exclusive to the apostles,[44] though it eventually includes Paul and Stephen.[45]

Stephen sees the risen Jesus standing at the right hand of God (Acts 7:55–6) so that Luke can later call him the Lord's witness (22:15). Paul is also described as having seen the risen Lord. Each time Paul's Damascus road experience is told he is said to see a bright light from heaven and to hear the voice of the Lord Jesus.[46] Luke understands this as the risen Jesus appearing to Paul, for Luke has Ananias say to Paul, 'you will be a witness for him to all men of what you have seen and heard' (22:15). Also, the risen Lord says to Paul, 'I have appeared to you for this purpose, to appoint you to serve and testify to the things in which you have seen me' (26:16). This extension of the witnesses to include Stephen and Paul opens the way

---

[42] Luke 24:48; Acts 1:8, 22; 2:32; 3:15; 5:32; 10:39, 41; 13:31; 22:15, 20; 26:16; 2 Tim. 2:2; 1 Pet. 5:1; Rev. 11:3.

[43] Luke 2:32; see also Acts 1:22; 3:15; 4:33; 5:32; 10:39, 41; 13:31; see also 22:15; 26:16.

[44] Luke 11:48 24:48; Acts 1:8, 22; 2:32; 3:15; 5:32; 10:39, 41; 13:31; 22:15, 20; 26:16.

[45] Acts 22:15, 20; 26:16.

[46] Acts 9:1–19; 22:3–16; 26:4–18.

to extending the role to the whole Church, as Jesus has prophesied to all his followers.[47]

An important aspect of Luke's view of a witness cannot be ignored. In the discourse, to which we have just alluded (about the times before the end), Jesus speaks of his followers being persecuted and brought before kings and governors for his name's sake. Then he says, 'This will be the time for you to witness' (Luke 21:13). Then, in Acts 10:43, Peter is said to speak of all the prophets bearing witness. Notably, the Septuagint describes the ministry of prophets with the verb 'to testify' or 'to bear witness' (*diamarturesthai*).[48] We have already noted that Luke considered all the prophets to suffer persecution and death at the hands of the Jews (§5.1 above). In turn, that Luke thought bearing witness involved suffering and martyrdom cannot be doubted. Stephen is the example par excellence. Also, as well as James being killed (Acts 12:2), we can note that when, like Jesus (Luke 9:51), Paul heads towards Jerusalem he will enter a period of considerable suffering and have to face death.[49] Notably, it is only when this journey of Paul's is complete, and Paul is in Jerusalem as a prisoner, that Luke uses the word 'witness' of Paul (Acts 22:15; 26:16). In short, being a witness involves a total re-enactment of the journey of Jesus, including his suffering in Jerusalem (see 10:39). For Luke, followers of Jesus are not witnesses because they suffer and die, but they suffer and die because they are witnesses.

§13.5.2 Message

In turning to consider the message of mission in more detail, we can begin by recalling that the preaching theme given to the twelve was the kingdom of God (§2.5.1 above). In fact, for Luke, preaching the kingdom is a synonym for preaching or evangelizing (Luke 9:6). In Acts the missionaries are portrayed as speaking about the kingdom. The kingdom is said to be expressly the theme of the preaching of Philip (Acts 8:12), Barnabas and Saul (14:22) and Paul.[50]

Yet, most often in Acts the theme of the preaching is summarized as 'the word', usually of God, but also of the Lord, or of salvation or of the gospel.[51] Jesus' message was also summarized in this way as, for example, when the people pressed upon him to hear 'the word of God' when he was standing by the lake of Gennesaret.[52]

In a number of speeches in Acts, Luke also gives some detail of what he considers to be the message of the followers of Jesus. He provides his readers

---

[47] Luke 21:13; cf. 20:45; 21:13; 24:9. See, also, the discussion at §2.5.3 above.
[48] See 2 Kgs 17:13; 2 Chr. 24:19; Neh. 9:26.
[49] Acts 19:21; 20:22–3; 21:11–13.
[50] Acts 19:8; 20:25; 28:23, 31.
[51] Acts 4:4, 29, 31; 6:2, 4; 8:4, 14, 25; 10:36, 37, 44; 11:1, 19; 13:5, 7, 26, 44, 46, 48; 15:7, 35, 36; 16:6, 32; 17:11, 13; 18:5, 11; 19:10; 28:25.
[52] Luke 5:1; see also 8:11–12; 11:28.

with five speeches by Peter[53] and one by Paul (Acts 13:16–41) that are directed to the Jews. Luke also gives two further speeches by Paul which are directed to Gentile audiences (14:15–17; 17:22–31). Whatever the historical value of these speeches, we can be certain that they represent what Luke considered to be the essential elements of the Christian message to the respective audiences: insiders and outsiders.

In the speeches to the Jews the basic message is that the long-awaited age of the coming of the Messiah had arrived in Jesus.[54] He performed powerful works and, though he is the Messiah,[55] was crucified and killed.[56] God raised Jesus from death making him Lord and Christ (Acts 2:33–36) or Leader and Saviour.[57] Also, God is involved in all that happened to Jesus: 'a man attested to you by God with deeds of power, wonders, and signs that God did through him among you'. Even his death took place 'according to the definite plan and foreknowledge of God'. And it was God who raised Jesus from death (2:22b–24, 32–33).

Apart from this basic message, a number of other aspects of these speeches stand out. Interestingly, in none of them is there a connection made between salvation and the cross or death of Jesus. The mention of the resurrection – as fundamental as it is – serves merely to substantiate the message (see Acts 17:31). The outline of Jesus' story is interspersed with explanations and proofs from Scripture.[58] There is the affirmation that the first followers are witnesses of these things.[59] The story of Jesus, including his receiving and, in turn, pouring out of the Spirit is applied to the present situation.[60] There is the call to repentance linked with the assurance of salvation.[61] Finally, there is the application of the message for the particular audience:[62] Jesus continued to work in the presence of the audience through the mighty works they were seeing (3:12, 16). The conclusion to this argument was that the hearers should repent and be baptized so that they could be forgiven and receive the gift of the Holy Spirit.[63]

Turning to the two speeches by Paul to Gentile audiences we see how Luke thought the good news should be presented to outsiders. As the first of them is very short and intended to persuade the people of Lystra not to worship him and Barnabas (Acts 14:15–17), we will focus our attention on Paul's longer speech to the Athenians (17:22–31).

---

[53] Acts 2:14–40; 3:12–26; 4:9–12; 5:29–32; 10:34–43.
[54] Acts 2:16; see also 3:18, 24; 13:23; cf. e.g. 2:36; 3:13; 5:30a; 10:36, 42.
[55] Acts 2:30–22; see also 3:22–24; 13:33.
[56] Acts 2:22–23; see also 3:13; 4:10; 5:30; 10:39; 13:28–29.
[57] Acts 3:13; 5:31; 13:30.
[58] Acts 2:25–31, 34–35; 3:18, 21, 22.
[59] Acts 2:32; 3:15; 5:31–32; 10:40; 13:31.
[60] Acts 2:33b, 36; see also 3:10c, 16, 25; 13:40–41.
[61] Acts 2:38; see also 3:19; 4:12; 10:43; 13:38–39.
[62] Acts 2:39; see also 3:25–26; 10:36; 13:26.
[63] Acts 2:38; 3:17, 19; 5:31–32; 10:43.

The speech begins with an engagement of the hearers through noting their incomplete understanding of religion: 'Athenians, I see how extremely religious (*deisidaimōn*) you are in every way. For as I went through the city and looked carefully at the objects of your worship, I found among them an altar with the inscription, "To an unknown god"' (Acts 17:22–23a). As Luke will use the term 'extremely religious' in a derogatory sense later, where it can be translated 'superstition' (25:19), here he is probably suggesting the irony of religiosity is no more than empty superstition. This leads to noting that Paul then identifies and corrects a misunderstanding. He says that what they worship as unknown is God the creator (17:23b–24).

Most notably, the central testimony about Jesus – that we could now expect from what we see in the speeches to Jews – has been abandoned for a statement about the nature and character of God as one not aided by mankind, but who is our creator who has put in us the need to worship him. Though thoroughly biblical, this material would have been equally accepted as Greek philosophy.[64]

This theological statement is supported not by scriptural texts but by imprecise allusions to Greek writers, material possibly from Plato and Aratus, but at least thoroughly compatible with the philosophy of Paul's hearers so that he is portrayed as using the terms of his hearers. Thus, in support of the message, Luke is happy to take over literature familiar to the audience and apply it to the creator.[65] Paul then draws the conclusion that since we are God's offspring we should not think of him as something we have created (Acts 17:29).

There follows the call to repentance: 'now he commands all people everywhere to repent' (Acts 17:30). The importance and urgency of this call is based on the conviction that God has appointed a time of judgement by a man, proved by raising this man from the dead (17:31).

Enlightened Greeks had attempted to overthrow the popular belief in a future judgement. Judgement was an ongoing part of life.[66] Thus, only at the point of mentioning a future time of judgement – of directly challenging his hearers – does Paul allude to the resurrection of Jesus. The impact of this strategy is said to cause debate among Paul's audience, some mocking him, some desiring to hear more, others joining him as believers (Acts 17:32–34).

§13.5.3 God's tangible presence

For Luke, the mission of the Church was not only talking about Jesus and the resurrection. The good news of Jesus was also expressed in terms we could call the tangible presence of God through particularly, though not exclusively, miracles or 'signs and wonders'.

---

[64] Acts 17:24–27; see also Ps. 50:7–15; Isa. 55:6; 65:1; 2 Macc. 14:35; 3 Macc. 2.9; Plutarch, *Stoic Self Contradictions* 1034b; Aristobulus in Eusebius, *Preparation for the Gospel* 13.12.9–12.

[65] Acts 17:28; see also Plato, *Sophist* 248e; *Timaeus* 37c; Aratus, *Phaenomena* 5.

[66] E.g. Plato, *Apology of Socrates* 40c; *Laws* 903b, 904c–d; see also Macrobius, *Commentarii in Somnium Scipionis* 1.10.7–17.

In this Luke is using the 'show-and-tell' combination familiar in his portrait of Jesus' ministry as the model for mission (Acts 2:19, 22). From his portrayal of Jesus' ministry in his Gospel we see that Luke considers the Spirit to be on Jesus not only to speak of release from sin[67] but also release from sickness[68] and evil spirits.[69] In Acts, when Luke sums up Jesus' ministry, he notes 'how God anointed Jesus of Nazareth with the Holy Spirit and with power; how he went about doing good and healing all who were oppressed by the devil, for God was with him' (10:38). Thus, even more so than preaching, the most often mentioned aspect or activity of the life of the followers of Jesus are the 'signs and wonders'.[70]

We can see what Luke had in mind in calling miracles 'signs and wonders' from the two uses of the term in the literature of the period. First, in Deuteronomy, where there is the largest number of occurrences of the phrase, 'signs and wonders' do not authenticate the prophet Moses as they do in Exodus (e.g. Exod. 4:1–17). Instead, being from God they point to his saving power, which can be known in the present.[71] Second, twice Philo uses the phrase 'signs and wonders' of the Exodus miracles validating the divine origin of an accompanying statement or revelation.[72]

In Acts we see that Luke has used these two understandings of signs and wonders. His initial specific example of a sign is in the extended story of Peter and John healing a man who had been lame from birth (Acts 3:1–10). Not only is this miracle story called a sign (4:16), it also has echoes of Luke 7:22 where Jesus' miracles demonstrate that he was the coming one. In turn, both Luke 7:22 and Acts 3:8 have echoes of Isaiah 35:6, indicating that this miracle, along with those of Jesus, is a present fulfilment of promised salvation. In other words, for Luke, signs and wonders are an essential and integral expression of the salvation being proclaimed. We can add that, from the story of Ananias and Sapphira, a sign also expressed judgement (Acts 5:1–12; Deut. 28:46).

Further, Philip's ministry in Samaria is portrayed as successful because the signs and wonders, as well as his message, cause the crowd to give attention to him.[73] Also, the story of the healing of Aeneas ends: 'And all the residents of Lydda and Sharon saw him, and they turned to the Lord' (Acts 9:35). Similarly, the story of the raising of Tabitha from the dead has, as part of its ending: 'And it became known throughout Joppa, and many believed in the Lord' (9:42). This point is made even more clearly in the story of the sons of Sceva. In the body of the story, Luke links the defeat of the Jewish exorcists with the name of the Lord Jesus being extolled (19:17), and the story ends with the line 'So the word of the Lord grew and prevailed mightily' (19:20).

---

[67] Luke 24:47; Acts 2:38; 5:31; 10:43; 13:38; 26:18.
[68] Luke 4:39; 7:22; 18:41–43.
[69] Luke 4:31–37; 8:26–39; 9:37–43.
[70] Acts 2:43; 4:30; 5:12; 6:8; 14:3; 15:12; see also 4:33; and §9.8 above.
[71] Deut. 4:34; 6:22; 7:19; 11:3; 26:8; 29:3; 34:11; see also 28:46.
[72] Philo, *Moses* 1.95; *Spec. Laws* 2.218; see also, *Moses* 1.210.
[73] Acts 8:6–7; see also 8:13; 9:32–43; 16:30; 19:20.

While these signs and wonders are not intended by Luke as conjuring tricks to induce belief, they do – and are intended to – cause observers to respond with amazement and have the effect of causing belief. The wonders and signs meant that God was so powerfully and obviously present that onlookers could not resist the message of the believers. As in his understanding of the miracles of Jesus, Luke thought the miracles of the followers of Jesus were an important basis for belief in the message about Jesus.

§13.5.4 The character of the community

For the sake of completeness, another aspect of Luke's understanding of the mission of the Church has to be added: the character of the community of believers. In two of his three sketches of the life of the Jerusalem church Luke includes the sharing of belongings as among the characteristics of the Church impressing observers. In Acts 2:44–45 he says that the believers 'had all things in common and they sold their possessions and goods and distributed them to all, as any had need' (cf. Acts 4:32—5:11). Luke also says, 'And day by day, attending the temple together and breaking bread in their homes, they partook of food with glad and generous hearts, praising God and having favour with all the people' (2:46–47). Luke goes on immediately to say that the Lord added to their number daily those who were being saved, highlighting the place of this continuous mood of joy and praise as important in attracting outsiders (2:48).

Then, through the opening chapters of Acts (2:1—6:8), Luke's narrative gives the impression that the life of the group of followers of Jesus is able to be observed by others and has a positive impact on them.[74] Thus, as well as speaking of and demonstrating the powerful presence of God in signs and wonders, which dominated Luke's understanding of the nature of mission, he considered the character of the community of believers to be significant in the success of mission. Brief though this point be, it is to be kept in mind for when we listen in the next chapter to what Luke might say in a conversation with us about the mission of the Church.

§13.6 Conclusions

Early in Acts Luke establishes that, until the consummation of history, God's people are to be involved in a universal mission. The *raison d'être* for the mission is not only preparation for the coming of God's Messiah but also, particularly, to fulfil the call of Jesus to model his own ministry which characterized God's love in rescuing the lost or poor. Not to be engaged in this mission is to cease being the Church. As the theme of mission looms so large in Luke-Acts, and from hints in the text, it is most likely Luke thought his readers were failing and needed encouragement in their mission.

---

[74] Cf. Acts 5:12–16, 39–42; 6:7.

The surprise and – in the face of contemporary ideas of mission – challenge is in Luke's portrayal of that mission. The mission as Luke describes it is not one of simply speaking about the Jesus event and its relevance to listeners. The mission is one of witnessing, primarily to the resurrection, through not only speaking but also demonstrating the powerful presence of God in signs and wonders. Social action, in terms of caring for the physical needs of the outsider, plays no part in Luke's view of mission.

What social care was enacted by the followers of Jesus in Acts was directed inwards to the body of believers. It bears repeating that, whereas we preach (and sometimes demonstrate) the gospel to each other on Sundays and seek to bring social justice to the world, Luke maintained that the Church should preach and demonstrate the gospel to the world and apply social justice within the Church. A discussion of the implications of this will be taken up in the next and final chapter. For the moment we can at least note that if we are to claim that social action, along with evangelism, is part of the mission, we will not find any support in Luke–Acts.

14

Listening to Luke

We began this study acknowledging that the Church is undergoing a crisis of a magnitude felt only a few times in its history. If the Great Schism (1054) between the East and the West left the Church with an indelible and unhealed fracture, if the Reformation (sixteenth century) further divided the Church and undermined established authorities, and if the Enlightenment (eighteenth century) denied the Church access to the supernatural, the present crisis of knowledge, taking place in a profoundly pluralist world culture, is draining the Church of its confidence.

Early in this study it was stated that, in looking to the New Testament, we were not seeking to ignore the present crisis or the two thousand years of hard won knowledge about the Church. Instead, we have turned to the New Testament because contemporary Christians continue to look to these foundational writings for guidance in belief and practice. Nevertheless, we further acknowledged that, in the New Testament, we would not find a uniform message about the Church; there are as many ecclesiologies as writers.

We have turned to Luke in particular for a number of reasons, though not because he can readmit us to an ecclesiastical Eden we had deserted. Nor are we able to apply what he says as an ecclesiological straitjacket, for other voices – ancient and modern – need to be heard as well as we seek to understand the Church and live in it. We want to listen to Luke because, of all those writers in our collection of foundational literature, it is he alone in the New Testament who has attempted to write so self-consciously and so extensively about the corporate life of the followers of Jesus. Also, of the New Testament writers it is Luke who has written the largest body of work, yet may have been heard the least. His voice is often drowned out by the more demanding and, apparently, more practical voice of Paul. Moreover, Luke's emphasis on the miraculous and the outward, focused mission of the Church is less appealing than Paul's comforting call to give attention to internal matters.

At first sight, it might appear that circumstances have so changed since Luke wrote that we will, in any case, be unable to take into account what he says. The Church is now a major world religion; in some countries the Church is either very influential or politically determinant. No longer is the Church restricted to handfuls of people meeting in one or a few homes in some cities. As well as small churches, there are now, across the globe, vast numbers of mega-churches that, this side of heaven, could hardly have been imagined when Luke was writing.

Yet, even though Luke and the other New Testament writers were not issuing timeless encyclicals, but were writing to their particular readers two thousand years ago, human nature and the way individuals relate to each other appear to have remained sufficiently similar for us to recognize ourselves in some of the characters and activities in Luke-Acts. Further, the way Luke writes of God's activity in human affairs after Easter bears sufficient resemblance to the way he is still claimed to act in human affairs that what Luke has to say is likely to remain of interest to readers in the twenty-first century.

That Luke is aware of the problem of bridging the gap between one generation of followers of Jesus and the next is seen in the way he has elevated Paul, in particular, to the apostolate. In Paul's elevation Luke is proposing that, in each new generation, the Church is carried forward in and by those who have encounters with, and are called by, the risen Jesus. From Luke's perspective we can suppose, then, that, if our generation is to be part of the Church and, in turn, hand on the good news to the next, it will do so not only with the aid of hermeneutical skills to help hear anew from the old texts. Rather, it will be primarily through its members having encounters with the risen Jesus to save, empower and direct them according to his will.

Indeed, we have argued that, broadly, Luke's descriptions are prescriptions. This is particularly obvious in his characterization. But his prescriptive intent is also borne out in his open-ended narrative that leaves the plot, involving the main character of the last part of Acts, to be taken up in the lives of the readers. Yet, perhaps most importantly, Luke's prescriptions come with a particular and clear warning for later generations. Embedded in Luke's understanding of God is not only that in recent history he has acted in new ways (notably, raising Jesus from the dead), but also that he has even more recently acted (in the inclusion of the Gentiles), and that he is presently doing a further new thing (directing the mission of the Church to the Gentiles). Therefore, if we take Luke's prescriptions seriously, we are bound to note that one of them is that God continues to act in new ways. We will need to hear more about this from Luke in a moment (§14.7 below).

With these confidences and cautions we are in a position to listen in more detail to what Luke would contribute to a conversation on the Church held in our time. In what follows, the successive chapters of this book will be our guide. However, we are not seeking to summarize the conclusions to each chapter, though some summarizing will be involved. Rather, in the light of those conclusions, we want to see what Luke would say to us in a conversation about the Church.

§14.1 Christo-centric not pneuma-centric

Perhaps, above all else, Luke would say that the Church is the present and ongoing embodiment of Jesus and his mission. It is not that the Church is simply Christ-like or is to mirror and maintain the ministry of Jesus through emulating his activities and message. Rather, through receiving the empowerment and direction of the Spirit, the Church embodies and expresses the same powerful presence of God apparent in Jesus and his ministry.

At the same time, the Church is not the outcome of the Spirit's creativity; the Spirit did not occasion or form the Church. The Church came into existence before the coming of the Spirit. It was in Jesus' simple choosing of the apostles – without any sacramental dimension – that the Church was born, not in the experience of Pentecost. The Church, created by Jesus and recreated by the risen Jesus, is Christo-centric not pneuma-centric. Concluding that the Church is Christo-centric is not to deny the importance Luke placed on Pentecost; Luke portrays the Church differently after Pentecost. It was in this post-Easter coming of the Spirit that the Church received the resource to empower and direct its life and ministry.

Not only does the life of the Church begin in Jesus' ministry, but also the life of Jesus continues in the ministry of the Church. Through both volumes – though less visibly in the second – Jesus remains the lead and directing character. Moreover, the kingdom or powerful presence of God, embodied and announced in Jesus and his ministry, remains an active theme not only through the two volumes, but also the open end of Acts invites Luke's readers to take up this ministry in their own narrative.

This positive conclusion that the Church is fundamentally and continually Christo-centric is a warning to our increasingly large Church in the twenty-first century. No matter how large, influential or significant the Church either becomes or is perceived to be, it is neither an end in itself nor does it exist for its own perpetuation. The Church is not its own master or mistress; it has no existence outside of service to Jesus in embodying and expressing his life and ministry. For Luke, the Church could be described as sacrament not in and of itself but only in so far as the life and ministry of Jesus can be seen in it.

The positive conclusion that the Church is fundamentally Christo-centric also stands as a critique of some contemporary understandings of the Church. For example, the Church is sometimes seen as essentially a community. But, for Luke, the Church is not fundamentally a community, though it is, in part, communal. In that Jesus is said to appoint a group (note Acts 1:21), Luke signals that he understood the Church was not a collection of individuals related to him but a community of his followers. Yet, for its identity, the Church depended on the call of Jesus not its collecting or being together. Also, the Church is sometimes seen as those gathered around the cross. However, for Luke, the community of the Church is not determined by gathering around or under the cross; it is gathered around the living Jesus. The Church is sometimes seen as gathered around or based on the gospel. Luke's writings do not suggest that he would agree. Yet again, the Church is sometimes seen as a community collected around a sacred meal as its focus. But, Luke's Church has no sacred meal (see §14.6 below). Instead, for Luke, the Church is called into existence by Jesus and has its *raison d'être* in its his ongoing embodiment of his life and mission.

§14.2 The purpose of the Church

In the way he portrays the creation of the Church Luke discloses another aspect of his understanding of its purpose. This is obvious in twelve being called, as well as in the reconstitution of their number after Easter, echoing the identity of Israel. The Church is to inherit all the genetic material of the people of God with their hopes, and to receive all the blessings God had promised his people. At one level, in calling the Church a sect, the Church is seen as a legitimate expression of Judaism and God's promises to his people. Yet, at another level, in so far as the message that Jesus is Messiah is rejected by the Jews, and the Church is forced to separate from the Jews, the Church becomes the new and true Israel. It is not only a sect or a faithful expression of Israel; it is 'the Way', the true and faithful expression of Israel.

Also, in the Church being Christo-centric – embodying the same powerful presence of God seen in Jesus – Luke establishes another aspect of the purpose of the Church. In particular, this is obvious in the use of the term apostle for those first involved in the infant Church. The heritage of the word apostle from the Old Testament prophetic call stories means that those who carry this name bring to the Church they represent the idea and charge that it represent God. So important to Luke is the notion of the Church being sent that he discards the separate idea of the disciples being with Jesus as part of this purpose. Instead, to be on mission is to be with Jesus. Not surprisingly, then, Luke makes much of the parallels between Jesus and his followers, both before and after Easter. Luke is likely to say to us, what we see in Jesus is what is to be reflected in the Church in representing a saving God.

However, we need to note that even though Luke took the purpose of the Church to be embodying Jesus – including being sent on mission – he did not mean that it dispensed salvation. Although Luke describes the Church as embodying the ministry of Jesus, he does not describe the Church as dispensing salvation. The missionaries remain mortals bringing and demonstrating the news that makes salvation possible. Moreover, although salvation is prior to and distinct from becoming part of the Church, belonging to the people of God is an assumed and natural expression of being saved. In short, although salvation comes prior to belonging to the Church, salvation is inconceivable without the Church. As I concluded earlier: we are saved individually but live corporately (§4.4 above).

§14.3 People of the Spirit

I have argued that it is highly probable that Luke inherited a number of post-Easter stories of Jesus sightings or experiences of the Spirit. I also argued that

Luke recast this tradition so that one of the Spirit stories was fixed in Jerusalem on the day of Pentecost after Easter. Luke has the story involve all the followers of Jesus, and the reported event is said to generate an immense public response to what he portrayed as a highly ecstatic event. Notably, the story involved a thoroughly eschatological interpretation of the coming of the Spirit. Luke would agree that the power of the life to come is experienced in the power of the Spirit in this world.

In all this Luke has raised the importance of the coming of the Spirit to overshadow that of the resurrection. As important as Easter is in Luke's narrative and in the constitution of the Church (cf. Acts 20:28), it is the Pentecostal coming of the Spirit that marks the realization of what the not-always-obvious eschatological rumblings in the ministry of Jesus were presaging.

Moreover, in going on to use this story as the model and template for later followers of Jesus, Luke establishes the coming of the eschatological Spirit as the defining event and experience of the Church. Christians are people of the Spirit. Thus, if Luke was asked what determined and characterized Christianity or the Church he would probably say that those who are part of it are people of the Spirit: they have had, and continue to have, experiences of the Spirit of God that are ecstatic and obvious.

However, Luke would go on to remind us that the coming of God's Spirit was not simply an ecstatic experience. The coming of the Spirit on the followers of Jesus filled them with the Holy Spirit and they were able to receive God's forgiveness and a Spirit-based relationship with him. Further, Christians are given a boldness and power for prophesying and performing miracles in order to carry out a universal mission of witnessing to the resurrection.

§14.4 Joining the people of God

Since Luke sees the coming of the Spirit as such an important aspect of joining the people of God, and as the topic is frequently discussed in the contemporary Church, we have been interested in putting a number of questions to him: what is the place of the coming of the Spirit in becoming a Christian? Is tongues the initial evidence for being filled with the Spirit? Does water baptism confer the Spirit or Spirit baptism? Also, is water baptism necessary for salvation? Are we to baptize those too young themselves to respond in faith to the message? From our reading of Luke it seems he would offer us something like the following response.

1 To begin with, lest we become preoccupied with an obvious or ecstatic beginning to the Christian faith, Luke is likely to point out that there is not one coming or filling of the Spirit for the followers of Jesus. Rather, followers of Jesus are understood to be repeatedly or even characteristically filled with the Spirit. Yet, to describe a person as filled with the Spirit is not to reduce the acceptable Christian life to a series of

Spirit-experiences or events. To be filled with the Spirit is to give rise to a life-disposition of being preoccupied or overcome with the character and desires of God.

2 Luke's shorthand for becoming part of the Church is for the person to exhibit some evidence of belief, which other believers affirm and accept through water baptism, joining them to the community. In some of Luke's stories we saw all four elements involved: belief, baptism in water, the coming of the Spirit and speaking in tongues, or some obvious response. At first it is not clear in what precise order Luke would say these steps took place, for in some of the stories the Spirit came on a person before water baptism. However, in these stories we saw that Luke was showing that God was overtaking and overruling human hesitancy in accepting certain people. Therefore, if Luke had a particular view he probably assumes that normally, having believed and been baptized in water, the person received the Spirit which was, in some way, obvious to bystanders.

3 Luke would tell us that the coming of the Spirit was not equivalent to becoming a Christian. Yet, without the Spirit a person could not be considered a Christian. Rather, with belief, repentance and water baptism, the Spirit's coming is one of the aspects of a person joining the followers of Jesus. Luke would say that, broadly, a person became part of the Church through repenting and the others in the community baptizing the person in water in preparation for God giving the gift of the Spirit.

4 In answer to the question as to whether or not speaking in tongues was the initial evidence for being filled with the Spirit Luke would say, no. It is not that tongues are unimportant. However, rather than drawing a close and firm link between tongues and the coming of the Spirit, Luke would want us to see that the Spirit's coming was inescapably obvious. The ecstatic or supernatural evidence of this sometimes involved tongues.

5 Does water baptism confer the Spirit or Spirit baptism? Again, Luke would answer, no. Water baptism is not the same as Spirit baptism and does not confer the Spirit. Luke never equates water baptism and Spirit baptism, nor does he think that baptism in water causes God to give his Spirit or render the baptism of the Spirit superfluous. We suggested that Luke thought Spirit baptism was evidence of faith and water baptism evidence of acceptance into the community.

6 On being asked if water baptism was necessary for conversion or salvation Luke would probably answer, yes. However, baptism is necessary – it appears in all of his stories – not because it alone saves but because it was the action to which a person was able to submit, indicating a faith response as well as a submission to an acceptance by the existing community. Thus, for Luke, baptism is necessary because belonging to the group of followers of Jesus or Christians is fundamental to becoming and being a Christian.

7 Should children below responsible age be baptized? Luke was probably not intending to answer this question for he has left us no direct evidence of his views. However, given that one of his heroes, Paul, would not have

baptized babies, that it was not until the turn of the second and third centuries that it is clear they were baptized, and that Luke is unlikely to have children in mind when describing a household that was baptized, it is unlikely that Luke would have considered baptizing them. In any case, given that, otherwise, Luke has a consistent emphasis on believing, we can say that not only is it highly unlikely that Luke would encourage us to baptize babies, it would probably also have been incomprehensible to him.

§14.5 Facing problems and persecution

To our great gain Luke has not portrayed a perfect or even triumphalist Church with which we would have difficulty identifying. As much as he idealizes and idolizes the Church and its leaders before him, not only does he acknowledge problems in the Church from the beginning but he shows how they can be handled.

In Luke's narrative, the greatest problem facing the Church from outside was that of persecution. From our reading of him, it would not be surprising to hear Luke say that the Church should not respond negatively – even in retaliatory prayer. The Church should pray for the persecutors and for boldness and the miraculous involvement of God to enable further witnessing.

Despite the pronounced theme of persecution, for Luke, the range of problems within the Church was even greater and more debilitating. Luke addressed the problem of rich and poor being in the Church; the high and low being in the Church; the damage to the life of the community caused by dishonesty and selfishness; the cultural tensions exhibited in the disagreement between the Hebrews and the Hellenists; and the role and care of women. All these problems stand over against Luke's high value of unity and the community of believers.

For all of these difficulties Luke provides the backdrop of teaching material from Jesus. He also emphasizes the example and encouragement of Jesus, and the other main characters in his narrative also provide models for his readers in the face of their difficulties. Further, Luke writes of the importance of being together and the pursuit of unity, along with the blessedness of being poor and the cost of being wealthy, and the importance of women, for example. It cannot go without notice that, in the face of even the most profound difficulties, Luke would also say that joyful fellowship is to characterize the Church.

§14.6 Luke on worship

Even though Luke and his first readers had no access to Jewish temple worship, he sees Christian worship as having its roots in faithful Jewish worship that was focused on the temple. Worship also took place in homes and synagogues, venues that remained part of the experience of Luke's first readers. In passing, we saw that Luke seems to have no particular interest in

Sunday as the preferred time of Christian worship. If Luke was asked about worship, and what should take place in worship, from what we know of his commitment to the prayer habits of his Jewish forebears, as well as the synagogue, he would probably give a number of ideas.

First, Luke would tell us that during the festivals and on the Sabbath, the religious activities would dominate: Scripture reading and its Christian interpretation, as well as worship or prayers that were said or sung from memory or extemporized. As healing and fasting were firmly part of the Christian tradition and seemed to have taken place in synagogues, Luke would probably have assumed they would take place at any Christian meeting. He would also tell us that at non-worship meetings those present could resolve leadership or charity issues, hear reports, distribute aid to the poor, eat together, plan mission work, or commission missionaries.

Second, Luke is likely to draw to our attention his expectation that Christian meetings would involve dramatic encounters with God. In these, God was experienced as tangibly present to fill those present with his Spirit or give direction of some kind.

Third, if we asked Luke what part the Eucharist should play in Christian worship we are likely to be surprised, for he does not show the Christians celebrating the Last Supper. Thus, we have already noted that Luke has given no evidence to support the view that the Eucharist was an instrument of grace or that the Church is to be understood as gathered around the Eucharist. As important as eating together is for Luke, it is a corporate expression of the joy of its life not its cause or means of cohesion. Thus, what Luke would probably say to us is that Christians eating together is the joyous remembering of their companionship with Jesus, no more and no less.

Perhaps, fourth, another comment that Luke might make in a contemporary conversation about worship would be his surprise as to how much worship preoccupies or dominates the life of our churches to the point of defining them and sometimes being the sole focus of Christian activity. From what he has written, Luke is likely to expect mission rather than worship to characterize and dominate the life of the Church (see below).

Finally here, if we asked Luke about the popular view in our time that the Church can be understood as a gathering around the word of God, he would probably fully understand. However, while the handing on of the word by the apostles was important to Luke, he gave no impression that this was confined to worship meetings or that it was the prime function of the Church. This leads to the next point.

§14.7 Scripture and experience

Here our questions to Luke are: how would he expect us to relate to and use our Scriptures, and what is the place of experience and Scripture in knowing God and his guidance? First, by way of preface, Luke would probably say that an interpretive tool or lens with which he approached his Scriptures was the idea that, so profound had been the Jesus event, the coming of the Spirit and the inclusion of the Gentiles that, not only were they taken to be predicted and explained by the ancient texts but that, reciprocally, those texts were now to be reinterpreted in the light of what God had done. However, even though there was a reciprocal relationship between the text and event or experience, it was, in Luke's view, the Jesus event, the coming of the Spirit and the Gentile mission, taken together, that were primary: the text remained interpretive.

In practice, for Luke and those who want to take up his interpretive lens, this means that God has moved the locus of revelation. In the beginnings of the history of his people, God was known to Abraham and Moses, for example, through his direct intervention in their lives. Subsequently, the traditions and writings kept alive knowledge of that experience as well as the hope that, in the future, God would similarly act and relate to his people. In the coming of Jesus, the coming of the Spirit and in the inclusion of the Gentiles, the locus of revelation has moved not simply from the ancient events or memories of them embedded in ancient documents, or even simply to events revolving around Jesus. Instead, in the coming of the Spirit and the inclusion of the Gentiles, the locus of revelation is now to be found in events or experiences in which all subsequent people of God can now be caught up.

Second, therefore, the contemporary preoccupation with Scripture would probably puzzle Luke. He would be surprised that most twenty-first-century Christians see themselves essentially as people of the book, seeking guidance and their identity through reading sacred texts. Luke would argue that, even though Scriptures are important in developing Christian theology and practice, we do not find God in, or our initial identity through, reading Scripture. Scripture explains what God has already done and what we have already experienced of him.

Therefore, Luke would urge that we are, fundamentally, people of the Spirit. What we have experienced and what we are has come about not through the exegesis of a text. Rather, what we are and experience has come about through a faith response to the demonstrated message about Jesus that brings the experience of the filling, empowering and guidance of God's Spirit. It is in the light of this experience that Luke would then expect us to look to ancient writings for further understanding.

We could not reply to Luke that we are now in a different position from him in relation to the defining events of Christianity, and so must depend on a text in a way that he did not. With Luke we share in being later generation Christians. He has provided us with his received traditions about Jesus and the early Church, so we have no more or no less access to these events than Luke and his readers.

Third, in privileging event or experience over Scripture, Luke would affirm to us that knowledge of God and his guidance comes through the Spirit enabling inspired speech, and in providing dreams, visions and also prophets who predict the future, teach, encourage and influence, as well as providing the direction of Spirit-filled leaders. Nevertheless, through the portrait and teaching of his heroes, Luke would also encourage us to see that texts – including those relating the traditions of Jesus – have their place to guide understanding and determine behaviour.

It may be in Luke's story of the Jerusalem council that we see how he understands the divine and the human relate in discerning God's direction. Luke portrays the divine as dominant through the initial, obvious and tangible activity of the Spirit. But this was only taken to be God's action, and understood, when the leader recognized and interpreted it in the light of perceiving an agreement with Scripture. Human involvement in discernment also had its place in the community witnessing and affirming the decision of the leader.

In this scenario, Luke's readers are provided with a model for discerning new acts of God and his direction for his people. That is, God's new acts are perceived through a group of believers debating and receiving reports. A Spirit-filled leader detects some continuity between what is reported and what God has said in the Scriptures. Finally, the group is involved in the affirmation of the leader's conclusion. An important implication of this is that, though anchored in being the people of God, Luke would agree that development and change are fundamental to the character of the Church.

Finally, Luke would be surprised at some Christians using Scripture to predict future events. Although Luke's view is that Scripture is predictive of events that have already taken place – to repeat what we have already stated – *Luke does not expect his readers to see still-future events predicted in the Scriptures, not even the Parousia.* The resurrection, not Scripture, guarantees the Parousia.

§14.8 Church structures and leadership

In describing the local church meeting in homes and in (or as) households, Luke is not thinking of the Church as a number of families as we would understand a family. Rather, as the notion of the Church as a synagogue shows, and as we would understand it, he would have in mind describing the Church as a community association or an institution.

In what we can see from his two volumes, it is unlikely Luke was promoting a church organization with Jerusalem as the headquarters. Yet, Luke clearly wanted his readers to understand that the Jerusalem church was the source of what became a self-propagating church. Therefore, on the one hand, since Luke saw that the Church needed to be firmly rooted in, though not controlled by, Jerusalem it is highly likely that he would be deeply grieved by both the dividing lines that characterize our contemporary Church and the immense number of local churches that are independent of all outside authority. On the other hand, I suspect Luke would be equally grieved at the overbearing control some denominations and leaders exercise over their constituents and people, thwarting both divine and human initiative.

The same comments apply in relation to the question of the succession of leaders. Luke would probably not endorse leadership based on formal apostolic succession. However, if he was advising us, I suspect he would encourage organizing leadership so that no part of the Church was isolated or independent from the whole. As we have noted, the idea of a completely independent church or leader seems not to have crossed Luke's mind.

Luke's view is clear on the way leaders are to take up their role: neither by appointment nor by charisma alone; both the Holy Spirit and other leaders, or followers of Jesus, are to be involved. Thus, once again, Luke has the divine and the human in concert realizing God's oversight of the Church.

Although Luke did not know the Church as a global phenomenon, he did know it as an international one. Therefore, it is reasonable to note that he would probably expect individual churches to be linked to each other through the travels of leaders.

At the local level Luke would most probably advocate a group of leaders with an individual, *primus inter pares*, exercising day to day leadership. At least some key individuals, Luke would assume, were travelling missionaries, only from time to time offering direct leadership. Thus, for long periods the group of elders was left to lead or care for the local church. From what Luke says, we can assume the key individual in a local church, as well as the group of leaders, would lead through interpreting Scripture and strengthening or supporting the believers.

The prominence of the servant dimension to leadership shows that Luke is not ignorant of leadership too often imperfectly realized. This also probably explains his emphasis on promoting leaders who are of good standing, full of the Spirit, full of faith, wise and dedicated to prayer and the ministry of the word. His assumption that leaders would perform miracles in conjunction with preaching the word is likely to be variously applauded and dismissed in our twenty-first-century churches.

§14.9 Mission

As Luke sees it, God is a missionary, Jesus is a missionary and so is the Church. Embodying Jesus so that he continues his mission is, for Luke, the prime function of the Church. Though not the light itself, the Church reflects the light of Christ for the world. Therefore, not to be 'on mission' is to cease being the Church. However, I argued that the theme of mission features so prominently in his writings that, along with assuring his readers that God's salvation had not passed them by, one of his purposes is to encourage them in the face of failing in their mission.

As we have already seen, it is on the nature of the mission of the Church that Luke's views appear most at variance with our own. In order to be clear about what Luke is likely to say to us about mission it is important to recall his understanding of salvation. We concluded that Luke has made a radical departure from his Scriptures in exchanging the military and material understanding of salvation for one that can be described in spiritual and personal terms such as forgiveness, the gift of repentance, the gift of the Spirit, healing, 'being found', escaping from the last days, eternal life, blessedness, peace, revelation and glory. *For Luke, salvation is the realization of the powerful presence of God in an individual's present as well as future experience* (see §4.4 above).

Some of what Luke would go on to say about communicating this salvation would not be surprising. For Luke may say to us that an attractive community of believers – or 'another sort of country', as Origen later put it (*Cels.* 8.75) – played an important role in causing people to become believers and join the followers of Jesus (cf. §13.5.4 above). This strategy of the Church in society being the society of the Church would find little disagreement in our contemporary churches.

However, for Luke to say that mission is not simply speaking about Jesus, but also demonstrating the powerful presence of God through the performance of signs and wonders, there would be a mixed response among churches of the twenty-first century. In developing-world churches Luke would find his most enthusiastic support for his interest in the miraculous. In the charismatic and Pentecostal churches in the West there would at least be affirmation, though the miraculous is more part of their doctrine than their practice. In yet other quarters of the Western church the miraculous will be seen as part of the mythological aspect of the early Church that can no more be part of our mission than it was, historically, theirs.

Even if we could agree with Luke on the role of the miraculous, the vast majority of the Church would part company with him in his seeing neither a political nor a social aspect to the mission. Social action, of which there is a considerable interest in Luke, is directed solely to the believers. To repeat, and put the point at its sharpest, I have argued that Luke would see that, whereas we preach the gospel to each other on Sunday and seek to bring social justice to the world, he maintains that the Church should preach the gospel to the world and apply social justice within the Christian community (cf. §13.4 above).

If my argument in reflecting Luke's view has been sound, it will require more space than is available here to explore its ramifications. Nevertheless, there are some pointers that can be offered.

- Luke takes seriously that the most profound human problem is not political or economic but the need for individuals to experience forgiveness, healing – the powerful presence or kingdom of God – and to belong to a caring body of believers.
- Luke does not ignore human physical need. However, it is met within rather than outside the community of believers.
- The portrayed strategy of mission in Luke-Acts is not devoid of care for the physical needs of outsiders. That care is in the form of miraculous healings and exorcisms – signs and wonders taken to be evidence of God's powerful presence.

- To adopt the strategies involved in Luke's view of mission would mean not necessarily fewer but different people would be helped economically or socially. Given a supposed holistic environment of the community of believers, it could be expected that the care of members would be deeper and longer lasting than care offered outside the context of the community. In turn, the Church would be equipped to reach an ever-increasing number of people.

- Luke raises the possibility that the Church would have had a greater impact on society if it had taken his view seriously, concentrating on proclamation accompanied by signs and wonders, and giving care to each other to the extent that outside observers would want to join the community of believers.

- The view that Luke takes on mission places a far greater store on the quality of the community of believers than is generally recognized. If the quality of relationships and care among Christians approached the order proposed by Luke, I suppose that the Church could hardly accommodate or assimilate those who sought to belong to it.

- It is highly unlikely that Luke would object to Christians taking up vocations of care — medics, social workers and psychologists, for example. Also, he is unlikely to speak against a Christian entering politics or diplomacy or economics. What he would want to maintain, however, is that the Church per se has as its mission helping people experience the powerful and transforming presence of God to enable them to receive salvation and then join other believers.

- What Luke would say about involvement in social action as a means of gaining hearers for the gospel is difficult to judge. I suspect he would still argue that such social action or attention rightly belongs to the believers and that evangelism, including the miraculous, ought to be the highest or only priority of the Church in relation to those outside.

- Luke's view of mission would probably be much more difficult to implement than the present two-pronged approach generally adopted: evangelism and social action. It is manifestly easier to send aid to distant strangers than it is, once a person becomes a believer, to share one's resources with them and to relate to them in such a positive way that observers would conclude that the community was an expression of God's presence and ought to be joined. Moreover, those involved in evangelism — from Luke to the present — report the difficulty and suffering involved in helping and encouraging people to believe, even with the aid of the miraculous!

- It is of little comfort to our present mission theory and strategies that Luke's views are probably not unique in the New Testament but were widely shared!

§14.10 Luke's voice

It can be difficult to hear Luke's particular voice in the choir of the New Testament, now accompanied by an increasingly vast interpretive orchestra that has assembled around it over the centuries. If we have correctly identified Luke's voice, he is likely to say to us that the Church is not understood by describing it primarily as a community. Nor would Luke describe the Church as essentially gathered around either the Eucharist as Sacrament or the preached word, or even both. Neither is the word of God the foundation or organizing principle of the Church in so far as the word is understood as a message or utterances or anything distinct from or less than Jesus. Nor, from Luke's perspective, is the Church the creation of the Spirit – though it already lives and breathes at the direction and in the power of the Spirit of the world to come.

Luke tells us that the Church is the renewed people of God called into being by Jesus not merely to represent him or to continue his ministry in his absence. Instead, though he remains distinct from and more than the Church, Jesus is embodied in his followers. The Church is Christ present in God's people. In other words, in experiencing and expressing the kingdom or powerful presence of God – now available through the outpouring of the Spirit – the Church maintains Jesus' presence and ministry between Pentecost and the Parousia.

Therefore, for Luke, the fundamental and active purpose of the Church – the reason for its existence – is neither worship nor the material reformation of the world. The purpose of the Church is the mission of proclaiming, and demonstrating in signs and wonders, the good news of God's salvation in Jesus so that others – everyone – can be saved and join the caring, joyful community of believers preparing for the return of Jesus.

Bibliography

Following the first three sections, this selection of books and articles is arranged according to the chapters of this book. More important or introductory items are identified by an asterisk, *.

Commentaries on Luke and Acts

*Barrett, C. Kingsley, *The Acts of the Apostles*, 2 vols (International Critical Commentary; Edinburgh: T&T Clark, 1994 and London: T&T Clark/Continuum, 2002).

*Bock, Darrell L., *Luke*, 2 vols (Baker Exegetical Commentary on the New Testament; Grand Rapids, Mich.: Baker, 1994, 1996).

Bovon, François, *Luke 1* (Hermeneia; Philadelphia, Pa.: Fortress Press, 2002).

Bruce, F. F., *The Acts of the Apostles* (Grand Rapids, Mich.: Eerdmans, and Leicester, UK: Apollos, 1990).

Conzelmann, Hans, *Acts of the Apostles* (Hermeneia; Philadelphia, Pa.: Fortress Press, 1987).

*Dunn, James D. G., *The Acts of the Apostles* (Epworth Commentaries; Peterborough, UK: Epworth, 1996).

Evans, C. F., *Saint Luke* (Trinity Press International New Testament Commentaries; London: SCM Press; and Philadelphia, Pa., Trinity Press International, 1990).

Fitzmyer, Joseph A., *The Acts of the Apostles* (Anchor Bible 31; New York: Doubleday, 1998).

*Fitzmyer, Joseph A., *The Gospel according to Luke*, 2 vols (Anchor Bible 28 and 28A; New York: Doubleday, 1981, 1985).

Gaventa, Beverly Roberts, *The Acts of the Apostles* (Abingdon New Testament Commentaries; Nashville, Tenn.: Abingdon, 2003).

Green, Joel B., *The Gospel of Luke* (New International Commentary on the New Testament; Grand Rapids, Mich., and Cambridge, UK: Eerdmans, 1997).

Haenchen, Ernst, *The Acts of the Apostles* (Oxford: Blackwell, 1971).

Johnson, Luke Timothy, *The Acts of the Apostles* (Sacra Pagina 5; Collegeville, Minn.: Michael Glazier/Liturgical, 1992).

Johnson, Luke Timothy, *The Gospel of Luke* (Sacra Pagina 3; Collegeville, Minn.: Michael Glazier/Liturgical, 1991).

Marshall, I. Howard, *The Acts of the Apostles* (Tyndale New Testament Commentaries; Leicester, UK: Inter-Varsity Press, 1980).

Marshall, I. Howard, *The Gospel of Luke* (New International Greek Testament Commentary; Exeter, UK: Paternoster, 1978).

Nolland, John, *Luke*, 3 vols (Word Biblical Commentary 35A, B, C; Dallas, Tex.: Word, 1989, 1993, 1993).

Parsons, Mikeal C., *Acts* (Paideia Commentary on the New Testament; Grand Rapids, Mich.: Baker Academic, 2008).

Pervo, Richard I., *Acts: A Commentary* (Hermeneia; Minneapolis, Minn.: Fortress Press, 2009).

Plummer, Alfred, *The Gospel according to S. Luke* (International Critical Commentary; Edinburgh: T&T Clark, 1922).

Tannehill, Robert C., *The Narrative Unity of Luke-Acts: A Literary Interpretation*, 2 vols (Philadelphia, Pa.: Fortress Press, 1986, 1990).

Witherington, Ben, *The Acts of the Apostles: A Socio-rhetorical Commentary* (Grand Rapids, Mich.: Eerdmans, and Carlisle, UK: Paternoster, 1998).

Studies on Luke-Acts

Bovon, François, *Luke the Theologian: Fifty-five Years of Research (1950–2005)* (Waco, Tex.: Baylor University Press, 2006).

Bovon, François, *Studies in Early Christianity* (Grand Rapids, Mich.: Baker, 2003).

Cadbury, Henry J., *The Making of Luke-Acts* (London: SPCK, 1961).

Cadbury, Henry J., *The Style and Literary Method of Luke* (Harvard Theological Studies VI; Cambridge, Mass.: Harvard University Press, 1920 and New York: Kraus, 1969).

Conzelmann, Hans, *The Theology of Saint Luke* (London: Faber and Faber, 1961).

Dibelius, Martin, *The Book of Acts: Form, Style, and Theology* (Minneapolis, Minn.: Fortress Press, 1956).

Esler, Philip F., *Community and Gospel in Luke-Acts: The Social and Political Motivations of Lucan Theology* (Society for New Testament Studies Monograph 57; Cambridge, UK: Cambridge University Press, 1987).

Fitzmyer, Joseph A., *Luke the Theologian: Aspects of His Teaching* (New York: Paulist, 1989).

Foakes-Jackson, F. J., and Kirsopp Lake, *The Beginnings of Christianity: The Acts of the Apostles*, 5 vols (Grand Rapids, Mich.: Baker, 1979).

Gasque, W. Ward, *A History of the Interpretation of the Acts of the Apostles* (Peabody, Mass.: Hendrickson, 1989).

Gaventa, Beverly Roberts, *From Darkness to Light: Aspects of Conversion in the New Testament* (Philadelphia, Pa.: Fortress Press, 1986).

Gaventa, Beverly Roberts, 'Towards a Theology of Acts: Reading and Rereading', *Interpretation* 42 (1988): 146–57.

Grassi, J. A., *God Makes Me Laugh: A New Approach to Luke* (Wilmington, Del.: Michael Glazier, 1986).

*Green, Joel B., *The Theology of the Gospel of Luke* (Cambridge, UK: Cambridge University Press, 1995).

Hemer, Colin J., *The Book of Acts in the Setting of Hellenistic History* (Wissenschaftliche Untersuchungen zum Neuen Testament 49; Tübingen: Mohr, 1989).

Hengel, Martin, *Acts and the History of Earliest Christianity* (London: SCM Press, 1979).

*Jervell, Jacob, *The Theology of the Acts of the Apostles* (Cambridge, UK: Cambridge University Press, 1996).

Jervell, Jacob, *The Unknown Paul: Essays on Luke-Acts and Early Christian History* (Minneapolis, Minn.: Augsburg, 1984).

Juel, Donald, *Luke-Acts: The Promise of History* (Atlanta, Ga.: John Knox, 1983).

Keathley, N. H., ed., *With Steadfast Purpose: Essays on Acts in Honor of Henry Jackson Flanders Jr.* (Waco, Tex.: Baylor University Press, 1990).

Keck, Leander E., and J. Louis Martyn, eds, *Studies in Luke-Acts* (London: SPCK, 1968).

Kümmel, Werner G., 'Current Theological Accusations against Luke', *Andover Newton Quarterly* 16 (1975): 131–45.

Luomanen, P., ed., *Luke-Acts: Scandinavian Perspectives* (Publications of the Finnish Exegetical Society 54; Göttingen: Vandenhoeck & Ruprecht, 1991).

Marguerat, Daniel, *The First Christian Historian* (Cambridge, UK: Cambridge University Press, 2002).

Marshall, I. Howard, *Luke: Historian and Theologian* (Exeter, UK: Paternoster, 1988).

Marshall, I. Howard, and David Peterson, eds, *Witness to the Gospel: The Theology of Acts* (Grand Rapids, Mich., and Cambridge, UK: Eerdmans, 1998).

Navone, John, *Themes of St. Luke* (Rome: Gregorian University Press, 1970).

Neyrey, Jerome H., ed., *The Social World of Luke-Acts: Models for Interpretation* (Peabody, Mass.: Hendrickson, 1991).

O'Collins, G., and G. Marconi, eds, *Luke and Acts* (New York: Paulist, 1993).

O'Toole, Robert F., 'Highlights of Luke's Theology', *Currents in Theology and Mission* 12 (1985): 353–60.

O'Toole, Robert F., *The Unity of Luke's Theology: An Analysis of Luke-Acts* (Good News Studies 9; Wilmington, Del.: Glazier, 1984).

Pao, David W., *Acts and the Isaianic New Exodus* (Grand Rapids, Mich.: Baker, 2000).

Penner, Todd C., *In Praise of Christian Origins: Stephen and the Hellenists in Lukan Apologetic Historiography* (Emory Studies in Early Christianity 10; New York: T&T Clark, 2004).

Penner, Todd C., and Caroline Vander Stichele, eds, *Contextualizing Acts: Lukan Narrative and Greco-Roman Discourse* (Society of Biblical Literature Symposium 20; Atlanta, Ga.: Society of Biblical Literature, 2003).

Reicke, Bo, 'The Risen Lord and His Church: The Theology of Acts', *Interpretation* 13 (1959): 159–69.

*Shillington, V. George, *An Introduction to the Study of Luke-Acts* (T&T Clark Approaches to Biblical Studies; London: T&T Clark, 2007).

Stronstad, Roger, *The Charismatic Theology of St. Luke* (Peabody, Mass.: Hendrickson, 1984).

Talbert, Charles H., ed., *Perspectives on Luke-Acts* (Danville, Va.: Association Baptist Professors of Religion; and Edinburgh, UK: T&T Clark, 1978).

Tannehill, Robert C., *The Shape of Luke's Story* (Eugene, Oreg.: Cascade, 2005).

Thompson, Richard P., *Keeping the Church in Its Place: The Church as Narrative Character in Acts* (New York and London: T&T Clark, 2006).

Thompson, Richard P., 'Keeping the Church in Its Place: Revisiting the Church(es) in Acts', *Wesleyan Theological Journal* 41 (2006): 96–115.

Thompson, Richard P., and Thomas E. Phillips, eds, *Literary Studies in Luke-Acts: Essays in Honor of Joseph B. Tyson* (Macon, Ga.: Mercer University Press, 1998).

Tiede, David L., *Prophecy and History in Luke-Acts* (Philadelphia, Pa.: Fortress Press, 1980).

Turner, M. M. B., *Power from on High: The Spirit in Israel's Restoration and Witness in Luke-Acts* (Journal of Pentecostal Thelogy Supplement 9; Sheffield, UK: JSOT, 1996).

Tyson, Joseph B., *The Death of Jesus in Luke-Acts* (Columbia, SC: University of South Carolina Press, 1986).

Wilson, Stephen G., *The Gentiles and the Gentile Mission in Luke-Acts* (Cambridge, UK: Cambridge University Press, 1973).

*Winter, Bruce W., I. Howard Marshall and David Gill, eds, *The Book of Acts in Its First Century Settings* (5 vols; Grand Rapids, Mich.: Eerdmans, 1993).

Witherington, Ben, ed., *History, Literature, and Society in the Book of Acts* (Cambridge, UK, and New York: Cambridge University Press, 1996).

Bibliographical aids

Bovon, François *Luke the Theologian: Fifty-five Years of Research (1950–2005)* (Waco, Tex.: Baylor University Press, 2006).

Green, Joel B., and Michael C. McKeever, *Luke-Acts and New Testament Historiography* (Institute for Biblical Research Bibliographies 8; Grand Rapids, Mich.: Baker, 1994).

Penner, Todd C., 'Madness in the Method? The Acts of the Apostles in Current Study', *Currents in Biblical Research* 2 (2004): 223–93.

Van Segbroeck, Frans, *The Gospel of Luke: A Cumulative Bibliography 1973–1988* (Bibliotheca Ephemeridum Theologicarum Lovaniensium 88; Leuven: Leuven University Press, 1989).

1 The issues

Brown, R. E., *The Churches the Apostles Left Behind* (London: Chapman, 1984).

Dunn, James D. G., 'Models of Christian Community in the New Testament', in *Strange Gifts: A Guide to Charismatic Renewal* (eds David Martin and Peter Mullen; Oxford: Basil Blackwell, 1984), 1–18.

Jenkins, Philip, *The Next Christendom: The Coming of Global Christianity* (New York: Oxford University Press, 2002).

Kurz, William S., 'Narrative Models for Imitation in Luke-Acts', in *Greeks, Romans, and Christians: Essays in Honor of Abraham J. Malherbe* (eds David L. Balch, Everett Ferguson and Wayne A. Meeks; Minneapolis, Minn.: Fortress Press, 1990), 171–89.

Luke's identity and date

Cadbury, Henry J., ' "We" and "I" Passages in Luke-Acts', *New Testament Studies* 3 (1956–7): 128–32.

Du Plooy, Gerhard P. V., 'The Author in Luke-Acts', *Scriptura* 32 (1990): 28–35.

Finn, T. M., 'The God-fearers Reconsidered', *Catholic Biblical Quarterly* 47 (1985): 75–84.

*Fitzmyer, J. A., 'The Authorship of Luke-Acts Reconsidered', in *Luke the Theologian: Aspects of His Teaching* (New York: Paulist, 1989): 1–26.

Gilbert, Gary, 'The Disappearance of the Gentiles: God-fearers and the Image of the Jews in Luke-Acts', in *Putting Body & Soul Together: Essays in Honor of Robbin Scroggs* (eds Virgiania Wiles, Alexandra Brown and Graydon F. Snyder; Valley Forge, Pa.: Trinity Press International, 1997): 172–84.

Glover, R., ' "Luke the Antiochene" and Acts', *New Testament Studies* 11 (1964–65): 97–106.

Haenchen, Ernst, ' "We" in Acts and the Intinerary', *Journal for Theology and Church* 1 (1965): 65–99.

Hemer, Colin J., 'First Person Narrative in Acts 27–28', *Tyndale Bulletin* 36 (1985): 79–109.

Kraabel, A. Thomas, 'The Disappearance of the "God-fearers" ', *Numen* 28 (1981): 113–26.

Overman, J. A., 'The God-fearers: Some Neglected Features', *Journal for the Study of the New Testament* 32 (1988): 17–26.

Pervo, Richard I., *Dating Acts: Between the Evangelists and the Apologists* (Santa Rosa, Calif.: Polebridge, 2006).

Praeder, Susan Marie, 'Acts 27:1—28:16: Sea Voyages in Ancient Literature and the Theology of Luke-Acts', *Catholic Biblical Quarterly* 46 (1984): 683–706.

Praeder, Susan Marie, 'The Problem of First-person Narration in Acts', *Novum Testamentum* 29 (1987): 193–218.

Robbins, Vernon K., 'By Land and by Sea: The We-passages and Ancient Sea Voyages', in *Perspectives on Luke-Acts* (ed. Charles H. Talbert; Danville, Va.: Association of Baptist Professors of Religion; Edinburgh: T&T Clark, 1978): 215–42.

Robbins, Vernon K., 'The We-passages in Acts and Ancient Sea Voyages', *Biblical Research* 20 (1975): 5–18.

Tyson, Joseph B., *Marcion and Luke-Acts: A Defining Struggle* (Columbia, SC: University of South Carolina Press, 2006).

Wilcox, M., 'The "God-fearers" in Acts: A Reconsideration', *Journal for the Study of the New Testament* 13 (1981): 85–9.

Unity of Luke-Acts

Beck, B. E., 'The Common Authorship of Luke and Acts', *New Testament Studies* 23 (1977): 346–52.

*Bird, Michael F., 'The Unity of Luke-Acts in Recent Discussion', *Journal for the Study of the New Testament* 29 (2007): 425–47.

Dawsey, J. M., 'The Literary Unity of Luke-Acts: Questions of Style – a Task for Literary Critics', *New Testament Studies* 35 (1989): 48–66.

Gregory, Andrew, 'The Reception of Luke and Acts and the Unity of Luke-Acts', *Journal for the Study of the New Testament* 29 (2007): 459–72.

Parsons, Mikeal C., 'The Unity of the Lukan Writings: Rethinking the *Opinio Communis*', in *With Steadfast Purpose: Essays on Acts in Honor of Henry Jackson Flanders Jr.* (ed. N. H. Keathley; Waco, Tex.: Baylor University Press, 1990): 29–53.

Parsons, Mikeal C., and Richard I. Pervo, *Rethinking the Unity of Luke and Acts* (Minneapolis, Minn.: Fortress Press, 1993).

Rowe, C. Kavin, 'History, Hermeneutics and the Unity of Luke-Acts', *Journal for the Study of the New Testament* 28 (2005): 131–57.

Rowe, C. Kavin, 'Literary Unity and Reception History: Reading Luke-Acts as Luke and Acts', *Journal for the Study of the New Testament* 29 (2007): 449–58.

Spencer, Patrick E., 'The Unity of Luke-Acts: A Four-Bolted Hermeneutical Hinge', *Currents in Biblical Research* 5 (2007): 341–66.

*Verheyden, Jozef, 'The Unity of Luke-Acts. What are we up to?', in *The Unity of Luke-Acts* (ed. Jozef Verheyden; Bibliotheca Ephemeridum Theologicarum Lovaniensium 142; Leuven: Leuven University Press, 1999): 3–56.

Genre of Luke-Acts

Alexander, Loveday C. A., 'Luke's Preface in the Context of Greek Preface-writing', *Novum Testamentum* 28 (1986): 48–74.

Alexander, Loveday C. A., *The Preface to Luke's Gospel: Literary Convention and Social Context in Luke 1.1–4 and Acts 1.1* (Society for New Testament Studies Monograph 78; Cambridge, UK: Cambridge University Press, 1993).

Aune, David E., 'The Problem of the Genre of the Gospels: A Critique of C. H. Talbert's *What Is a Gospel?*', in *Gospel Perspectives, vol. 2, Studies of History and Tradition in the Four Gospels* (eds R. T. France and David Wenham; Sheffield, UK: JSOT, 1981): 9–60.

Balch, David L., 'The Genre of Luke-Acts: Individual Biography, Adventure Novel, or Political History?', *Southwestern Journal of Theology* 33 (1990): 5–19.

Barr, David L., and Judith L. Wentling, 'The Conventions of Classical Biography and the Genre of Luke-Acts: A Preliminary Study', in *Luke-Acts: New Perspectives from the Society of Biblical Literature Seminar* (ed. Charles H. Talbert; New York: Crossroad, 1984): 63–88.

*Burridge, Richard A., *What Are the Gospels? A Comparison with Graeco-Roman Biography* (Society for New Testament Studies Monograph 70; Cambridge, UK: Cambridge University Press, 1992).

Callen, T., 'The Preface of Luke-Acts and Historiography', *New Testament Studies* 31 (1985): 576–81.

Gentilli, Bruno, and Giovanni Cerri, *History and Biography in Ancient Thought* (London Studies in Classical Philology 20; Amsterdam: J. C. Gieben, 1988).

Palmer Bonz, Marianne, *The Past as Legacy: Luke-Acts and Ancient Epic* (Minneapolis: Fortress Press, 2000).

Pervo, Richard I., 'Must Luke and Acts Belong to the Same Genre', *Society of Biblical Literature Seminar Papers* 28 (1989): 309–16.

Pervo, Richard I., *Profit with Delight: The Literary Genre of the Acts of the Apostles* (Philadelphia, Pa.: Fortress Press, 1987).

Phillips, Thomas E., 'The Genre of Acts: Moving towards a Consensus?', *Currents in Biblical Research* 4 (2006): 365–96.

Praeder, Susan Marie, 'Luke-Acts and the Ancient Novel', *Society of Biblical Literature Seminar Papers* 20 (1981): 269–92.

Robbins, Vernon K., 'Prefaces in Greco-Roman Biography and Luke-Acts', *Perspectives on Religious Studies* 6 (1979): 94–108.

Sterling, G. E., *Historiography and Self-Definition: Josephos, Luke-Acts and Apologetic Historiography* (Leiden and New York: Brill, 1992).

Talbert, Charles H., *What Is a Gospel? The Genre of the Canonical Gospels* (Philadelphia, Pa.: Fortress Press, 1977).

Luke's aims

Bruce, F. F., 'Paul's Apologetic and the Purpose of Acts', *Bulletin of John Rylands University Library of Manchester* 69 (1986–7): 379–93.

Franklin, Eric, *Christ the Lord: A Study in the Purpose and Theology of Luke-Acts* (London: SPCK, 1975).

Creech, R. R., 'The Most Excellent Narratee: The Significance of Theophilus in Luke-Acts', in *With Steadfast Purpose: Essays on Acts in Honor of Henry Jackson Flanders Jr.* (ed. N. H. Keathley; Waco, Tex.: Baylor University Press, 1990): 107–26.

Dillon, Richard J., 'Previewing Luke's Project from His Prologue (Luke 1:1–4)', *Catholic Biblical Quarterly* 43 (1981): 205–27.

Donfried, K. P., 'Attempts at Understanding the Purpose of Luke-Acts: Christology and the Salvation of the Gentiles', in *Christological Perspectives: Essays in Honor of Harvey K. McArthur* (eds R. F. Berkey and S. A. Edwards; New York: Pilgrim, 1982): 112–22.

Du Plessis, I. I., 'Once More: The Purpose of Luke's Prologue (Lk 1:1–4)', *Novum Testamentum* 16 (1974): 259–71.

Fearghail, Fearghus Ó., *The Introduction to Luke-Acts: A Study of the Role of Luke 1, 1– 4, 44 in the Composition of Luke's Two-Volume Work* (Analecta Biblica 126; Rome: Pontifical Biblical Institute Press, 1991).

Houlden, J. L., 'The Purpose of Luke', *Journal for the Study of the New Testament* 21 (1984): 53–65.

*Maddox, Robert, *The Purpose of Luke-Acts* (Studies of the New Testament and Its World; Edinburgh: T&T Clark, 1982).

*Marshall, I. H., 'Luke and His "Gospel"', in *The Gospel and the Gospels* (ed. P. Stuhlmacher; Grand Rapids, Mich.: Eerdmans, 1991): 273–92.

Mattill, Andrew J., 'The Date and Purpose of Luke-Acts: Rackham Reconsidered', *Catholic Biblical Quarterly* 40 (1978): 335–50.

Mattill, Andrew J., 'The Purpose of Acts: Schneckenburger Reconsidered', in *Apostolic History and the Gospel: Biblical and Historical Essays Presented to F. F. Bruce on His 60th Birthday* (eds W. Ward Gasque and R. P. Martin; Exeter: Paternoster, 1970): 108–22.

Minear, Paul S., 'Dear Theo: The Kerygmatic Intention and Claim of the Book of Acts', *Interpretation* 27 (1973): 131–50.

Nielsen, A. E., 'The Purpose of the Lucan Writings with Special Reference to Eschatology', in *Luke-Acts: Scandinavian Perspectives* (ed. P. Luomanen; Publications of the Finnish Exegetical Society 54; Göttingen: Vandenhoeck & Ruprecht, 1991): 76–93.

O'Toole, Robert F., 'Why Did Luke Write Acts (Lk-Acts)?', *Biblical Theology Bulletin* 7 (1977): 66–76.

Talbert, Charles H., *Luke and the Gnostics: An Examination of the Lucan Purpose* (Nashville, Tenn.: Abingdon, 1966).

Van Unnik, Willem C., 'The "Book of Acts": The Confirmation of the Gospel', *Novum Testamentum* 4 (1960): 26–59.

Van Unnik, Willem C., 'Remarks on the Purpose of Luke's Historical Writing', in *Sparsa Collecta: The Collected Essays of W. C. van Unnik*, Part 1: *Evangelia-Paulina-Acta* (Novum Testamentum Supplement 29; Leiden: Brill, 1973): 6–15.

Walaskay, Paul W., *'And So We Came to Rome': The Political Perspective of St. Luke* (Society for New Testament Studies Monograph 49; Cambridge, UK: Cambridge University Press, 1983).

2 Origins and purpose

Agnew, Francis H., 'On the Origin of the Term Apostolos', *Catholic Biblical Quarterly* 38 (1976): 49–53.

*Agnew, Francis H., 'The Origin of the NT Apostle-Concept: A Review of Research', *Journal of Biblical Literature* 105 (1986): 75–96.

Barrett, C. Kingsley, *The Signs of an Apostle* (Philadelphia, Pa.: Fortress Press, 1972).

Horbury, William, 'The Twelve and the Phylarchs', *New Testament Studies* 32 (1986): 503–27.

Kirk, John Andrew, 'Apostleship since Rengstorf: Towards a Synthesis', *New Testament Studies* 21 (1975): 249–64.

Kodell, J., 'Luke's Use of *Laos*, "People", Especially in the Jerusalem Narrative (Lk 19,28–24,53)', *Catholic Biblical Quarterly* 31 (1969): 327–43.

Lightfoot, J. B., 'The Name and Office of Apostle', in *St. Paul's Epistle to the Galatians* (Grand Rapids, Mich.: Zondervan, 1957): 92–100.

Menoud, Philippe Henri, 'The Additions to the Twelve Apostles according to the Book of Acts', in *Jesus Christ and the Faith: A Collection of Studies* (Pittsburgh Theological Monograph 18; Pittsburgh, Pa.: Pickwick, 1978): 133–48.

Menoud, Philippe Henri, 'Jesus and His Witnesses: Observation on the Unity of the Work of Luke', in *Jesus Christ and the Faith: A Collection of Studies* (Pittsburgh Theological Monograph 18; Pittsburgh, Pa.: Pickwick, 1978): 149–66.

Munck, Johannes, 'Paul, the Apostles, and the Twelve', *Studia Theologica* 3 (1949): 96–110.

Pfitzner, V. C., '"Pneumatic" Apostleship? Apostle and Spirit in the Acts of the Apostles', in *Wort in der Zeit: Neutestamentliche Studien. Festgabe für Karl Heinrich Rengstorf zum 75. Geburtstag* (eds W. Haubeck and M. Bachmann; Leiden: Brill, 1980): 210–35.

Rengstorf, Karl Heinrich, *Apostolate and Ministry: The New Testament Doctrine of the Office of the Ministry* (Saint Louis, Mo., and London: Concordia, 1969).

Schmithals, Walter, *The Office of Apostle in the Early Church* (Nashville, Tenn.: Abingdon, 1969).

Stanley, David M., 'Paul's Conversion in Acts: Why the Three Accounts?', *Catholic Biblical Quarterly* 15 (1953): 315–38.

Sweetland, Dennis M., 'Following Jesus: Discipleship in Luke-Acts', in *New Views on Luke and Acts* (ed. Earl Richard; Collegeville, Minn.: Liturgical, 1990): 109–23.

3 Jesus: the Church modelled

Clark, Andrew C., *Parallel Lives: The Relation of Paul to the Apostles in the Lucan Perspective* (Carlisle, UK, and Waynesboro, Ga.: Paternoster, 2001).

Mattill, Andrew J., 'Jesus-Paul Parallels and the Purpose of Luke-Acts: H. H. Evans Reconsidered', *Novum Testamentum* 17 (1975): 15–46.

Moessner, David P., '"The Christ Must Suffer": New Light on the Jesus–Peter, Stephen, Paul Parallels in Luke-Acts', *Novum Testamentum* 28 (1986): 220–56.

O'Toole, Robert F., 'Parallels between Jesus and His Disciples in Luke-Acts: A Further Study', *Biblische Zeitschrift* 27 (1983): 195–212.

*Praeder, Susan Marie, 'Jesus–Paul, Peter–Paul, and Jesus–Peter Parallels in Luke-Acts: A History of Reader Response', *Society of Biblical Literature Seminar Papers* 23 (1984): 23–39.

Spencer, F. Scott, *The Portrait of Philip in Acts: A Study of Roles and Relations* (Journal for the Study of the New Testament 67; Sheffield, UK: JSOT, 1992).

Sweetland, D. M., *Our Journey with Jesus: Discipleship according to Luke-Acts* (Good New Studies 23; Collegeville, Minn.: Liturgical, 1990).

Talbert, Charles H., *Literary Patterns, Theological Themes and the Genre of Luke-Acts* (Missoula, Mont.: Scholars Press, 1974).

The Ascension

Davies, J. G., 'The Prefiguration of the Ascension in the Third Gospel', *Journal of Theological Studies* 6 (1955): 229–33.

*Dillon, Richard J., *From Eye-Witnesses to Ministers of the Word: Tradition and Composition in Luke 24* (Analecta Biblica 82; Rome: Biblical Institute, 1978).

Epp, Eldon Jay, 'The Ascension in the Textual Tradition of Luke-Acts', in *New Testament Textual Criticism: Its Significance for Exegesis* (eds Eldon Jay Epp and Gordon D. Fee; Oxford: Clarendon Press, 1981): 131–45.

*Fitzmyer, Joseph A., 'The Ascension of Christ and Pentecost', *Theological Studies* 45 (1984): 409–40.

Franklin, Eric, 'Ascension and the Eschatology of Luke-Acts', *Scottish Journal of Theology* 23 (1970): 191–200.

Menoud, Philippe Henri, 'Observations on the Ascension Narratives in Luke-Acts', *Jesus Christ and the Faith: A Collection of Studies* (Pittsburgh Theological Monograph 18; Pittsburgh, Pa.: Pickwick, 1978): 107–20.

Parsons, Mikeal C., *The Departure of Jesus in Luke-Acts: The Ascension Narratives in Context* (Journal for the Study of the New Testament Supplement 21; Sheffield, UK: JSOT, 1987).

Schubert, Paul, 'The Structure and Significance of Luke 24', in *Neutestamentliche Studien für Rudolf Bultmann* (ed. Walther Eltester; Berlin: Alfred Töpelmann, 1954): 165–86.

Van Stempvoort, P. A., 'The Interpretation of the Ascension in Luke and Acts', *New Testament Studies* 5 (1958–9): 30–42.

Zwiep, Arie W., *The Ascension of the Messiah in Lukan Christology* (Supplements to Novum Testamentum 87; Leiden: Brill, 1997).

Structure and end of Acts

Cook, C., 'Travellers' Tales and After-dinner Speeches: The Shape of Acts of the Apostles', *New Blackfriars* 74 (1993): 442–57.

Fowler, Don, 'First Thoughts on Closure: Problems and Prospects', in *Roman Constructions: Readings in Postmodern Latin* (Oxford: Oxford University Press, 2000): 239–83.

Fowler, Don, 'Second Thoughts on Closure', in *Roman Constructions: Readings in Postmodern Latin* (Oxford: Oxford University Press, 2000): 284–307.

Kodell, Jerome, 'The Word of God Grew: The Ecclesial Tendency of Logos in Acts 6,7; 12,24; 19,20', *Biblica* 55 (1974): 505–19.

Kurz, William S., 'The Open-ended Nature of Luke and Acts as Inviting Canonical Actualisation', *Neotestamentica* 31 (1997): 289–308.

Marguerat, Daniel, 'The End of Acts (28.16–31) and the Rhetoric of Silence', in *Rhetoric and the New Testament: Essays from the 1992 Heidelberg Conference* (eds Stanley E. Porter and Thomas H. Olbricht; Journal for the Study of the New Testament Supplement 90; Sheffield, UK: Sheffield Academic Press, 1993): 74–89.

*Marguerat, Daniel, 'The Enigma of the Silent Closing of Acts (28:16–31)', in *Jesus and the Heritage of Israel: Luke's Narrative Claim upon Israel's Legacy* (ed. David P. Moessner; Harrisburg, Pa.: Trinity Press International, 1999): 284–304.

Menoud, Philippe Henri, 'The Plan of the Acts of the Apostles', in *Jesus Christ and the Faith: A Collection of Studies* (Pittsburgh Theological Monograph 18; Pittsburgh, Pa.: Pickwick, 1978): 121–32.

Roberts, Deborah H., Francis M. Dunn and Don Fowler, eds, *Classic Closure: Reading the End in Greek and Latin Literature* (Princeton, NJ: Princeton University Press, 1997).

*Talbert, Charles H., *Literary Patterns, Theological Themes, and the Genre of Luke-Acts* (Society of Biblical Literature Monograph 20; Missoula, Mont.: Scholars Press, 1974).

Talbert, Charles H., *Reading Acts: A Literary and Theological Commentary on the Acts of the Apostles* (Reading the New Testament; New York: Crossroad, 1997).

Thomas, John Christopher, 'The Charismatic Structure of Acts', *Journal of Pentecostal Theology* 13 (2004): 19–30.

4 Salvation and the Church

Barrett, C. Kingsley, 'Salvation Proclaimed: Acts 4:8–12', *Expository Times* 94 (1982): 68–71.

Clifford, Richard, and Khaled Anatolios, 'Christian Salvation: Biblical and Theological Perspectives', *Theological Studies* 66 (2005): 739–69.

Danker, F. W., 'Theological Presuppositions of St. Luke', *Currents in Theology and Mission* 4 (1977): 98–103.

Giles, Kevin N., 'Salvation in Lucan Theology', *The Reformed Theological Review* 42 (1983): 10–16, 45–9.

*Green, Joel B., '"The Message of Salvation" in Luke-Acts', *Ex Auditu* 5 (1989): 21–34.

Karris, Robert J., 'Luke's Soteriology of With-ness', *Currents in Theology and Mission* 12 (1985): 346–52.

Larkin, W. J., Jr., 'Luke's Use of the Old Testament as a Key to His Soteriology', *Journal of the Evangelical Theological Society* 20 (1977): 325–35.

Neyrey, J. H., *The Passion according to Luke: A Redaction Study of Luke's Soteriology* (New York: Paulist, 1985).

Plunkett, Mark A., 'Ethnocentricity and Salvation History in the Cornelius Episode', *Society of Biblical Literature Seminar Papers* 24 (1985): 465–79.

Powell, Mark Allan, 'Salvation in Luke-Acts', *Word & World* 12 (1992): 5–10.

Punayar, Sebastian, 'Salvation in the Gospel of Luke', *Jeevadhara* 24 (1994): 360–72.

Steyn, Gert Jacobus, 'Soteriological Perspectives in Luke's Gospel', in *Salvation in the New Testament: Perspectives on Soteriology* (Supplements to Novum Testamentum 121; ed. J. G. Van der Watt; Leiden: Brill, 2005): 67–99.

5 The Church as the people of God

Barbi, Augusto, 'The Use and Meaning of (*Hoi*) *Ioudaioi* in Acts', in *Luke and Acts* (eds Gerald O'Collins and Gilberto Marconi; New York/Mahwah, NJ: Paulist, 1991): 123–42, 243–5.

Brawley, R. L., 'Ethical Borderlines between Rejection and Hope: Interpreting the Jews in Luke-Acts', *Currents in Theology and Mission* 27 (2000): 415–23.

Brawley, R. L., *Luke-Acts and the Jews: Conflict, Apology, and Conciliation* (Society of Biblical Literature Monograph 33; Atlanta: Scholars Press, 1987).

Carroll, J. T., 'Luke's Portrayal of the Pharisees', *Catholic Biblical Quarterly* 50 (1988): 604–21.

Dupont, D. Jacques, 'The Salvation of the Gentiles and the Theological Significance of Acts', in *The Salvation of the Gentiles: Essays on the Acts of the Apostles* (New York: Paulist, 1979): 11–33.

*Fitzmyer, Joseph A., 'The Designations of Christians in Acts and Their Significance', in *Unité et diversité dans l'église: texte officiel de la Commission Biblique Pontificale et travaux personnels des membres* (eds Martins Terra, João Evangelista and Antonio Moreno Casamitjana; Vatican City: Libreria Editrice Vaticana, 1989): 223–36.

Harland, Philip A., *Association, Synagogues, and Congregations* (Minneapolis, Minn.: Fortress Press, 2003).

Jervell, Jacob, 'God's Faithfulness to the Faithless People: Trends in Interpretation of Luke-Acts', *Word and World* 12 (1992): 29–36.

*Jervell, Jacob, *Luke and the People of God: A New Look at Luke-Acts* (Minneapolis, Minn.: Augsburg, 1972).

Matera, F. J., 'Responsibility for the Death of Jesus according to the Acts of the Apostles', *Journal for the Study of the New Testament* 39 (1990): 77–93.

Moessner, David P., 'Paul in Acts: Preacher of Eschatological Repentance to Israel', *New Testament Studies* 34 (1989): 96–104.

Pathrapankal, J., 'Christianity as a "Way" according to the Acts of the Apostles', in *Les Actes des Apôtres: traditions, redaction, theologie* (ed. Jacob Kremer; Leuven: Leuven University Press, 1979): 533–9.

Räisänen, H., 'The Redemption of Israel: A Salvation-Historical Problem in Luke-Acts', *Luke-Acts: Scandinavian Perspectives* (ed. P. Luomanen; Publications of the Finnish Exegetical Society 54; Göttingen: Vandenhoeck & Ruprecht, 1991): 94–114.

Richardson, Peter, David M. Granskou and Stephen G. Wilson, *Anti-Judaism in Early Christianity* (Studies in Christianity and Judaism 2; Waterloo, Ont.: Wilfrid Laurier University Press, 1986).

Sanders, Jack T., 'The Jewish People in Luke-Acts', in *Luke-Acts and the Jewish People* (ed. Joseph B. Tyson; Minneapolis, Minn.: Augsburg, 1988): 51–75.

Sanders, Jack T., *The Jews in Luke-Acts* (Philadelphia, Pa.: Fortress Press, 1987).

Sanders, Jack T., 'Who Is a Jew and Who Is a Gentile in the Book of Acts?', *New Testament Studies* 37 (1991): 434–55.

Simon, Marcel, 'From Greek Hairesis to Christian Heresy', in *Early Christian Literature and the Classical Intellectual Tradition* (ed. W. R. Schoedel and R. L. Wilken; Paris: Beauchesne, 1979): 101–16.

Slingerland, David, 'The Jews in the Pauline Portion of Acts', *Journal of the American Academy of Religion* 54 (1986): 314–19.

Tannehill, Robert C., 'Israel in Luke-Acts: A Tragic Story', *Journal of Biblical Literature* 104 (1985): 69–85.

Tyson, Joseph B., *Images of Judaism in Luke-Acts* (Columbia, SC: University of South Carolina Press, 1992).

Tyson, Joseph B., ed., *Luke-Acts and the Jewish People: Eight Critical Perspectives* (Minneapolis, Minn.: Augsburg, 1988).

Weatherly, J. A., 'The Jews in Luke-Acts', *Tyndale Bulletin* 40 (1989): 107–17.

Wills, Lawrence M., 'The Depiction of the Jews in Acts', *Journal of Biblical Literature* 110 (1991): 631–54.

Wilson, Stephen G., *Luke and the Law* (Society for New Testament Studies Monograph 50; Cambridge, UK: Cambridge University Press, 1983).

Ziesler, John A., 'Luke and the Pharisees', *New Testament Studies* 25 (1979): 146–57.

6 Luke's Pentecosts

Barrett, C. Kingsley, 'Light on the Holy Spirit from Simon Magus (Acts 8,4–25)', *Les Actes des Apôtres: traditions, rédaction, théologie* (Bibliotheca Ephermeridum Theologicarum Lovaniensium 48; ed. Jacob Kremer; Gembloux: J. Duculot, 1979): 231–95.

Brown, Schuyler, '"Water Baptism" and "Spirit-Baptism" in Luke-Acts', *Anglican Theological Review* 59 (1977): 135–51.

Bruce, F. F., 'The Holy Spirit in the Acts of the Apostles', *Interpretation* 27 (1973): 166–83.

*Dunn, James D. G., *Baptism in the Holy Spirit* (London: SCM Press, 1970).

Dunn, James D. G., 'Spirit-and-Fire Baptism', *Novum Testamentum* 14 (1972): 81–92.

Giblin, Charles H., 'Complementarity of Symbolic Event and Discourse in Acts 2,1–40', in *Studia evangelica*, vol. 6, Papers presented to the 4th International Congress on New Testament Studies held at Oxford, 1969 (Texte und Untersuchungen zur Geschichte der Altchristlichen Literatur 112; ed. Elizabeth A. Livingstone; Berlin: Akademie Verlag, 1973): 189–96.

Giles, Kevin N., 'The Significance of the Day of Pentecost', *Lutheran Theological Journal* 17 (1983): 137–9.

Grogan, G. W., 'The Significance of Pentecost in the History of Salvation', *Scottish Bulletin of Evangelical Theology* 4 (1986): 97–107.

Hull, John H. E., *The Holy Spirit in the Acts of the Apostles* (London: Lutterworth, 1967).

Hur, Ju, *A Dynamic Reading of the Holy Spirit in Luke-Acts* (Journal for the Study of the New Testament 211; Sheffield, UK: Sheffield Academic Press, 2001).

Lampe, G. W. H., 'The Holy Spirit in the Writings of St. Luke', in *Studies in the Gospels: Essays in Memory of R. H. Lightfoot* (ed. Dennis E. Nineham; Oxford: Blackwell, 1955): 159–200.

*Lincoln, Andrew T., 'Theology and History in the Interpretation of Luke's Pentecost', *Expository Times* 96 (1985): 204–9.

*Marshall, I. Howard, 'The Significance of Pentecost', *Scottish Journal of Theology* 30 (1977): 347–69.

Noack, Bent, 'The Day of Pentecost in Jubilees, Qumran, and Acts', *Annual of the Swedish Theological Institute* (Leiden: Brill, 1962): 73–95.

Pereira, Francis, *Ephesus, Climax of Universalism in Luke-Acts: A Redaction-Critical Study of Paul's Ephesian Ministry (Acts 18:23–20:1)* (Series X Jesuit Theological Forum Studies 1; Anand, India: Gujarat Sahitya Prakash, 1983).

Richard, Earl J., 'Pentecost as a Recurrent Theme in Luke-Acts', in *New Views on Luke and Acts* (ed. Earl Richard; Collegeville, Minn.: Liturgical, 1990), 133–49.

Samkutty, V. J., *The Samaritan Mission in Acts* (Library of New Testament Studies 328; London: T&T Clark, 2006).

Shelton, James B., *Might in Word and Deed: The Role of the Holy Spirit in Luke-Acts* (Peabody, Mass.: Hendrickson, 1991).

Turner, M. M. B., 'The Spirit of Prophecy and the Power of Authoritative Preaching in Luke-Acts: A Question of Origins', *New Testament Studies* 38 (1992): 66–88.

7 The Spirit, tongues and baptism

Balch, David L., and Carolyn Osiek, *Families in the New Testament World: Households and House Churches. Family, Religion, and Culture* (Louisville, Ky: Westminster/ John Knox, 1997).

Barrett, C. Kingsley, 'Apollos and the Twelve Disciples of Ephesus', in *The New Testament Age: Essays in Honor of Bo Reicke*, vol. 1 (ed. William C. Weinrich; Macon, Ga.: Mercer, 1984): 29–39.

Bradley, Keith R., *Discovering the Roman Family: Studies in Roman Social History* (New York and Oxford: Oxford University Press, 1991).

Ervin, Howard M., *Conversion-Initiation and the Baptism in the Holy Spirit* (Peabody, Mass.: Hendrickson, 1984).

*Ervin, Howard M., 'Hermeneutics: A Pentecostal Option', *Pneuma* 3 (1981): 11–25.

*Fee, Gordon D., 'Baptism in the Holy Spirit: Issues of Separability and Subsequence', *Pneuma* 7 (1985): 8–99.

Lampe, G. W., *The Seal of the Spirit* (London: Longmans, 1951).

Matson, David Lertis, *Household Conversion Narratives in Acts: Pattern and Interpretation* (Journal for the Study of the New Testament Supplement 123; Sheffield, UK: Sheffield Academic Press, 1996).

Menzies, Robert P., *The Development of Early Christian Pneumatology with Special Reference to Luke-Acts* (Journal for the Study of the New Testament Supplement 54; Sheffield, UK: JSOT, 1991).

Menzies, Robert P., *Empowered for Witness: The Spirit in Luke-Acts* (London and New York: T&T Clark, 2006).

Rawson, Beryl, ed., *The Family in Ancient Rome: New Perspectives* (Ithaca, NY: Cornell University Press, 1986).

Turner, M. M. B., 'The Significance of Receiving the Spirit in Luke-Acts: A Survey of Modern Scholarship', *Trinity Journal* 2 (1981): 131–58.

Turner, M. M. B., 'Spirit Endowment in Luke-Acts: Some Linguistic Considerations', *Vox Evangelica* 12 (1981): 45–63.

Speaking in tongues

*Cartledge, Mark J., ed., *Speaking in Tongues: Multi-Disciplinary Perspectives* (Milton Keynes, UK: Paternoster, 2006).

Davies, J. D., 'Pentecost and Glossolalia', *Journal of Theological Studies* 3 (1952): 228–31.

Esler, Philip F., 'Glossolalia and the Admission of Gentiles into the Early Christian Community', *Biblical Theology Bulletin* 22 (1992): 136–42.

Goodman, Felicitas D., *Speaking in Tongues: A Cross-Cultural Study of Glossolalia* (Chicago: University of Chicago Press, 1972).

Graves, Robert W., 'Documenting Xenoglossy', *Paraclete* 21 (1987): 27–30.

Gundry, Robert H., '"Ecstatic Utterance" (N.E.B.)', *Journal of Theological Studies* 17 (1966): 299–307.

Hovenden, Gerald, *Speaking in Tongues: The New Testament Evidence in Context* (New York: Sheffield Academic Press, 2002).

Mills, Watson E., ed., *Speaking in Tongues: A Guide to Research on Glossolalia* (Grand Rapids, Mich.: Eerdmans, 1986).

Stevenson, Ian, *Unlearned Language: New Studies in Xenoglossy* (Charlottesville, Va.: University Press of Virginia, 1984).

Water baptism

Aland, Kurt, *Did the Early Church Baptize Infants?* (Philadelphia, Pa.: Westminster, 1963).

Beasley-Murray, G. R., *Baptism in the New Testament* (Grand Rapids, Mich.: Eerdmans, 1962).

Cullmann, Oscar, *Baptism in the New Testament* (Studies in Biblical Theology 1; London: SCM Press, 1950).

Jeremias, Joachim, *Infant Baptism in the First Four Centuries* (The Library of History and Doctrine; London: SCM Press, 1960).

Larere, Philippe, *Baptism in Water and Baptism in the Spirit: A Biblical, Liturgical, and Theological Exposition* (Collegeville, Minn: Liturgical, 1993).

O'Neill, John C., 'The Connection between Baptism and the Gift of the Spirit in Acts', *Journal for the Study of the New Testament* 63 (1996): 87–103.

*Porter, Stanley E., and Anthony R. Cross, eds, *Baptism, the New Testament and the Church: Historical and Contemporary Studies in Honour of R. E. O. White* (Journal for the Study of the New Testament Supplement 171; Sheffield, UK: Sheffield Academic Press, 1999).

Porter, Stanley E., and Anthony R. Cross, eds, *Dimensions of Baptism: Biblical and Theological Studies* (Journal for the Study of the New Testament Supplement 234; Sheffield, UK: Sheffield Academic Press, 1999).

Laying-on of hands

Coyle, John Kevin, 'The Laying-on of Hands as Conferral of the Spirit: Some Problems and a Possible Solution', *Studia Patristica* 18 (1989): 339–53.

Ferguson, Everett, 'Laying-on of Hands: Its Significance in Ordination', *Journal of Theological Studies* 26 (1975): 1–12.

Oulton, John E. L., 'Holy Spirit, Baptism, and Laying-on of Hands in Acts', *Expository Times* 66 (1955): 236–40.

Parratt, John, 'Laying-on of Hands in the New Testament: A Re-examination in the Light of the Hebrew Terminology', *Expository Times* 80 (1969): 210–14.

Tipei, John F., 'The Function of the Laying-on of Hands in the New Testament', *Journal of the European Pentecostal Theological Association* 20 (2000): 93–115.

8 Problems in the early Church

Suffering and persecution

Brown, Schuyler, *Apostasy and Perseverance in the Theology of Luke* (Analecta Biblica 36; Rome: Pontifical Biblical Institute, 1969).

Cunningham, Scott, *'Through Many Tribulations': The Theology of Persecution in Luke-Acts* (Journal for the Study of the New Testament Supplement 142; Sheffield, UK: Sheffield Academic Press, 1997).

Kilgallen, John J., 'Persecution in the Acts of the Apostles', in *Luke and Acts* (eds Gerald O'Collins and Gilberto Maroni; New York/Mahwah, NJ: Paulist, 1993): 143–60.

Mittelstadt, Martin William, *The Spirit and Suffering in Luke-Acts: Implications for a Pentecostal Pneumatology* (New York: T&T Clark, 2004).

Moessner, David P., 'Suffering, Intercession and Eschatological Atonement: An Uncommon Common View in the Testament of Moses and in Luke-Acts', *The Pseudepigrapha and Early Biblical Interpretation* (Journal for the Study of the Pseudepigrapha 14; ed. James H. Charlesworth and Craig A. Evans; Sheffield, UK: JSOT, 1993): 202–27.

Scheffler, Eben, *Suffering in Luke's Gospel* (Abhandlungen zur Theologie des Alten und Neuen Testaments 81; Zürich: Theologischer Verlag, 1993).

Prayer

*Crump, D. M., *Jesus the Intercessor. Prayer and Christology in Luke-Acts* (Tübingen: Mohr Siebeck, 1992; and Grand Rapids, Mich.: Baker, 1999).

Green, Joel B., 'Persevering Together in Prayer: The Significance of Prayer in the Acts of the Apostles', in *Into God's Presence: Prayer in the New Testament* (ed. Richard N. Longenecker; Grand Rapids, Mich.: Eerdmans, 2001): 183–202.

O'Brien, Peter T., 'Prayer in Luke-Acts', *Tyndale Bulletin* 24 (1973): 111–27.

*Plymale, Stephen F., 'Luke's Theology of Prayer', *Society of Biblical Literature Seminar Papers* 29 (1990): 529–51.

Plymale, Stephen F., *The Prayer Texts of Luke-Acts* (New York: Peter Lang, 1991).

Smalley, Stephen S., 'Spirit, Kingdom and Prayer in Luke-Acts', *Novum Testamentum* 15 (1973): 59–71.

*Trites, Allison A., 'Prayer Motif in Luke-Acts', in *Perspectives on Luke-Acts* (ed. Charles H. Talbert; Danville: Association of Baptist Professors of Religion, and Edinburgh: T&T Clark, 1978): 168–86.

Trites, Allison A., 'Some Aspects of Prayer in Luke-Acts', *Society of Biblical Literature Seminar Papers* 11 (1977): 59–77.

Turner, M. M. B., 'Prayer in the Gospels and Acts', in *Teach Us to Pray: Prayer in the Bible and the World* (ed. D. A. Carson; Grand Rapids, Mich.: Baker, and Exeter, UK: Paternoster, 1990): 72–5.

Twelftree, Graham H., 'Prayer and the Coming of the Spirit in Acts', *Expository Times* 117 (2006): 271–6.

Rich and poor, high and low

Capper, Brian, 'Reciprocity and the Ethic of Acts', in *Witness to the Gospel: The Theology of Acts* (ed. I. Howard Marshall and David Peterson; Grand Rapids, Mich., and Cambridge, UK: Eerdmans, 1998): 499–518.

Capper, Brian, 'Review Article: Two Types of Discipleship in Early Christianity', *Journal of Theological Studies* 52 (2001): 105–23.

Donahue, John R., 'Two Decades of Research on the Rich and Poor in Luke-Acts', in *Justice and the Holy: Essays in Honor of Walter Harrelson* (ed. D. A. Knight and P. J. Paris; Atlanta, Ga.: Scholars Press, 1989): 129–44.

D'Sa, Thomas, 'The Salvation of the Rich in the Gospel of Luke', *Vidyajyoti* 52 (1988): 170–80.

Gillman, J., *Possessions and the Life of Faith: A Reading of Luke-Acts* (Collegeville, Minn.: Liturgical, 1991).

Johnson, Luke Timothy, *The Literary Function of Possessions in Luke-Acts* (Society of Biblical Literature Dissertation 39; Missoula, Mont.: Scholars Press, 1977).

Johnson, Luke Timothy, *Sharing Possessions: Mandate and Symbol of Faith* (Philadelphia, Pa.: Fortress Press, 1981).

Kim, Kyoung-Ji, *Stewardship and Almsgiving in Luke's Theology* (Journal for the Study of the New Testament Supplement 155; Sheffield, UK: Sheffield Academic Press, 1998).

Mealand, David L., 'Community of Goods and Utopian Allusions in Acts II-IV', *Journal of Theological Studies* 28 (1977): 96–9.

*Phillips, Thomas E., *Reading Issues of Wealth and Poverty in Luke-Acts* (Studies in the Bible and Early Christianity 48; Lewiston, NY: Edwin Mellen, 2001).

Phillips, Thomas E., 'Reading Recent Readings of Issues of Wealth and Poverty in Luke and Acts', *Currents in Biblical Research* 1.2 (2003): 231–69.

Schmidt, T. E., *Hostility to Wealth in the Synoptic Gospels* (Journal for the Study of the New Testament Supplement 15; Sheffield, UK: JSOT, 1987).

York, John O., *The Last Shall Be First: The Rhetoric of Reversal in Luke* (Journal for the Study of the New Testament Supplement 46; Sheffield, UK: JSOT, 1991).

Meal scenes and hospitality

Finger, Reta Halteman, *Of Widows and Meals: Communal Meals in the Book of Acts* (Grand Rapids, Mich.: Eerdmans, 2007).

Heil, John Paul, *The Meal Scenes in Luke-Acts: An Audience-oriented Approach* (Society of Biblical Literature Monograph 52; Atlanta, Ga.: Society of Biblical Literature, 1999).

Just, Arthur A., *The Ongoing Feast: Table Fellowship and Eschatology at Emmaus* (Collegeville, Minn: Liturgical, 1993).

Moxnes, Halvor, 'Meals and the New Community in Luke', *Svensk Exegetisk Årsbok* 51–2 (1986): 158–67.

Smith, Dennis E., 'Table Fellowship as a Literary Motif in the Gospel of Luke', *Journal of Biblical Literature* 106 (1987): 613–28.

Hebrews and Hellenists

Ferguson, Everett, 'The Hellenists in the book of Acts', *Restoration Quarterly* 12 (1969): 159–80.

*Hengel, Martin, *Between Jesus and Paul* (London: SCM Press: 1983).

Hill, Craig C., *Hellenists and Hebrews: Reappraising Division within the Earliest Church* (Minneapolis, Minn.: Fortress Press, 1992).

Lienhard, Joseph T., 'Acts 6:1–6: A Redactional View', *Catholic Biblical Quarterly* 37 (1975): 228–36.

Moule, C. F. D., 'Once More, Who Were the Hellenists', *Expository Times* 70 (1959): 100–2.

Richard, Earl J., *Acts 6:1—8:4: The Author's Method of Composition* (Society of Biblical Literature Dissertation Series 41; Missoula, Mont.: Scholars Press, 1978).

Seccombe, David P., 'Was There Organized Charity in Jerusalem before the Christians?', *Journal of Theological Studies* 29 (1978): 140–3.

Simon, Marcel, *St Stephen and the Hellenists in the Primitive Church* (London: Longmans, 1958).

Spencer, F. Scott, 'Neglected Widows in Acts 6:1–7', *Catholic Biblical Quarterly* 56 (1994): 715–33.

Tyson, Joseph B., 'Acts 6:1–7 and Dietary Regulations in Early Christianity', *Perspectives in Religious Studies* 10 (1983): 145–61.

Women

*D'Angelo, Mary Rose, 'Women in Luke-Acts: A Redactional View', *Journal of Biblical Literature* 109.3 (1990): 441–61.

Levine, Amy-Jill, ed., *A Feminists Companion to Luke* (London and New York: Continuum/Sheffield Academic Press, 2002).

Reid, Barbara E., 'Luke: The Gospel for Women?', *Currents in Theology and Mission* 21 (1994): 405–14.

*Reimer, Ivoni Richter, *Women in the Acts of the Apostles: A Feminist Liberation Perspective* (Minneapolis, Minn.: Fortress Press, 1995).

Spencer, F. Scott, 'Out of Mind, Out of Voice: Slave-Girls and Prophetic Daughters in Luke-Acts', *Biblical Interpretation* 7 (1999): 133–55.

Stricher, Joseph, 'The Men–Women Parallels in the Work of Luke', *Bulletin Dei Verbum* 53 (1999): 14–17.

Watts, R. E., 'Women in the Gospels and Acts', *Crux* 35.2 (1999): 22–33.

9 Worship

Burtshaell, James Tunstead, *From Synagogue to Church: Public Services and Offices in the Earliest Christian Communities* (Cambridge, UK: Cambridge University Press, 1992).

Hahn, Ferdinand, *The Worship of the Early Church* (Philadelphia, Pa.: Fortress Press, 1973).

Hamm, Dennis, 'Acts 4:23–31 – a Neglected Biblical Paradigm of Christian Worship (Especially in Troubled Times)', *Worship* 77 (2003): 225–37.

Hamm, Dennis, 'The Tamid Service in Luke-Acts: The Cultic Background behind Luke's Theology of Worship (Luke 1.5–25; 18.9–14; 24.50–53; Acts 3.1; 10.3, 30)', *Catholic Biblical Quarterly* 65 (2003): 215–31.

Lindquist, Jack E., 'The Emmaus Story (St Luke 24:13–35) as "Early Catholic" Liturgical Catechesis', in *Ecclesia, leiturgia, ministerium: studia in honorem Toivo Harjunpaa* (Publications of the Luther-Agricola Society B 9; eds Martti Parvio, Eric Segelberg and Jan L. Womer; Helsinki: Loimaan Kirjapaino, 1977): 68–88.

Moule, C. F. D., *Worship in the New Testament* (London: Lutterworth, 1961).

Van der Waal, C., 'The Temple in the Gospel according to Luke', *Neotestamentica* 7 (1973): 44–59.

Weinert, Francis D., 'The Meaning of the Temple in Luke-Acts', *Biblical Theology Bulletin* 11 (1981): 85–9.

10 Scripture and knowing God

Alexander, Loveday C. A., ' "This Is That": The Authority of Scripture in the Acts of the Apostles', *Princeton Seminary Bulletin* 25 (2004): 189–204.

Archer, Kenneth J., *A Pentecostal Hermeneutic for the Twenty-first Century: Spirit, Scripture and Community* (Journal of Pentecostal Theology Supplement 28; London: T&T Clark/Continuum, 2004).

Barrett, C. Kingsley, 'The Old Testament in the New Testament: Luke/Acts', in *It Is Written: Scripture Citing Scripture* (ed. D. A. Carson and H. G. M. Williamson; Cambridge, UK: Cambridge University Press, 1988): 231–44.

Bellinger, W. H., Jr., 'The Psalms and Acts: Reading and Re-reading', in *With Steadfast Purpose: Essays on Acts in Honor of Henry Jackson Flanders Jr* (ed. N. H. Keathley; Waco, Tex.: Baylor University Press, 2000): 127–43.

Bock, Darrell L., *Proclamation from Prophecy and Pattern: Lucan Old Testament Christology* (Journal for the Study of the New Testament Supplement 12; Sheffield, UK: Sheffield Academic Press, 1987).

Brodie, Thomas L., 'Towards Unravelling Luke's Use of the Old Testament: Luke 7.11–17 as an *Imitatio* of 1 Kings 17.17–24', *New Testament Studies* 32 (1986): 247–67.

Bruce, F. F., 'Paul's Use of the Old Testament in Acts', in *Tradition and Interpretation in the New Testament: Essays in Honor of E. Earle Ellis for his 60th Birthday* (ed. G. F. Hawthorne with O. Betz; Grand Rapids, Mich.: Eerdmans and Tübingen: Mohr, 1987): 71–9.

Denova, Rebecca I., *The Things Accomplished among Us: Prophetic Tradition in the Structural Pattern of Luke-Acts* (Sheffield, UK: Sheffield Academic Press, 1997).

Doeve, J. W., *Jewish Hermeneutics and the Synoptic Gospels and Acts* (Assen, Netherlands: Van Gorcum, 1954).

Dupont, D. Jacques, 'Apologetic Use of the Old Testament in the Speeches of Acts', in *The Salvation of the Gentiles: Essays on the Acts of the Apostles* (New York: Paulist, 1979): 129–59.

Evans, Craig A., and James A. Sanders, eds, *Luke and Scripture: The Function of Sacred Tradition in Luke-Acts* (Minneapolis, Minn.: Fortress Press, 1993).

Green, Joel B., 'The Problem of a Beginning: Israel's Scriptures in Luke 1—2', *Bulletin of Biblical Research* 4 (1994): 61–85.

Hanson, A. T., *The Living Utterances of God: The New Testament Exegesis of the Old* (London: Darton, Longman and Todd, 1983).

Jervell, Jacob, 'The Center of Scripture in Luke', *The Unknown Paul: Essays on Luke-Acts and Early Christian History* (Minneapolis, Minn.: Augsburg, 1984): 122–37.

*Johnson, Luke Timothy, *Scripture and Discernment: Decision Making in the Church* (Nashville, Tenn.: Abingdon, 1983).

Kilpatrick, George D., 'Some Quotations in Acts', in *Les Actes des Apôtres: Traditions, Rédaction, Théologie* (ed. Jacob Kremer; Bibliotheca Ephemeridum Theologicarum Lovaniensium 48; Leuven: Leuven University Press, 1979): 81–97.

Kimball, Charles A., *Jesus' Exposition of the Old Testament in Luke's Gospel* (Journal for the Study of the New Testament Supplement 94; Sheffield, UK: JSOT, 1994).

Koet, Bart J., *Five Studies on Interpretation of Scripture in Luke-Acts* (Studiorum Novi Testamenti Auxilia 14; Leuven: Leuven University Press, 1989).

*Moyise, Steve, *The Old Testament in the New: An Introduction* (Continuum Biblical Studies; London and New York: Continuum, 2001).

Sanders, Jack T., 'The Prophetic Use of the Scriptures in Luke-Acts', in *Early Jewish and Christian Exegesis: Studies in Memory of William Hugh Brownlee* (ed. Craig A. Evans and William. F. Stinespring; Atlanta: Scholars Press, 1987): 191–8.

Sanders, James A., 'Isaiah in Luke', *Interpretation* 36 (1982): 144–55.

Seccombe, David P., 'Luke and Isaiah', *New Testament Studies* 27 (1981): 252–9.

Steyn, Gert Jacobus, *Septuagint Quotations in the Context of the Petrine and Pauline Speeches of the Acta Apostolorum* (Contributions to Biblical Exegesis and Theology 12; Kampen: Kok Pharos, 1995).

Talbert, Charles H., 'Promise and Fulfillment in Lucan Theology', in *Luke-Acts: New Perspectives from the Society of Biblical Literature* (ed. Charles H. Talbert; New York: Crossroad, 1984): 91–103.

Tyson, Joseph B., 'The Gentile Mission and the Authority of Scripture in Acts', *New Testament Studies* 33 (1987): 619–31.

11 Experience and knowing God

Aune, David E., *Prophecy in Early Christianity and the Ancient Mediterranean World* (Grand Rapids, Mich.: Eerdmans, 1983).

*Dunn, James D. G., *Jesus and the Spirit: A Study of the Religious and Charismatic Experience of Jesus and the First Christians as Reflected in the New Testament* (London: SCM Press, 1975).

Ellis, E. Earle, 'The Role of the Christian Prophet in Acts: Source', in *Apostolic History and the Gospel* (eds W. Ward Gasque and R. P. Martin; Exeter, UK: Paternoster, 1970): 55–67.

Fowl, Stephen E., 'How the Spirit Reads and How to Read the Spirit', in *The Bible in Ethics: The Second Sheffield Colloquium* (Journal for the Study of the Old Testament Supplement 207; eds John W. Rogerson, Margaret Davies and M. Daniel Carroll R.; Sheffield, UK: Sheffield Academic Press, 1995): 348–63.

Hanson, J. S., 'Dreams and Visions in the Graeco-Roman World and Early Christianity', *Aufstieg und Niedergang der Römischen Welt* II.23.2 (1980): 1395–427.

Hill, David, *New Testament Prophecy* (Basingstoke, UK: Marshall, Morgan & Scott, 1979).

Koet, Bart J., *Dreams and Scripture in Luke-Acts: Collected Essays* (Studiorum Novi Testamenti Auxilia 42; Leuven: Leuven University Press, 2006).

*Nolland, John, 'Acts 15: Discerning the Will of God in Changing Circumstances', *Crux* 27 (1991): 30–4.

*Pilch, John J., *Visions and Healing in the Acts of the Apostles: How Early Believers Experienced God* (Collegeville, Minn.: Liturgical, 2004).

Stronstad, Roger, 'Pentecostal Experience and Hermeneutics', *Paraclete* 26 (1992): 14–30.

Thomas, J. Christopher, 'Reading the Bible from within Our Traditions: A Pentecostal Hermeneutic as Test Case', in *Between Two Horizons: Spanning New Testament Studies and Systematic Theology* (eds Joel B. Green and M. M. B. Turner; Grand Rapids, Mich. and Cambridge, UK: Eerdmans, 2000): 108–22.

Turner, M. M. B., 'The Spirit of Prophecy and the Power of Authoritative Preaching in Luke-Acts: A Question of Origins', *New Testament Studies* 38 (1992): 66–88.

12 Early Catholic, Protestant or Charismatic?

Campbell, Alastair V., 'The Elders of the Jerusalem Church', *Journal of Theological Studies* 44 (1993): 511–28.

Campbell, R. Alastair, *The Elders: Seniority within Earliest Christianity* (Studies of the New Testament and Its World; Edinburgh: T&T Clark, 1994).

Giles, Kevin N., 'Is Luke an Exponent of "Early Protestantism"? Church Order in the Lukan Writings (Part I)', *Evangelical Quarterly* 54 (1982): 193–205.

Giles, Kevin N., 'Is Luke an Exponent of "Early Protestantism"? Church Order in the Lukan Writings (continued)', *Evangelical Quarterly* 55 (1983): 3–20.

Giles, Kevin N., *Patterns of Ministry among the First Christians* (Melbourne, Australia: Collins Dove, 1989).

Harvey, A. E., 'Elders', *Journal of Theological Studies* 25 (1974): 318–32.

Käsemann, Ernst, 'Ministry and Community in the New Testament', *Essays on New Testament Themes* (London: SCM Press, 1964): 63–94.

*Marshall, I. Howard, '"Early Catholicism" the New Testament', in *New Dimensions in New Testament Study* (eds R. N. Longenecker and M. C. Tenney; Grand Rapids, Mich.: Zondervan, 1974): 217–31.

Nelson, Peter K., *Leadership and Discipleship: A Study of Luke 22:24–30* (Society of Biblical Literature Dissertation 138; Atlanta, Ga.: Scholars Press, 1994).

Parsons, Mikeal C., 'The Place of Jerusalem on the Lukan Landscape: An Exercise in Symbolic Cartography', in *Literary Studies in Luke-Acts: Essays in Honor of Joseph B. Tyson* (eds Richard P. Thompson and Thomas E. Phillips; Macon, Ga.: Mercer University Press, 1998): 155–71.

Schweizer, Eduard, *Church Order in the New Testament* (London: SCM Press, 1961).

Smith, Abraham, '"Full of Spirit and Wisdom": Luke's Portrait of Stephen (Acts 6:1–8:1a) as a Man of Self-Mastery', in *Asceticism and the New Testament* (eds Leif E. Vaage and Vincent L. Wimbush; New York: Routledge, 1999): 97–114.

Tyson, Joseph B., 'The Emerging Church and the Problem of Authority in Acts', *Interpretation* 42 (1988): 132–45.

Young, Frances M., 'On Episkopos, and Presbyteros', *Journal of Theological Studies* 45 (1994): 142–8.

13 Mission: evangelism or social action or both?

Biggar, Nigel, 'Showing the Gospel in Social Praxis', *Anvil* 8 (1991): 7–18.

Cassidy, Richard J., *Jesus, Politics and Society: A Study of Luke's Gospel* (Maryknoll, NY: Orbis, 1978).

Christenson, Larry, *A Charismatic Approach to Social Action* (Minneapolis, Minn.: Bethany Fellowship, 1974).

Gallagher, Robert L., and Paul Hertig, eds, *Mission in Acts: Ancient Narratives in Contemporary Context* (Maryknoll, NY: Orbis, 2004).

Green, Joel B., '"Proclaiming Repentance and Forgiveness of Sins to All Nations": A Biblical Perspective on the Church's Mission', in *The Mission of the Church in Methodist Perspective: The World Is My Parish* (ed. Alan G. Padgett; Lewiston/Queenston/Lampeter: Edwin Mellen, 1992): 1–43.

Hauerwas, Stanley, 'The Politics of Charity in Luke', *Interpretation* 31 (1977): 251–62.

Miller, M. P., 'The Function of Isa 61:1–2 in 11Q Melchizedek', *Journal of Biblical Literature* 88 (1969): 467–9.

Penney, John Michael, *The Missionary Emphasis of Lukan Pneumatology* (Sheffield, UK: Sheffield Academic Press, 1997).

Sanders, Jack T., *Ethics in the New Testament* (London: SCM Press, 1975).

Senior, Donald P., and Carroll Stuhlmueller, *The Biblical Foundations for Mission* (Maryknoll, NY: Orbis, 1983).

Sloan, R. B., Jr., *The Favorable Year of the Lord: A Study of Jubiliary Theology in the Gospel of Luke* (Austin, Tex.: Schola Press, 1977).

Yoder, J., *The Politics of Jesus* (Grand Rapids, Mich.: Eerdmans; and Carlisle, UK: Paternoster, 1994).

Poor and marginalized

Abesamis, C., 'Good News to the Poor', *Concilium* 198 (1988): 25–32.

Abraham, M. V., 'Good News to the Poor in Luke's Gospel', *Bangalore Theological Forum* 19 (1987): 1–13.

Beavis, Mary Anne, '"Expecting Nothing in Return": Luke's Picture of the Marginalized', *Interpretation* 48 (1994): 357–68.

Bergquist, James A., '"Good News to the Poor" – Why Does This Lucan Motif Appear to Run Dry in the Book of Acts', *Bangalore Theological Forum* 18 (1986): 1–16.

Brawley, Robert L., 'The Blind, the Lame and the Poor: Character Types in Luke-Acts', *Currents in Theology and Mission* 25 (1998): 218–19.

*Donahue, John R., 'Two Decades of Research on the Rich and the Poor in Luke-Acts', in *Justice and the Holy: Essays in Honor of Walter Harrelson* (eds Douglas A. Knight and Peter J. Paris; Atlanta, Ga.: Scholars Press, 1989): 129–44.

Dupont, D. Jacques, 'The Poor and Poverty in the Gospels and Acts', in *Gospel Poverty* (ed. M. D. Guinan; Chicago: Franciscan Herald, 1977): 25–52.

*Green, Joel B., 'Good News to Whom? Jesus and the "Poor" in the Gospel of Luke', in *Jesus of Nazareth: Lord and Christ. Essays on the Historical Jesus and New Testament Christology* (eds Joel B. Green and M. M. B. Turner; Grand Rapids, Mich.: Eerdmans, 1994): 59–74.

Hamm, Dennis, 'Sight to the Blind: Vision as Metaphor in Luke', *Biblica* 67 (1986): 457–77.

Keck, Leander E., 'Poor among the Saints in the New Testament', *Zeitschrift für die Neutestamentliche Wissenschaft und die Kunde der Älteren Kirche* 56 (1965): 100–29.

*Meadors, Gary T., 'The "Poor" in the Beatitudes of Matthew [5:3] and Luke', *Grace Theological Journal* 6 (1985): 305–14.

Mealand, David L., *Poverty and Expectation in the Gospels* (London: SPCK, 1980).

Pilgrim, Walter E., *Good News to the Poor: Wealth and Poverty in Luke-Acts* (Minneapolis, Minn.: Augsburg, 1981).

Roth, S. John, *The Blind, the Lame, and the Poor: Character Types in Luke-Acts* (Journal for the Study of the New Testament Supplement 144; Sheffield, UK: Sheffield Academic Press, 1997).

Seccombe, David P., *Possessions and the Poor in Luke-Acts* (Linz: SNTU, 1983).

Stegemann, Wolfgang, 'The Following of Christ as Solidarity between Rich, Respected Christians and Poor, Despised Christians (Gospel of Luke)', in *Jesus and the Hope of the Poor* (eds L. Schottroff and W. Stegemann; Maryknoll, NY: Orbis, 1986): 67–120.

Wansbrough, Henry, 'The Lowliness of Mary', *Way* 20 (1980): 176–83.

Ethics

Brown, Raymond E., 'The Beatitudes according to Luke', *New Testament Essays* (Ramsey, NJ: Paulist, 1965): 265–71.

Cassidy, Richard J., *Society and Politics in the Acts of the Apostles* (Maryknoll, NY: Orbis, 1988).

Hays, Richard B., *The Moral Vision of the New Testament: A Contemporary Introduction to New Testament Ethics* (Edinburgh: T&T Clark, 1997): 113–37.

Karris, Robert J., 'Mary's Magnificat', *The Bible Today* 39 (2001): 145–9.

Kirk, Alan, '"Love Your Enemies," the Golden Rule, and Ancient Reciprocity (Luke 6:27–35)', *Journal of Biblical Literature* 122 (2003): 667–86.

Leoh, Vincent, 'Toward Pentecostal Social Ethics', *Journal of Asian Mission* 7 (2005): 39–62.

O'Hanlon, John, 'The Story of Zacchaeus and the Lucan Ethic', *Journal for the Study of the New Testament* 12 (1981): 2–26.

*Phillips, Thomas E., and Stanley E. Porter, ed., *Acts and Ethics* (New Testament Monographs 9; Sheffield, UK: Sheffield Phoenix, 2005).

Piper, John, *'Love Your Enemies': Jesus' Love Command in the Synoptic Gospels and the Early Christian Paraenesis* (Grand Rapids, Mich.: Baker, 1991).

Talbert, Charles H., 'Martyrdom in Luke-Acts and the Lukan Social Ethic', in *Political Issues in Luke-Acts* (ed. Richard J. Cassidy and Philip J. Scharper; Maryknoll, NY: Orbis, 1983): 99–110.

Luke 4:16–30

Chilton, Bruce D., 'Announcement in Nazara: An Analysis of Luke 4:16–21', in *Gospel Perspectives, vol. 2, Studies of History and Tradition in the Four Gospels* (ed. R. T. France and David Wenham; Sheffield, UK: JSOT, 1981): 147–72.

Kodell, Jerome, 'Luke's Gospel in a Nutshell (Lk. 4:16–30)', *Biblical Theology Bulletin* 13 (1983): 16–18.

Menezes, Franklin, 'The Mission of Jesus according to Lk 4:16–30', *Bible Bhashyam* 6 (1980): 249–64.

Prior, Michael, *Jesus the Liberator: Nazareth Liberation Theology, Luke 4:16–30* (The Biblical Seminar, 26; Sheffield: Sheffield Academic Press, 1995).

Sanders, James A., 'From Isaiah 61 to Luke 4', in *Christianity, Judaism and Other Greco-Roman Cults: Studies for Morton Smith at Sixty*, part one: *New Testament* (ed. J. Neusner; Leiden: Brill, 1975): 75–106.

*Schreck, Christopher J., 'The Nazareth Pericope: Luke 4:16–30 in Recent Study', in *L'Evangile de Luc = The Gospel of Luke* (ed. Frans Neirynck; Bibliotheca Ephemeridum Theologicarum Lovaniensium 32; Leuven: Leuven University Press, 1989): 399–471.

Tannehill, Robert C., 'The Mission of Jesus according to Luke 4:16–30', in *Jesus in Nazareth* (ed. Erich Grässer; Berlin: de Gruyter, 1972): 51–75.

Miracles in Luke-Acts

*Achtemeier, Paul J., 'The Lucan Perspective on the Miracles of Jesus: A Preliminary Sketch', in *Perspectives on Luke-Acts* (ed. Charles H. Talbert; Danville, Va.: Association Baptist Professors of Religion; and Edinburgh, UK: T&T Clark, 1978): 153–67.

Gen, Raymond M., 'The Phenomenon of Miracles and Divine Infliction in Luke-Acts: Their Theological Significance', *Pneuma* 11 (1989): 3–19.

Hardon, John A., 'Miracle Narratives in the Acts of the Apostles', *Catholic Biblical Quarterly* 16 (1954): 303–18.

Klauck, Hans-Josef, *Magic and Paganism in Early Christianity: The World of the Acts of the Apostles* (Edinburgh, UK: T&T Clark, 2000).

Klauck, Hans-Josef, 'With Paul in Paphos and Lystra: Magic and Paganism in the Acts of the Apostles', *Neotestamentica* 28 (1994): 93–108.

Kolenkow, A. B., 'Relationships between Miracles and Prophecy in the Greco-Roman World and Early Christianity', *Aufstieg und Niedergang der Römischen Welt* II.23.2 (1980): 1470–506.

Lampe, G. W. H., 'Miracles in the Acts of the Apostles', in *Miracles: Cambridge Studies in Their Philosophy and History* (ed. C. F. D. Moule; London: A. R. Mowbray, 1965): 163–78.

McCord Adams, Marilyn, 'The Role of Miracles in the Structure of Luke-Acts', in *Hermes and Athena* (University of Notre Dame Studies in the Philosophy of

Religion 7; eds Eleonore Stump and Thomas P. Flint; Notre Dame, Ind.: University of Notre Dame Press, 1993): 235–73.

Maloney, Linda M., *'All that God had Done with Them': The Narration of the Works of God in the Early Christian Community as Described in the Acts of the Apostles* (American University Studies 7 Theology and Religion 91; New York and Bern: Lang, 1991).

May, Eric, '"... For Power Went Forth from Him ..." (Luke 6, 19)', *Catholic Biblical Quarterly* 14 (1952): 93–103.

Menzies, Robert P., 'Spirit and Power in Luke-Acts: A Response to Max Turner', *Journal for the Study of the New Testament* 49 (1993): 11–20.

Neirynck, Frans, 'The Miracle Stories in the Acts of the Apostles', in *Les Actes des Apôtres: traditions, rédaction, théologie* (ed. Jacob Kremer; Duculot, Paris-Gembloux and Leuven University Press, 1979): 169–213.

Pilch, John J., 'Sickness and Healing in Luke-Acts', *The Bible Today* 27 (1989): 21–8.

Reimer, Andy M., *Miracle and Magic: A Study in the Acts of the Apostles and the Life of Apollonius of Tyana* (Journal for the Study of the New Testament Supplement 235; London and New York: Sheffield Academic Press, 2002).

Talbert, Charles H., 'Excursus B: Miracle in Luke-Acts and in the Lukan Milieu', *Reading Luke: A Literary Theological Commentary on the Third Gospel* (New York: Crossroad, 1984): 241–6.

*Turner, M. M. B., ' "The Spirit and the Power of Jesus" Miracles in the Lucan Conception', *Novum Testamentum* 33 (1991): 124–52.

Twelftree, Graham H., *In the Name of Jesus: Exorcism among Early Christians* (Grand Rapids, Mich.: Baker Academic, 2007).

Williams, Benjamin E., *Miracle Stories in the Biblical Book* Acts of the Apostles (Lewiston, NY: Edwin Mellen, 2001).

Eschatology

Bruce, F. F., 'Eschatology in Acts', in *Eschatology and the New Testament: Essays in Honor of George Raymond Beasley-Murray* (ed. W. H. Gloer; Peabody, Mass.: Hendrickson, 1988): 51–63.

Cadbury, Henry J., 'Acts and Eschatology', in *The Background of the New Testament and Its Eschatology: In Honour of Charles Harold Dodd* (eds W. D. Davies and D. Daube; Cambridge, UK: Cambridge University Press, 1954): 300–21.

Carroll, John T., *Response to the End of History: Eschatology and Situation in Luke-Acts* (Society of Biblical Literature Dissertation 92; Atlanta, Ga.: Scholars Press, 1988).

Chance, J. Bradley, *Jerusalem, the Temple, and the New Age in Luke-Acts* (Macon, Ga.: Mercer University Press, 1988).

Ellis, E. Earle, *Eschatology in Luke* (Philadelphia, Pa.: Fortress Press, 1972).

Ellis, E. Earle, 'Eschatology in Luke Revisited', in *L'Évangile de Luc – The Gospel of Luke* (Bibliotheca Ephemeridum Theologicarum Lovaniensium 32; Leuven: Leuven University Press, 1989): 296–303.

Francis, Fred O., 'Eschatology and History in Luke-Acts', *Journal of the American Academy of Religion* 37 (1969): 49–63.

*Gaventa, Beverly Roberts, 'The Eschatology of Luke-Acts Revisited', *Encounter* 43 (1982): 27–42.

Hiers, Richard H., 'The Problem of the Delay of the Parousia in Luke-Acts', *New Testament Studies* 20 (1974): 145–55.

Mattill, Andrew J., *Luke and the Last Things: A Perspective for the Understanding of Lukan Thought* (Dillsboro, NC: Western North Carolina Press, 1979).

Mattill, Andrew J., 'Naherwartung, Fernerwartung, and the Purpose of Luke-Acts: Weymouth Reconsidered', *Catholic Biblical Quarterly* 34 (1972): 276–93.

Moessner, David P., 'Paul in Acts: Preacher of Eschatological Repentance to Israel', *New Testament Studies* 34 (1988): 96–104.

Sabourin, Léopold, 'The Eschatology of Luke', *Biblical Theology Bulletin* 12 (1982): 73–6.

Wilson, Stephen G., 'Lukan Eschatology', *New Testament Studies* 16 (1970): 330–47.

Speeches in Acts

Balch, David L., 'The Areopagus Speech: An Appeal to the Stoic Historian Posidonius against Later Stoics and the Epicureans', in *Greeks, Romans, and Christians: Essays in Honor of Abraham J. Malherbe* (eds David L. Balch, Everett Ferguson and Wayne A. Meeks; Minneapolis, Minn.: Fortress Press, 1990): 52–79.

Barrett, C. Kingsley, 'Paul's Address to the Ephesian Elders', in *God's Christ and His People: Studies in Honour of Nils Alstrup Dahl* (eds Jacob Jervell and Wayne A. Meeks; Oslo: Universitetsforlaget, 1977): 107–21.

Bowker, John W., 'Speeches in Acts: A Study in Proem and Yelammedenu Form', *New Testament Studies* 14 (1967–8): 96–111.

*Bruce, F. F., 'The Significance of the Speeches for Interpreting Acts', *Southwestern Journal of Theology* 33 (1990): 20–8.

Conzelmann, Hans, 'The Address of Paul on the Areopagus', in *Studies in Luke-Acts* (eds Leander E. Keck and J. Louis Martyn; Nashville, Tenn.: Abingdon, 1966): 217–30.

Ellis, E. Earle, 'Midrashic Features in the Speeches of Acts', in *Mélanges Bibliques en hommage au R. P. Béda Rigaux* (eds A. Descamps and A. De Halleux; Gembloux: J. Duculot, 1970): 303–12.

Gasque, W. Ward, 'The Speeches of Acts: Dibelius Reconsidered', in *New Dimensions in New Testament Study* (eds Richard N. Longenecker and Merrill C. Tenney; Grand Rapids, Mich.: Zondervan, 1974): 232–51.

Hemer, Colin J., 'The Speeches of Acts 1: The Ephesian Elders at Miletus', *Tyndale Bulletin* 40 (1989): 77–85.

Hemer, Colin J., 'The Speeches of Acts 2: The Areopagus Address', *Tyndale Bulletin* 40 (1989): 239–59.

Hilgert, Earle, 'Speeches in Acts, and Hellenistic Canons of Historiography and Rhetoric', in *Good News in History: Essays in Honor of Bo Reicke* (ed. Ed. L. Miller; Scholars Press Homage; Atlanta, Ga.: Scholars Press, 1993): 83–109.

Horsley, G. H. R., 'Speeches and Dialogue in Acts', *New Testament Studies* 32 (1986): 609–14.

Schweizer, Eduard, 'Concerning the Speeches in Acts', in *Studies in Luke-Acts* (eds L. E. Keck and J. L. Martyn; Nashville, Tenn.: Abingdon, 1966): 208–16.

Schubert, Paul, 'The Final Cycle of Speeches in the Book of Acts', *Journal of Biblical Literature* 87 (1968): 1–16.

*Soards, Marion L., *The Speeches in Acts: Their Content, Context, and Concerns* (Louisville, Ky: Westminster/John Knox, 1994).

Tannehill, Robert C., 'The Functions of Peter's Mission Speeches in the Narrative of Acts', *New Testament Studies* 37 (1991): 400–14.

Townsend, John T., 'The Speeches in Acts', *Anglican Theological Review* 42 (1960): 150–9.

14 Listening to Luke

Bockmuehl, Markus, and Alan J. Torrance, eds, *Scripture's Doctrine and Theology's Bible: How the New Testament Shapes Christian Dogmatics* (Grand Rapids, Mich.: Baker Academic, 2008).

*Davis, Ellen F., and Richard B. Hays, *The Art of Reading Scripture* (Grand Rapids, Mich.: Eerdmans, 2003).

Fee, Gordon D., 'Hermeneutics and Historical Precedent: A Major Problem in Pentecostal Hermeneutics', in *Perspectives on the New Pentecostalism* (ed. Russell P. Spittler; Grand Rapids, Mich.: Baker, 1976): 118–32.

*Fee, Gordon D., and Douglas K. Stuart, 'Acts: The Question of Historical Precedent', *How to Read the Bible for All Its Worth* (Grand Rapids, Mich.: Zondervan, 2003): 107–25.

France, R. T., ' "It seemed good to the Holy Spirit and to us"? . . .', *Churchman* 108 (1994): 234–41.

Green, Joel B., and M. M. B. Turner, eds, *Between Two Horizons: Spanning New Testament Studies and Systematic Theology* (Grand Rapids, Mich., and Cambridge, UK: Eerdmans, 2000).

Michiels, Robrecht, 'The "Model of Church" in the First Christian Community of Jerusalem: Ideal and Reality', *Louvain Studies* 10 (1985): 303–23.

Schnackenburg, Rudolf, *The Church in the New Testament* (New York: Herder and Herder, 1965).

Stibbe, Mark W. G., 'This Is That: Some Thoughts concerning Charismatic Hermeneutics', *Anvil* 15 (1998): 181–93.

Stuhlmacher, Peter, *Historical Criticism and Theological Interpretation of Scripture* (Philadelphia, Pa.: Fortress Press, 1977).

Thiselton, Anthony C., *New Horizons in Hermeneutics: The Theory and Practice of Transforming Biblical Reading* (London: HarperCollins, 1992).

Thompson, Richard P., 'Keeping the Church in Its Place: Revisiting the Church(es) in Acts', *Wesleyan Theological Journal* 41 (2006): 96–115.

*Wedderburn, A. J. M., 'New Testament Church Today?', *Scottish Journal of Theology* 31 (1978): 517–32.

Xavier, A. Aloysius, 'Church according to the Acts of the Apostles', *Jeevadhara* 15 (1985): 94–104.

The contemporary Church

Abbot, Walter M., and Joseph Gallagher, eds, *The Documents of Vatican 2* (London and Dublin: Chapman, 1966).

Barth, Karl, *Church Dogmatics* Vol. IV *The Doctrine of Reconciliation*: Fragment Part 4 (Edinburgh: T&T Clark, 1969).

Bonhoeffer, Dietrich, *Sanctorum Communio: A Dogmatic Inquiry into the Sociology of the Church* (London: Collins, 1963).

Clapp, Rodney, *A Peculiar People: The Church as Culture in a Post-Christian Society* (Downers Grove, Ill.: InterVarsity Press, 1996).

Clifton, Shane, 'Pentecostal Ecclesiology: A Methodological Proposal for a Diverse Movement', *Journal of Pentecostal Theology* 15 (2007): 213–32.

Collins, Paul M., and Michael A. Fahey, eds, *Receiving 'The Nature and Mission of the Church': Ecclesial Reality and Ecumenical Horizons for the Twenty-First Century* (London and New York: T&T Clark, 2008).

Congar, Yves, *The Mystery of the Church* (London: Chapman, 1965).

Dulles, Avery, *Models of the Church* (Dublin: Gill and Macmillan, 1976).

Gelder, Craig Van, *The Essence of the Church: A Community Created by the Spirit* (Grand Rapids, Mich.: Baker, 2000).

Gibbs, Eddie, and Ryan Bolger, *Emerging Churches: Creating Christian Communities in Postmodern Cultures* (London: SPCK, 2006).

Grdzelidze, Tamara, *One, Holy, Catholic and Apostolic: Ecumenical Reflections on the Church* (Geneva: WCC Publications, 2005).

*Grenz, Stanley J., 'Ecclesiology', in *The Cambridge Companion to Postmodern Theology* (ed. Kevin J. Vanhoozer; Cambridge, UK: Cambridge University Press, 2003), 252–68.

Grenz, Stanley, *Theology for the Community of God* (Grand Rapids, Mich.: Eerdmans, 2000).

Hauerwas, Stanley, *Resident Aliens: Life in the Christian Colony* (Nashville, Tenn.: Abingdon, 1989).

Kärkkäinen, Veli-Matti, *An Introduction to Ecclesiology* (Downers Grove, Ill.: IVP, 2002).

Kenneson, Philip D., 'Selling [Out] the Church in the Marketplace of Desire', *Modern Theology* 9 (1993): 319–48.

Küng, Hans, *The Church* (London: Search, 1968).

Lathrop, Gordon, *Holy People: A Liturgical Ecclesiology* (Minneapolis, Minn.: Fortress Press, 2006).

Lennan, Richard, *The Ecclesiology of Karl Rahner* (Oxford: Clarendon Press, 1995).

Lohfink, Gerhard, *Jesus and Community* (Philadelphia, Pa.: Fortress Press, 1982).

McLaren, Brian D., *The Church on the Other Side: Doing Ministry in the Postmodern Matrix* (Grand Rapids, Mich.: Zondervan, 2000).

*Mannion, Gerard, *Ecclesiology and Postmodernity: Questions for the Church in Our Time* (Collegeville, Minn: Liturgical, 2007).

Matthey, Jacques, and Alan Falconer, eds, *International Review of Mission* 90 (No. 358, July, and No. 359, October 2001): 227–454. Papers presented at the consultation by the Faith and Order and Mission and Evangelism teams of the World Council of Churches at the Coptic Orthodox Monastery, Höxter-Brenkhausen, Germany, 8–15 July 2000.

Milbank, John, Catherine Pickstock and Graham Ward, eds, *Radical Orthodoxy: A New Theology* (London and New York: Routledge, 1999).

Moltmann, Jürgen, *The Church in the Power of the Spirit: A Contribution to Messianic Ecclesiology* (Minneapolis, Minn.: Fortress Press, 1993).

Newbigin, Lesslie, *The Household of God: Lectures on the Nature of the Church* (London: SCM Press, 1953).

Rahner, Karl, *The Church and the Sacraments* (New York: Herder and Herder, 1963).

Sweet, Leonard, ed., *The Church in Emerging Culture: Five Perspectives* (Grand Rapids, Mich.: Zondervan, 2003).

Volf, Miroslav, *After Our Likeness: The Church as the Image of the Trinity* (Grand Rapids, Mich.: Eerdmans, 1998).

Index of ancient and biblical texts

245

248

24:24 121
24:25–28 141n6
24:25–27 102n4
24:25 145
24:26 142n9
24:27 142n7, 145
24:28–35 116
24:30 37n27, 126n7,
  131
24:32 141n6
24:33 26, 75n30
24:34 26–7
24:36–53 36
24:36–49 68n14
24:36–40 68
24:36 154n3
24:39 142n8
24:41 35, 80
24:44–49 26–7, 145
24:44–47 32, 141n6
24:44 26, 102n4,
  103n6, 142n7,
  154n3
24:46–47 141, 178n5
24:46 26, 142n9, n10
24:47–49 81–2
24:47–48 26n65,
  111n27, 194
24:47 39, 45, 75n30,
  90n23, 112, 142,
  186n30, 188, 201n67
24:48 20, 26, 26n63,
  n65, 197, 197n44
24:49–53 66, 109,
  167n14
24:49 23, 38, 68, 76,
  80, 142n11, 154n2
24:49b 75
24:50–53 26, 37
24:50–52 38
24:50 37n27, 126n6,
  n7
24:51 37n25, n27,
  38, 126n7
24:52–53 37, 47,
  75n30, 80, 126
24:52 35
24:53 37n27, 54n7,
  108n23, 125, 125n5,
  126n7

John
1:41 62
3:13 37n26
4:3 186n30
4:28 186n30
4:52 186n30
6:62 37n26
7:33 37n26
8:14 37n26
8:17 65n1
8:21 27n26

8:29 186n30
9:1–41 185n25
10:11–16 4n6
10:12 186n30
10:13–17 4n6
10:16 4n5
11:44 186n30
11:48 186n30
12:7 186n30
12:40 149n27
13:1–3 37n26
13:16 18n20
13:33 37n26
14—15 68
14:2 37n26
14:4 37n26
14:13 37n26
14:18 186n30
14:27 186n30
14:28 37n26
16:5 37n26
16:7 37n26
16:10 37n26
16:17 37n26
16:28 37n26, 186n30
16:32 186n30
17:20–21 3
18:8 186n30
20:17 37n26
20:19–29 68n14
20:19–23 68
20:19 68n14
20:23 186n30
21:1–14 68n14

Acts
1—7 78n39
1 17
1:1–26 15, 28
1:1–11 178
1:1–2 6n9, 7
1:1 9, 10, 16, 30,
  32, 36, 38, 43, 129,
  153–4, 165, 179,
  182
1:2–11 17, 18
1:2 15, 17, 18n20,
  20n41, 21, 37n25,
  38n31, 129, 147
1:3–9 38
1:3 6n9, 24
1:4–5 65n1, 154
1:4 68, 75, 75n30,
  76, 80, 124, 167n14
1:5 16n8, 38n34, 70,
  75, 84, 84n2, 91
1:6–8 17, 17n18, 194
1:6–7 179
1:6 21n44, 24,
  38n30, 75, 78n38,
  180–1, 194
1:7–8 76

1:7 194
1:8 11n36, 16n8, 23,
  24, 26n63, n65, 34,
  38–9, 41, 44, 46n12,
  75, 75n30, 76, 81,
  81n49, 82, 85, 85n6,
  147, 177, 177n1,
  178, 180–1, 183n18,
  190, 194, 197n42,
  n44
1:8b 81
1:9–11 17, 37
1:9 38, 38n30, 78n38
1:10 38n30
1:11 38, 38n31,
  180n11
1:12–14 126, 166
1:12–13 15, 16, 126,
  167n14
1:12 75n30, 78n38,
  135n30
1:13 6n9, 17, 17n14,
  65, 118, 165n2
1:14–15 15, 17, 65,
  167
1:14 16, 16n4, 17,
  17n17, 31, 33, 77,
  109, 120, 121, 126,
  127n9, 131, 168,
  196
1:15–26 17, 127,
  129, 138, 153,
  165n1, 167
1:15 11n36, 15n3,
  17n14, 56, 66, 77,
  85, 127, 132, 165n2
1:16–22 17n18
1:16 11n36, 142, 150
1:17 174
1:19 75n30
1:20 142, 152
1:21–25 171n28
1:21–22 16, 25, 154,
  172
1:21 21n44, 206
1:22–23 110
1:22 11n36, 26n63,
  n65, 38n31, 172,
  197nn42–4
1:23 118
1:23–26 21
1:24–25 17n18,
  133n23
1:24 21, 21n44,
  28n71, 31, 36,
  106n18
1:25 174
1:26 18n20, 21, 24
2—5 28n70
2 65–8, 70, 74–5,
  77, 80, 90–1, 153,
  157, 163

2:1—6:8 202
2:1–42 8n27
2:1–13 31, 65
2:1–4 65, 112, 128
2:1 15, 15n3, 16n4,
  38n35, 65–6, 66n5,
  71, 76–7, 80, 85
2:2–4 71
2:2–3 75, 133
2:2 65–6, 71, 75,
  132n22
2:3 78–9
2:4 21, 31n2, 38n34,
  65, 66n5, 69, 70n18,
  n19, 72, 72n23, 73,
  73n27, 75, 77, 85,
  85n3, 90, 90n24,
  97–8, 142, 150, 157,
  161, 179n9
2:5–13 71n20
2:5–6 73
2:5 75n30, 78
2:6 78
2:8 73, 73n27
2:11 73, 73n27, 90,
  158
2:13 88, 142
2:14–40 31, 199n53
2:14–39 80
2:14–36 65, 81, 178
2:14–21 25, 140n2
2:14 17n14, 24,
  31, 75n30, 91n25,
  104, 129n14, 150,
  165nn1–2, 167
2:16–21 82
2:16 199n54
2:17–35 142,
  142nn10–11
2:17–21 98
2:17–18 122, 157–8
2:17 24, 31n2, 47,
  70, 70n18, n19,
  75–7, 85n5, 112n28,
  121, 148n25, 155,
  156n8, 157, 168,
  178n6
2:18 31n2, 70n18,
  n19, 85n5, 121
2:19–21 151
2:19 82, 82n51, 201
2:21 45n1, 46n12,
  n14, n15, 47, 49n37,
  50n42, 77, 78n41,
  95n32, 112n28
2:22–36 81
2:22–23 199n56
2:22 35, 82, 129n14,
  161n16, 201
2:22b–24 199
2:23 53
2:24–28 109

Index of subjects

Abraham 76, 143, 145, 156, 189, 212
adelphoi 11n36, 110
Agabus 157–8, 160, 163, 171
Ananias of Damascus 69, 74, 89–90, 94, 148,
154, 156, 197
Ananias and Sapphira 16n10, 117, 120, 159, 201
anti-Marcionite Prologue 7n18
Antioch, Pisidian 53, 134, 146
Antioch, Syrian 6–7, 32, 34, 87–8, 105, 111,
113, 118, 134–6, 154, 157–60, 162, 165,
168–9, 172, 175, 196; ministry model 165,
169–71
aphesis/release 31, 182, 186–7, 193, 196, 201
Apollos 55, 70, 74, 85, 93–4, 122, 154
apostle, apostolate 9, 15–29; Barnabas 25–7, 29;
chosen 19–22, 129, 144n16, 166; defined 25,
26; extended by Luke 25; miracle worker 23,
33–4, 72, 195; origin of Church 21–2; Paul
18n20, 19, 26–9; and purpose of Church
22–5; and the twelve 19–21; *see also* tradition;
twelve
Aquila *see* Priscilla and Aquila
Ascension 17, 20, 25–6, 33, 36–8, 43, 63,
78, 106, 109, 126, 143, 167, 172, 178, 180;
see also witness

Babel reversed 78
baptism (water) 28, 48, 50, 83, 84–7, 91–3, 95,
97, 98, 99, 122, 146, 170, 209; and belief
90–4, 96, 99, 209; confers the Spirit 5, 84,
87, 90, 93, 95, 96, 98, 99, 208, 209; and
conversion 49, 88, 95; defined 99; with fire
71, 79–80; and forgiveness 95; infant 91–2,
93, 95, 100, 208, 209–10; with laying on of
hands 94; necessity 99, 208, 209; passive act
86, 88, 89, 91, 92, 93, 99; by Paul 100; and
salvation 50, 95; and the Spirit 13, 49, 70, 75,
79, 86, 87, 89–91, 95, 96, 98, 99, 208, 209;
see also household; Jesus; John the Baptist;
repentance; Spirit baptism
Barnabas 31, 32, 34, 40, 50, 55, 72, 88, 102,
109, 111, 115, 117, 118, 123, 129, 135, 137,
147, 154, 157, 158, 159, 160, 161, 170–2,
175, 181, 198, 199; *see also* apostle
Beatitudes 115, 182, 187–8
belief *see* faith
biography 7–10, 146
bishop(s) 5, 13, 135, 164
blood 53–4, 62–3, 112, 130, 160, 174
boldness 26–7, 43, 69, 72, 74, 81–3, 107–9, 133,
144, 154, 181, 208, 210
breaking bread 110, 116, 128, 130–2, 137, 139, 202

characters as models (narrative technique) 30–44,
123, 150, 174

charis see grace
charisma see Spirit, gift(s) of
charismatic(s) movement 5, 13, 73, 215
child(ren) 91–2, 119, 167, 100; *see also* baptism
Church/church: birth 28, 75, 206; as
brotherhood 3, 13; 'catholic' 62; as charismatic
13, 159–60, 164, 172, 157, 176; Christo-
centric 206; as community 2, 3, 16, 60, 110,
124, 206, 213, 216, 217; conception 12, 15,
28–9, 52, 75, 153, 206; congregational model
13, 164, 176; contemporary 1, 14, 73, 84,
95, 100, 137, 140, 164, 172, 176, 177, 196,
197, 203, 204, 206, 208, 211, 212, 213, 215;
defined 205–7, 217; 'of God' 62, 171; growth
39–41, 55, 170, 178, 201; house/as household
13, 32, 52, 57, 63–4, 66, 116, 121, 124, 126,
130, 132, 134, 137–8, 202, 204, 210, 213;
joining 48–9, 86, 98, 116, 131, 208–10,
215–17; names for 11n36; problems in 3, 13,
29, 40, 49, 50, 101–23, 147–8, 181, 205, 210;
purpose 207, 217; and salvation 12, 44, 45–52,
207, 216; as sect 11n36, 13, 52, 58–61, 64,
105, 110, 207; as synagogue 52, 56–8, 64,
65–6, 124, 127, 130, 130–2, 134, 138, 162,
213; relation to synagogue 11, 55, 56, 60,
63–4, 69, 77, 92, 102, 104–5, 107, 124, 126,
133–4, 138, 151, 155, 210–11; universal
Church 3, 4, 61–2, 112; Western 1, 215;
see also early catholic; *ekklēsia*; Israel
community: of goods 113, 117, 168, 202;
imperative of 110, 123; breaches of 116–19,
123, 210; character of 202, 216, 217; joining
209; and prayer 127–8, *see also* Church; unity
Cornelius 37, 49, 63, 70, 84, 88–91, 94–8,
111–13, 116, 118, 156, 161
covenant 76, 78–9, 128, 130n
Crispus 55, 92–3, 97
cross: bearing 103; and Church 206; focus of
Church 206; of Jesus 80, 107, 113, 120, 199;
see also Jesus
Cynics 59

daily distribution 113, 118–19, 168, 195
Damascus: Christians 60, 69–70, 90, 105, 108,
133; and Paul 94, 108, 134, 197
deacon(s) 5, 13, 135, 164, 168
dead, raising 33, 34, 47, 137, 195, 200, 201
Dead Sea Scrolls 60–1, 80, 128, 184–5, 187;
see also Essenes; Qumran
deeds of power *see* miracle(s)
demon(s) 22–3, 29, 33–4, 81, 174, 192, 194;
demoniac 188, 194; demonic 122, 182–7, 196
devil 33, 81, 106, 186, 192, 201; *see also* Satan
devoted 17, 25, 33, 110, 116, 127, 128, 129,
131, 154, 168, 173, 181; *see also* *proskartereō*

264